An Idea of Dante

Opuntia is an imprint of Agincourt Press

Opuntia Books are published by
Luigi Ballerini
Beppe Cavatorta
Gianluca Rizzo
Federica Santini

Agincourt Press is a non-profit chaired by Berardo Paradiso

The publisher gratefully acknowledges the financial contribution
of the Italian Cultural Institute of New York

All rights reserved.

ISBN: 978-1-946328-31-1

AGINCOURT PRESS
P.O. Box 1039
Cooper Station
New York, NY 10003
www.agincourtpress.org

© 2021 by Agincourt Press

The publisher welcomes enquiries from copyright-holders he has been unable to contact

Gianfranco Contini

An Idea of Dante

*Translated by
Stephen Sartarelli*

*with a Foreword by
Fabio Finotti*

Agincourt Press
New York, 2021

Table of Contents

7 Foreword *by Fabio Finotti*
11 Translator's Note *by Stephen Sartarelli*

AN IDEA OF DANTE

17 Introduction to the *Rime* of Dante
35 Exercise in Interpreting a Sonnet by Dante
47 Dante as Character/Poet in the *Commedia*
75 Dante Today
81 One Interpretation of Dante
129 Philology and Dantean Exegesis
161 Cavalcanti in Dante
177 On Canto XXX of the *Inferno*
189 Some Notes on *Purgatorio* XXVII
209 An Example of Dante's Poetry (Canto XXVIII of the *Paradiso*)

Appendix

233 An American Book on Dante
241 Dantean Postscript
249 Postscript on Celestine
251 Sicilian Stylemes in the *Detto d'Amore*
259 A Crux of Medieval Culture: *Roman de la Rose – Fiore – Divina Commedia*

Foreword

Gianfranco Contini revolutionized Dante studies. To him goes the credit for having recognized *La Divina Commedia* as the text that radically re-thinks the medieval world's relationship to the *auctoritates*. The repetitive use of sources, and the appeal to the commonplace—the focus of Curtius's seminal 1948 study, *Europäische Literatur und lateinisches Mittelalter*—become, in Dante, an impassioned dialogue, a radical re-writing of the past, an intertextuality precisely in the sense we understand it today, after Kristeva. From this perspective, the *Divina Commedia* is an extraordinary secular Bible, because within its confines it contains not only itself, but an entire library, re-read, reviewed, put into perspective, and judged, with no less rigor and intensity than that involved in judging souls.

Demonstrating the metatextual dimension of Dante's masterpiece is one of Contini's principal achievements, and his work in this area underlies many of the more interesting and stimulating Dantean interpretations that emerged during his latter years, starting with that of John Freccero. And the dynamic power of Dante's voice in uttering the words of the past informs, to my mind, the most important accomplishment of the greatest living Dante scholar, Teodolinda Barolini: Dante does not limit himself to responding to his sources with total autonomy, but often re-creates them, or at least re-constructs them, and as a result, the positivist paradigm collapses. It is no longer the cause that produces the effect, but—at least in literature—the (apparent) effect that produces the cause. Indeed, how much history has been invented to justify Dante's text?

A second fundamental point of Contini's hermeneutics is the category of the *personaggio poeta*, the "poet as character," thanks to which we have learned to understand that Dante spans not only the universal reality of his omnivorous readings, but that of his own self, both as a man and as a writer. The *Commedia* is also the autobiography of a poet, and thus the question that arises concerning history must be re-applied concerning literature. How much literature (beginning with the *stil novo*) derives from the categories that Dante uses to give form not only to his present but also to that same past that seems to generate it? How much of the *Divina Commedia* is bound up with a continual discourse on the limits, possibilities, practices, and mission of poetry?

Contini's emphasis on this point is also his way of overcoming an absolutizing vision of literature such as that implied even in Croce's distinction between "poetry" and "non-poetry." Poetry, for Contini, is a process of creation that transcends mere intuition and includes an internal dialectics, a history of techniques and practices, a variability of perspectives and objectives. And within this diachronic, intertextual movement, words may look the same, yet they change with each new appearance, because their meanings are conferred by the epochs, and even the individual texts, in which they appear. One need only think of Contini's splendid pages on the idea of love and the courtly lineage embodied, in part, in Francesca da Rimini.

Through the category of "poet as character," Contini tackles a theme dear to the narratology of the 1960s and 1970s (Contini's essay on the subject is from 1957-1958), finally separating autobiography from textuality: The author is not the producer of the text—such as we ourselves know it—but a product of the text, and just as fictitious as the other characters brought onto the stage.

The emphasis on Dante's modernity, in Contini, is owing to the poet's more general concern for linguistic creativity and his ability to take innovation to a level not simply subversive (like so many twentieth-century avant-gardes) but also productive, in regard to both the signifier and the signified. In this way Contini's pages give proper relief to Dante's experimentalism (in the *Rime*, for example) and its particularity: never any blind proceedings, but always a concreteness combining research and realization.

Quintessentially Continian is the attention he pays to the Italian tongue itself: the language is experienced as living matter in ceaseless evolution and carrying history within its words. Thus do philology and exegesis keep pace with each other in Contini's pages, engaging both the relationship the *Commedia* establishes with tradition and the one the great poem establishes with itself. The *Commedia* is everywhere threaded within itself, through an extremely dense intertextuality, a compact fabric of echoes lending meaning to images, characters, and words.

Dante's prodigioius memory likewise acts upon the text's rapport with itself and provides the best proof of the metalinguistic dimension of the verbal language—a language that is continually able to reflect upon itself (as Dante does explicitly in the *Vita Nuova* and the *Convivio*), and to confer new meaning upon itself, confirming that "production of the text" of which Michele Riffaterre spoke in times closer to us.

For us students entering Contini's seminars in the late '70s, his Dante lectures offered an extraordinarily fascinating model and guided us as well in our approach to other authors of the Italian literary tradition.

Who can forget his "let us explain the Etruscans with the Etruscans," which Contini would repeat so often as he set about examining Dante's text? In this motto the hermetic element (the almost impenetrable mystery of the Etruscan language) combined with philological discipline, which did not shy from traveling a path a bit like that of Champollion, finding the tools to the text's interpretation within the text itself.

Who can forget forget the lectures on the *Fiore*, in which the poet's prodigious memory in quoting passages remote from one another in the *Roman de la Rose* was matched only by Contini's own in tracking them down?

And who can forget the deep, thoughtful, intimate tone of voice with which Contini delivered his lectures to us students, who came to them from the somewhat unruly classrooms of post-'68 Italian *licei*? It felt like entering a sort of church and participating in a ceremony that had something religious about it.

In the lecture halls of the Normale we thus learned that poetry demands patience and listening, and has little to do with facile emotivity. The first step of cognitive activity was rather to recognize the distance between ourselves and the text. That distance, which Contini's analysis of the sonnet, *Tanto gentile e tanto onesta pare*, presented in the clearest possible way, gave us in fact an inkling of the very essence of Continian poetics and the solid certainty on which it blossomed: namely, the conviction that poetry is a language set by the poet into a motion intended to detach it from himself and project it into a new sphere in which the text will gain its own autonomy, where nobody—not the author, and not the readers—can claim in reality to possess it.

Fabio Finotti

Translator's Note

The highly specialized critical prose of Gianfranco Contini is quite unlike any other form of writing I have ever undertaken to translate. Highly allusive and often drawing spontaneously from a seemingly endless store of source materials, it assumes, first and foremost, an already deep familiarity on the part of the reader with the subject at hand. Since the English-language audience for whom the present translation is intended will not, except in rare cases, possess the same body of knowledge as the author concerning early Italian literature and its Classical and medieval European influences, I have taken the liberty of providing footnotes for those allusions and citations that might not be immediately evident to a reader educated mostly in the English and American literary traditions and whose knowledge of foreign literatures is limited principally to reading translations. And since, moreover, so much of Contini's analysis is directly textual, his essays are bursting with citations of primary texts, often in archaic Italian, not to mention Latin and Occitan, necessitating the creation of a sort of bridge to facilitate comprehension of the author's arguments for those not steeped in Italian literary history or Romance philology.

For this purpose I have taken to providing "service translations" of those passages of quoted text for which a comprehension of the literal meaning is essential to Contini's argument. When such passages are limited to one or a few lines of verse, as they often are, the translation, being itself limited to the fragment of text being cited, cannot be aesthetically adapted to the fuller context of the source text, as the differences between the languages and their respective syntaxes are such that a fully realized translation would not reflect the same breakdown of lines in the poem and thus not necessarily the same words as in the quoted original. My service translations are therefore only that: quasi-literal renderings permitting the reader to engage as fully as possible the original text being treated by the author.

The same logic also dictates, however, that when the author's analysis involves exclusively, or primarily, a discussion of the specifically *physical* aspects of the poetry or usage—whether morphology, or meter, rhyme, assonances and other assorted aspects of prosody—I leave the Italian text under examination untranslated, since in such cases the actual meaning of the words, at the moment of analysis, is irrelevant to the argument and would simply further clutter the already very busy visual aspect of Contini's text. This, then, is why the reader will find that some quoted text is translated, while some is not.

A further inconsistency—with respect to general convention—that may strike the reader is that some of my service translations are embedded within the main text, while others are relegated to footnotes. This apparent discrepancy was dictated by dual concerns of space and aesthetics, with the latter involving specifically the desire to maintain the flow of the author's arguments without too much interruption. A similar concern also informs the decision, when the translated quotes are embedded, to feature sometimes the English version first, before the original (especially when the citation is in prose), to preserve the logical concatenation of the sentence in question. Given the extremely complex nature of Contini's jigsaw puzzle of references, many of these decisions were made on the fly in the process of translating him, and the present system, if we can call it that, is what I have arrived at by force of necessity and expediency within the relatively brief time allotted for completing the project. It is my hope that my "variable" approach to providing the information necessary to satisfactory comprehension has yielded as smoothly flowing a text as is possible within the limits imposed by the need to harmonize so many diverse elements.

Given this complexity, it would be nearly impossible, if not absurd, to hew too strictly to scholarly publishing conventions when translating Contini, as the great philologist's own manner of exposition relies so heavily on his prodigious memory and his ability to summon references for his purposes at a moment's notice, without regard for systematic bibliographical documentation to justify every reference in his rapid-fire manner of citation. As the reader will see, much of the documentation of Contini's references is my own, contained in my body of footnotes, alongside the author's often more extensive notes, which are distinguished from mine by the inclusion of his intials in parentheses (GC) at the end of each.

The service translations are predominantly mine, except in those cases where, for some of the more problematic quotes, I draw from already existing translations, which are duly credited. The Latin translations are also my own, with some valuable help from Luigi Ballerini and Gianluca Rizzo, except in those relatively frequent cases where I quote from prior renderings.

Translating a collection of such documentary richness as these essays possess would, in the past, have taken years of research in libraries both specialized and general. Luckily, thanks to the miracle of the internet and its seemingly infinite store of source materials, I was able to complete the work in a relatively short span of time. For their invaluable assistance in this task, I am especially indebted, among others, to such websites as Teodolinda Barolini's brilliant "Digital Dante" site (https://digitaldante.columbia.edu/dante/divine-comedy/) and Terrill Soules's Dante Concordance website, both of which make it possible to engage in split-second consultation of Dantean passages, bypassing the much slower process of digging through books for fragments one does not always find. Also of crucial importance, for rapid consultation of other medieval Italian poets referenced, was the Italian website, letteraturaoperaomnia.org. More traditional ink-on-paper sources for similar research include the Charles Singleton critical edition of *The Divine Comedy* (Princeton: Bollingen, 1970); the Vandelli critical edition of *La Divina Commedia* with Scartazzini's commentary (Hoepli, Milan [1928] 1989); Dante, *Vita nuova e rime*, Guido Davico Bonino, ed. (Milan: Mondadori, 1985); F. Bausi, M. Martelli, *La metrica italiana* (Florence 1989); and Contini's own anthology of early Italian poetry, *Letteratura italiana delle origini* (Florence 1976).

Stephen Sartarelli

AN IDEA OF DANTE

Introduction to the Rime *of Dante*

Rather than speak of a *Canzoniere* for Dante, as seems to have become the habit after Charles Lyell (1835), it is more prudent to speak of his *Rime* (i.e., "lyric poems"), since the sixteenth-century meaning of *canzoniere* ("songbook") is automatically associated, after the example set by Petrarch, with the idea of a unified body of work, the organic adventure of one soul. Such a position tends to hark back to the thirteenth century and its need for a conscious psychological as well as stylistic construction enclosed within the clear framework of a personal history in which style itself becomes primarily an endless effort of elimination and simplification.

In Dante, too, we find attempts at unification, especially in the *Vita Nuova*. But it is a unification after the fact, consisting of things of the past from the end of his youth, whose purpose is to dispense, lyrically, with a period of life in preparation for another more splendid one (*"io spero di dicer di lei quello che mai non fue detto d'alcuna"*) ["I hope to say of her what has never before been said of any woman"; *V.N.* XLII]. It is therefore a partial, anecdotal unification, one that presupposes plurality, and at the same time a transcendent unification, sought through a system of *razos*[1] and within a narrative structure.

Leaving aside other spontaneous groupings (although that designated by *Parole mie* is a conscious one), we find another interrupted and much less solid attempt at unification in the *Convivio*, a collection of the most demanding allegorical *canzoni*, in which the intention that beautiful form should be, without distinction, a celebration of the highest moral virutes, is constant. In this manner, the so-called Dantean *canzoniere* revolves around the absence of the *Vita Nuova*

---

[1] The *razo* (old Occitan for "cause" or "reason") was traditionally a text accompanying a troubadour poem and explaining the circumstances and meaning of the composition. The convention carried over to a degree in Italian medieval poetry, and was refined by Dante to include himself as his own commentator. The authors of the Occitan *razos* were never the poets themselves.

at the very least, includes the remaining excluded poems and the many novelties that came after the period of pure *stilnovismo*, and can be defined as a magnificent collection of "outliers."

It is stating the obvious to assert that the history of Italian lyric poetry at its origins is still organized around Dantean schemas that corresponded to general critical demands of the time, but which continued to exist after Dante's imperative (the constitution of the Sicilian School, the Dolce Stil Nuovo, the Sicilian limitation of *Guittonismo*)[2]; all the more reason, then, that the same should be true of his own poetry. We are dealing here not only with nominal definitions, such as the *nove rime* ("new poems"), the poems of *la loda*, and the *bello stile* that won Dante praise, exemplified by the lofty Tragedy of Virgil,[3] and the great *canzoni*, which have been legitimately singled out, every one of them, as an application of the tragic style; but also with the fact that Dante's critical judgment of his predecessors and contemporaries—from the Provençal troubadours to Cino da Pistoia—functions in relation to his own poetics. Those elements of Dantean literary history are of course contained in a theoretical work such as the *De vulgari Eloquentia*, which also stands as a justification of the abovementioned *bello stile* and significantly leaves off when the *fragmenta* in the tragic style definitively give way to the wholeness of the great poem. And yet they are also found, at least in equal measure, in the *Commedia*, which in its vital richness is also a stylistic *summa*. I am thinking specifically of the essential roles played by the apologia for the vernacular tongue and the justification of the ideal banquet in the *Convivio*, which, following the youthful *Vita Nuova*, would pull together in a single whole the allegorical *canzoni* of the mature period. And this perpetual addition of a technical reflexion to a work of poetry, this association of concrete poetic creation and stylistic intelligence, would become a constant of Dante's personality. It grants Dante's oeuvre a unique appearance, not quite of discontinuity, but of cadenced periodicity. In him there is never peace, but always the torment of dialectics.

Precisely because of these residues of poetic transcendence, then, it is less illegitimate, in regard to Dante, than for the other poets, to apply the didactic approach (without of course any universal applicability), according to which one may recognize, in an author's *opera omnia*, the signs of an ideal chronology.

---

[2] *Guittonismo*: the stylistic conventions of those following and imitating Guittone d'Arezzo (1235-1294).

[3] That is, the *Aeneid*.

Residues of poetic transcendence; exercising style not as an absolute tendency according to what would become the Petrarchian and later the Platonic Renaissance model, but as a "local" attempt; that sense not so much of a general limit to form as of the specific limitations of the Scholastic styles; his downgrading of a prior experience, depriving it of any intrinsic finality and exploiting it as an element of a new experience. In this sense, Dante's "outliers" actually follow a linear unity, but in the same restless manner of procedure as we find from one Dantean essay to the next. And the whole "songbook" is fragmentary not only for those looking for flashes of brilliance and pure intuition, but also as a series of attempts, as was recognized by so implacable a Dante specialist as E. G. Parodi, who in so doing scandalized a good half of the secluded world of Dante scholars.

Dante's teachers and friends already displayed a considerable range in taste and technical possibilities. I'm not referring to the Sicilians, however, for whom it would be problematic to raise the question of stylistic consistency. The first Guido (Guinizzelli, that is) was a magistrate writing in the manner of Guittone, and so docile as to merit—after he had *mutata la mainera* ["transformed the manner"][4]—from another strictly observant vernacular poet in Bonagiunta, not only personal reproaches but the precise critical objection that poetry is not knowledge. Except that his novelty was not only the doctrinal one we find (apparently) in *Al cor gentil*; and neither did it stop at the myth of the salvational woman, but went so far as to embrace bourgeois anecdotalism in *Chi vedesse a Lucia un var cappuzzo* and primitive "realism" in *Diavol te fera*.

Even more nonchalant was Cavalcanti, who was able to reproduce all the "genres" of lyric poetry—the transalpine *pastorella* (*In un boschetto*), the Sicilian *canzonetta* (*Fresca rosa novella*), the naturalistic Panism invented by Guinizzelli (*Beltà di donna*)—with the freshest of virtuosity; and in matters of doctrinal rigor and esoterism he outperformed even the most learned (*Donna mi prega*) and managed to carry psychological analysis to the level of parody. Nor—as these were all rather aristocratic manners—did he ever compromise his somewhat snobbish, gentlemanly, splenetic melancholy.

As for Cino da Pistoia, if we look closely, his unity of tone—which, according to the cliché, prefigured Petrarch—proves just a wee bit involuntary or,

---

[4] "Voi ch'avete mutata la mainera" is the first line of a sonnet by Bonagiunta Orbicciani (13th cent.) addressed to Guido Guinizzelli and the latter's transformation of vernacular Italian poetry.

let us say, psychologistic (which is where we encounter the limits of his Petrarchianism *avant la lettre*). And what better place, than amidst so much dread and tears and fear of death, for a sonnet on a set motif (*Tutto ciò ch'altrui aggrada*), a text which no one today would dream anymore of reading as a redoubtable romantic document, as it clearly echoes the caricatural vein of Cecco Angiolieri and Trecento *giullaresco* modes?

Dante's variety, which is certainly no less considerable, materially speaking—from the *ballata della ghirlandetta* or that for Violetta to the so-called *rime petrose*,[5] from the sonnet for la Garisenda to the canzone *Tre donne* or *la montanina*—is of an entirely different order. In him there is never so much as a hint of scepticism. There are jokes, of course, in his work, but they are always far from the centers of inspiration. Deep down, there's a terrible seriousness to it all. All the "imitations" are allowed to leave their deposits, down to the last, and achieve the final results (some fruits of the poet's reading of the Sicilians would remain indelible in the *Rime*), but they never deviate into the sort of cynical amplifications that could give rise to parody. In reality, technique in Dante is something belonging to the sacred order of things; it is the path of his ascetic practice, indistinguishable from the striving for perfection. There is, on the one hand, overall and throughout the wealth of Dante's attempts, a sweet technique that wishes to cancel out its own effort, and which resolves in a smooth writing texture that is modulated but without unevenness—and yet it is still the same world as that of the *Vita Nuova*, with the renunciation of earthly matters and the devotion to a woman who is all the more real the less reality is granted the poet, and who becomes most real when she is physically dead. And in this atmosphere the triumph over sin—that is, the effort of the triumph over sin—tends to lose its exceptional quality and become normalized in the everyday acceptance of an ideal.

Thus (given our fairly summary distinction between these two opposite poles of inspiration), we can say that there is also, in Dante, a harsh technique, one that underscores the effort and explicitly accentuates the most salient points of the rhythm, especially in the rhyme—but it is all one with the sentiment of love and the difficulty of life, obstacles, and their overcoming. One particular

---

[5] The term by which are generally designated the sestina *Al poco giorno e al gran cerchio d'ombra*; the canzone *Io son venuto al punto de la rota*; the double sestina *Amor tu vedi ben questa donna*; and the canzone (considered the most emblematic of the "petrose"), *Così nel mio parlar voglio esser aspro*.

example should more than suffice to demonstrate this second aspect—in it Dante finds himself in contact with one of his most intimate friends. A sonnet by Cino to the Marchese Malaspina is a lament for the suffering experienced from a new love, consisting of rather facile rhymes, as well as a pun on the nobleman's name and a little residue of Guittonian esoterism at the start and at the end. The answer from the character called Moroello in the poem was written by Dante, and it stresses the motif, which recurs elsewhere, of Cino's volubility, contrasted on the one hand by the charm of his poetry, on the other by the respondent's genuine passion.

Casting a comparative glance at the quatrains' rhymes suffices to demonstrate the abyss of knowledge separating the two artificers. Cino: *oro, inchina, spina, moro, ploro, fina, destina, dimoro*; Dante: *tesoro, latina* (in the archaic sense of "clear, intelligible"), *disvicina, fóro, poro, medicina* (as a verb), *affina, discoloro*. Here we already encounter the lexical breadth of the *Commedia*, indeed already that of the two last *cantiche* (i.e., the *Purgatorio* and the *Paradiso*): *fóri* [holes] for "wounds" break the person of Jacopo del Cassero; the sun *discolora* the metaphorical grass in Oderisi's simile; and the representation of Piccarda Donati will be *latina*. And if the verb *medicinare* is a Provençalism, the fine litotes contained in *disvicinare* bears the same inventive trademark of such verbal creations as *dismentare*, *immillare*, and *indovare*. It is instructive to see such a robust vocabulary make its way back up the verse lines, propagating itself in reverse compared to the rhyme, which itself is the "center of difficulty": "*ma volgibile cor ven disvicina*" ["but the movable heart takes you away"]; or: "*ove stecco d'Amor mai non fe' foro*" ["to where Love's thorn pricks me not"]; or even "*del prun che con sospir si medicina*" ["of the wood that medicates with sighs"].

If the glow radiates from the rhyme, that amounts to saying that the springboard of inspiration is the obstacle (what was called, more or less properly, the "resistance of the medium"). And the obstacle is the enemy to be defeated each and every day, the permanent state of war, the awareness of the dangerous eros to which the poet succumbs, and in which he finds perfection and glory. One could make similar observations concerning the tercets (Cino: *conte* [meaning "known"], *gioia, noia, moia, monte, fonte*; Dante: *fronte, poia, croia, ploia, conte* [meaning "skilled"], and *ponte* in a highly idiomatic expression), highlighting the difference in the fact that Dante here emphasizes, polemically, the counter-role opposed to the always accepted torment, the dishonesty of inconstancy. The technical "medium" is merely a tool of self-investigation; more precisely, it is religious thirst itself in action, whereby one does not wish to exclude, in practice, even the frequent lapsing into the dangers of abstract technicalism. And although the correspondence between specific techniques and specific moments within Dante's soul could destroy from the start the hypothesis of a potential equidistance from specific experiences and a fundamental uninterest in them (which one cannot rule out for any of his colleagues) and thereby appear to belong to customs of the time and the sphere of moral life, this variety stands out, on the other hand, as a spiritual evolution in its circulation, and therefore as a fact of form.

If in discussing Dante's lyric poetry one turns continuously to his contemporaries, this circumstance stems not from the superstition of literary history, nor from the usual didactic artifice of defining through differentiation and antithesis, but indeed from the nature of the subject treated, which is reproduced in the critic. The Dolce Stile is the school that most self-consciously and gracefully features a sense of collaboration in a work of objective poetry—in other words, the school most deserving to be called a "school." It is not enough, and imprecise, to imagine a common stylistic ideal shared by every adept. We find in the Dolce Stile all the sentimental premises of a congruence in the work composed, first and foremost the idea of a friendship that recalls, in these fallen noblemen and high-culture bourgeois, the equality and solidarity of the Occitan knights. The sonnet, *Guido, i'vorrei*, is in general correctly interepreted as a typical product of the *stilnovista* taste, not because one may gather from this lyric the motif of fateful escape towards remote, exotic places in which one recognizes without much effort the tradition of Provençal/troubadour *plazer*, but rather because this flight towards an unreal world is something to be taken affectionately among close friends, with their beautiful consorts. And in this very vicinity, made warmer by its imaginative nature, the desires would be the same, and the wish to remain together would increase. An absolute break from reality converted into friendship: this is the true content of the lyric, friendship being the defining emotional element of the Stil Novo.

In the practice of the poetic event, the potential lack of differentiation between the poets, their lack of interest in or refusal to emphasize distinctions of individuality, are facts somewhat thorny to grasp for the Western mentality, especially after the exaltation of subjectivity effected by the great European Romantic movement. For this is not a case of the same involuntary equivalency that supposedly makes it ever so difficult to attribute specific authorship, or affective and national-historical meaning, to certain texts, when anonymous, of even minor Romantics, and later of minor Symbolists and, today, of minor Surrealists; and neither is this merely a case of the objective poetics of "classical" epochs (the demand of the "*Hic est*" as affirmed, in Antiquity, by Martial, himself an author of epigrams…). Rather, we are dealing with something more resolute, because the classical author, like a good craftsman, believes in a canon of *ars*, a workman's canon, and the *stilnovista* believes in absolute inspiration—he keeps himself close, in the Dantean expression, with his pen, to the "dictator": Amore. The frequent interchangeability of attribution in the manuscripts, and the fact that within certain limits, without any specific documentary evidence, the stylistic aspects would not appear to be sufficient to buttress any definitive "expert opinions" concerning certain pairs of authors writing texts together, are the pale outward reflection of what is, indeed, above all a theoretical interchangeability. The watershed between Dante and Cino is, to cite a typical case (while leaving aside the circumstances that made the exchange possible, and the fact that outside the Middle Ages they would not have been able to act so broadly), less than certain. Uncertain in a juridical sense—and perhaps even too obvious to mention—demonstrating the unimportance of property and the individual.

In truth, what Dante says in the Bonagiunta episode we alluded to just now is the fundamental text for understanding the Dolce Stile. One must, however, interpret it in full, and understand that the inspiration (*Amor mi spira*) is not a private, occasional inspiration, nor even an inspiration of an amorous order[6] (war too, the *De vulgari* recognizes, can be the subject of the tragic style, though at this point the consideration of a "general" style will have been abandoned for a "particular" one, technically speaking). It is, rather, nothing less than an inspiration arising from a transcendent principle, a total surrender to Love. The inspiration is obejctive and absolute, and for this reason, if the normal content of Stil Novo lyric poetry is the phenomenon of love subjected to minute analysis and then hypostatized in its elements, this analysis must not be applied to the empirical individual, but rather, beyond this initial adventure of his, to a universal exemplar of man: he too an objective, absolute individual.

This explains how the person of the new troubadour, far from asserting himself, dissolves in a chorus of friendship; and how this friendship, aside from representing the general possibility of this particular poetry, is actually assumed

---

[6] In the *Vita Nuova* (XXV 6), Dante marshals arguments "contra coloro che rimano sopra altra matera che amorosa" ["against those who rhyme on subjects other than love"]. (GC)

in the guise of an initial poetic motif. To the chorus of friends within which the poet loses himself comes a reply, like a twin poetic motif, from the other side, the choral background of ladies from which *la beatrice* (i.e., the inspiration) stands out like a queen and as the fundamental seat of their honor and the source of their beauty. It is clear that, in this atmosphere of prehistoric earthly paradise, if on the side of Adam there exist men of flesh and blood, the lesser feminine clientele have only the task of underscoring Eve, and live through the metaphor of those friends gathered round the poet. The fact remains that, like him, the character who speaks in the first person is the "absolute individual," and the woman, too, loses all historical attributes, all possibility of genuine plurality. And if the field of observation, in this process, is gradually broadened, one notes that the whole experience of the *stilnovista* is depersonalized, transposed to a universal order: losing all memory of circumstance, it crystallizes at once.

In a rather elementary, empirical manner (coming indeed from empiricism's land of origin), this truth has been elaborated upon, as we shall see below, by the most illustrious of today's English poets, right after he had just denied that Dante's "romance" could have the present-day meaning of a confession: "It is difficult to conceive of an age (of many ages), when human beings cared somewhat about the salvation of the 'soul,' but not about each other as 'personalities.' Now Dante, I believe, had experiences which seemed to him of some importance; not of importance because they had happened to him and because he, Dante Alighieri, was an important person who kept press-cutting bureaux busy; but important in themselves; and therefore they seemed to him to have some philosophical and impersonal value."[7]

It is always useful to bear in mind our Romantic education as modern men, raised in the aesthetic cult of subjective reactions that present themselves to us in all their nakedness, to measure how much, by comparison, the *stilnovista* rendered such reactions figurative and symbolic. A plastic approach, so to speak, to relations between things is the only way in which the objets of his dream, for him, will tolerate being expressed in orderly fashion—what some very recent and rather eccentric English-language readers, based on premises they have read, call by the rather suggestive formula of "objective correlative." Caring only that the representation not be without relation and worrying little

---

[7] T.S. Eliot, "Dante," in *The Selected Essays of T.S. Eliot*, Harcourt, Brace & Co, NY, 1932, p. 233.

about the concrete hidden meaning, these fanciful interpreters will prove exegetically wanting; practically speaking, however, an effort of transliteration of *stilnovista* objective figuration within the schemas of "Romantic" subjectivistic representation could, today, be pedagogically useful in helping to demonstrate that incarnation in plastic terms.

When Dante, in the sonnet, *Sonar bracchetti*, hears an amorous *pensamento* (that is, a "preoccupation"), a reproach—or more precisely a "taunt"—addressed to him as if by a sprite, for preferring the bourgeois pleasures of the hunt to the courtly duty of the *joi d'amor*, we have before us the externalized "action" of an inner remorse. Instead of the myths of conscience, a miniature *sacra rappresentazione* (though we must not forget that, from this perspective, inner drama, indeed theatricality, is typical of medieval art). And when, elsewhere (as in the sonnet *De gli occhi de la mia donna*), Dante returns to the most dangerous of moments ("*e tornomi colà dov'io son vinto*") ["and I returned to where I was vanquished"], and before his lady's eyes he closes his own and his desire dies, this troubled multiple and spatial figuration would translate as *giving in to temptation and succumbing*. A man seeking to banish dark thoughts as unmanly, and finding himself unable to do so, who only through the onset of amorous desire manages to give precise expression to that disquiet in the pressing sensation of his beloved's mortality: this is the translation of *Un dì si venne a me Malinconia*—which nevertheless lets slip the fundamental essence of the sonnet; that is, the concretization of the private, tangible presentiment glimpsed in a vision: the reality of the angel.

One final example, indeed the clearest of all, as well as the most legendary, is that of Lisetta, a graphic representation of the victory over temptation in a strong man. Desire is bold until it wanders onto the *terrain vague* of velleity, but it cannot breach the solidity of moral decisiveness. It is clear, given the mentality driving medieval poetics, that we are not dealing, in this sonnet, with a physical phenomenon—that is, with an actual, rejected Lisetta. Indeed at this point, the fruit that Dante could still gather from the Sicilian separation of the woman from her image, as painted in the lover's heart, is plain as day. Lisetta is real (we are not speaking, of course, in absolute terms—it would be superfluous to do so—but in terms of the poet's initial awareness) in as much as she is a fantasy in Dante's mind. Thus when the laboriously and discordantly elaborated identification and differentiation of the so-called women loved by Dante is not aimed at clearly isolating poetic experiences—a process deemed extraneous by aestheticist critics—it becomes extraneous to Dante's poetics themselves. Another important consequence follows in descending progression: as his inner events are separated and rendered distant, the poet can dispense with the frown that induces self-obsession in the Romantic (with an ultimate escape in the grotesque), and then pass through a series of touching emotions or confusions, of self-recoveries and smiles ("prendo vergogna, onde mi ven pesanza" ["I feel shame, which weighs heavy on me"]; "Amore / lo mira con pietà ..." ["Love / looks on him with pity ..."]; "Che hai, cattivello?" ["What is wrong, naughty one?"]; "Or ecco leggiadria di gentil cuor..." ["And now behold a grace of noble heart..."]; "passa Lisetta baldanzosamente" ["Lisetta passes boldly by"]).[8] Thus in Dante, who is dead serious as to his method, a possibile germ of "irony" begins to take shape.

It is precisely the mentioned lack of "lyricism" in Dante's lyric poetry that better explains how, at a general historical glance, there appears to be no clear, distinct stylistic "development" in it, but rather a process of permanent restlessness. The first shift that one is able to notice in the formula is represented by the *nove rime* ["new poems"]. But there is no way we can speak of an actual shift away from *guittonismo* for *stilnovismo* because, from the point of view of the school, Dante's Guittonian lyrics are gallantries, gambles, *peccata iuventutis*, and the presumed conversion is merely a sliding from one friendship to another (we've seen the importance of friendship), from friendship with another Dante, da Maiano, to Lippo, possibly to Chiaro Davanzati and Puccio Bellondi, to that with Guido Cavalcanti and Lapo Gianni, and even Guido Orlandi and Meuccio Tolomei. From the point of view of the practice, on the other hand, traces of the Guittonian Dante who breaks up the word *parla* in a number of different ways to multiply the homonymous rhymes, and has *ch'amato* rhyme with the rare *camato* (almost a *hapax legomenon*!), and indulges in repetitions ("ciò che sentire / dovevano a ragion senza *veduta*, / non conobber *vedendo*")[9], will nevertheless reappear in the Dante of the *Commedia*, who, after years of abstaining from such procedures in the "tragic" atmosphere of the great moral *canzoni* (the "expanses" of that Boccacciesque collection), will, for example, put a *non ci ha* in the mouth of mastro Adamo to rhyme with *oncia* and *sconcia*, have Pier della Vigna lament the harlot who enflamed everyone's spirits against him, even

---

[8] Quotes drawn from, respectively, *Sonar bracchetti*; *Ne le man vostre, gentil donna mia*; *Un dí si venne a me Malinconia*; *Rime*, LXI; *Per quella via che bellezza corre*.

[9] From *Rime*, LI. Contini's emphasis.

as the enflamed souls enflamed Augustus, and will pray and re-pray (*pregare / ripregare*) Virgil to see that one prayer is worth a thousand.

The commentators repeat, and they are not wrong, that the counterfeiter is indeed cursing his own tremendous immobility ("potessi in cent'anni andare un'oncia" ["if I could move an inch in a hundred years"; *Inf.* XXX, 83]), while a humanly ridiculous vista expands frighteningly before him until we reach the strained rhyme ("e men d'un mezzo di traverso non ci ha" ["and it is less than half a mile across"; line 87]). And they repeat, with equal legitimacy, that a prince-dictator's speech is rather fitting for a minister of Frederick II, and that in these orations all the ornaments of that century's rhetoric are on display. This is the way they explain how the Guittonian Dante is no longer freely gadding about but is encapsulated and put to account within the Dante of the *Commedia*; and how the latter, in speaking disdainfully of Guittone, can engage in discourse from a time long surpassed within himself. The Guittonian who once existed, naively, in a pure state, is now subordinate and docile, serving a rather different purpose from mere abstract exercise. And clearly the same distinction must be made within Guittone himself; and the historian, who must be effortlessly reverent to the great ones fallen in the battle for glory, has the obligation to recognize that something else and much more essential, having passed through Dante and into the highest Italian literary consciousness and tradition—namely the lyrical-essayistic construction—would move through the culture from an initiative that we owe to none but Guittone, Friar Guittone. The eloquent, energetic vein that flows from *Poscia ch'Amor* to *Doglia mi reca* clearly follows in the wake of his moral *canzone*. Dante's ingratitude towards the old master, not unlike the anti-D'Annunzianism of many of our contemporaries, is indeed an indication, among other things, of having beaten him on the turf most his own, and one of great merit, of having fulfilled and surpassed his highest ambition.

If for Dante *stilnovismo* is, as we have said, essentially a faithfulness to the "dictator" (Love), and therefore a poetics of the objectification of feelings, its culmination and point of greatest innovation lies in the moment in which the organization of Love's faithful becomes so complete as to include the justification of speech. The myth is certainly one of the most beautiful of those marking the story of his poetics (*Vita Nuova* XVIII): If happiness no longer resides in even the slightest thing outside the lover, the lady's greeting, which heretofore was the ultimate purpose of his life, it will now be found in something permanent, "in quelle parole che lodano la donna" ["in the words that praise the woman"]; and since the noble ladies—again the pairing of theme of the feminine "chorus" and that of the "objectification" of remorse—reproach him for having used other words than those intended for her praise, he will propose to "prendere per matera" his "parlare sempre mai quello che fosse loda di questa gentilissima" [to "take as his material" . . . "only ever that which were praise for this noblest of ladies"]. What spurs Dante's mind and determines the *nove rime* is therefore a demand for unity (the *razo* of *Donne ch'avete* gives us a glimpse, moreover, of the relationship between the inspiration, the *est deus in nobis*— from which the *"cominciamento"* ["beginning"] draws its origin: "Allora dico che la mia lingua parlò quasi come per se stessa mossa..." ["And so I say that my tongue spoke as if moved by itself"]—and the work itself, the thought of "alquanti die" ["a good number of days"]).

The same necessity inspires the extension of love poetry into moral poetry, and allows the *nove rime* to give way to the *bello stilo*. This transition is allegorized in the sonnet *Due donne in cima de la mente mia*, in which the uniqueness of love is first split into the aspects of beauty and virtue, then comes back together in its primordial oneness, proclaimed, mind you, by Amore as the "fonte del gentil parlare" ["font of noble speech"]—as "dictator," in other words. Of course the risk always remains that this unity will break: the risk of allegorical poetry. So far there has been no question of allegorization, in the contemporary (i.e., dualistic) sense of the term; indeed the "objective" poetry we've described is more or less the opposite of allegorization, as it is taken up entirely with the eminently unitary concern for the perceptible presentation of internal events. Allegorization begins with a divorce from meaning; and thus *Voi che 'ntendono* will close with the pathetic exclamation, "Ponete mente *almen* com'io son bella" ["take note *at least* how beautiful I am"; emphasis added], while the *Convivio* (II xi 4) will gloss: "la bontade e la bellezza di ciascuno sermone sono intra loro partite e diverse; ché la bontade è ne la sentenza, e la bellezza è ne l'ornamento de le parole; e l'una e l'altra è con diletto, avvegna che la bontade sia massimamente dilettosa."[10]

Thus, on the one hand, we have a plurality of meanings, a duality of planes sliding one over the other, interfering with one another and never perfectly coinciding; and on the other, the possibility that the philosophical exposition, the "prose" of the idealistic definition, might remain solitary and neglected—an

---

[10] "...the goodness and beauty of every avowal separate and different from one another; for goodness lies in the statement, and beauty lies in the ornamentation of the words; and while both provide delight, it is true that goodness gives the most delight."

extreme example of this being in another of the *Convivio*'s canzoni, *Le dolci rime*. During this period, Dante, to justify the varying and increasing isolation of moral themes, will construct an entire mythology, one based on the abandonment—at least temporary—of Love, in the sweet, delightful sense of the notion. And yet Love still remains deep down the source of goodness, along with beauty, "a vertú solamente formata" ["created only for virtue's sake"], of which the canzone *Doglia mi reca* speaks. And thus the *cantor rectitudinis* issues from the *cantore d'Amore*. And this abandonment *a parte obiecti* becomes likewise an abandonment *a parte subiecti*; that is, human love finds a competitor in the love of virtue, and through this "objective" poetics, the competition is represented as a rivalry among women, so that in its initial phase it becomes possible to hesitate exegetically between a literal interpretation and an allegorical one (think of the case of the *pargoletta*[11]). Is the woman real? Or just a symbol? The puzzlement of commentators gains meaning and seriousness exclusively as pertains to this moment of poetic "transition."

In Dante's moral poems we encounter the zeal of the neophyte having just stepped into the disputations of the philosophizers. We find a similar enthusiasm in Dante the poetry lover and literary scholar such as those fields were being developed in his time (scholarly and moral enthusiasm, and the enthusiasm for Occitan culture, are contemporaneous in the *De vulgari*.) In his youth Dante had experienced a second-hand and, so to speak, specialized—that is, mannered—Provençalism through the Guittonians and Sicilians. And even the Provençal precedents of the Dolce Stile, and thus the irresponsible ancestors of the Dante of the *Vita Nuova*, had been indicated in secondary authors entirely devoid of grace, such as the boring Guilhem de Montanhol, and possibly Guiraut Riquier, who were astute adminstrators of poetry in the general decline that began with the death of Folquet (in so saying we are of course neglecting the only true poet of this period, the great, archaizing Peire Cardinal, because he was not a *chef d'école*). Is there any need to point out that an Occitanism so indirect could only become a concern in times of abstraction and then ritualized? "Se volemo cercare in lingua d'oco," says the *Vita Nuova* (XXV 4), "noi non troviamo cose dette anzi lo presente tempo per cento e cinquanta anni." ["If we wish to search

---

[11] A series of poems in the *Rime* about a beautiful young girl (*pargoletta*) descended from heaven to display her charms but who is loath to fall in love.

in the langue d'oc {...} we find nothing said for one hundred and fifty years before the present time."]

And across this rather limited, compact sphere, there isn't much outward variety, since the Provençal soul can be subtly gathered from the craft. But if indeed Dante destined himself to gathering the essential thing it has to teach him—style—he still had to backtrack across that brief span of a century and a half and differentiating the generations. Such is the intelligence of this philology nourishing poetry! And thus Dante's first-hand Provençalism becomes his meetings with the troubadours of the "golden age", those in the *Commedia*: Giraut de Borneil, Bertran de Born, Folchetto (Folquet), Sordello (the latter being chronologically out of phase and a peripheral author); and, above all, Arnaut Daniel. Within the *Rime*, this genuine Provençalism is represented by the experience of the so-called *rime petrose*: an experience that will remain, in lesser form, in the *Commedia* as a verbalization of difficulty, of obstacle, a grasping of a troubling reality, in keeping with the definition that has been imposed on it.

This recourse to interpretation in the *Commedia* is not merely a didactic artifice, nor does it concern a reversion to precedent or to material normally imposed on authors in one's own already accomplished poetry; rather, it concerns the need to integrate those immobile lyrics and the lack of any complete self-sufficiency. The current legitimate admiration for this suggestive series[12] must nevertheless make it clear that, even more than the "fragments" of *poesia petrosa* articulated in the *Commedia* (such as, for example, in the traitors' circle), the inspiration of the *petrose* themselves appears to be radically "fragmentary."

Alongside the sentiment of difficult reality in itself, as an object, such as we find in the *petrose*, Dante's *tenzone* (*tenso*) with Forese presents a reality known through a gamut of resentments and the violent distortion of caricature. And the representation is already rich therewith, and technically witty. Just one example, from the first quatrain of the second sonnet. We know that the height of Provençal stylistic artifice was the sestina, the versification of which careers vehemently towards the end, which is designed to feature the most decisive words and thus a spectacle of the hardest reality. It is in keeping with such a procedure that the "petti delle starne" ["the partridges' breasts"]—with the indicated fleshliness of their tempting appearance—appear in the verse and follow in this

---

[12] Croce, in *La poesia di Dante* (pp. 46-47), has a few reservations in this regard. (GC)

fashion the strongly idiomatic and allusive "nodo Salamone"[13]; while, just below, the ingenious collation of the fates of the flesh, buried in the physiology of the glutton, with those of the skin—converted into parchment for registering ruinous debts—is presented with a noble appearance somewhere between the riddle and the *trobar clus* ("ma peggio fia la lonza del castrone / ché 'l cuoio farà vendetta de la carne" ["but the loin will be worse than mutton / for the leather will take revenge for the flesh"]). The looming threat takes on a physical concreteness in the insistence of the alternating rhymes (among the rhymes we have *San Simone*—the prison—and *l'andarne*: the painful need to flee, uttered with joyous ferocity): for Dante knows how to vary the patterns skillfully, and saves the closed rhymes for the tranquil and much more triumphant ending. And paying tribute, in the *tenso*, are all the sciences of the encyclopedia, from physiology (the ancient humours, as used in marriage) to mineralogy (the origin of rock crystal from ice, fittingly evoked in a *petrosa*). *Sieti raccomandato il mio Tesoro*: Let my Tesoro, my book, be a boon to you... We are far, here, from the ascetic leveling of the *Vita Nuova* (which, like all asceticism, is renunciatory); and the new sense of reality postulates a richer fabric, with complements and components not traceable to the *canzoniere* of the second period. Once again, as the initial stilnovistic unity (which now seems temporary) is broken, we find ourselves in the presence of very fine fragments that certainly conspire towards a unity. But this unity exists outside of these precincts; we won't repeat where, alone, it is achieved.

It is nevertheless certain that the poetics of resentment quite singularly grafts itself onto the poetics of moral living, when the resentment becomes disdain for the cowardice of the prior generation, and the virtues become tattered, scorned women like Poverty in the Franciscan canto. It is their mistreatment that guarantees Dante's faithfulness, and above all their own poetic existence; and through it the moral life acquires a figurative reality, just as the hyperbolic conventions of the cult of unrequited love, or rather, self-requited love, possessed a figurative reality. The *cantor rectitudinis* and the self-avenger live together, and in cohabitation with the well-practiced draughtsman of symbolic compositions, in the canzone *Tre Donne*—in which we find the ill-fated damage of an entire century, a disaster in precisely the etymological sense ("e dolgasi la bocca / de li uomini a cui tocca") ["and may the mouths of the men / whom it

---

[13] In heraldry, the "Solomon's knot" is an intricate, allegorical system of knots.

touches lament"], as well as personal experience ("E io, che ascolto nel parlar divino . . .") ["And I, who listen to this speech divine..."].

The diagram of Dante's poetry would appear, in our quick review, to draw to a close in the poem *Tre donne*; and yet the divergence of the two chronologies—the ideal and the literary—reasserts itself here, since a surviving trace of biographical concern lets us see that the canzone should be situated in the very earliest phase, indeed the first months, of his exile. And the poems of his exile, now that the astronomical argument has removed the *petrose* from their number, show anything but an organic stylistic consistency. I am not talking about his correspondence with Cino (and, for his less uncertain but still problematic part in it, his correspondence with Giovanni Querini), which, while being a far cry from the invariability of his friend's, is still dotted with technical wizardry, a constant that preserves some aspects of the old fidelity. Nor am I talking about the sonnet for Lisetta, which, if anything, is genuinely archaizing (as well as quite playful, being, deep down, a kind of jest) and has been attributed to this period on the slightest of evidence.

Historical reasons, however, show two great canzoni to come after *Tre donne*: *Doglia mi reca*—for its allusive *envoi* to a lady of the Conti Guidi—and the "montanina," *Amor, da che convien*, for its epistle to Moroello Malaspina. What is new about *Doglia mi reca* is its loose syntax and enthusiastic assertions and pronouncements; but, skipping over *Tre donne*, it links back up, with its airy structure, to the didactic poems of the *Convivio*, specifically *Le dolci rime*, which contains a similarly swift alternation of hendecasyllables and *settenari* in the long strophe (we think for example of sequences such as: "né la diritta torre / fa piegar rivo che da lungi corre"; and "Ubidiente, soave e vergognosa / è ne la prima etate..."). And there are certainly more vestiges of the figurative reality of the virtues in that one: Discretion's quick action in the second stanza, honest birding in the sixth; note, however, the lack of clarity in precisely one of the most suggestive moments for the presence of extremely real, everyday things in poetry: ("Maladetto lo tuo perduto pane, / che non si perde al cane!" ["Cursed be bread lost on you, / not on a dog!"]).

Strictly speaking, then, are we not still at the construction stage? And it's not atelier-related questions the "*montanina*" calls to mind, but old and somewhat lazy conventions—a fact that on the one hand undoubtedly condemns the experience of the *petrose*. But we mustn't exaggerate: the text is stiff in content or "motif," and finds linguistic fertility only in the opening of the fifth stanza, "Così m'hai concio, Amore..." ["To this pass have you brought me, Love"].

Still, for a broad portion, and in the overall tone, the poet falls back into a Sicilianization deprived of the earlier Sicilians' merits of naïveté (the painting of the image, the distinction between woman and image). Here the chronological conflict becomes a peremptory indication of the fundamental crisis of the *Rime*, as they are about to end (and not in vain). One of their most astute, ideal organizers—and certainly the most elegant—Ferdinando Neri, states: "This canzone is a problem that even I refuse to explain: there is, in it, courtly love, a few Cinoesque moves, and a few other 'petrose.'"

Beyond the anecdotal, the "problem" is the same general one of the Dantean *canzoniere*'s insufficient ability to justify itself, its inexplicability *iuxta propria principia*[14]. The *montanina* is the only lyric poem of Dante's for which we are able to assign, with assurance, a relatively late date, and even so, it is in following a regressive, and almost erroneous, sequence. Can there be, in conclusion, any better argument for reconfirming that the obsession with the *Commedia*, in the mind of the exegete of the *Rime*, is not a useless phantasm moved by the principle of authority? Only from such a critical perspective are we able to see Dante's exploratory struggle, and the furor of his practice, find fulfillment.

(1938)

[Introduction to the 1939 edition (Turin, Einaudi) of Dante's *Rime*, and to all subsequent editions.]

---

[14] "...according to its own principles," quoting the lesser-known second part of the title of Lucretius' magnum opus, *De rerum Natura iuxta propria principia*.

Exercise in Interpreting a Sonnet by Dante

    Tanto gentile e tanto onesta pare
la donna mia, quand'ella altrui saluta,
ch'ogne lingua deven, tremando, muta,
e li occhi no l'ardiscon di guardare.

    Ella si va, sentendosi laudare,
benignamente d'umiltà vestuta,
e par che sia una cosa venuta
da cielo in terra miracol mostrare.

    Mostrasi sí piacente a chi la mira
che dà per li occhi una dolcezza al core
che'ntender no la può chi no la prova;

    e par che de la sua labbia si mova
un spirito soave pien d'amore
che va dicendo a l'anima: "Sospira."

*

So open and so self-possessed appears
my lady when she's greeting everyone,
that every tongue, in trembling, falters dumb,
and eyes don't dare to watch her as she nears.

She senses all the praising of her worth,
and passes by benevolently dressed
in humbleness, appearing manifest
from heaven to show a miracle on earth.

She shows herself so pleasing to the one
who sees her, sweetness passes through the eye
to the heart—as he who's missed it never knows.

> So from her face it then appears there blows
> a loving spirit, as if spring's begun,
> which breathes upon the soul and tells it: Sigh.)[1]

I should think there is no need to justify the choice of illustration. Considered typical of Dante's lyric poetry, or more precisely of the *stilnovista* phase of his youthful lyrics, this poem is, as such, committed to memory by any even moderately cultured Italian during his secondary school education. It is my ambition that the present interpretative exercise also be seen by the eyes of secondary school students in particular; so that, when being committed to memory, this sonnet will be registered with a different meaning from the one usually retained. Indeed it passes for the kind of linguistically limpid composition that requres no explanation—as something that "could have been written yesterday." Whereas we can confidently say that there is not a single word in it—or at least not any of the essential words—that has kept in the modern language the same meaning it had in the original. From the start, therefore, we are confronted with a problem of literal—indeed lexical—exegesis.

What, at best, can a commentator say? That *labbia*, which has disappeared from the modern language, means "face," in keeping with Dante's frequent use of the noun (thus in *Inf.* VII 7, we have the *infiata labbia* of Pluto; in XIV 67, the *miglior labbia* of Virgil when he moves from Capaneus to Dante; in XXV 21, Cacus the centaur covered with snakes where *comincia nostra labbia*, that is, where begins the human aspect of the bimorphous creature; in *Purg.* XXIII, 47, *la cangiata labbia* of Forese, later specified as *faccia*). But since it turns out, from these examples, that the respective significations of *labbia* and "face" do not entirely overlap (the latter being more physical, the former more spiritual and for that very reason physically broader, as in the case of Cacus), and since *labbia* is different from *faccia*, we shall settle for "physiognomy" as the least imprecise translation. Indeed translating merely means determining new relationships among synonyms and cognates in the culture represented by our language, a new redistribution, so to speak, in words, of a reality considered to be objective and constant. It is noteworthy, meanwhile, concerning Dante's particularity—or at least the particularity of this lyric poem of his—that the most

---

[1] Translation by Andrew Frisardi, by permission, from *Vita Nova*, Northwestern University Press, 2012.

material, the most physical word referring to the woman ends up involving her relation to the subject: "face" disappears, and "physiognomy" enters the picture.

And so what can the commentator say? He could diligently point out the (seemingly minimal) grammatical aspects that nevertheless help to situate the text's archaic Italian. Or the role as impersonal pronoun played here by the word *altrui* (as the objective case of *altri*), whose real function is to provide an object to a transitive verb that remains without any precise complement, and which becomes neutral, such as *salutare* here, or, for example, *camminare*. Or he could point out the placement of the pronoun object in line 4, right in front of the verb on which the infinitive supporting it depends, even though it is not a helping verb and indeed there is a preposition in the middle of it all: modern Italian cannot assert this sort of conjunction of the two verbs (that is, the interpenetration of the implied action), aside from cases such as *non la possono guardare*. Or the commentator might indicate the "median" or "deponent" signification of *si va*, an action reflecting on the subject, a meaning today lost in the fossil of *se ne va*. And there is also the absence of the article (after the preposition) before the word *cielo*, no less normal than in front of *terra*, and comprehensible only if one writes *da Cielo in Terra*. Of note as well is the placement of the object *miracol* (probably, but not inevitably, in the singular), between the preposition and the governing verb, asserting a conjunction, similar to the one mentioned above, between object of the verb in the action described (in another sonnet we find *"per mia lettera mandare"* ["my letter to send"]). And we can point out the obligatory nature of *Mostrasi*, which is in no way interchangeable with *si mostra*, since at the start of a sentence (and in early times also after *e* and *ma*), an unstressed particle[2] can only come after the verb: this is the so-called Tobler and Mussafia law, a syntactical bond discovered in Old French by the former—a Swiss professor in Berlin—and corroborated in Old Italian by the latter, a Dalmatian doing honor to Italian culture in Vienna.

And our commentator will also dwell on the true meaning of *che* at the start of line 11, which is not at all a conjunction (as in "una dolcezza *tale* che …'), but rather—today it would be considered an anacoluthon to be rooted out in elementary school—a relative pronoun combined with a pleonastic *la*. (Nor is there any lack of parallel examples in Dante, to say nothing of his contemporar-

---

[2] This is a translation of the more precise *particella*, which in Italian grammar refers to a non-autonomous grammatical morpheme that forms, with a lexical morpheme, a word or accentual unit.

ies: in *Inf.* V 69, "ombre ... / ch'amor di nostra vita dipartille"; in the canzone *Poscia ch'Amor*, "cosa / che lo 'ntelletto cieco non la vede.") And he will not fail to mention the perfectly acceptable use of *un* before *spirito*,[3] as we often find in Dante, and we can even find similar examples in the ever-so-smooth Petrarch—which means that the so-called "impure *s*" didn't always require a vowel preceding it (e.g., *ispirito*), a condition from which the use of the article *uno* would inevitably derive; but it means above all that one mustn't measure so-called euphony on subjective, arbitrary taste or a limited tradition.

And with these pedantic notes, which meanwhile help to situate the language historically (never mind its natural harmony), we can consider the task of the ordinary commentator fulfilled. Now begins the important part.

No less than three words in the first line have meanings entirely different from those assigned them in the contemporary tongue. *Gentile* means "noble," practically a technical term in the language of courtly love; *onesta*, a natural Latinism, is a synonym for it, but in the sense of outward decorum (we recall Virgil's *onestade* being compromised by his haste in *Purg.* III, 10-12). But it is more important, indeed essential, to establish that *pare* does not in fact mean "seem" or even simply "appear," but rather "appears in all clarity," or "is clearly manifest." This meaning of *pare*, a key word, reappears in the second quatrain and the second tercet—that is, at strategic points in every one of the sentences that go to make up the sonnet.[4] It appears missing in the first tercet, but only because that strophe begins with the equivalent *Mostrasi*, repeating thus the last word of the second quatrain. Let us not forget that the sonnet is a strophe of a *canzone*, where the quatrains are the feet of the *fronte* (the first part of a Petrarchian canzone), and the tercets are the *volte* of the *sirima*—which leads us to conclude that this connection between *fronte* and *sirima* is the very same as that we so often encounter between the strophes of archaic canzoni (*coblas capfinidas*[5] in Provençal), as for example in the celebrated *Al cor gentil* by Gunizzelli.

---

[3] In modern Italian, the article would have to be *uno*, because of the "impure *s*" in *spirito*—that is, an *s* combined with another consonant.

[4] This meaning of *par che* (quite illustratively charged in our example) remains in Petrarch, however in somewhat attenuated form (LXIV: "Ché gentil pianta in arido terreno / Par che si disconvenga, et però lieta / Naturalmente quindi si disparte.") (GC)

[5] *coblas capfinidas*: a link between successive stanzas in which the last line of one stanza contains a word repeated in the first line of the following stanza.

This allows us to put our finger on the structurally foremost concept of the composition.

Moving forward, we shall have less opportunity for discoveries. But we should point out that *donna* here exclusively has its early meaning as the "lady (of one's heart)"; it is, in short, a term with a purely grammatical feminine ending, in which the gender does not imply any opposite—think of the Portuguese poetry of the time, where one can address one's (female) beloved with the masculine *senhor*; same with the Provençal *midons*. To connote "woman," the prose commentary of the *Vita Nuova*, uses *femmina*, in opposition to *angeli*. On this subject, however, one mustn't grant the poet's additional prose too much exegetic value as for our area of concern: that would risk relating (as "discrete") the sonnet's *onesta* with the "*dolcezza onesta e soave*" the onlookers receive in their hearts, or even with the *onestade* of the intimidated gazer, whereas, on the contrary, these instances are a result of it. Thus we must not limit the import of line 6 with the gloss "nulla gloria mostrando di ciò ch'ella vedea e udia " ["showing no self-satisfaction from what she saw and heard"], which in fact is illuminated by it as a corollary: that *umiltà*, confirmed by *benignamente*, is, in the courtly context, the opposite of the cruelty and pride of the insensitive woman: it is benevolence. The metaphor of the dress (*vestuta*), so common in Dante and the Stil Novo in general, brings us back to that visible manifestation of a feeling and a quality that we've seen concentrated in the word *pare*. Even the word *cosa* stands inside a network of relationships entirely different from its modern meanings. Nowadays a *cosa*, a thing, ranks well below the ontological level of a person (a woman can become her lover's "thing," his tool, an object without autonomy, through self-abnegation[6]); here, on the other hand, *cosa* is more broadly a human being, in as much as the "thing" indeed evokes feelings and impressions. The effect is a *miracol*, explained in the gloss to mean a *maraviglia*; which would be equivocal, once again, if there wasn't the addition of a blessing to the Lord, "che sì mirabilmente sae adoperare" (that is, the poem sheds light on the prose, not the inverse).

"Questo sonetto è sí piano ad intendere," adds the commentary, and the tercets describe the process of the physics of love in terms so ordinary that there

---

[6] As for example, in Balzac (*Splendeurs et misères des courtisanes*): "cette bonne fille [...] qui fut si bien ta chose" (Vautrin, to Lucien). The naturalistic meaning can also be obtained with other specifications: "Le train s'éloigna, et je la vis, petite chose résignée, évoluer à travers les gros colis vers la sortie de la gare" (Barrès, "Le jardin de Bérénice," quoted by Lanson). (GC)

isn't much to add to it. Still, there is always something. *Piacente* (moreover derived from the Occitan *plazen*), does not describe the simple subjective pleasantness for the onlooker. And just as everything stresses the manifestation of the beloved's qualities, the relationships of essences, from a dynamic, not static, point of view (and for this reason we have not "face" but "physiognomy"), so *piacente* alludes to an objective attribute in as much as she becomes manifest, "equipped with beauty," and "obtaining the effect that beauty necessarily produces." It is not for nothing that *piacere*, in stilnovista language, means "beauty," even "beautiful face," and indeed the prose commentary itself states: "ella si mostrava sì gentile e sì piena di tutti li piaceri" ["she showed herself so noble, so full of all the beauties"]. The theme of line 11, on the incommunicability of the experience, would crop back up at the start of the *Paradiso* (line 70):

> Trasumanar significar *per verba*
> non si poria: però l'essemplo basti
> a cui esperïenza grazia serba.[7]

It is impossible to transcribe, in precisely technical fashion, the *spirit* as typically conceived, the hypostasis of a vital activity.

But, finally, a word on the phrase *va dicendo*: nowadays this sort of periphrasis has a clearly iterative import and can only refer to a repeated, resumed action. In the ancient language it stands in natural opposition to the simple form of the verb in so far as the latter represents an absolutely instantaneous action (that is, perfective, to use the terminology pertaining to the category of verb aspects, so important in Greek and Slavic grammar); but it refers to a duration so generic (imperfective aspect) that today, the nuance having been lost, it is absorbed into the simple form of the verb.

A few examples from Dante's lyric poetry. In *Movi, ballata senza gir tardando*, which speaks to poetry itself (the dubious *In abito di saggia messaggiera*), we have something like a durative "*tardare*," a kind of "lingering." In *Non v'accorgete voi d'un che si smore / e va piangendo*—the opening of a sonnet more likely by Cino than by Dante—the periphrasis almost means "won't stop crying." At the start of a known Dante sonnet—*O dolci rime che parlando*

---

[7] Contini's emphasis. Possibly the most untranslatable lines in the *Commedia*. Roughly: "Transcending the human cannot be conveyed / *in words*: let the example therefore suffice / for those for whom grace has reserved the experience."

andate—and also in the canzone *Amor, da che convien*, we find the phrase *va dicendo*. Here we have a poem hypostatized as a *spirit*, which is a kind of personification, more than *dire* and *parlare* momentarily "expressing" anything in their continuous non-physical activity.

Thus summing up and schematically paraphrasing our exposition, we more or less arrive at the following:

"So apparent is the nobility and decorum in the greeting of the woman who is my lady, that every tongue so trembles as to fall mute, and eyes dare not gaze upon her. And so she steps forward, hearing the words of praise, outwardly manifesting her inner benevolence, and making apparent her nature as a being descended from heaven onto the earth to represent divine power in physical form. Such representation, to those who look upon her, is so laden with beauty that a sweetness knowable only through direct experience enters their hearts by way of the eyes. And from her physiognomy emanates a gentle amorous inspiration made physical and visible that can only prompt the soul to sigh."

There is no need to point out that such a paraphrase is purely semantic, and that in this semantic equivalency it stresses the logical connections and relationships. It should be seen as a kind of watermark to be interpolated behind the text such as it sits in our memory (with thanks to those who put it there) to correct as gently as possible any involuntary interpretation in keeping with the Italian language's present-day system. The "translation" thus obtained—and philosophers are correct to point out that any text (or rather, any work of any art) must inevitably be translated—will no doubt seem inadequate, indeed a distortion, in that it takes into account only the language's instrumental meanings and not those pertaining properly to expression; and thus it throws the poem out of balance, making it logical, and neither is the residue thus obtained particularly significant. It is also true, meanwhile, that one can only arrive at an objective acquaintance with the expressive meanings after clearing the instrumental meanings away from the ground of ignorance—for who better than a philologist knows the negative import of his own exegetical operation? Whereas a vague and ineffable textual reading so rationally precise risks adding an aura of spurious enchantment to the object, which one can say at this point would overrate the sonnet in the overall context of Dante's lyric body of work. What remains to be done is to reconstruct mentally the sonnet's charm using the new semantic elements. But, in order to do this, we will have to have defined it from the very start of the new, attempted interpretation. One will probably say: phonic values, further specifying, perhaps, that these are pure phonic values, ones, that is, that lie clearly outside of the general cultural resonance of vocables *qua* vocables (such as we find in the aestheticism of the Parnassians, of D'Annunzio and Rilke et al.: the pleasure of the word as object).

But what would be the meaning here (and I say "here" because it would indeed have some meaning if drawn from a text by Mario Luzi or Alfonso Gatto) of a mere "sound score" in which, for example, we underscored the most logically prominent tonic vowels (ranging from two to four per line), subordinating all the remaining elements to them? Such an attempt could yield only one important result, but one no more verifiable in a "sonorous" than in a "semantic" context: which is that expression can do without any intention and expressive aim, quite unlike what happens for example in Dante's own *"poesia petrosa"*[8] (broadly speaking) and in one of the dominant tonalities of the *Commedia*. In this way, my "translation" neither adds nor subtracts anything—in the sense that, with respect to the average Italian tongue of today, and with respect to the average Italian tongue of the late 13th century, none of the semantic energy's equilibrium has been shifted in any way. Our anachronistic distortion leaves one essential aspect of the poem completely unaltered and undamaged. Moreover, as implicitly alluded to above, the imaginary sound score would be utterly inconceivable without rhythm—and here the hendecasyllabic line is clearly much slower (one can invoke, if you wish, the metaphors of *largo* and *andante*) than, for example, the henecasyllabic line of the *Commedia*, and we frequently encounter the presence of three strong logical accents (particularly typical in lines 1, 4, 6 and several others), and even interjections (3) and analytically serialized substantives (8, 10), intended to complicate and slow the line's forward progress. But this amounts to saying simply that the poem's rational/mythic statements become the object of a calm, relaxed, engrossed contemplation.

One may point out how the sonnet should be read, but one may also point out how it should not be read. Interpreting it through lexical anachronisms is far less grievous than juxtaposing the text, mentally, with a visual representation. This is what has happened starting with Rossetti the younger and with his Pre-Raphaelitism going forward; and the beloved is certainly not plastically modeled on the robust frames of Giottesque women (or those depicted by the major Pisan sculptors), nor on the telluric deities rather emphatically discussed by Emilio Cecchi, nor on the forms of Cimabue (spiritually the artist least dis-

---

[8] See note 4 on p. 19 of the first essay in this collection.

tant from Dante's symbolism) or of Sienese painting, but rather on the exquisite, slender, bloodless schemas of a Botticelli. Chronologically speaking, Pre-Raphaelitism doesn't go in much for subtlety, almost as if Raphael himself did not actually represent the culmination of a long aspiration to objective beauty. The beloved (*la beatrice*) is more or less consciously translated (and this, on the other hand, is indeed a dangerous translation) into an "icy Pre-Raphaelite virgin," lilylike, snow-white, and long-limbed. The fact is, not just this awkwardly aestheticizing visualization, but all visualizations are foreign to Dantean figuration. Dante's expressive problem is not at all that of representing a spectacle, but rather that of enunciating, almost theoretically, an incarnation of heavenly things and describing their necessary effect on the spectator. He is not concerned with sensations, but with amatory metaphysics and general psychology. When, four centuries later, Lorenzo Magalotti sings Platonically of his imaginary woman, it will be well in this traditional ontological vein, which is in fact that of true lovers—almost foreshadowing the woman of Leopardi's *canti*.

But let us leave off these rather dreamy evocations and return to the text. Where do we see the woman? The only mention is in her undisturbed movement: *Ella si va* . . . And yet this allusion, too, finds itself in a strategically well-shielded situation. It is preceded by the first *pare*, which refers to the woman's manifestation, and by the description of her physical effect on others. The mention itself is immediately corrected, in the line that follows, by an affirmation of the correspondence between exterior and interior, and this is followed by the second *par*, and then by *mostrare*. As for the tercets—the first revolving around the repetitive *Mostrasi*, the second around the final *par*—they are devoted exclusively to her effects on the onlooker.

More objective on the one hand and more subjective on the other, or even more illustrative of the modern mentality—in a word, more speculative: such are the qualifications by which one may summarize the *chiquenade* (in the Pascalian sense) that must be impressed upon the minds of those studying the sonnets of the *Vita Nuova*, to steer them away from the usual distortions of the schools.

[From *L'immagine*, number 5, November-December 1947]

Addendum 1975

Rereading this old piece after such a long time, I have figured that the "phonic values" of the sonnet could be concretely investigated, without this constituting a retraction and indeed with the result of corroborating the thesis of tonal balance and *medietas*. Such an inquest yields solid and other gradually dominant norms that are of course consistent with an operational spontaneity that has not yet a perfectly rule-establishing and therefore reflexive level (as with the required points of rhyme, rhythm, etc.). Once we distinguish the (E) extreme vowels (*i*, *u*) from the absolutely (*a*) or relatively (*e*, *o*) intermediate vowels (I), we find that the quatrains have I externally and E externally, while the block of tercets, chiastically, have E external and I internal (and there are two distinct rhymes, but with a common tonic [accent] and for the most part in [an] open variant: ò); the realizations are opposite for E (*u*, *i*), different for I (*a*, *o*). Thus excluded from our inventory is *e*, which is the first of the last syllables of the rhyme, in which role it alternates only with the other intermediate, but absolute, vowel: *a*. Between the accented and final vowels there is only a single, identical consonant (*r*) for the first rhyme of the quatrains and the first two in the tercets.

More flexible but easily discernible is the pattern of the dominant internal vowel. In the first quatrain, this is *i* (i.e., the extreme opposite of what figures as the tonic final), both in the lines of A rhymes and those of B rhymes: *gentile, mia, lingua, ardiscon*. But in the penultimate case, and especially the last one, no cesura follows, and so the libretto of stressed vowels becomes enriched and differentiated (4 ó í Á; 3 with every possible variety in the slowed-down ó í é á Ú). Something similar reappears in 7 (*sia*, libretto á í ó Ú), which, with its echo of the first quatrain cuts into the second's entirely different status, characterized by intermediate secondary á's (a possible foreshadowing of Á) and *e*'s, 5 á é Á, 6 chiastically é á Ú, after the abovecited incision 8 with an iteration of é é á Á. In the tercets, the rhyme with *I* is preceded by é (*piacente, dicendo*), next to which we find, in the first case, ó, which prefigures the formula of ó é Ó (line 10), or é ó Ó (line 11) in the remaining first tercet (Ó prepared by ó), á in the second case, which thus comes to resemble the remaining second tercet (*par* and *labbia, soave*).

The rhymes could not be less harsh or affected. Suffice it to say that we encounter here the sublimely banal rhyme (in Saba's inimitable formulation) of *core / amore*. But there are also more desinential, that is, facile, rhymes concentrated in the second quatrain—a facility compensated by a richness in reverse. The rhyme of *venuta* and *vestuta* is broadened into a veritable consonantal pun, while alliterations appear in the peripheral lines (*si va sentendosi, miracol mostrare*); and one hears better the particular tonal context of the central distich, as described above. The alliterative tendency continues beyond the key (mostrare / Mostrasi) between *fronte* and *sirima*: line 9, M*ostrasi sí*; line 10, dà ... *dolcezza*; line 11, *può* ... *prova*; and then comes to an end in the second tercet (*spirito soave*, perhaps introduced by *sua* ... *sì*).

If, as Domenico De Robertis justifiably points out (in *Il canzoniere Escorialense e la tradizione "veneziana" delle rime dello Stil Novo*, Turin 1954, pp. 26, 30, 41-42; *Il libro della "Vita Nuova"*, Florence 1970 (2nd ed.), pp. 145-47), the most substantial variants taken from the Escorialense and similar codices are early authorial versions: 7 instances of *Credo* for *E par*; 10 *fier* for *dà*; 13 *fiero* for *soave* and *ardore* for *amore* (the *ard* group apparently re-echoes 4 cases of *ardiscon* and *guardare*, the latter however replaced by *mirare* in one part of the tradition of the *Vita Nuova*[9])—then a number of the facts highlighted in the present addendum would seem to mirror a "soft" modification effected at the moment in which the "loose" sonnet was included in the "romance." There is a general subsitition of é for á (with the associated implications), the long-distance confusion of *fier/fiero* gives way to the mild alliterations of *d/d* and *s/s*, and the same key-word *par* is reconfirmed.

---

[9] *Ardore* surely harks back to "Amore è uno spirito d'ardore," by Guido delle Colonne (*Ancor che l'aigua*, l. 24). *Mira* (line 9), which, moreover echoes the preceding *miracol*, makes the introduction of *mirare* less likely. (GC)

Dante as Character/Poet in the Commedia

All history is contemporary history, goes Benedetto Croce's famous theorem. If such an assertion is correct, not every attempt to appeal to current events to shed light on events from long eclipsed or remote cultures will fall into anachronism. And the Dantean scholar, too, may perhaps legitimately resort expeditiously to this same artifice. Nowadays, the general approach is to emphasize one feature of the character who says "I" in *The Divine Comedy*. But to articulate the subject in ths manner is already using, or abusing, for purposes other than hermeneutic, a linguistic cell born within the tissue of the literary criticism of the Moderns. Marcel Proust, in other words, serves as a metaphor for a not entirely elementary discourse on Dante. I won't hide the perhaps unappreciative, one might even say snobbish, effect that such a catachresis has had on me; it is enough to recall my perplexity at seeing our Quasimodo and Vittorini being used by a barbarian certainly not devoid of brilliance to explain Chrétien de Troyes. And yet the greatest writer of our times indeed seems equal to the task presented to him.

    Let us try. The person who says "I" in the *Recherche du temps perdu* has no name—belonging thus to the category of "he"; but the rare times—two in all—and not before *La prisonnière*—that any name appears, it is necessarily recorded as Marcel. Is he the author? Is he someone other than the author? The essential problematic of Proust lies in this ambiguity, this gap. I am not referring to the near-endless diligence of the book's specific erudition, especially in the final years, which allows one to distinguish a little better which parts are straight autobiography, which are transposed autobiography, and which involved thematic interpolation or rhythmic or structural adjustment—in short, what at school is called the "inevitable imaginative transformation" of the great French novel. It is the equivalent of stopping at the surface of the question. What should be asked is instead: Is Proust's "I" (once established that it is not a banal inflective means of converting a third-person novel into a first-person one, as has been the custom from Apuleius's *Metamorphoses* to any number of modern creations) the subject of a limited, definite, unrepeatable historical experience, or is it the transcendent subject of any adventure of life or the mind?

We know that the answer is neither alternative nor disjunctive. The microscopic dimension and the telescopic dimension, as Proust himself said, like the anecdotal dimension and the legal dimension, mutually condition one another. Anecdote or custom: the *Recherche* is also, as defined, a Balzacian novel, and therefore a storytelling based on verisimilitude—let us call it a bourgeois verisimilitude. And yet the insufficiency of such a reading—which bolsters the perhaps sociologically or folkloristically naïve interpretation that has been given of certain key episodes in keeping with a magical mentality and primitive conception of the sacred—is yet to be demonstrated. The symbol stands alongside the "entertainment" of the literal: a second level. At this point, the link between the two "I"s is to be found in the inevitable corollary that the novelistic component of the *Recherche* finds its specificity within the story of a literary vocation. The character who says "I" recognizes himself as a poet, and the arc of the development lies in the evolution of this observation into a representation. Life has acquired a meaning, even as its contents remain unchanged.

Let us now see whether, *a minore*, i.e., from the "lesser" instance (I mean *minore* only chronologically speaking), we can gain some understanding of Dante's case. This twofold, ambiguous aspect of the *Commedia*'s structure has been brought into a clear didcactic light thanks to some very recent contributions. Particular homage should be paid to the American Italianist Charles Singleton, who in a single penetrating essay (which is not, however, immune to a certain captiousness) has noted how Dante's "I"—which is the "I," we must add, of a Saint Paul revealing himself, an "I" that speaks of the vicissitudes of an Aeneas from the Virgilian Tragedìa, all lined up in "he"—brings together "man" in general, the subject of living and acting, and the historic individual, bearer of an experience determined *hic et nunc*, in a specific place and at a specific time. Today we would call this dichotomy the transcendent "I" as opposed to the existential "I". Even grammatically speaking, Singleton points out, the telltale signs are many, since, right from the start we find, in opposition to "nostra vita"—the life of the "I" that is "us"—the phrase "mi ritrovai", an action of the "I" that is only I. As we can see, compared to the compactness and unprecedented case of the monistic modern author, the medieval one displays first a possible linguistic divorce, that is, an external separation, of the two levels; and second, a radical cultural connection, a solid bond, with precedents and with the authorities ("Io non Enëa, io non Paulo sono"; *Inf.* II, 32). The double semantic level itself already has institutional confirmation, which lies in the juxtaposition of the literal meaning—that concerning the historical "I"—and the spiritual or mystical meaning, that concerning the "I" who is all men.

Such polysemy was initially reserved for Biblical exegesis. Indeed the Bible never stopped being a book of history merely because it contains the revelation of universal truths: the Hebrews never cease crossing the Red Sea (to use the clearly sacred example which Dante's famous letter to Cangrande cites to illustrate the plurality of meanings of the Scriptures), because this exit of theirs comes to signify redemption and the passage into a state of grace. These are exegetical—in other words, *mutatis mutandis*, critical—propositions. (In the *Convivio*, and in the letter, Dante is his own exegete.) And the exegesis is of the holy book, laying, moreover, the theoretical foundation for allegorism (even if on occasion, in the wake of Macrobius and Fulgentius, it can obtain as well for human books—but books that verge on sacred prophecy, such as the *Aeneid*).

And this means: first, that Dante "applied" elaborate critical principles *a priori* to his own creation; and second, that he is working in a poetic "genre" that is not a "genre": i.e., the "sacred poem" is not merely an image. Sacred in the theological, dualistic, and intellectual sense (even if the aim, says the letter, is action, not speculation), they are sermons that go together, and they account for the particular formulation adopted by the character who says "I" in the voice of a genius in the summer of the Middle Ages.

And here a digression is in order, to state that the distinction between symbol and allegory so clearly drawn in Singleton would seem to be far more clearly demarcated in theory than in fact. Nor is Singleton the first to re-assert this in our time: we will recall that critic of Chrétien, Reto Bezzola. And the matter is quite understandable as a form of self-defense instituted by specialists averse to the eradication of any literalism that is not a literal reading in service of a criticism based on pure sentiment; added to this is the effective re-evaluation of a reading that is not exclusively literal—that is, a reading also of allusive meaning transcending normal semantics, such as one finds in almost all poetics after Baudelaire, unless we start digging further back, into the "mysterious" vein of European Romanticism. Bezzola's approach, like that of many Dante scholars, at least *in pectore*, is more or less to save what can be saved: to abandon, that is, to its dark destiny any literalism that is not the literal meaning, in order to recuperate a literal reading that is not ONLY literal—otherwise the medievalist's heart would bleed at the enormity of the sacrifice demanded. And indeed, how many literal readings that have nothing literal about them are thus smuggled in! Take, to cite just one example, the long elucubrations on numbers attributed to Chrétien, which, if indeed they correspond to any intentions discovered by the new initiate, relegate a good part of the literal meaning, which at first seemed neutral and anodyne, to an insipid nothingness.

Truth be told, Singleton never descends to this level. The literal meaning in allegorical poetry, for him, has value as historical testimony that can never be taken away from it. The opposition between symbol and allegory is no less tainted, in him, than the poison of idealism (which does not disqualify him from rejecting its texts as pernicious), as it is essentially (and perhaps quite anachronistically) a travesty of the opposition between poetry and non-poetry. Rather, it corresponds to two quite distinct dimensions of the medieval book, which are nevertheless linked by the principle of imitation. In as much as it is an imitation of a sacred book, it has a literal meaning and a mystical one: the allegory; yet, in as much as it is a mimesis of the book of nature, the objects of the literal meaning divide and become doubled in themselves and in their meaning, the symbol, just as the thing of nature—whether stone or plant or beast—in medieval herbariums and bestiaries, is at once itself, eventually with its own individuable story that can be told, and also an ensemble of qualities and customs transferrable to the moral realm.

The distinction is very sharp on the theoretical level, but it seems to me less relevant as pertains to exegetical results. Even setting the experiment aside (which says it all!), how can you practice a symbolic hermeneutics appreciably distinct from an allegorical hermeneutics if not, at the most—where there is a hidden meaning—as a hermeneutics of the static hidden meaning and the dynamic hidden meaning (which would correspond to the Dantean distinction between science and history, *doctrinae* and *historiae*)? An eagle is... (aside from a *simpliciter* eagle): a symbol. An eagle that swoops down and effects such-and-such an operation is... (aside from the historical fact of the act): allegorical. The advantage has its limits. And it behooves us to specify the reason. The ever so irresistible garment of interpretation that medieval man—when engaged in interpretation, of course—superimposed upon reality does not cling, and thus reality does not die of asphyxiation. The intellectuals of the Scholastic era may well have been rationalists, but not in the same sense as Enlightenment rationalists. The armor does not fit for the simple reason that, reality being total and in some way already exhausted *a priori* (being in some areas entirely known), it is not *more geometrica demonstrata*, even if it is geometrically researched passage by passage, in keeping with singular, adventurous necessity. Truth has not one but two sources: if one is reason, the other is the writing (*scrittura*) in which it is recorded, which is not only Holy Scripture, but *auctoritas*. This is demonstrated in lawerly fashion by the tradition of the rhetoricians and the sophists; many propositions of one's adversaries can be dialectically recuperated, so that the word takes on a staggering breadth, elasticity, and semantics. And so I leave aside the patriarchs of speculation, but the philosophizers of average initiative , such as we might characterize Dante—who are, so to speak, short-term rationalists—let themselves be caught in obvious contradictions. Since the subject here is mimesis in nature, we see towards what kind of contrary consequences these concepts are taken by Dante. If art imitates nature, and nature imitates God, then art is secondary. Is the natural therefore superior to the artificial (the Latin language, in this case), being closer to the Creator? This is the thesis, in linguistics and rhetoric, of the *De vulgari Eloquentia*, and even, in other respects, of the *Commedia*. Or is there greater nobility in that which is not transformed into an "artificialized" pleasure (in this case the vernacular tongue)? This is the thesis, in the same context, of the *Convivio*. I say "thesis," but I should probably say "themes," variably applicable to the mutable needs of the (rhetorical) argument, even though the aim, justification, and celebration of the vernacular are all the same. This, in my opinion, should occasion more than a little caution on our part. I'm afraid that the splitting of allegory and symbol in two, in as much as it can be traced back to the radical difference between sacred history and natural history, still teaches very little about the hierarchization and distribution of the referenced categories in our mental space. In other words, in this context, not only the actual poetry of Dante, but also his (conjectural) poetics, seem hardly univocal. We have difficulty reconstructing them for the simple reason that they cannot be easily defined.

I conclude this protracted digression hoping that it does not prove entirely devoid of material useful in defining the matter of interest to us here. We were in the process of looking for certain features of the medieval character who says "I": a character who steps into a premeditated, heteronomous framework. The dimensions are not his own; they come from without. For modern man, the poet alone can identify himself as both onlooker and legislator/representor. But the fact remains that Dante's protagonist, too, is a poet/character: he is entrusted to the patronage of a "famous sage" and commends himself to him for having long studied his volume; someone welcomes him by performing or quoting his *canzoni*,[1] actually hailing him as the founder of a new manner; he entrusts himself to Apollo and the Muses, and will be crowned with the beloved laurel wreath.

The connection may not appear as necessary and logical as with the modern poet who has no sources of knowledge outside his intellectual intuition; but we have seen how the prefabricated armor of medieval knowledge allows frequent play for adaptation. And the effective, one might even say biological, onset of instinct restores symmetries and relationships into which the theoretical justification perhaps had trouble bending itself to fit. It goes without saying that the medieval poet did not possess the logical autonomy of the modern one (even though in Proust there is an emphasis on cognitive and declarative necessity—a mission less optional than inevitable, "art as progressive anthropology," according to Novalis's motto quoted by Benn—rather than on the aestheticizing, athletic triumph of the Word: "verse is all," "*im Wort sammelt sich die Erde*")[2]. The medieval poet is always justifying himself as a sage and a prophet; he produces *auctoritates*—that is, he contributes to one of the sources of knowledge (here too, a cultural attitude precedes concrete action) and is a revealer, and acts as such on humanity's destinies. Virgil is overflowing with grave pronouncements, but also marches on with his Sibyl behind the figures of the Ancient Law, in the processions of the prophets for Advent and Lent. Sage and prophet, man of science and, in some ways, of action: here is a meeting of opposite poles leading to the double "I" of the *Commedia*—an "I" that is not select, not socially supreme, since that would have necessitated the tragic style; but rather a common "I", one that adequately represents all of humanity.

Here an exquisite terminological problem comes to mind, one upon which a piece by Francesco Mazzoni sheds some definitive light. In the letter to Cangrande, whose authenticity Mazzoni's critical essay, armed with nineteenth-century hypercriticism, was able to prove, one of the categories that defines the work of art is the "*agens*." This is the subject of moral activity, of practical

---

[1] Dante's self-quotations (*Purg.* II, 112; XXVI, 51; *Par.* VIII, 37), all of them openings of canzoni collected in the *Vita Nuova* or the *Convivio* (and we have the last one already in the sonnet *Parole mie*) are of course culturally justified above all by the self-quotations, of sections II and III, made by Menalca in the *Bucolica*, V, 86-87. In the same way, the signature and repertoire inscribed by Chrétien de Troyes before the *Cligés* have an authoritative precedent in the verse lines (of uncertain Virgilian attribution) at the start of the *Aeneid* and the signing of the *Georgics*. (GC)

[2] "In the Word the Earth gathers."

action—in short, the character who says "I." Already in the 14th century, the commentators confused the *agens* for the *auctor*, the subject who makes poetry. But we're indulgent of the defective dialectics of these rather approximative readers. Their confusion stems from the common circumstance whereby *agens* and *auctor* coincide, and therefore on the fact that the *Commedia* is, after all, also the story—I was about to say the autobiography—of a poet.

The fact is even, clearly, too elementary. It nevertheless remains to be seen whether or not it is possible to use it in a slightly less truistic, superfluous way—in other words, whether certain episodes of the tale of the *Commedia* will prove to be readable in greater depth, and the sudden appearance of certain interlocutors better justified, when we pay special attention to the circumstance that the traveller from beyond the grave is a man of letters. But this is hardly a guaranteed, surefire criterion. On the contrary, the limited use to which it has been put is scarcely free of abuse, to the point that it can in fact serve, with some stimulation, as an admonition to be careful. We are at too eminent a level to adopt the trope of the drunken Helot.

Indeed it is no less a figure than De Sanctis who gets the ball rolling, when he says of Pier delle Vigne: "We hear in him not the man, but the courtier and the troubadour." This explicit focus is introduced only in the reprinting of the essay in book form; but even beforehand, and starting even with his Turinese lecture, he writes: "Not only does he express himself with delicacy, but also with grace and elegance, as would a cultured man, brilliant and well-bred: with antitheses, metaphors, conceits, and sentences in pairs." But here, I'm afraid, some naturalistic illusion might creep in. The rhetoric in question is the generic sort of rhetoric of all official and celebratory speech, which is no less valid for Mastro Adamo (who is, at least, a university "graduate") or—just to cite another example, for Vanni Fucci, who was the protonotary of the Imperial court. It is, in short, the rhetoric of Dante, not of Pier delle Vigne. The troubadour was known to Dante more or less from one of those same *canzonieri* (songbooks) of the kind we too still peruse; but the *De vulgari* does not quote him, just as it does not name Stefano Protonotaro, even though in them the strong new imagery springs almost urgently from the much-admired Guido delle Colonne, indeed a precursor of Guinizzellian heuristics. Nor do we happen upon any memory of those verses in the entire episode. This, moreover, is consistent with a constant habit in the *Commedia*, which is that of presenting the great men of the world (Frederick II, but also Folquet and Bertran de Born) just as they are, without the superfluous laurels.

We can easily imagine, however, that modern Dante scholars are better trained to discover professional echoes in the *Commedia*. One borderline case is that of an eminent Frenchman, André Pézard, who in his highly erudite volume, *Dante sous la pluie du feu*, manages to undermine the traditional interpretation of the vice of Brunetto Latini, Prisciano, Andrea de' Mozzi and other intellectuals, taking that episode for a contemporary polemic in favor of the native vernacular and claiming that that the "mal protesi nervi" (*Inf.* XV, 114) are a rhetorical figure and that the author of the *Tesoretto* (Brunetto) is expiating a waste of intellect. But the more we go back to the context, the less, we must admit, it seems to jibe with this ingenious solution.

In compensation, Pézard appears ever more brilliant for having put his finger on a theoretical connection as important as the linguistic question, concerning the principle of imitation and the theological evaluation of nature—a problem whose solution we've seen to be changeable, at least in its verbal expression. And there are also, truth be told, exegetes for whom everything runs smoothly. Bruno Nardi, for example, reads only great harmony in Dante's forays into the linguistic question, and sees its evolution conspiring to a single end: that of exalting the temporal mutability of language. One could claim that this dialectic is far less serene and more dramatic than he thinks. Practically (but not theoretically) speaking, it is certain—indeed obvious—that Dante is increasingly on the way to justifying the use of the vernacular. What level of sentiment should the cardinal notion of mutability have aroused in him? The Humanist inference *perituro, dunque da cogliere* ("perishable, therefore to be plucked") surely does not square with the Christian yearning for eternity. And here (since the answer is in the *Commedia*—in the literal meaning of the *Commedia*, that is, and therefore not unrelated to our present task) the question of linguistic mutability stands as a case in point of the question of the relativity of taste (also echoed by the "uso moderno," *Purg.* XXVI, 113, in the Guinizzelli episode), which is resolved elegiacally, and not triumphally, in the Oderisi canto (*Purg.* XI). The mutable vernacular's competition with the immutable "*gramatica*" is an underlying motif of Dante's oeuvre: the institutional immutability of artificial Latin seems tacitly counterbalanced and contested, in conformity with the *Convivio*, by the poetic connection whereby the vernacular works towards its own preservation (whence the institutional necessity of poetry).

We might as well, therefore, highlight this dangerous intercessionary notion and assert, as is done in Canto XXVI of the *Paradiso*—in recantation of his own treatise, and using the very example drawn from the name of God—the mutability even of Hebrew, the presumed language of grace, for which an exception is made in the *De vulgari* for a very arguable reason. Those lines on the language of Adam are a sort of *mise-en-abîme* within the *Commedia*, to self-justify the paradox of the sacred poem in a perishable language—whose inevitable course of ephemerality is slowed, perhaps, by the very poeticalness holding it together. Such a courageous, and by no means overreaching assumption blooms in the lines of the *Commedia*. Indeed the desire is to establish the necessarily anthological sampler of corollaries to the principle of the poet/protagonist on the basis of textual givens, though read between the lines. And the passage on the language of Adam may be the first such instance.

Not all such instances in the *Commedia* are encounters with literary professionals and colleagues of the poet. Francesca da Rimini, for example, is one who enjoys the fruits of literature, indeed a reader, not a producer of literature herself. It is true that the culture assigns her a vital role, perpetrated outside the strictly technical sphere. If ever there were a quarry for psychological literary criticism, even of the highest tenor, a pretext for sentimental extrapolations (oh, the sovereignty of love, oh, the "rights" of the heart—teleologically safe from damnation—oh, George Sand, oh Ibsen!), it is she, Francesca. It should pain me—and in fact it is not so easy—to have to play the part of the provincial intellectual and cast her aside. It is even less important, for the reasons hinted, that her rhetoric is flawless: utter expertise in her periphrasis, agile, perfect symmetries, speech that keeps to the rules of the *ars dictandi*. . . Where indeed is any rhetoric of Francesca's that isn't Dante's own?

I too, if anything, would lay the emphasis on the triple anaphora: "Amor ch'...," "Amor ch'...," "Amor..." (*Inf.* V, 100-106), an unusual indicator of a special situation, as it is not only a threefold cry to a love that, alas, will never be able to rise to the trinitarian procession, but a form in which the contents most pressing to Dante are poured and which requires illustration in some detail. In this episode the book becomes an instrument of biography—though a contemporary variant (as demonstrated by scholarship[3]) and not a text among the most archaic and select: a sort of *roman-fleuve* on the Breton theme. And so we have

---

[3] Especially by Zingarelli (in *Studi Danteschi*, I, 65-90); by Rajna (in *Nuova Antologia*, June 1, 1920, pp. 223-247); and by Crescini (in *Studi Danteschi*, III, 5-57). The first author's article is reprinted among his *Scritti di varia letteratura* (Milan 1935), pp. 203-220. (GC)

a eulogy of the book, within that eulogy of that particular book (thus a courtly mediator, as courtly as Galehaut himself); and the courtesy of the quotation, with its underscoring of the interlocutor's adherence to that *auctoritas*: "(i)l tuo dottore"—in the rhetorical, not philosophical sense (and who indeed was not Virgil, as so many commentators have made contortions to "prove," but in fact Boethius, "*infelicissimum genus infortunii est fuisse felicem*" ["the unhappiest kind of misfortune is to have been happy"]).[4] But if we examine the tercets of the amorous anaphora from closer quarters—the central lines of the episode for all intents and purposes—we can see, with some surprise, that they open with an *ad hominem* quotation or paraphrase: "*Amor ch'al cor gentil ratto s'apprende.*"[5]

I say *ad hominem* quotation because, while the line indeed harks back to the same Guinizzelli *incipit*, "*Al cor gentil rempaira* [or '*repara*' in the *De vulgari*] *sempre Amore*," when combined with the start of the second stanza, "*Foco d'amore in gentil cor s'aprende*," it can also be seen to harken implicitly—let's say to a second degree—to two lines from the *Vita Nuova* (XX):

> Amore e 'l cor gentil sono una cosa,
> sí come il saggio in suo dittare pone.

(We note, in passing, that "the sage" ("*il saggio*") is not an antonomastic reference to Guido Guinizzelli, but a depersonalization of the author, as is the "dottore" for Francesca, his reduction to a vector and anonymous vessel of knowledge. Cecco Angiolieri similarly cites, to one who has heard it, a pronouncement by Guido delle Colonne as the statement of an "*om saggio*.")

Francesca, in short, takes refuge behind a familiar *auctoritas* acceptable to Dante, and applies it the same way as in his sonnet, at least according to the declaration in the *Vita Nuova*, where, first saying, of love, "in quanto è in potenzia," then reducing it to the act, the sudden falling in love, an act of which the woman—and not for nothing—is just as capable as the man ("E simil face in donna omo valente"). As concerns documentary verisimilitude one could add that it is not to be ruled out that the Dantean composition—which, as the *Vita*

---

[4] I cite the pronouncement as it was proverbially excerpted from Antonio da Tempo (p. 115 Grion). But (for "*recolentem*," whence "ricordarsi," and "in...", whence "nella miseria"), see the whole passage in *De consolatione Philosophiae* II, pr. 4: "*Sed hoc est, quod recolentem vehementius coquit; nam in omni adversitate fortunae infelicissimum est genus infortunii fuisse felicem.*" (GC)

[5] "Love, in a noble heart so quickly rapt..."; *Inf.* V, 100.

Nuova states, is a sonnet of correspondence spurred by the reading of *Donna ch'avete*—was publicly known in Romagna at the time of such cases, verified to be around 1285 (nor did the text, in this "loose" state, present any variation with respect to the version received in the *libello,* as another valiant young Florentine, Domenico De Robertis, has shown). But this disputable detail is not what matters here. What matters is that the sinning woman "shelters" her sin in the shadow of a morality one could describe—with qualities that could be called into question—as "stilnovistic" (it is not lost on me that Guinizzelli was from the same region as the enchained, indeed enflamed Francesca of Ravenna), even while inserting a suddenness, implanting a *coup de foudre* ("ratto"), into the pastiche of the double allusion.

This stilnovistic principle of the noble heart is closely linked to the so-called "bourgeois solution"—i.e., the Scholastic and, as concerns vernacular poetry, the already Guittonian solution—to the problem of nobility, such as it is developed (by quoting Guinizzelli, whether or not by name) in the canzone *Le dolci rime* and in the fourth treatise of the *Convivio*—in contrast to the aristocratic solution, that is, the hereditary-patrimonial one assigned to Frederick II. (Just to be clear, the Emperor, though Dante takes care to hide it from us, returns before us as a poet, since there seems to be no doubt that Dante had in mind, however slightly blurred, a nasty little sonnet by Frederick rediscovered a few years earlier by his friend Angelo Monteverdi.) But in the specialized field of the philosophy of love[6] I cannot see how such a principle differs in any substantial way from that of the "*morum probitas*," which is so often repeated, and central to Andreas Cappellanus's *De amore*, the much-disparaged materialistic theorization of courtly love from the turn of the twelfth to the thirteenth centuries. Here is its most explicit passage:

> Moral valor alone makes a man's nobility shine forth, and his appearance of resplendent beauty. We men were all descended from one, and we have one birth as second nature: not beauty, not bodily ornaments, not wealth, but moral valor alone was what men first knew as nobility and to which they taught deference across the generations. [...] Thus valor alone is worthy to wear the crown of love.

---

[6] Since outside of this context it is naturally a commonplace, as the biography assembled by Curtius (*Europäische Literatur und lanteinisches Mittelalter*, Kap. 9, § 7) has proved. The *Carmina Burana* in particular incorporate nobilitas with probitas (ed. Hilka-Schumannn, I, I, p. 8). (GC)

And in summary (as represented by number XVIII of the Rules for Love, a series of epiphonemes that were in circulation at the time, even in isolated form): *Probitas sola quemque dignum facit amore.*[7]

Did Dante know Gualtieri, as Cappelanus was called in his time?[8] A strictly rhetorical question, though he wraps this name in a cloak of the most total omission and, by extension, disdain. Aside from the connection established by posterity (where they incorporated a sort of apocryphal paralipomenon of the *Vita Nuova* into a vulgarization of Cappellanus's *De amore*),[9] I recall that Gualtieri and Cappellanus are inferred and counter-inferred in the poetic correspondance between Cavalcanti and Gianni Alfani. And then Cino: "Io studio solo nel libro di Gualtieri / per trarne vero e nuovo intendimento" ["I study only Gualtieri's book / to draw new and true understanding therefrom"]. The interpretation Francesca gives to this principle is physical ("la bella persona"; *Inf.* V, 101), and her enactment adulterous. Nothing could be more in keeping with the theories of Cappellanus. Who rules out, by dint of syllogisms, that love could ever be conjugal.

Let us see whether Francesca remains true to these positions in the second tercet, "Amor ch'a nullo amato amar perdona" (line 103). Reciprocity and irrefutability are, however marginally formulated, also principles in Cappellanus. Rule IX: "*Amare nemo potest nisi qui amoris suasione compellitur*;"[10] and rule XXVI: "*Amor nil posset amori denegare*".[11] As for the third tercet, "Amore condusse noi ad una morte" (line 106), the rhythmical highlighting of *una* implicitly infers the identity of even the ultimate fate from the identity of the lovers' will, a principle that was current in the medieval doctrine of love, but which Cappellanus receives ("*omnia de utriusque voluntate* [...] *praecepta compleri*")[12] only

---

[7] "Probity alone makes one worthy of love."

[8] In Italy, that is.

[9] Upon Dante's death, poor Pieraccio Tebalda dared write that he was "più copioso in iscienza / che Catone o Donato o ver Gualtieri" ["more abundant in knowledge / than Cato or Donato or Gualtieri"]. On Cappellanus in Italy, and the name Gualtieri, the fundamental text is still that published by Pio Rajna in 1890 in *Studj di Filologia Romanza*," V. fasc. 13, especially pp. 205-224 and 242-245). (GC)

[10] "No one can love unless he is compelled by the persuasion of love." This and subsequent English translations of the Rules are by John Jay Parry, *The Art of Courtly Love*, New York: 1960, Columbia University Press.

[11] "Love can deny nothing to love."

[12] "...to wish above all other things ... the embraces of the other ... and to carry out all of love's precepts in the other's embrace..."

to reduce it crudely to a conjunction of mutual pleasure. In the famous *canzone*, Dante's *Doglia mi reca* pronounces "di due potere un fare" ["to be able to make two from one"] as a prerogative for love. Actually, Dante could have found this principle in a saying familiar to all in the Middle Ages (*"unum velle atque unum nolle"*[13]), whether or not people recognized the provenance of the line from Sallust's *Catiline Conspiracy*.

Still, a closer echo of the letter can be found in a number of troubadour propositions, such as the following from Aimeric de Peguilhan: *"E fai de dos cors un, tant ferm los lia"* ["And made of two hearts one, so strong the bond"]. Except that the *auctoritas*, clearly transcribed from the Occitan, must necessarily, I'm afraid, be mediated by an interpreter whom I think Dante might not so readily admit: Guittone, who in his letter number X, says "de dui cori fa uno." It is therefore a position that ideally sends us back beyond Guinizzelli.

But the matter is not yet settled. In the story of their love, even as concerns Paolo, Francesca describes a phenomenology of Ovidian lineage entirely consistent with Cappellanus's description: "e scoloròcci il viso" ["and it uncolored our faces"], "la bocca mi baciò tutto tremante" ["he kissed my lips all trembling"][14]. Rule XV indeed says: *"Omnis consuevit amans in coamantis aspectu pallescere"* ["Every lover turns pale in the presence of his beloved"]; and Rule XVI: *"In repentina coamantis visione cor contromescit amantis"* ["When a lover suddenly catches sight of his lover his heart palpitates"].[15] But the worst of it is that even Dante's language, in the question he asks, comes from the case history of the manner here described. He wants to know how the lovers came to know of their mutual love and speaks of "dubbiosi disiri" ("doubtful desires"). This is not a formula from curial convention; it is pure Cappellanus: "before the love of each party is weighed, there is no greater anguish which therefore one of the lovers fears," etc. It is understood that in the *De amore*, in the "If Love is Passion" insert (even Saint Thomas will set himself the task of proving the same proposition!), the argument is more general (rule XX: *"Amorosus semper est timorosus"*[16]) and extends as well to requited love that is by its nature based on

---

[13] "to like and dislike the same things"
[14] Lines 131 and 136, respectively, of *Inf.* V.
[15] Translations of the *Rules* are by John Jay Parry, *op. cit.*
[16] "A man in love is always apprehensive."

an imbalance and fed by jealousy, "*zelotypia*," linking back up with the theorem minted in a famous Ovidian pentameter: "*Res est solliciti plena timoris amor.*"[17]

What a cruel cultural dissection of a human heart, and such a passionate heart at that! But the lovers from Rimini or Gradara on which the philologist works his scalpel are, clearly, only intermediaries. He wants to poke around in Dante himself. Why the affective complicity of the itinerant "I", why the pity, the fainting, indeed the tenderness even before the two are identified, accompanied by a condemnation of the avenging demiurge? Is it only a kind of mental honesty, or is this process of participation and objectivity, of identification and differentiation (this *Aufhebung*—this "sublation"—if we wish to inject the Hegelian term into the discussion), the usual dialectics of the beyond? In the Mastro Adamo episode, Dante is chided for having aired his, let's call it "comical-realistic" fondness for gossip—which he then satisfies and gets past in a single movement. Whether or not this episode is also inspired by a literary opportunity (that hinted in my double adjective), it is exemplary. Dante's *Inferno* (and *Purgatorio*) is also the place of the sins he has overcome, the temptations he has left behind. Francesca, we sometimes forget, is the first of the damned who speaks to Dante; lust the first vice he detaches from himself, examines and judges. That Dante surpasses Paolo, and Beatrice surpasses Francesca (after all, Platonism aside, neither Dante nor Beatrice could have produced a certificate that they were free), means that the stage of courtly love, of mere *probitas*, of worldly ethics, which endures in the Stil Novo and is extended into the *Vita Nuova*, has likewise been surpassed. The sublimation of Beatrice is effected through analogy. In the face of the pure experimentality of eros, and the plurality of those falsities "che nulla promission rendono intera" ("that keep no promise in full" *Purg.* XXX, 132), one must safeguard, or indeed redeem the totality of the amorous experience: it becomes the analogue of a definitive intention aimed at the "perfect good" (*buon perfetto*) which is the radical end of love. Francesca is, in short, a stage, a lower, sympathetic but rejected stage of Dante's itinerary, a stage for which it would be pointless to attempt to distinguish whether it stems more from literature or from life. And so it becomes clear to what the canon of the poet/protagonist lends itself: to the status of exegetical criterion, and at the same time of heuristic probe. Let us continue to make use of this function, while descending into the topographical order of the poem itself.

---

[17] "Love is a thing full of anxious fears."

Let us search, meanwhile, for the first point where the new Beatrice finds herself attacked by a polemic we can still keep calling "literary." The attack comes from Guido Cavalcanti, and can be extracted from the brief, sudden colloquium with Cavalcanti *père*, who inserts himself into the conversation with Farinata, Guido's father-in-law. The literal meaning of this passage has, in truth, been the target of lively controversy. One can apparently say, moreover, that, concerning the line "forse cui Guido vostro ebbe a disegno" (*Inf.* X, 63), modern interpreters are now in agreement in referring the pronoun "cui" to Beatrice, not to Virgil or to God. Grammar and context do not allow any other solution. Which Beatrice, however? (Indeed the episode is too elliptical and accelerated for him not to be there stating how, on an equal basis of "altezza d'ingegno" [X, 59],[18] the great experiment brings merit to Dante; or how it is, from a more subjective point of view, that it is being carried out by him, not by Guido.) As long as "monna Vanna e Monna Bice" go together, as in the sonnet *Io mi senti' svegliar*, the agreement is perfect. Between Guido and Beatrice, or between Guido and Dante. What follows in the *Vita Nuova*, in fact, further confirms (end of Chapter XXV) the solidarity between the two poets: "E questo mio primo amico e io ne sapemo bene di quelli che così rimano stoltamente" ["And my first friend and I knew all about those who thus rhyme inanely"].

But solidarity in what? In interpreting the metaphors of love poetry as a "licenzia" already granted "a li poete" (that is, to those writing in Latin) and therefore, by analogy, "a li rimatori" (that is, those writing in the vernacular). And this is the gloss given for none other than our sonnet (*Io mi senti'*), which speaks of "Love as if it were a thing in itself, and not merely a substance of the mind, but as if it were a bodily substance; which, in truth, is false; for Love is not a substance in and of itself, but an attribute of substance"—an artifice already adopted by Ovid, in no less a work than his *Remedium amoris* (now *there* is a reference which would sound rather odd when cited in the context of the *Divine Comedy*!). It is known that the presentation of the sonnet (Chapter XXIV) adds things that for good reasons did not figure in the poem ("silencing certain words which seemed to need silencing, as I believed that his [Guido's] heart still contemplated the beauteousness of this noble Spring.") This addition is an interpretation, as puzzle, of the *senhal* "Primavera" (Spring): clearly Cavalcanti's

---

[18] To be compared, obviously, to the nearby "*alto ingegno*" (apostrophized with the Muses) in *Inf.* II, 7. (GC)

"Fresca rosa novella, / piacente primavera," from his *canzonetta* in the archaic Bonagiunta manner, which features the happy concordance of nature ("vostro fin pregio mando – a la verdura," "e cantin[n]e gli auselli, / ciascuno in suo latino, / da sera e da matino / su li verdi arbuscelli" ["to the greenery I cast your rare worth" ... "and may the birds sing, / each in his own fine tongue, / evenings and mornings / in the little green saplings"]); but also Guido's sonnnet "Avete 'n vo' li fior' e la verdura."

This is the theme of nature as perennial metaphor of woman, invented by Guinizzelli ("Io vogl' del ver la mia donna laudare / ed asembrarli la rosa e il giglio" ["I wish in truth to praise my lady / and liken her to rose and lily"], reprised by Cavalcanti in the sonnet *Biltà di donna*, one line of which—"e bianca neve scender senza venti" ["and white snow falling windless"]—is borrowed, with slight circumstantial variation, in a line of the *Inferno*. Dante, however—and by Dante I mean Dante the exegete—pretends that Giovanna ("Vanna") was generically called Primavera "for her beauty, by others' belief" ("per la sua bieltade, secondo che altri crede"), and from this derives the word-play of "prima-verrà" ("will come first"), to signal her function as pure herald and forerunner of the highest beauty, and in this way investing her with a noteworthy identification with the widespread courtly equation of Love with the lady beloved (Love himself says: "e quell'ha nome Amor, sí mi somiglia" ["and she is called Love, so like me is she"]). A clever promotional procedure, to be sure; but then there is no saying that the essential value of Chapter XXV is retrospective. If it were instead proleptic, it would serve to call the (Chapter XXVI) sonnets *Tanto gentile* and *Vede perfettamente* (lightly retouched, as proved by Domenico De Robertis, when incorporated into the little book) back to their competent metaphorical interpretation, as they further develop the motifs of the angel, salvation, and the chorus, which in Guinizzelli are still short-lived and occasional (especially in *Io vogli' del ver*). The sonnets, and their *razo*, even more so.

And here allow me to probe a little: "Diceano molti, poi che passata era: 'Questa NON È FEMMINA, anzi è uno de li bellissimi angeli del cielo'" (in verse this becomes less emphatic: "*e par* [that is, it becomes clear] *che sia una cosa* [a creature] *venuta / da cielo in terra a miracol mostrare*"; while the first draft had simply: "Credo che sia...") Whether or not Cavalcanti (if we wish facetiously to magnify our observation) felt in agreement with this surreptitious hierarchization of their women, the Cavalcanti-*Vita Nuova* lineage thus emerges as clearly literary. The "instruction manual" represented by Chapter XXV means to say: Careful, I'm laying it on a little thick here, but the lady-as-angel is no longer but a hyperbole.

Cavalcanti mocks Orlandi, who'd believed himself to be competent in matters of love for having read a bit of Ovid. Dante, as we can see, teaches the truth about Ovid. There is a shade of refinement and taste, not necessarily involving knowledge. And so the heuristic value of the theological ingredients is openly stated, but on a poetic level. These include her arrival: "*Chi è questa che vèn...?*" ("Who is this woman who comes...?), derived from the Song of Songs (which in the Vulgate is "*Quae est ista quae ascendit de deserto...?*") crossed with Isaiah ("*Quis est iste qui venit de Edom...?*"); the endless analogy, also from the Song of Songs (to the point of "*Equitatui meo in curribus Pharaonis assimilavi te, amica mea*"); the chorus of praise, again from the Song (not for nothing does the *Convivio* comment on the passage "*Sexaginta sunt reginae...*"); and love-as-fear or love-as-death, which Guido earnestly recuperates from obsolete Occitan and anthological reservoirs (including Guittone), and which in him means blind, irrational passion, according to the metaphysical, perhaps heterodox rule, but cannot be severed from death, thus signaling a mystical conception of death, the fundamental text for which is, once again, the Song of Songs ("*fortis est ut mors dilectio*," "*quia amore langueo*").

When does the disagreement between Dante and Guido begin? I would be the happiest man in the world if I could enclose the celebrated sonnet *I' vegno 'l giorno a te* in this wrapping. Is this a sonnet of the "*rimenata*"?[19] Or is it merely abjection, discouragement, heartache over the death of Beatrice or some other event? However intense the desire may be to coax the texts, it seems hard to get any traction on this one. It is probably referring an overly generous body of correspondence between Dante and poets of the old guard, one not deemed worthy of being collected by a follower of the modern mode. That would put us at an earlier time. Whereas the dispute occurred when Dante found himself contemplating Beatrice, who was, by Gilson's illuminating observation, at once woman, woman in love, and saint (without ceasing to be real), with this cultural experience being mediated not only by her death (the death of the beloved having inspired in the troubadouric tradition, up to and including Pier della Vigna and Giacomino Pugliese, some even gracious corrollaries, however tenuous),

---

[19] I.e., the "scolding" of Guido Cavalcanti by Dante, traditionally believed to have been occasioned by Guido's friendship with Forese Donati and his "intimacy" with the latter's circle.

but also by the inanity of the *pargoletta*, the fetching girl, love-as-libido. To conclude, the duality of the Dantean "I" is objectively mirrored (which is what Dante seems to be wanting to say to Cavalcanti) in the duality of Beatrice. Guido's recalcitrance is not only quite likely that of the atheist refusing grace, but also that of the poet satisfied with literature and its systems of metaphors. Dante, as with Francesca of the *"morum probitas,"* makes amends with Guido for a theology applied as a trope.

Let me now jump ahead to Forese Donati. And here, too, we would seem to be again rather far from the literary realm. Nor is Forese's offense, like Francesca's or Guido's, lethal, but sentimentally or metaphysically ostentatious. There is nothing here to confer praise on the "water-drinking" Dante. He certainly cannot purge himself of his own physical vices through Donati. And yet in the famous *tenzone* Dante already proffers the reproach of gluttony: "Ben ti faranno il nodo Salamone / [...] e' petti delle starne," "giú per la gola tanta roba hai messa") ["Much good will the Solomon's knot / {...} and the partridge breasts do you," "so much have you stuffed down your throat"]. It seems therefore obvious, with all doubt as to the texts' authenticity now dispelled, that the episode is a compensation for so much defamation—especially, as they know even in school, of "la vedovella mia che molto amai" ("my little widow, whom I loved so much"; *Purg.* XXIII, 92), who had been treated so psychologically cruelly as in the tenzone sonnet *Chi udisse tossir*. According to Francesco D'Ovidio, on the other hand, rhyming "Christ" with itself repeatedly in the *Paradiso* is a "making amends" (since the expression "per ammenda" is given the same rhyming treatment—in *Purg.* XX, 65-67—thus, as it were, "Cristo per ammenda", "Christ as amends"), amends made for the "Cristo" in an impious rhyme and irreverent context in the sonnet *Bicci novel* (and also, adds D'Ovidio, in the *Fiore*). I myself would add that the "faccia," the repetition of "faccia" ("la faccia di Forese," "la faccia tua") in the *Purgatorio* scene, turning up as it does at the end of a *variatio* that I will venture to call ostentatious ("testa," "viso," "aspetto," "labbia"), redeems "la faccia fessa" of the same sonnet (though I am not thereby asserting that the connotation of "faccia" in these cases is necessarily derogatory); I'm not even sure that the "difetto di carne" isn't, indeed, a "vendetta de la carne." All this is indisputable; and Forese, even in the guise of an offended party in search of redress, re-enters the realm of literature, as expected. But he does so, in my opinion, in triumph over the most disputable point of all:

>...Se tu riduci a mente
> qual fosti meco, e qual io teco fui,
> ancor fia grave il memorar presente.
>   Di quella vita mi volse costui... (*Purg.* XXIII, 115-118)

> [...If you recall to mind
> how you were with me, and how I was with you,
> the present remembrance will still be grave.
>   From that life was I turned away by the man {before me}...]

And here we see Dante's presumed "straying" re-emerge, giving rise to interpretations sometimes so catastrophic that they are not borne out by the quotation. I do not question the moral straying on his part, but in this case I think that it would all make sense if the shame expressed were simply a condemnation of a shared stylistic experience ("e qual io teco fui") that took precedence over the "tragic" model: the bawdy and precious in the pure state; the *trobar clus* over the dregs of Sinon and MastroAdamo; the charming rhymes in virtuosic passages of insult, pornography, and coprolalia that become a genre in themselves, breaking with the tradition of parallelism and satirical counterpoint to the tragic, which runs—leaving out the Occitans—from Lentini and Guittone (even Rustico di Filippo, like Pieraccio Tedaldi after him, figure in the ranks of the typical love-sonneteers) to a few stilnovistic sparks between Guinizzelli and Cino. Is it really an accident that, not Rustico, but Cecco Angiolieri, his a bit too confidential correspondent, does not make Dante's roll call (taking as well into acount that Book IV of the *De vulgari*, intended to discuss the humble, mediocre style, was never written)? Forese manages to cover them all. That sort of upside-down virtuosity is like the direct virtuosity of Arnaut Daniel (Dante may not have known that Daniel himself had had his own "*tenso* with Forese," in his case with Truc Malec), for which he must be judged as the *De vulgari* does for the ultimate fruit of his imitation, Dante's own double sestina *Amor, tu vedi ben*. It is like the prerogative of the day one dubs oneself knight—in other words, a youthful exacerbation of technique. They are all stylistic experiments that demand to be silenced, subdued, in a comprehensive *summa* of tonalities.

Another glutton is Bonagiunta, "Bonagiunta da Lucca," as the listing in the *canzonieri* has it. It is pointless to speculate where—if part of oral tradition—Dante learned of the man's fame as a big eater and drinker (the second worldly passion of the intelligentsia). I am indulging in this pseudo-biographical triviality because, if we use only heuristic criteria, we will find nothing to grasp onto in the *canzoniere* that has come down to us (at the most, and this is probably just a cavil, some hint of his punishment might be provided by the concluding line of a canzone of his: "ancor mi sia cangiata la figura" ["may my appearance change yet again"]. Nor does the fact that he is introduced by his old companion, and that his appearance is framed in the Forese episode, lend itself to being considered particularly significant. It would, moreover, be indiscreet to spill too much more ink over the definition of "dolce stil novo" such as it appears on the lips of Bonagiunta; it is enough to point out, at most, that "novo," like "dolce," are technical terms. *"Nove rime"* is in fact Dante's manner, starting with *Donna ch'avete*—that is, the transcendental description of Love, praise of the beloved; no longer, so to speak, feudal and merely formalistic poetry, but verse devoted and obedient to its object. Cognitive poetry. The mythological aspect of this approach is inspiration (leaving aside the "sincerity of inspiration" of the careless interpreters, and actually *Donna ch'avete* is a composition whose first line, according to the *Vita Nuova*, was GIVEN to the poet ("Allora dico che la mia lingua parlò quasi come per se stessa mossa" ["And so I say that my tongue spoke almost as if moving by itself"]) and solicits its continuation by him ("Queste parole io ripuosi ne ne la mente con grande letizia, pensando di prenderle per mio cominciamento" ["I set these words down in my mind with great delight, thinking I would use them for my beginning"]).

But perhaps, since we may posit Dante as a self-critic on the basis of a verb ("mi spira"), we could investigate the matter a little further, even beyond what pertains to the strict letter of the *Purgatorio*, while still shedding light on an epithet ("novo") within it. Now, the "libello" (i.e. *La Vita nuova*) points out that the device of *la lode* is enacted by speaking "to women in the second person," but only to ladies who are "gentili" ("noble") and not "pure femmine." "Gentile" is a pregnant, technicalized term, whose implications were indicated to us by the analysis of the "cor gentil." Wherever Dante says "donna gentile" (and we know the prominence this expression assumes for the internal biography), we must read, between the lines, an extension of the nobility of the lady ("E simil face in donna omo valente")—not "pure femmine," and thus germinally not a woman but an angel (see above). This virtually involves an ontological promotion of the object of the poetry, and is the novelty asserted by Dante; contributing to its formation are the choral theme already mentioned, with its allusively mystical language (indeed, one could more specifically call it a veritable secular carbon copy of the dogma of the Communion of the Saints), and the folk motif that must certainly date back to the relationship of the chorus with the queen of the dance, the ladies and demoiselles, maidens and wives in Cielo d'Alcamo (and not surprisingly, in Cielo, but also in Bonagiunta, in a *ballade*).

As for "dolce," it too is one of these elements of the normal language which, despite their outward, non-intellectualized aspect, a mentality less abstract than our own can use for a technical purpose, like the *unito* of Stefano Fiorentino in Vasari, so magisterially translated by Roberto Longhi. One need only think of the "*dolci rime d'amor,*" indeed the melodic (more than expressive) phase of the poetry of Dante in the tragic vein, of the "*dulcior* [...] *loquela*" in the *De vulgari*, of the vernacular poets (i.e., he and Cino) who made "*dulcius*" poetry; and, not too far off, the "dolci detti" ("sweet sayings") of Guinizzelli, and the "dolci e leggiadre" ("sweet and graceful") poems of those who can claim him as their progenitor.

This "sweet," "new" manner is really Dante's own poetry. Lentini, Guittone, and Bongiunta, three *chefs d'école* cited with all due honors (this holds as well for Bonagiunta, whom an age-old oversight passes off as a strict Guittonian acolyte),[20] remain positively on this side of it. It is not certain whether the unmentioned greats, the two Guidos, really stand on the other side of this frontier. They are left out of the non-participation only negatively, and they do contribute decisively to the Dantean manner; but Dante himself does *not* produce the definition of a school. His position is always that presented in the Oderisi Canto (*Purg*. XI), where the "glory of the tongue" wasn't a limitation, but the refinement of an art that is not "*pintura*": with Guittone as the dogmatic representative of the old style, and the three—Dante and the two Guidos—as his replacements, though in a gradated chronology, just as they certainly are in worth as well. So why is the recognition of the break in continuity assigned to none other than Bonagiunta (who in the *De vulgari* holds a slavish rear-guard position linked to the manuals of the day)? The reason lies also in the public domain: because it was Bonagiunta who denounced Guinizzelli—however humoristically, in my opinion—as a dangerous innovator and accused him of having "mutata la mainera / de li plagenti ditti de l'amore" ("transformed the manner / of the pleasant ditties of love"), and more precisely of having twisted poetry in the illustration of propositions ("*scrittura*"), in accordance with the intellectualism of the university milieu.

---

[20] Note that, at the current stage of our biographical knowledge, Bonagiunta would appear to be actually older than Guittone. (GC)

Dante limited himself to accepting this anecdotal given, including of course the submission to the "alta spera" ("lofty sphere") of Guittone (which I am not sure is a formula for modesty, coming from Bonagiunta)—not, obviously, not even in reverse, the preamble on intellectualism, which was destined instead to come down to Romantic critics and the "science" of De Sanctis. Francesco Novati assumes, it's true, a stylistic evolution in Bonagiunta, but I'm afraid he's the victim of a short circuit. The rigidified definition extracted from this same canto, since become a scholastic norm, has led to an exclusivistic conception also of the characteristics experimentally perceived in the authors of the so-called school. The opposite is true: that the so-called school, or at least Cavalcanti himself (he too being, in one *canzoniere*, a correspondent of his), is clearly indebted to this noble vernacular poet.[21]

Let us then look at the face—or at least into the Dantean mirror—of the presumed founder (or, as others say, "precursor") of the Stil Novo. We find him at last among the lustful,[22] along with Arnaut Daniel. Having already atoned for the infernal eros of courtly ethics in the Francesca episode, Dante now expiates the purgatorial eros of the highest Occitan tradition and even the *cor gentil* (whose contribution to Francesca's ruin we've already seen). And it is a veritable amphictyony of vernacular poets. Cino had so well understood this that, if the sonnet *Infra gli altri difetti del libello* ("Among [La Vita Nuova's] other defects"] is indeed his, he reproaches Dante for not having said a word about Onesto da Bologna, who was close to Arnault. In that girone, Bosone da Gubbio, responding to Cino, has Dante himself and Immanuel Giudeo consumed by flames.

Returning, however, to Guinizzelli, I am not certain whether his lust was known to Dante from documentary sources. For us, of course, the official personality of Guinizzelli, not to mention his flaws, *non liquet*: between the two archival candidates for identification, I fear that the final choice would still be inappropriate. And the scarce political and genealogical findings, however suggestive (to the point of lending themselves to Zaccagnini's exaggerations as to a

---

[21] As is Dante as well, if the "succiso" in *Tre donne* (a connection made by Torraca) is indeed owing to Bonagiunta, and especially if the latter is the author of the beginning "Ben mi credea in tutto esser d'Amore certamente allungiato," which seems to have inspired Dante's "Io mi credea del tutto esser partito." (GC)

[22] Guinizzelli, that is.

murky family drama), turn out to be vitiated by this same conjecturality. Given our paucity of information, it is perhaps legitimate to presume that Dante didn't know any more than this; and Vittorio Rossi's wonderful suggestion that the sin is known through the literature and not through the biography—that Dante, in short, was taking aim at Guinizzelli's sonnet for Lucia ("Ah prender lei a forza, ultra su' grato..."), even though the sinful action in it ("seguendo come bestie l'appetito" *Purg.* XXVI, 85; "following our appetite like beasts") was coerced by the pious fear that it might create "forse non poco" ("maybe more than a little") damage and displeasure for others.

As for Daniel, leaving aside what the *Vidas* have to say on the matter (the line from which the *Commedia* steals the beginning, "*Ieu sui Arnautz qu'amas l'aura*," can be read in the Provençal biography), one interpretation is certain: that Dante borrowed from the verbal-fantastical delirium around the "*cambra*" and the desire for closeness in Arnaut's sestina. The salient aspect of his surpassal of the Occitan master is not of a solely moral nature, but stylistic and moral at once. In Arnaut's fire (a refining fire, like the fire of love in the Provençalizing currents of the time) Dante burns his *rime petrose*—he burns, that is, if not actually style as an end in itself that invents and concretizes its own obstacle, then the fleshliness of style, language specialized as expressiveness (as was, even more specifically because it was dipped in the sestina, the language of the *tenzone* with Forese), before it is corrected and assumed into the synthesis and encyclopedia of styles: into, indeed, the *Commedia*. The experience of Daniel is, moreover, so decisive for Dante's career as vernacular poet that he considers him the flower of the Occitan phase, and places him ahead of Giraut de Borneilh (while the third great Occitan of the *De vulgari*, Bertram de Born, is, as usual, folded into his public and historical functions). We will recall that, when Crescini's *Manuale* came out as an upgrade of his *Manualetto provenzale*, in the major announcement made in the most widely read daily newspaper in Italy, the reviewer boastfully placed himself, on his own, among the ranks of the ignorant. The date of this publication was not, despite your surprise, so lost in the mists of time: 1926. Since then, a great deal of headway has been made: Academic triflers may find no audience in such precincts, but Arnaut's stock has risen in our marketplace. Why does Dante limit Giraut? Is it Because he's *a bon à tout faire* available for any need of a poetic nature, fluttering between *trobar leu* and hermeticism, and, to top it off, a bit cynical? Or is it because his commitment to "*rectitudo*" (see the *De vulgari*) brings him closer to Guittone than to the moral Dante?

A less obvious question, though probably also a bit less cumbersome, is the one raised by the surpassing of Guinizzelli. A radical source (when not also systematic) of many attitudes considered stilnovistic, Guinizzelli lends himself to being recuperated by Dante also as a single source: if the *nove rime* begin with *Donne ch'avete*, his dialogue in the skies would have been inconceivable without the dialogue—admittedly and unquestionably more epigrammatic and almost wittier—which closes *Al cor gentil*. He is, above above all, "dolce," that is, a master of tone, as we have seen. And therefore a patron saint of the "modern mode" (*"uso moderno"*), and a "father" to Dante's betters (the other Guido and Cino) and no less to Dante himself.

The surpassing is fully expressed in the fact that a supernal lady is proclaimed Dante's salvation within the very *girone* of the lustful ("donna è di sopra che m'acquista grazia" ("there is a lady above who wins me grace"), and the empyrean (the sky "ch'è pien d'amore") is augured his imminent abode. Not woman but angel; and on top of that, not metaphor, but reality. An analogical leap. Hereabove, then, are enough passages to assert, even if it's along one same line, the progress of both Cavalcanti and Dante; and we won't hide the fact that, through the interpretation of "Primavera" and its declassing, Dante's progress over Cavalcanti is hinted at in the *Vita Nuova* itself. Still the fact remains that Dante's beginnings, between fear and spirits, are Cavalcantian. The Dolce Stile—if we can stretch things and speak of a school, is the Tuscan, indeed Florentine variant, of the "uso moderno." Let us keep this "Florentine variant" in mind, and meanwhile, just to be certain, we must say first that none other than Guinizzelli himself, and certainly not for the sake of conversational convention, proclaims Arnaut as the "miglior fabbro del parlar materno." (*Purg*. XXVI, 117) *Fabbro*: artificer, artisan. Against any eventual nationalists or parochialists, those for whom the *De vulgari*'s city of Pietramala is the entire universe, Dante, for whom the world is *"patria velut piscibus aequor"* ("a homeland, as water is to fish"), first asserts the greatness of a non-Tuscan, then, having himself drunk not from tributary streams but from the primary sources of Occitan *saber*, the greatness of a non-Italian. He remains faithful to his literal and ideal chronology. He has gone beyond the *rime petrose*, but that difficult stage of awkward business was unavoidable; analogy serving to perfect, yet while still connected to the laboratory.

This surpassing of the Stil Novo experience contributed greatly, if I am not mistaken, to reducing Guinizzelli's hegemony and points to a less emphatic reading of the episode. The Bolognese master continued being viewed as the traditional *Wendepunkt*[23] ratified by Bonagiunta. Still, the historical Guinizzelli paid homage to Guittone, sending his way—under the guise of asking him to bestow his knowledge upon him—an original canzone (presumably the hyper-Guittonian *Lo fin pregi' avanzato*), to which Guittone replied in rhyme, but with increased skill, adding equivocation to the makeweight of expressive terms. "O caro padre meo," began Guido's sonnet; and in parody and antithesis, and throwing in an enjambment, Dante calls him "padre / mio."[24] "De vostra laude," Guido went on, "non bisogna ch'alcun omo se 'mbarchi" (rhymed with "marchi" and repeated four times by Guittone, each time with a different meaning). It is a rather peregrine word, as is necessary for the phrase "*esperienza imbarche*," which Dante puts in Guido's mouth, to carry the precise allusion assigned to it[25]—an allusion brought into focus by critics of Guittone's fame, whose number he will soon explicitly join.

---

[23] "Turning point."

[24] The comparison was already suggested by S. Santangelo (*Dante e i trovatori provenzali*, Catania, s.a., p. 222), but for an entirely different purpose ("it is not out of the question to think that, in that mode of address, he wished to present the modesty of a genuine master in opposition to the false modesty of a false great poet"). And this writer, too, reads what I will call a "bovarysm" on Dante's part in the episode, that is, a transposed autobiography; and he perceives in it more anti-Guittonism than any exaltation of Guido. He re-evokes Oderisi's words (believing moreover that the "two Guidos" are Guittone and Guinizzelli). But the specific hypothesis he puts forward—trapped inside a much vaster castle of conjecture—is the presumed "anti-Bologna" purpose of the canto: the Guittonians of Bologna had supposedly humiliated Dante during his sojourn there in 1304-1306, and this would constitute his revenge. Guido, Giraut, and Arnaut are supposedly just stand-ins, the last two for Guittone and Dante (including the "amorous passion" he felt "in his mature years"), while the first supposedly serves the purpose of putting the condemnation on the tongue of a famous Bolognese. It would therefore be pointless to look for sources for reports of the poets' sins of lust; one would do better indeed to look for documentation of the salvation of Arnaut, which we gather from reports of his becoming a monk, as divulged by Benvenuto da Imola. As for what is suggested in the text, it should be added that, according to Santangelo, Dante was not familiar with the *Vidas*; and that the *sirventès* for Truc Malec (whose putative relationship to Dante informs the useless elucubrations of Kolsen, in *Deutsches Dante-Jahrbuch*, VIII, 51-52) does not figure in the tradition close to the Provençal *canzoniere* used by Dante, in Santangelo's estimation (whereas it does appear in songbooks related to the one reconstructed by Bartsch). What matters here is not a general judgment of this book, which is less known than it should be, but was fortunately reprinted shortly after the present writing, and remains bold though debatable, since the eventual dismantling of the individual texts can only be done after due consideration. (GC)

[25] A connection generally inferred by Torraca, in *Nuovi studi danteschi etc.*, Naples 1921, p. 448. (GC)

To summarize: the episode of the first Guido is, in short, far less a declaration of Guinizzellism than an anti-Guittonian proclamation in the form of a palinode. Another overlap: an unbridled fame graced ("*extollere*" is verb used in the *De vulgari*)[26] the poet from Arezzo only "fin che l'ha vinto il ver con piú persone" ["until the truth won out with more people"]. *Il ver* being, of course, reality as it is lived. Now Guido, replying to Bonagiunta's attack and his profession of Guittonian faith—in a courteous reply not in rhyme and actually detached, over time, from the correspondence, the better to attribute it to Guittone, and limited to liberally asserting the plurality of opinion, a reply at once courteous, *ad hominem*, and ironic, since the initial formulation "Omo ch'è saggio" retraces an *incipit* by Bonagiunta,[27] itself derived in turn from a line of the cited sonnet by Frederick II, and even the "despàri senni" echo a poetic correspondence of Bonagiunta's—Guido, in replying, inferred on the contrary that the prudent man should refrain from pronouncing a judgment "infin a tanto che 'l ver l'asigura" ["until such time as the truth should assure it"]. Here too, *il ver* is reality as it is lived.

It remains for us to establish the true reason for Dante's anti-Guittonism. It's a position that he in fact gets from that same "Florentine variant," since the first anti-Guittonian was not Guinizzelli, but Cavalcanti, in an obscure sonnet that attacks the rational claims of "fra Guittone," thereby wrongfooting Bonagiunta's argument against the other Guido. For Dante, the *Commedia* isn't enough, and so we must consult the *De vulgari*. Generically speaking, we can always presume a natural impatience towards any cultural dictator, especially a national, indeed local monopolist, if we think of such conduits of Guittonism in Florence as Monte Andrea and (considerably less so) Chiaro Davanzati (who are never cited in compendiums which do not otherwise lack for presences, and absences, such as the *Commedia* and some minor texts). Nor would I insist too strongly on an antipathy, on Dante's part, towards the Frati Gaudenti (Guittone's order), who are limited to a brief, painful appearance in Malebolge (and one of whom,

---

[26] The "*ignorantiae sectatores*" who do this are the originals of the "stolti" who extol Giraut in the *Purgatorio*. There is therefore no need to go looking for other forefathers for them, particularly, as Torraca states, the "*fatz*" whose praise Linhaure (Raimbaut d'Orange) rejects in his *tenso* with Giraut on the *trobar clus* (refuted by Giraut). (GC)

[27] Compare moreover the opening of an anonymous sonnet to Bonagiunta: "Eo so ben ch'om non poria trovar saggio / sí come voi, maestro Bonagiunta." (GC)

Loderingo, is honored by Guittone). We could even narrow the motive by taking a closer view, when we note that Dante, first with the great moral canzoni, then with the prose of the *Convivio*, had experimented—by compensating, restoring, renovating—precisely where the other had indicated the path. These are precedents without which both the canzoni and the *Convivio* are unthinkable; and some of us (let us honor Giuseppe De Robertis in this regard) have taken the trouble to track down precise echoes, even in the *Commedia*, of the maligned predecessor. It is always a good tactical rule to get rid of one's neighbor and competitor first. But since the *De vulgari* places him among the "*numquam* [...] *plebescere desuetos*" ["never ... become commonplace"] right where he discusses (adding the "*vocabula*") the degrees of the "*constructio*," a border zone between syntax and style (even Cavalcanti's sonnet to Guittone mocked the "profferer, che cade in barbarismo," due to a "difetto di saver"[28]), we shall infer that Guittone, in remaining on this side of the "dolce" manner—i.e., that of melody and nuance—trusted only the expressiveness of the language, which in itself might even be harsh and vernacular. The moral Guittone, Fra Guittone (though Dante never calls him that), is prosaic: "Ami nel drappo suo card' e non sciugna" ["Love the carder in the cloth and not the grease"], he says, preaching. It's a technology of the lower arts, where Cecco Angiolieri digs out the error that drags Dante into his mire ("s'eo cimo 'l panno, tu vi freghi il cardo" ["if I trim the cloth, you scrape the carder"])." He directly versifies his actual biography, like some thirteenth-century Bettelloni, for which Torraca gives him well-deserved credit. But Dante is hardly a bourgeois realist.

In any case, Guinizzelli and Arnaut Daniel are the last souls in Purgatory with whom Dante will engage in conversation—the last, like Francesca, the first of the damned, under the same epigraph. Guido was able to do his penance effectively "prima ch'a lo stremo" ["before the end"]; whereas Francesca had been surprised by her violent death (thus "e il modo ancor m'offende" ["and the manner still offends me"], as the suddenness of her end did not allow her a chance to save her soul). The circle closes: Brunetto's lines: "sai che sem tenuti / un poco mondanetti" ["you know we are taken / for being a bit worldly"], seem a rather fitting motto for such intellectuals.

---

[28] The sonnet being "Da più a uno face un sollegismo," dedicated to Guittone d'Arezzo. Translation of cited phrases: "...the offering, which falls into barbarism," due to a "lack of knowledge."

The circle of sinners, whether forsaken or redeemed, and in whom the "I"—who is us—objectifies and ransoms his possible guilt, begins and ends there. This can be glossed from Dante's own ethics:

> Quinci comprender puoi ch'esser convene
> amor sementa in voi d'ogni virtute
> e d'ogne operazion che merta pene.
>
> [You can thus understand that love
> must plant in you the seed of every virtue
> and every action meriting punishment.] (*Purg.* XVII, 103-105)

And now the pilgrim can ascend to where love is entirely directed "nel primo ben." But the journey belongs to Dante's historical "I," to the "I" that is I, the poet—and all the poetry, as we heard in the confession to Bonagiunta, is love poetry. Every stage and stopping point of his journey beyond the earth is a victoriously traversed modality of his former "I"; and his interlocutors are themselves historical and at the same time, other: they are symbol and function. In them too, therefore, is realized the planar duality characterizing Dante and, in his mirror, Beatrice. If a structural analysis is the right one, it is reflected from the macrocosm to the microcosm. Its validity, now verified in the particular, is a perfect "casting out of the nines" for an overall interpretation.

[Lecture from 1957, later printed in *Approdo letterario*, January-March 1958, and reprinted that same year in the volume, *Secoli vari*, of the Libera Cattedra della Civiltà fiorentina, Florence, Sansoni.]

Dante Today

A few months ago, on Montreal radio, a nice interviewer asked me whether I considered Dante an *engagé* writer. I will use this memory to orient my discussion of the most current aspect of Dante's *engagement*: the linguistic one.

That the *Commedia* is the only masterpiece of the European Middle Ages still linguistically alive today is an advantage that no doubt also has its silent repercussions in the immobility of Italian culture's structures and its aristocratic stigma. While making the most of such an advantage, we must also praise Dante's ingenious responsibility in directly converting the poetic problem into a linguistic one. Art historians are often surprised to discover, when comparing the history of painting from Cimabue to Giotto (including the illuminations of such mysterious figures as Oderisi da Gubbio and Franco Bolognese) to the history of poetry from Guinizzelli and Cavalcanti to Dante, that he rescued figurative dignity from manual effort. But historians of poetry should be no less surprised that the "glory of the language" should be invoked in his case. In his artisanal operation Dante rules out no expressive possibility whatsoever. He is helped by the belief in the continuity between Latin and the vernacular tongue, which allows him to link up with any tradition at the moment he gives himself over to any innovation.

In the *Vita Nuova*, the symoblic and anthropomorphic characters speak in Latin; Dante and the others in Italian; and Amore condescends to use vernacular words, in a similar fashion to Cacciaguida, or the representation of Cacciaguida, who, from "O sanguis meus," lowers himself to more confidential forms, though translated (whatever their expressive value) into a less "moderna favella" ("less modern speech"). The undertaking to describe the entire universe in depth is not a task for a "lingua che chiami mamma o babbo," and yet it is for a language that *says* "mamma" and "babbo." Although on some even spoken level, an Italian may be embarrassed of "mamma" and inflate it to "madre," the Dante of the *Paradiso*, with an apologetic argument that scoffs at all theological rationality, desires the resurrection of the flesh "per le mamme." I am pointing out a familiar, affective borderline case to avoid casting certain words as taboo, but I can state more specifically that, where Giacomo da Lentini more or less felt "*prurito*" ("itch"), Dante feels "*pizzicore*" ("itch, tingling"). The—let's say it—*social* importance of such an attitude is immense, even if enacted in the only culturally possible manner: that is, by emulsifying the natural language in a multiplicity and totality of tones, unshackling it from the slightly artificial specialization of "comic" literature, and yet deriving from this limitation the actual program and title of the great poem. Assuming that the poem's linguistic sublimity, which competes directly with Latin, is already known, we must not, however, neglect the fact that Dante, outstanding with extremes, equally excels in the mid-range tones, particularly speech, and especially in the dissociation between rhythmic monotony and syntactical freedom, which reminds us of his quality as a first-rate prose writer as well: "O mantoano, io son Sordello / de la tua Terra."

Master of every kind of excessive and violent expression, Dante also cultivates in his breast the refined man of letters, discreet and possessed of good taste, the "artist" in the De Sanctis sense of the term and the fountainhead of melodic poetry, without whom not even Petrarch would be conceivable. Imagine Dante having died before writing the *Commedia*, and even before the *Convivio*: while more univocal but perhaps no less arcane, the author of the *Vita Nuova* would remain a decisive stopping point perhaps less linearly rich than Petrarch, but still not developed along a single plane like him. And it is this same duality, the semantic surpassing of the immediate sphere of the word, that explains the particular audience granted this Dante, and his associate Cavalcanti, by a rather recent and still quite contemporary sector of the Symbolists in the English, or indeed neo-English, language. Even the most well-known parts of the *Vita Nuova* do not lend themselves to naïve readings: "benignamente d'umiltà vestuta" confirms a relationship between outside and inside, here rendered perceptible to the senses; the "cielo" from which the creature has descended is a figurative compendium of everything that transcends phenomena.

Yet not even the Dante of the *Commedia* is the bearer of a merely precise reality (but please let us not call him "impressionistic"). "E come a gracidar si sta la rana" ("And as the frog lies [with head half out of the water]"; *Inf.* XXXII, 31): this and the countless other fragments of reality have no contextual autonomy, and if we claim for ourselves the authority to free them in our minds and admire the prodigious speaker who detached them from contingency and uttered them for all time—just as the task of edifying or purifying does not mar the bursting vitality of the characters—the fact still remains that this *rana* stands etymologically for that "*come*," for that comparison. We have before us Dante's twofold condition: perennial representer on the one hand, man of established culture on the other. To better grasp the situation, we could propose—at least at a time when so much figurative material on Dante is in circulation, not always, truth be told, of the highest quality—the situation of an illustrator wanting to dispense with the narrative structure of the *Commedia*. This is not a fictional scenario. The illuminator of the age-old codex that Cortona lent to the Biblioteca Nazionale di Firenze for the large exhibition currently on view, behaves just like those masters who would insert and nearly forget "gratuitous" details in the workshops of the Middle Ages, as he assigns indeed frogs, cranes, goldfinches the function, or pretext, of reference marks from quinternion to quinternion. Hardly abstract, but indeed decorative, this enchanting illuminator is thus one of the most appropriate visualizers of the *Commedia*. And yet it is the "structure"— in the sense of that which Croce opposes to "poetry"—that fascinates other readers. If the German Dante Society was the first of so many to be born across the world—indeed it is celebrating its first centenary this year—it is because the work's Gothic monumentality is still viewed up north as homogeneous.

In the dialectical pairings, which never match, employed to define Dante's critical positions—poet vs artist, structure vs poetry—his *engagement* concerns the former pairing. And yet Dante's *engagement* has an essential connotation thus far inadequately investigated: its coincidence with the absolutism of the values of form. It is possible, that, in counterposing representationalism with calligraphism, our rhetoric has been a bit rough, but certainly no rougher than bureaucratic rhetoric in its rapport with reality. The fact remains that in certain precincts the need is perceived as current. Think, for example, that revolutionary Russian lyric poetry is closely related to critical formalism, or that there still exists in Hungary a literary etiquette well founded on phonetic interplay, one corollary of which—and for which they cannot be forgiven—demands that the translator imitate the rhythm of the original. Such experiences are a rather long way from modern Italian ones when one very basic characteristic of the *Commedia* does not seem flagrant enough: the continued repetition of purely rhythmic and phonetic figures undetermined by context, such as the exact reiteration of one formula from Charon ("ch'intorno a li occhi avea di fiamma viva"; *Inf.* III, 99) to the blessed ("Le facce tutte avean di fiamma viva" *Par.* XXXI, 13), from Brunetto ("ficca' li occhi per lo cotto aspetto"; *Inf.* XV, 26) to the final vision ("ficcar lo viso per la luce etterna"; *Par.* XXXIII, 83); or the closeness, on the level of sound and lexicon, though not at all on the level of meaning, of the clause on creatures "ch'hanno intelletto ed amore" (*Par.* I, 120) to that of the famous opening "*Donne ch'avete intelletto d'amore*" (*VN*, XIX). Dante is an *engagé* whose speech is music: rhythm and timbre, not just melody.

What constitutes this particular formalism is the contiguity of the data outside the system of signs—that is, the freedom of memory being inflected with such ideological passion. Proceeding further into the formal question, let us look at another example of contiguity. It is by now a well accepted notion that the dispute between Sinon and Maestro Adamo—a squabble that Dante will confusedly think he has heard, but in the meantime will indeed have heard—is a "comical" *tenzone* (from the Occitan *tenso*), a form already practiced in its pure state by Dante together with Forese Donati and that same Cecco Angiolieri about whom he says not a word (Dante's parts have been lost). Sinon's line, "S'io dissi falso, e tu falsasti il conio" ("If I spoke falsely, you falsified the coin"; *Inf.* XXX, 115), repeats Cecco's reproach to Dante, which only makes sense if taken as a reply, "s'i' desno con altrui, et tu vi ceni" ("if I lunch with others, you dine with them"). And Cecco goes on in this fashion for all the quatrains. Now the *bolgia* of the counterfeiters opens with the grotesque celebration of the freakish, clownish, goliardic wastrels of Siena. The evocation of the Sienese stirs in Dante the memory of the Sienese *rimeria*, a poetry circle he frequented directly in his days of "straying," and it is assimilated as inspiring the other "tonal" sources of this episode: classics such as Ovid and Virgil, and the Bible as read through the lens of the *Vita Nuova*.

These disputes unfold in a fully caricatural vernacular, thus bringing us back to a theorem of Dante the critic. The fact that the poet is supplemented by the critic constitutes Dante's borderline" condition, so that when, however improbably, we get fed up with his poetry, we can still derive sustenance from his intelligence. The first critic in Italian literature—and not only chronologically—Dante worked out the categories by which thirteenth-century poetry is still classified. Among other things he described, in the *De vulgari Eloquentia*, that parodic "*improperium*" of "indigenous mediocrities," sometimes even in unassailable technical form, that stands, where it exists, in opposition to literary poetry, thus giving us to understand how the polarization of spontaneous and reflective dialect poetry, which Croce placed in the Baroque period, needs to be pushed all the way back to its origins. It is curious to note that De Sanctis, with Nannucci's manual in hand, begins his history with the figure known as Cielo d'Alcamo; precisely the contemporary counterforce to Lentini and to Sicilian *trobar* of lofty intention. If we look to that rather prominent front line of contemporary Italian literature currently and broadly introducing regional elements into the language (but in the finest and by now re-evaluated naturalistic and *scapigliata*[1] tradition), we can only conclude that we have come full circle.[2] Dante with his "comical" practice; Galileo with his passion for the Padovan Ruzzante, who celebrated the *snaturale*, the "unnatural," pried open in all its truth, even for those who didn't know Latin; Manzoni with his fondness for Carlo Porta; and we can add De Sanctis with his nevertheless moderate praise of the likes of Folengo and Goldoni, Croce with his affection for Domenico Basile:[3] no great name of Italian linguistic "democracy" is missing from this lineage. And if Dante is so teeming with vital and contradictory virtualities as to cast hooks in every direction, the most telling picture we can draw from it is that of an irrepressible experimentalism, an absolute open-mindedness towards the real.

[From the *Corriere della Sera*, July 30, 1965]

---

[1] The "*scapigliati*" (the "dishevelled ones") were the members of la Scapigliatura, an avant-garde literary-artistic movement in northern Italy in the late 19th century.

[2] In the first decades following the end of World War II, there was a nationwide revival (Pasolini, Gadda, et al) in the use of regional dialects as literary vehicles.

[3] Ruzzante (Angelo Beolco, 1496-1542); Carlo Porta (1775-1821), Gerolamo Folengo (1491-1544), Carlo Goldoni (1707-1793), and Domenico Basile (1596-1633) were all (except Folengo) writers who composed a significant part of their *oeuvre* in their respective native dialects; Folengo was famous for his compositions in macaronic Latin.

One Interpretation of Dante

This essay will be a sincere soul-searching on the part of one to whom has fallen some responsibility, or perhaps custodianship, of all things Dante. And so I must begin with a simple, drastic question: Does anyone still read *The Divine Comedy*? I don't mean because you're required to read it at school, or do so out of a sense of cultural duty; I mean as the free, cheerful choice of someone undertaking to follow the story from beginning to end, putting his trust in the narrator, lending himself to his game, anticipating the surprises in store, the way one always does for the Homeric epics and the *Aeneid*, for the *Orlando Furioso*, *Don Quixote*, *The Betrothed* and every other great novel of the nineteenth century, and for the *Recherche du temps perdu* and for *Ulysses*. I don't doubt that the general answer would be no. Just as, on the other hand, I also have no doubt that, upon opening the book, or upon searching one's memory, the style will have, in every single word, the overwhelming, irresistible power of apparitions seen suddenly for the first time.

In the "light-hearted" forward motion of the tercets, in the well-oiled, freewheeling flow of the eschatalogical adventure, the major sequences dissolve and fade a little, and the lapidary words, etched for centuries in the national memory, begin to relax and release a little of their grip. But the reader who then slows down, lingers, and in fact looks back at the poem's technique of fits and starts, will feel at once the bite of the imagination and succumb to the overwhelming verbal intensity. For enthusiasts, the discrete prevails over the continuous.

So, the "little book" no longer holds up? Let us admit straight out that it holds up all too well, like a thread woven into a fabric but never fully assimilating. And not exactly, or not only, because it has been eclipsed ideologically. The pious modern reader will certainly prefer, as a vehicle for the truths of the faith, the Catechism of Pius X; and in searching for a Christian novel he will require that it be a book of Christian morals, say, Manzoni's *The Betrothed* (also because, let us say straight away, the *Commedia*'s intention is not aimed at "a better life," but at a "better here and now").[1] Only by *poussées*, fragmentarily, can the argument scoff at the official parenesis: no manual on the resurrection of the flesh can advance the primary argument put forward by so "rough" a voice as this:

> forse non pur per lor, ma per le mamme,
> per li padri e per li altri che fur cari [...] (*Par.* XIV, 64-65)
>
> (perhaps not just for themselves, but for their mamas,
> for their fathers, and for others who were dear to them [...])

The fact remains that the protagonist of the fable, the character whom recent criticism has taught us is bifrontal in nature—as ineffable individual and as man in general—is not caught up in plausible, imitable relationships. And the odd thing, though entirely attributable to the poet's merit, is that the vision becomes all the more touching as the traveler ascends: in these more compact zones, where the episodic samplings slow down a little, he digs into his personal background, encounters the *"piota"* ["root"] of his family tree, celebrates, more or less, his own birthday, and meanwhile chats only with Adam and the Patriarchs and Church Fathers and engages in an astronautical contemplation of the planet he has transcended. But what would his normal regimen be? The eager sigh of relief we breathe at the start of the *Purgatorio* seems and is pure—that is, detached from any connection with the presumed anguish of Hell's valley. And so, goodbye journey. All the same, don't put too much trust in those enchanting reeds that you see bending but not breaking at the water's edge; in fact they hide and imply a miracle: "oh maraviglia"—plucked by Virgil's hand, "l'umile pianta" ["the humble plant"] is reborn identical as before. The more she appears pacific, the more nature points to the marvelous. The register of our adherence, which is discontinuous and recurrent, divorces us from the register of the narration.

Dante's poetry, then, resides less in the book, where the material flows and unwinds, than in the memory, which halts its terrifying potency and then sets it slowly back in motion. Every slightly tense reading should re-start on virgin ground and wipe clean the slate of the history of criticism. But there's a limit

---

[1] Contini's phrase *una vita migliore* ("a better life") appears to be playing on a common Italian euphemism for death, *passare a miglior vita* ("to pass on to a better life"), and thus in saying "a better life," he is actually referring to the afterlife, since we are, after all, talking about Dante.

to an acquired ignorance of the precedents; and one cannot fail to recognize that whoever applies any kind of dichotomy within the *Commedia* is paying homage to the Crocian problematics of "structure" and "poetry." The irritating avalanche of lawyerly interpretations that have been unintentially stirred up therefrom (most of them aimed at reconnecting the poetry to the so-called structure) is not enough to make us forget that Croce's essay on the subject was the first reminder of the work to the modern intelligence, proving far more relevant, I must say, than all the centuries of hermeneutics combined.

The pragmatic aspect of this manner lies surely in Dante's attainment of lyricism, a preoccupation of the autonomous, exhaustive cultivation of sentiments of less concern to us nowadays, now that the poet's attempted fusion of lyric and narrative seems consonant with modern demands—with those endless series of "Ed io a lui…", "Ed elli a me…", "Io li rispuosi…," which rather amusingly call to mind the "he said, she said" of the contemporary Americans and those derived from them. Here there is a meeting and friction between levels that revives the Crocian problematics of the double register. Indeed the philosopher took supreme care to locate the paradigm's ancestor in the opposition between "system" and poetry, as posited by a German Romantic, but his distinction has a decided advantage over similar ones, especially over the famous case in which De Sanctis, in detaching the "effectual world" from the "intentional world," took it upon himself to protect Dante even against Dante, providing a theoretical foundation to the choice that has more or less always been exercised within that great poetic body of work. Croce's superiority lies in qualifying the rejected part as other than poetry. Croce declares quite rightly that "schema and poetry, theological romance and lyric, cannot be separated in Dante's work"; but it is the very spatial nature of his metaphors that matters in his praxis and in subsequent interpretations—the tendency to disassociate physically the poetic parts and the unpoetic structural parts, with the goal of establishing an ultimate collection of lyric poems.

An operation of this sort can, of course, be realized. In Croce's example, the four stars seen by Dante at the opening of the *Purgatorio*, which may represent the four cardinal virtues, "but in poetry are nothing but the emotion of wonderment and ravishment experienced at the sight of so unexpected and beautiful a spectacle," are specifically said in the poetic text to be as "never seen before except by the first people" ("non viste mai fuor ch'a la prima gente")—in other words, never before seen except at the very instant of their first perception. Most importantly, the distinction is not necessarily between the two sides of the writing, between the global event and the specific utterance.

If, therefore, the opposition is not so much between medium and poetic object as between manner and manner of reading, perhaps mathematical images inspired by continuity, discretion, and speed are preferable to metaphors lending themselves to merely spatial interpretion. Slowing down freezes the invention; gradual acceleration highlights its fertility, which, however, meets its limit in the perfect continuity of the book, which becomes atonic where it does not meet the conditions for poetry.

For this reason I would like to speak a bit about "states" of poetry, just as one speaks of solid states and liquid states of matter. Try as Dante's culture might to forbid him the direct approach and the autonomous conception of individual inventions, it was the very mark of the great poet to have pushed beyond these cultural restrictions, leaving a limitless margin for the collaboration of the future culture, even though we must admit that such a double-register system—with one ideological register almost entirely foreign to us, the other imaginative-verbal register almost entirely accessible to us (whereas the χωρίζουτες, including De Sanctis and Croce, call energetically for curtailing it)—may not be rescued by any corresponding parallel, with the result that Dante's much-deprecated uniqueness emerges more clearly than ever.

In other words, if a criterion exists for measuring the debatable category of a poet's greatness, it can only be that poet's translatability—especially from one cultural system to another. And no claim shall be made as to the absoluteness of his own sphere of transferral. Nevertheless, if Dante's dimensions survived the dramatico-passional readings of the Romantics, they withstand a linguistic reading and "execution" far better. Which, moreover, does not fail to translate. It knows that proverbial spells such as that cast by the words "Trivïa ride tra le ninfe etterne" ("Trivïa smiles among the eternal nymphs," *Par.* XXIII, 26-27) are bound and subjected to a discourse as metaphors and allusions, which meanwhile exonerates them from a fragmentary aestheticism. The "ravishment" (*rapimento*) of which Croce spoke is equivalent to a state of the text. A variable state.

To claim hat the true seat of the *Commedia* should reside in the memory and not in the book itself might give rise to accusations of *lèse-philologie*. I must confess that the common idolatry of the book would seem to me a rather primitive instance of the "patriotism" of my profession ("party patriotism," as they say), since good philology seems to me the ability to recognize the specific situation of each text. If memory allows a well-fitted reconstruction of Dante's text, where all the passages fall into their assigned order yet with a simultaneously clamorous novelty, then memory, too, necessarily becomes an object of philological study. The latter is neither neutral nor exclusive as to values, and it cannot exclude from its interests any surprise felt in the face of the brilliance and open-mindedness with which the need for concatenation is exploited step by step. Now, if this proposition contains even a scintilla of not purely metaphorical truth, some kind of reflection thereof should also be able to be found upon technical scrutiny. No one would ever suspect that the transmission of the *Commedia* could be more oral than written in nature. The fact remains, however, that, still more than any other work of such broad and sudden diffusion, Dante's poem oozes with variants that cannot be reduced to any "vertical" rationality exclusive to the written tradition. The constellations that arise in the presence of variants that are not manifestly erroneous—such as "e durerà quanto il moto / mondo lontana" or "anche di qua nuova schiera / gente s'auna"—do not overlap with one another, almost as though the copyists had a variety of versions available from which to make their choices. In cases like this, one gets around the obstacle by resorting to the escape-valve of considering the manuscripts on the same level as composite editions, which collate and contaminate a number of autoritative copies according to their own tastes (I am here ignoring the hypothesis—which in certain cases should not be dismissed but to this date has not been sufficiently investigated—of authorial variants, a hypothesis that the excellent Domenico De Robertis has at least recognized for the lyric poems of the *Vita Nuova*). But for this to happen it would be necessary for all the incriminated codices to maintain an addressable appearance of critical intention; and since this happens very rarely, we are forced to conclude that these asymmetries prove the blending of the oral tradition into the written one—i.e., that the scribes indeed copied but, as we are ourselves would do, with their minds overflowing with remembrances. They will have been excised, of course, but by the same token, this situation will also have given rise to more than a few of those variants. And if they are not, in the end, quite so numerous as the text's popularity would dictate, that means that the text, having entered in large chunks into all good Italian memories, carries a linguistic charge so differentiated, so inimitable, so—we cannot help but say—memorable as to brake any spontaneous attempt at imitative substitution. The passage into memory is an historical reflexion of objective memorability, a passage distinguished by the anecdotes of the petit-bourgeois and artisan classes in the legend of Dante. And in this legend there is even room for editorial variants: "tramestava i versi suoi, smozzicando e appiccando" ["he shuffled his lines around, cutting and pasting"], Franco Sacchetti says of the craftsman, and then has Dante say, in the subsequent short story of the donkey driver: "Cotesto *arri* non vi mis'io" ["*I* didn't put that *arri* there"].

The equating of memory and memorability has living, popular witnesses in the craftsman and the donkey driver (and thus Sacchetti foolishly inserts Dante's wrath in the face of such torment and grief). This equation eludes the hagiographer on duty, the delegated administrator of the dark cult devoted to Dante by generations of mercantile Florentines who'd only recently been rescued from their illiteracy. These insufferable shopkeepers, pushing the idea that Dante and his vast syncretism are excessive to the extreme, are incapable of grasping the reasons for Dante's true popularity and tremendous learning. Popularity of course also implies the billboard and its frame, violent coloring, precipitous rhythms through multiplying concatenations, and therefore vocal repertoire. (I was about to say *Verdian* repertoire.) And learning, on the other hand, because the most violent of the poet's formal energy is not pure nature without fathers or paradigms, but rather falls ideally within the framework of the claims which the *rimatori*,[2] as he calls them in the *Vita Nuova*, make for the status of *"poete"* (i.e., those writing in Latin).

And what, for Dante, is nourishment through the Classics, the "lungo studio" of and "grande amore" for Virgil's epic, the *Aeneid*, his "mamma" and "nutrice?" Plucking rhetorical figures and stylistic procedures from both fields and dissecting them in comparative herbariums was not without its usefulness, but it doesn't help us to answer this question directly. The teachings of the Classics for Dante lay instead entirely in the authority of their utterance, in their simultaneously new and definitive aspect, their quotability, their memorability. A "classic" is something from which—at least in a chosen circle of users—certain unmodifiable words can be extracted, words that one finds verified in one's own experience, however unprecedented. If I had to define the figures constituting such a circle, I don't think I could find any loftier, more appropriate examples than Montaigne and Sainte-Beuve, great men of letters, indeed exemplars, yet secondary (and thus free of hedonism) to the production of the poetic object, living in the warmth of its fruition. The Classics, the Latins in particular and Virgil more than anyone, together constitute (and in this respect Virgil differs from the more modern storytellers of the canon cited at the start of this essay) a tight-woven fabric and enjoy the ability of being quoted in snippets that immediately resolidify with all their meaning inact.

---

[2] Or, "rhymers," Dante's term for vernacular lyric poets.

On a plane infinitely more vernacular than that upon which those refined spirits move, *"amica silentia lunae"*[3] fits the measure of a nocturnal enchantment well known to all, even if, contextually speaking, *amica* carries a tactical connotation—good weather conditions for a military expedition—here replaced by a sentimental syntony with nature; but it is precisely in this latitude of abuse, of imitative reading, in the possibility of being translated autonomously, that the vitality of the Classics lies. And by repeating *"maioresque cadunt altis de montibus umbrae"*[4] ["and from high mountaintops fall the greater shadows"] one expresses the visual sensation of the mountain's silhouette projected onto the slope opposite and the associated irremediability of the decline of a season more than simply the end of a day—even if in the original that twinge is less mournful, less deathly, and is merely a fitting, colorful symbol to mark the conclusion of the poem.

This use of the classics as a reservoir of quotations is outstanding in Dante; this is the "maternity" of the *Aeneid*. Naturally, in Dante the operation takes on a less papillary character, and in fact the true nature of his commerce with those warehouses of *"geflügelte Worte"*[5] we can glean above all from what is his own production: a production of quotables destined for a society of users all the less exclusive and all the broader not in as much as it is opposed to affectedly precious readers and negates them, but only insofar as it includes them and subordinates them—with a brusqueness typical of Dante's exhaustive, pluralistic mentality. He therefore does not imitate, but reproduces and highlights an ontological situation that stands open, not closed. Imitation, in the Renaissance sense, is indeed programmatically posthumous; it moves through the realm of what has already occurred, inserting a series of variations therein, where one may admire the retrospective skill in reproducing the formal relationships and working out the situational extension of the model. Indeed, in a unitary, etymologically monotonous world, variants—whether static in value (that is, occurring inside the work) or dynamic in value (that is, occuring in the course of its elaboration)—are fundamentally variants of placement. And this in fact happens first, with convincing chronological succession, within Petrarch, then among the Petrarchists, then among the Latin-writing Humanists. And since Dante's own method of comic style goes beyond prior experiences without destroying them,

---

[3] "The friendly silence of the moonlight," quoted from Yeats.

[4] Virgil, *Eclogues*, I, l. 83.

[5] I.e., dictums.

the necessary premises of the Petrarchian style—that is, that of the stilnovista Dante, bearer of a limited, closed, and relatively impersonal language that is also a corporative, group expression, following, formally speaking, in the wake of the courtly tradition—are also included here. The more sublime, indeed Classical Dante pressuposes an open world and an ability to verbally record any experience that resists all slowing of the rhythm down to stasis, and is rekindled whenever the threat arises. Anything, therefore, that is eminently quotable. From this perspective Dante is a producer of *auctoritates*. Culturally, he is a medieval man for whom (even leaving revealed truth aside) the utterance, the spoken word in which human wisdom is deposited, is no less a source of knowledge than, and indeed precedes, reasoning and direct experience—except that, instead of limiting himself to mounting memorable sayings like jewels and glossing them, as the schools used to do, he produces his own and confers the same legislative command, the same lapidary syllabification, upon all of his pronouncements. His protestation, "Io non Enëa, io non Paulo sono," means—*e contrario* (even in the stylistic sense)—that his paradigm is the peremptoriness and unpredictability of the "famous sage" and the Scriptures. Linguistically, he is, and already wants to be, a prophet and a classic.

If this is Dante's classicism, an initial point of reference lies in the translated quotations, whose emulative value yields a concision that is at times even a little too terse. It is this compression, bursting with an expressiveness that may get the better of precision, that we see in action when the original is Virgil himself, as in:

> Perché non reggi tu, o sacra fame
> de l'oro, l'appetito de' mortali?[6]

Or in:

> Secol si rinova;
> torna giustizia e primo tempo umano,
> e progenïe scende da ciel nova.[7]

---

[6] "'Why, O holy hunger for gold, / do you not resist the appetite of mortals ?'" *Purg.* XXII, 40-41.

[7] "'The ages are renewed;/ justice and man's first time on earth return; / from Heaven a new progeny descends.'" *Purg.* XXII, 70-72, trans. Mandelbaum.

This does not happen, of course, out of stubbornness to meet the challenge—the same that, centuries later, will stimulate Davanzati with regard to Tacitus—since Dante pursues linguistic equivalents as any other great translator would do. Here the solemn detachment of *nova* from the noun it modifies, *progenie*, corresponds, through its shifted word order, to the analogous displacement we see in "*caelo demitttur alto*" or in "*magnus ab integro saeclorum nascitur ordo*"; and together, by making possible the etymological rhyming of *nova* with *rinova*, it is equivalent to the iterated anaphora of "*Iam redit... iam nova progenies...*" and "*redit et Virgo; redeunt Saturnia regna.*"[8] The contraction is thus inspired not by any sense of challenge but by the prominence—not entirely recognized, I daresay—which the *Commedia* assigns to rhythm, whereby the discourse marks a withdrawal from an extended unit such as the hexameter, one which, moreover, is not strophic, but "blank" or "loose," in favor of a reduced and still relatively autonomous meter such as the hendecasyllable, where in any case the meaningful decisiveness of the utterance cannot exceed the confines of the *terzina*.

The condensation is naturally less insistent, even as the intensity endures, when the model is prosaic and conceptual, as is the case with the other great examplar, Holy Scripture, as we see in:

> fede è sustanza di cose sperate,
> ed argomento de le non parventi.[9]

Of utmost importance, however, since it belies the possible hypothesis of any rhythmical stiffness on the translator's part, is how the prosaic model may contribute to loosening the verse lines into a sort of quasi-prose. We know that Francesca quotes a true *auctoritas*, uttering a saying by Boetheius ("il tuo dottore"); the result is:

> ...Nessun maggior dolore
> che ricordarsi del tempo felice
> ne la miseria...[10]

---

[8] Virgil, *Eclogues*, IV, ll. 5-8.

[9] "faith is the substance of things hoped for, / and the argument for things not seen." *Par.* XXIV, 64-65.

[10] "...No greater sorrow / than recalling happy times / when in misery ... " (*Inf.* V, 121-123)

This is all the more reason why any memorable utterance presenting itself entirely on its own assumes a precise, and not stenographic, appearance in which the energy is invested in the pure relationship between timbre and meaning, disregarding such things as alterations, ellipses, and syntactical contortions:

> Lunga promessa con l'attender corto
> ti farà trïunfar ne l'alto seggio.[11]

But the sampler of quotations could never extend any further without contradicting the central assumption of the argument, which strives to describe, if not transcribe (and so much the worse if it does not succeed), constant clues within the poem; to allude to a fact that may be documented not in this place or another, but by the totality of the work, and in support of whose truth the speaker may well put his trust in the national memory.

This collective memory, which perpetuates the traumatic impression made on the very first readers by the timbre of the utterance, teems not only with genuine *auctoritates* such as "Nessun maggior dolore," "seggendo in piuma,"[12] "sta come torre ferma,"[13] and whatever happens to follow in each case, but also with everyday, now outdated applications of metaphors and ever so crafty conjunctions, from "mezzo del cammin" to "l'amor che muove il sole e l'altre stelle,"[14] which take up such a large percentage of the Dantean fabric. To limit ourselves to the first cantos: "selva selvaggia," "uscito fuor del pelago a la riva," "falsi e bugiardi," "tremar le vene e i polsi," "qui si parrà la tua nobilitate," "color che son sospesi," "la vostra miseria non mi tange," "il ben dell'intelletto," "dentro a le segrete cose," "sanza infamia e sanza lodo," "a Dio spiacenti ed a' nemici sui," "sciaurati che mai non fur vivi," "bianco per antico pelo"—all these are raw linguistic material since become so ordinary as to seem hackneyed. But since the spark of imaginative synthesis has died out in so many fossilized parts of our language, and yet an effort of the imagination can still resuscitate the creative instant of such wizened imagery (as *paragone, sparuto, tramontare*), one must find proof, in this perhaps tedious heritage, of the irrresistibility, for virgin minds, of its novelty and original acuity. It is, moreover, true that the anthology

---

[11] "Long promise soon fulfilled / will make you triumph on the lofty seat." (*Inf.* XXVII, 110-111)

[12] "sitting on feathers, "*Inf.* XXIV, 47.

[13] "be like a solid tower," *Purg.* V, 14.

[14] "the love that moves the sun and the other stars"—the last line of the *Divine Comedy*.

created by the poem's public fame has left a great deal of gold currency of utterly sparkling coinage undamaged by circulation, and in no need of renewal, and which as recently as yesterday allowed, via brilliant, still fresh quotations, a poet, Giorgio Caproni, to entitle his songbook *Il seme del piangere*, and a novelist, Vasco Pratolini, to call his novel (turning, in his case, to the *Vita Nuova*) *La costanza della ragione*. Not to mention Giorgio Orelli, with *L'ora del tempo*.

If the national memory is a corollary, an imprint of the objective memorability of Dante's text, we may also ask ourselves whether it does not in its way act upon the author himself. We in fact know quite well, thanks to Curtius's study, how he felt about books in general, possibly towards the book of his "memory"; less attention has been paid to his attitude towards his own "book" and the part therein that was taken from his "memory." Usually a catalogue of stylemes is compiled by attributionists for heuristic ends (we shall later see how this can also be valid for Dante), but one might get better results from an investigation that—author by author, literary society by society—sheds some light on their nature. In Petrarch, as more generally is the case in the authoritative tradition from which he proceeds and more specifically in Dantean *stilnovismo*, among others, such a catalogue is the inventory of a closed world, with interchangable entities within it; and it is only normal that the *canzonieri* of Petrarchist poets (there are even traces of it in Leopardi) exhibit signs of variation and prolongation of the *Rerum vulgarium fragmenta*. This is all miles away from the comical Dante, who operates in an open world and counts on the novelty of his wellsprings. One may therefore presume that his repetitions are not so much words, semantic connections, and images, as relationships, deposits, and contacts; and that they do not, moreover, correspond to any programmatic intention, but rather pay spontaneous homage, by way of renewal, to the incontrovertibility of the result such as it appeared the first time it came into being. The regular typology of repetition, of words and images, affects mostly the less observant practitioners of *dantismo*: not only the slipshod efforts of Boccaccio's worst production and other more squalid Trecento scribes, but also at a less depressed level of craft, where Monti has his *zebe* ("goats") graze. It is clearly not entirely absent from Dante when he imitates himself, but vanishes for those who examine only the essential. To "Danticize" was therefore as illegitimate, indeed impossible, as it was legitmate and possible to "Petrarchicize": the absolute is, by definition, repeatable and mass-producible; excess is happy with its own unique, incomparable fruits.

The difficulty of illustrating, summarily, the echoes of Dante within Dante—echoes which, in their wholeness, are very eloquent and in no need of explanation—lies solely in making sure that the choice, necessarily rather spare, should be done in sequence so as not to compromise the obviousness of the inferences. Let's try.

When (*Purg.* I, 52-53) Virgil justifies himself to Cato:

> ...Da me non venni:
> donna scese dal ciel, per li cui preghi
> de la mia compagnia costui sovvenni,[15]

it is obvious that this calls to mind and mirrors, in the formal details of its argument, Dante's justification (*Inf.* X, 61-63) to Cavalcante de' Cavalcanti:

> ...Da me stesso non vegno:
> colui ch'attende là, per qui mi mena
> forse cui Guido vostro ebbe a disdegno.[16]

If this *cui*, the object of the phrase *ebbe a disegno*, is Beatrice, as most tend to believe now, then she links up other comparably similar tercets with her personal identity as well. And she thus accounts for the graftings whereby the Virgil-Cato conjunction becomes a parallel to the Beatrice-Virgil conjunction. Virgil says to Cato:

> grazie riporterò di te a lei [*Marzia*],

just as Beatrice had said to Virgil:

> di te mi loderò sovente a lui [*the Lord*];

and Cato to Virgil:

> bastisi ben che per lei [*Beatrice*] mi richegge,

---

[15] "...I came not on my own; / a lady descended from heaven, through whose prayers / I aided this man with my company, [...]"

[16] "...I come not on my own: / the man waiting there brings me here, / a man your Guido held perhaps in disdain."

just as, earlier, Virgil to Beatrice:

> tal che di comandare io la richiesi.[17]

The verbal resemblance, however pre-planned or spontaneous, could be merely reproducing, here as in so many other cases, a thematic and ideological proximity. But if we look back at the tercet that started it all (*Purg.* I, 52 ff.), and particularly at its central line, which, via the relative clause introduced by *per*, slides into

> donna scese dal ciel, per li cui preghi [...],

the memory infallibly unveils an entirely different central tercet line coordinated with a prior hemistich that slides into the line that follows:

> ...Elli stesso s'accusa;
> questi è Nembròt, per lo cui mal coto
> pur un linguaggio nel mondo non s'usa.[18]

The reader's memory or the author's? At any rate, the schema is renewed, this time not at all as a function of the content, but as a sort of original organizing principle.

Similar exercises of mnemonic dismantling could be easily repeated. From one same tight-grained episode the memory can sift out continuous backward and foreward echoes, as reverberation or prolepsis. Take the vision of the rapacious eagle in the *Purgatorio*. The tercet begins:

> in sogno mi parea veder sospesa
> un'aguglia...[19]

These lines, following their sequence's opening of "Ne l'ora che..." (*Purg.* IX, 13), prefigure the start of a later tercet in the *Purgatorio* (the one following the tercet similarly beginning "Ne l'ora, credo, che...," *Purg.* XXVII, 96), which continues:

---

[17] In order: "I shall report to her your goodness" (*Purg.* I, 83); "I shall sing to him your praises" (*Inf.* II, 74); "let it well suffice that for her sake you ask me" (Purg. I, 93); "such that I asked her to command me" (Inf. II, 54).

[18] "...He accuses himself on his own; / this man is Nimrod, by whose wicked mind / but one language in the world is not used." (*Inf.* XXXI, 76-78)

[19] "in dream I seemed to see aloft / an eagle..." (*Purg.* IX, 19-20)

> giovane e bella in sogno mi parea
> donna vedere andar...²⁰

The burning heat of the fire

> ... convenne che 'l sonno si rompesse.
>   Non altrimenti Achille si riscosse,
> li occhi svegliati rivolgendo in giro
> e non sappiendo là dove si fosse.²¹

This awakening is a parallel of the one from his sleep in Hell (especially if we read it with a few opportune cuts):

> Ruppemi l'alto sonno [...]
> un greve truono, sí ch'io mi riscossi [...];
>   e l'occhio riposato intorno mossi [...]
> per conoscer lo loco dov'io fossi.²²

However, that same "Non altrimenti..." (followed by the hero's name) also introduces an entirely different memory:

> Non altrimenti Tidëo si rose [...].²³

The sequence of *non altrimenti* plus name is entirely comparable to that whereby an illustrious name is accompanied by the verb *dipartire* (depart):

> là onde poi li Greci dipartiro²⁴

or here:

> vide'l carro d'Elia al dipartire²⁵

---

[20] "young and beautiful in dream I seemed / to see a woman walking..."
[21] "...caused my sleep to be broken. / No differently did Achilles stir himself, / looking round with now wakened eyes, / not knowing where he might be." (*Purg.* IX, 33-36)
[22] "My deep sleep was broken [...] / by heavy thunder, and I gave a start [...]; I cast my rested eye about [...] / to understand where indeed I might be." (*Inf.* IV, 1-2; 4, 6)
[23] "No differently did Tydeus gnaw [...]" (*Inf.* XXXII, 30)
[24] "there whence the Greeks then departed" (*Purg.* IX, 39)
[25] "[he ...] saw Elijah's chariot as it departed" (*Inf.* XXVI, 35)

or

> ...Quando
> mi diparti' da Circe...[26]

On the other hand

> e 'l viso m'era a la marina torto[27]

echoes

> Ond'io, ch'era ora a la marina volto,[28]

due to the identical position of *a la marina* and the exclusively phonetic similarity of the two-syllable word that follows in each case. This analysis could go on at great length and take its cues from any point in the text, but from the information already here adduced, we can grasp the essentials towards validly defining Dante's memory. His is not purely verbal, functioning through stimuli from similar objects; rather, it is organized by rhythmical figures. Proper to rhythm, in keeping with the twofold nature, phonic and symbolic, of language, is its additional association with the mental schema of the utterance, the categorical value of the element (this or that part of speech), and the tonal realization of the word. I hesitate to say whether it is the semantic or the musical aspect of the language that prevails in this selection; but, if the homogeneity in the articulation of the thought is predictable, the intensity of the purely formal values is surprisingly striking.

I believe that the solidity of my conclusion will be confirmed once we are able to reach it not only by proceeding through the examination of passages selected almost by chance, but through a sampling—a very reduced one, naturally, but also gradual and rationally arranged. In this case we would start with the plainest examples, such as the repetition of formulas in rhyme; that is, in specific and especially flagrant rhythmical instances, such as, for example, *caldi e geli* (the latter rhymed with *cieli* and *si sveli* or *si reveli*), where we go from

---

[26] "...When / I departed from Circe..." (*Inf.* XXVI, 91)

[27] "and my face to the sea was turned." (*Purg.* IX, 45)

[28] "Where I, who now shoreward was turned" (*Purg.* II, 100).

> A sofferir tormenti e caldi e geli[29]

to

> lievemente passava caldi e geli[.][30]

To these can be added the infinite instances that even a cursory reading of the rhyme indexes will reveal: *mondo errante, andavam forte, di giro in giro, la virtú che vole, con sí dolce nota* (or in the plural), *tra cotanto senno*, and I know not how many others. Equally flagrant are the renewals of opening formulas such as *Ma dimmi, se tu sai, Non ti maravigliar* (or *Non vi maravigliate*), *fannomi* (or *faccianli*) *onore e…, subitamente, nel mondo su*. But occasionally a well-displayed formula will be associated with a more hidden one, so that when we compare

> Com'a l'annunzio di dogliosi danni

with

> con tristo annunzio di futuri danni

what emerges is the reality of a rhythmical pattern whose regularity has been broadened with tonal weight. Until we come to the rather unusual and immediate realization that such locutions occupy a fixed rhythmic niche. When Guido Gozzano writes the famous line from *Signorina Felicita*,

> Donna: mistero senza fine bello![,]

which hendecasyllablic line from the *Commedia* is breathing life into his pastiche? Is it

> per la tua fame sanza fine cupa

or

> e sarai meco sanza fine cive

---

[29] To which we could add "ne le tenebre etterne, in caldo e ''n [variant *e*] gelo" (*Inf.* III, 87); see also the similar "onde Perugia sente freddo e caldo" (*Par.* XI, 46). (GC)

[30] Repectively, *Purg.* III, 31, and *Par.* 21, 116. "Caldi" and "geli" are, literally, "heats" and "frosts."

or is it

>Giú per lo mondo sanza fine amaro,

considering that in each case *sanza fine* appears right before the attributive or predicated final bisyllable? What Gozzano[31] is imitating is not a specific line of verse, but a figure, a rhythmic abstraction; just as the fixed position (always at the start of the tercet) of the word *licito* is a rhythmic abstraction in

>Molto è licito là, che qui non lece

and

>Ma se licito m'è, o sommo Giove[;]

Or like another, truly striking instance, where the word preceding *spesso* is frequently a *sdrucciolo* (dactyl)—"una pegola spessa," "nuvole spesse," and even "volgonsi spesso"—and most of the time a *sdrucciolo* with a dental first consonant:[32]

>[*nube*] lucida, spessa, solida e pulita;
>[*lampo*] subito e spesso a guisa di baleno,

or in a clausula:

>...una rena arida e spessa;
>...i vapori umidi e spessi;
>[la selva]... di spiriti spessi.

Here it is entirely clear why we must speak of memory. This sort of rhythmic—or even rhythmico-tonal—synthesis can only come into being because, having worked once, the conjunction, which was *a priori* abitrary, seemed to its inventor to be worth imitating.

---

[31] Elsewhere (in *L'onesto rifiuto*) he inlays or regenerates "Non son colui, non son colui che credi" ("I am not the one, I am not the one you think"), *Inf.* XIX, 62. (GC)

[32] The *sdrucciolo* can also be created by addition: "pietre-che-spesse moviensi," "dentro-piú spesse," "foco-di spessa nube." At any rate the presence of the dental is not infrequently found in the preceding word: "turba spessa," "o 'l tatto spesso," "foresta spessa e viva," or in what follows (the frequent "spesse volte" or "fïate"). (GC)

As the abstractive process progresses, it may seem that we arrive at purely grammatical figures, such as superlative iterations along the lines of *lento lento*, whose musical reality is certainly not highlighted by its banal dropping at the close of a line (*bruna bruna, vago vago*), but rather by the regularity of the bisyllabic mass, even when it falls in the middle of the line, as in

> e così chiusa chiusa mi rispose.

The same is true for paired gerunds, which appear to be only a grammatical figure, perhaps stressed at the start of the line, as in

> serrando e diserrando, sí soavi

or

> provando e riprovando, il dolce aspetto;

but when in the middle,

> sí che, pentendo e perdonando, fora

it allows the regularity of the syllabic measures to subsist,[33] as they grow from one point in the coordination. In reality, in the two lines

> la notte che le cose ci nasconde

and

> da essa, da cui nulla si nasconde

the duplication of the rhymed word is only a pretext for discovering a perfect duplication of the metrical score. The experiences I have so rapidly summarized here should now enable us to recognize an identical duplication of pattern, grammatical structure, conjunction-article-substantive-adjective-verb, and the syllabic meter of each individual component, in lines (both opening lines in their respective tercets) such as

---

[33] This in "venir, tacendo e lagrimando, al passo", and also, with a perhaps Virgilian dislocation (see "parcere subiectis et debellare superbos?"), "calcando I buoni e sollevandi i pravi." (GC)

> E quando il dente longobardo morse

and

> Poi che la gente poverella crebbe.

That *gente* rhymes with *dente* is merely an appreciated further confirmation drawn from the timbre.

A final series of surveys may serve to capture the dissimilarity, indeed the contextual antitheticality of the verbal congruences. The "secondo regno" ("second realm") repeated at the end of a line first means *Purgatory* (*Purg.* I, 4), then the sky of Mercury (*Par.* V, 93).

> ...Notabili fien l'opere sue,

Cacciaguida prophesizes about Cangrande's "works" in Paradise (XVII, 78), which sends the mind back to the "works" of Guido da Montefeltro in Hell (XXVII, 74-75):

> ...L'opere mie
> non furon leonine, ma di volpe;

a pairing not only peremptory but equally unflattering for the arts patron and object of involuntary memory. There's also:

> per entro il cielo scese una facella,

("from within the heavens a torch descended," *Par.* XXIII, 94), who turns out to be sweet Gabriel; but just a few cantos earlier (*Par.* IX, 29), we have:

> Là onde scese già una facella,

("therefrom once descended a torch") who is none other than the sinister tyrant Ezzelino. But then:

> di quella spera ond'uscì la primizia,

and this time, descending from "that sphere" (*Par.* XXV, 14), is the "first fruit," St. Peter—but clearly in echo (note the quasi-pun of *schiera* with *spera*) of

> cotali uscîr de la schiera ov'è Dido,

where those emerging from Dido's *schiera* are none other than Paolo and Francesca (*Inf.* V, 85). What else? The line (*Par.* XXX, 11) that concentrates God in the empyrean:

> sempre dintorno al punto che mi vinse,

mirrors the very famous line (*Inf.* V, 132) concerning those same sinners:

> ma solo un punto fu quel che ci vinse;

and just above the evocation of the Almighty we have (*Par.* XXIX, 138):

> quanti son li splendori a chi s'appaia

which is clearly referring to

> Molti son li animali a cui s'ammoglia.[34]

These are borderline cases, from which clearly emerges the preponderance of the signifier over the signified. And from this we may draw an even more general inference: that, if we accept as valid the Dante-Petrarch dichotomy in DeSanctis's heady terms of "poet" vs "artist", an unquestionable "poet" such as Dante displays formal extremes that one would think the exclusive domain of the pure "artist," but which in Petrarch, who is, in short, much more a "man of letters" than a "musician," do not crop up with the same vehemence. Of course, the moral and pragmatic intention with which we might renew the dichotomy of "poet" vs "artist" is entirely alien to the original one, since it not only does not involve a choice, it refuses it. For us, such an antithesis becomes inverted into one implying an inclusive position and an exclusive position, irreconcilable "projects" nevertheless of equal dignity between which it would be inconceivable to impose any hierarchy or preference.

And since Petrarch's name has come up in this discussion, what emerges at this point is a strange, unforeseeable confirmation. If the Dante of the *Commedia*'s memory turns to the same Dante of the *Commedia* for inspiration, and only very rarely (as I of course will have to demonstrate) to his predecessors, particularly the *stilnovista* Dante; and if, moreover, the *Commedia* reverberates

---

[34] "Many are the beasts with whom she wives" (*Inf.* I, 100), as opposed to (in the *Paradiso*): "Many are the splendors with which it [the light] joins."

throughout the history of our literature in trivial echoes of centonical quotations, always involving content, not form (so that in this respect Dante—and even here he stands alone—distances himself from the troubadour module by inserting into his verbal gestation an entirely melodic gestation, but at the same time opens and closes this twofold approach), a rhythmical-tonal remembrance of the *Commedia* most certainly occurs in the rather illustrious exception that is Petrarch. That Petrarch, so selective and unitonal, distanced himself as much as possible out of self-defense from the comical Dante—who is so pluralistic, inclusive, and versatile in the swift passage between opposites—should be considered a fair judgment. And therefore one should not be too shocked that, being a man of unexceptional logical intelligence, grappling, moreover, with a corresondent of scarce intellect, a runaway popularizer and mercantile plunderer of Dante's magnanimousness—i.e., Boccaccio—he fell into a flagrant lie. That Petrarch may have intended to erase all conscious memory of his reading of Dante is a plausible hypothesis; but since such reading had indeed, to use the metaphor of an illustrious friend of mine, "salted his blood," he ends up showing his hand in his involuntary memory—as involuntary as the Dantean memory we've just now examined—and probably not even his verbal memory, but his rhythmic but no longer tonal memory. I will leave out the predictable Petrarchian echoes of the lyric poems of the *Vita Nuova* and the rather frequent echoes of the *rime petrose*, and concentrate solely on the *Commedia*. And since there are so many available, I will favor the camouflaged Danteisms, which, because they are masked, tend to evade the diligent eyes of the commentators.

> Conven che 'l duol per gli occhi si distille
> dal cor...

From *Quel foco*, a ballata, these lines, according to the ever so attentive Ezio Chiòrboli, are reminiscent of Dante's:

> Ma voi chi siete, a cui tanto distilla
> Quant' i' veggio dolor giú per le guance?[35]

---

[35] Petrarch: "It fits that through the eyes sorrow is distilled / from the heart"; Dante: "But who are you, in whom I see so much / sorrow distilled down your cheeks?"

And the association of the verb *distillare* with *duolo* in the former case and *dolor* in the latter, is clear; Subtler than this evident echo, however, which is semantic in nature, is the connection with

> ...ed ancor mi distilla
> nel core il dolce...[36]

It is subtler, but also irrefutable, because the verb falls in the rhyming position, anticipating from there, and through the enjambment, a function of *core*. It is an unnecessary relationship, being notional, yet bound up in the rhythm—thus less mental, but more vital.

The opening of a Petrarch sonnet, which for the sake of clarity I will present with some abridgement as follows,

> I dolci colli ov'io lasciai me stesso [...]
> mi vanno innanzi; et èmmi ogni or a dosso
> quel caro peso...

undoubtedly revives another indelible Dantean memory, that of Maestro Adamo:

> Li ruscelletti che de' verdi colli [...]
> sempre mi stanno innanzi, e non indarno. [37]

The *colli* of the opening, which are *dolci* in the former, *verdi* in the latter; the interval marked by the relative clause; the verb followed by *innanzi*; the *e* that follows this; all these bring to light the thematic affinity in an identical articulation.

The interpolated clause we find in Petrarch's sestina, *Giovene donna*:

> ...i' l'ò dinanzi agli occhi,
> ed avrò sempre, ov'io sia, in poggio o in riva

as in his canzone, *Una donna*,

> ...et èvvi ancora,
> e sarà sempre, fin ch'i' le sia in braccio

---

[36] "and still in my heart / is distilled sweet [sorrow]"...
[37] Petrarch: "The sweet hills where I left myself [...] / go before me; and every hour now I bear / that precious weight"; Dante: "The green hills with their little streams / lie still before me, and not in vain."

proceed, with phonetic diminution, from such Dantean lines as

> ...onde mi vien riprezzo,
> e verrà sempre, de' gelati guazzi

and

> al punto fisso che li tiene a li *ubi*,
> e terrà sempre, ne' quai sempre foro.

Dare I add that, since the canzone *Una donna* speaks of the ice in the heart, it seems clear to me, by virtue of the connection between subject and rhythm, that the origin of Petrarch's memory, the first step, lies in the *Inferno*? Still, moving along the path of reduction to pure pattern, we shall see how, in the Petrarchian sonnet *Solo e pensoso*,

> Ma pur sí aspre vie né sí selvagge
> cercar non so...

especially in light of another (*I'ò pien di sospir'*) sonnet's

> né fiere àn questi boschi sí selvagge...;

come from (*Inf.* XIII, 9-10)

> non han sí aspri sterpi né sí folti
> quelle fiere selvagge...;

and how Petrarch's

> che già fece di me sí lungo stratio

from the sonnet *Morte à spento*, recalls (*Inf.* XXVII, 43):

> La terra che fe' già la lunga prova[.]

On a purer level still, because the echo lies not in any identical words, but only in identical parts of speech and the syllabic mass, is the opening to Petrarch's famous sonnet

> Al cader d'una pianta che si svelse

--which keenly recalls the opening line of *Inferno* VI:

> Al tornar della mente, che si chiuse.

And for the final example, we can see that Saint Anne's line in the *Paradiso* (XXXII, 134),

> tanto contenta di mirar sua figlia

gives rise to Petrarch's line, in the sonnet *Zefiro torna*:

> Giove s'allegra di mirar sua figlia[.]

This could be called a profaning variant, if not for the fact that the Petrarchian poem's purely emblematic mythology (exegetes are still in dispute as to the exact translation of the meteorological opening line) represents a strong reduction of the reality, which is so vibrant in Dante's voice and imagination, to an arabesque in the International Gothic style. It is extraordinary that Dante's vocal material—if not also his timbres and rhythms—should still be useful to Petrarch for such an operation, since we are, after all, near the end of that epoch.

Just as Petrarch (since it required no less formal ability than his) constitutes the sole exception to the non-Dantean memory we have of Dante, he also calls to mind an exception to the exclusively internal nature of the memory that resonates throughout the *Commedia*. And this exception is *Il Fiore*.[38] Which can be seen to satisfy even the attributive criteria said to be proper to the usual catalogues of stylemes. On the level to which we've risen, or rather descended, it seems rather unlikely, in our deep auscultation of the inner voice, that the author of the *Fiore*, the third in this list with Dante and Petrarch, could be anyone other than Dante himself, to whom so many well-studied outward clues point. I can hardly display here the whole rich case-file of evidence;[39] but I will extract a few examples that are consistent with Dante's own echoes of himself.

---

[38] *Il Fiore* is a narrative poem consisting of a cycle or *corona* (It.) of 232 sonnets retelling the principle episodes of the *Roman de la Rose* and written sometime between 1283 and 1287. Based principally on Contini's scholarship, most Dante scholars are in agreement in attributing it to the young Dante.

[39] Which is presented more summarily in *Cultura e Scuola*, January-June 1965 (the article "La questione del 'Fiore'" in fact closes the dossier), and more comprehensively in the article under the heading (Il) "Fiore", in the *Enciclopedia Dantesca*. One specific point is covered, in the present volume, in the chapter titled "Cavalcanti in Dante." (GC)

In one sonnet of *Il Fiore*, *Pietà* (piety, pity) is, with *Franchezza* (sincerity), an ambassador of the God of love: a situation somewhat similar to that of Beatrice with regard to Virgil at the start of the *Commedia*, a similarity underscored by coincidences less of textual sameness than of a similarities of rhythm and tonal nature. The *Fiore*'s line

> di non far GRAzia al meo dOMANDAMENTO

prefigures Virgil's line in the *Commedia*

> tanto m'agGRAda il tuo cOMANDAMENTO.

A bit further on in the *Fiore*:

> ... Or avem detto [...]
> ... la cagion per che no' siam venute;

and Virgil says to Dante:

> dirotti perch'io venni...;

then to Beatrice:

> Ma dimmi la cagion che non ti guardi
> De lo scender qua giuso...[40]

Then immediately in the *Fiore*:

> molt'è crudel chi per noi non vuol fare!

which displays the same strucure as Ugolino's pure *ternario*:

> Ben se' crudel, se tu già non ti duoli.

In the light of these experiences, the affinity between the *Fiore*'s enjambment

> ...e ciò ci ha procacciato
> lo Schifo...

---

[40] "...Now we have said [...] / the reason why we have come;" then: "I shall tell you why I came..."; and then: "But tell me the reason you have not avoided / coming down here..."

and the one we find in the *Paradiso*

> ...ciò li fece
> Romeo...[,]

or between the grandiloquence of Reason:

> Ed i'ho tal vertú dal mi' segnore
> che mi criò, ch'i'...

and Beatrice's declaration;

> Io son fatta da Dio, sua mercé, tale
> che ...[,]

seems even more decisive than a comparison between

> Quando Bellaccoglienza sentí 'l caldo
> di quel brandon...

and

> anzi che Chiarentana il caldo senta

or between

> ...condotto al passo stretto

and

> menò costoro al doloroso passo.

We should add that the connections between the *Commedia* and the *Fiore* are accompanied by highly similar connections between the *Fiore* and the lyrics of the *Vita Nuova* and that period (whereas such connections were lacking, or very rare, between the *Commedia* and the lyric poems). This proves that Dante found himself in the "comic" genre, to the point that it provided him with the title to his great poem; and that *Il Fiore* represents the link in a chain that would otherwise elude us in documentary terms. If I may excuse myself for dragging my listeners into a triple excursion through the laboratory, while providing only tenuous samplings of rather extensive experiments, I would also, however, flatter myself for having based, on tested foundations, not dialectical speculations, the definition of Dante's throbbing, epigrammatic utterance, which is capable of imprinting itself on our memory like a Classical quotation, and the realization of this memory in Dante through periodic recurrences of rhythmical and vocal figures. If I am not mistaken, this brings down to more correct dimensions that excess of ideological interpretation towards which Dante scholars feel irresistibly inclined.

But what does the memorability of Dantean utterance involve? There is no experience that does not incite and feed this imagination, and every datum maintains its proper value if taken singularly, while not losing it when taken in multiplicity. But it is by other means that Dante's rarity becomes clear. He is not at all a lyrical or interjective sort of writer, even if he holds up quite well to such a reading; but neither does he repeat his truth and efficacy through copying and accumulation, even if the pressure of the "high register" remains constant. He is, in sort, an incomparably inventive "local" writer, but one who allows the reader and user to linger—he himself does not linger, driven as he is by his nature "di collo in collo" ("from height to height"; *Par.* IV, 132), like one pursuing truth, as he describes, in logical concatenations.

The meteorological reality—of snowfalls, hoarfrosts, maritime horizons quivering at dawn, full moons—the biological, particularly animal reality, of the inexhaustible bestiary of fireflies, cranes, frogs, and lions, all evoke an entirely whole observer of nature, and a primordial contact with basic everyday events occurring within an ancient rural context only moderately furrowed with touches of urban landscape (such as, just a few steps away, the turreted defense wall of Monteriggioni, the pinecone of San Pietro, the leaning Garisenda tower...). But—and let this stand as one of those explanations aimed at immediately thwarting any unilateral interpretations in otherwise appropriate commentaries—this observer is a major loner, one who lends equal attention, out of a classicizing equanimity, to external as well as internal reality, not only to the mechanisms of passion over which the Romantic critics grew so ecstatic (such as when Guido da Montefeltro meets Boniface VIII: "...e io tacetti, / perché le sue parole parver ebbre", *Inf.* XXVII, 98-99; ["...and I remained silent / for his words sounded drunk"]), but also to the workings of the intellect, whereby the truth is not dissociated from the process of research, even if unremunerated. And here indeed, crowning the work, stands the surveyor skilled at squaring the circle, who doesn't find "the priniciple he needs" ("quel principio ond'elli indige"; *Par.* XXXIII, 135); here is the "bachelor" (in the medieval sense) who "arms himself and doesn't speak" ("s'arma e non parla"; *Par.* XXIV, 46), in order to set up the question—note well—with proper dialectics, but not to resolve it. Also note that, on the contrary, the Scholastic excess of didacticism is not, in the *Commedia*, a pedagogical dogmatism, but rather a perpetual resolution—constantly moving back-and-forth between the two sides—of the student's truth, whether in the form of the pupil or in the form of the teacher.

This historicity, moreover, applies not only to the cultural citations but to those from nature as well. The wonderful summer scene (*Inf.* XXVI, 25-27),

> Quante il villan ch'al poggio si riposa [...]
> vede lucciole giú per la vallea,
> forse colà dove vendemmia e ara
>
> (As many firefiles as the peasant resting [...]
> on the hillside sees down in the valley,
> where perhaps he picks the grapes and tills the fields),

which comes alive for all of us with birth certificates from the Florence city hall every evening in which those electric flocks climb back up the slopes between the Affrico and Mensola torrents, would seem less pertinent outside an Appenninic geology. For it to come alive, the farmer must, at sunset, leave the unsafe, insalubrious plain behind, withdraw up the low ridges, beyond the reach of the miasmas and infestations of the major roads; meanwhile the insects of the stables give way to other nasty bugs risen from the bogs: "as the fly gives way to the mosquito" ("come la mosca cede alla zanzara"; ibid, line 28), Dante specifies, in a powerful interjection oblivious to the wise rules against troublesome tangential details. I'll leave uncommented the fact that historicity quite often turns out to be an implicit element of fantasy. This happens not infrequently among modern authors: Hemingway's posthumous memoirs show that he demanded that his readers themselves work out the unrevealed end of a certain character of his. It is an attitude inherent not in ellipses such as "We read no further that day" ("Quel giorno piú non vi leggemmo avante") or Manzoni's "The wretched woman replied" ("La sventurata rispose"), for which there is only one explanation, but in those of the sort reflected in the elaboration of the *Vita Nuova*, where, for example, Dante says, about the canzone *Morte villana* (though it must be said that such similarly abbreviated discourse is the general rule for the *Vita*): "I turn to speak to an undefined person, as much as to my own understanding this person is defined" ("mi volgo a parlare a indiffinita persona, avvegna che quanto a lo mio intendimento sia diffinita"). The cannibalism—which is, to my mind, beyond doubt—of Count Ugolino, who is forced by the "new Thebes" to partake in that "Thyestes' supper" whose tragic situation was evoked by Horace, is the best known such example. Dante dismisses Averroism by quoting, in rhyme, Cavalcanti's "il possibile intelletto" from the latter's great canzone, *Donna mi prega*, thus tacitly but squarely involving Guido in the polemic. And why does Guido da Montefeltro compare himself and Boniface to Saint Sylvester and Emperor Constantine, if not because the baptism and donation of Constantine are among the favorite subjects of that pope?

The historicity of nature in Dante comes alive and prominent if we look at it through the artificial lens of its opposition to Petrarchian modules—such as "Quel rosignuol che sí soave piagne," or "garrir Progne e pianger Filomela" ("That nightingale so gently singing"; "Procne twittering and Philomel weeping"...)—which are cosmopolitan miniatures beyond all geographical situation: eternal objects, Platonic ideals. And we can continue our experiement by following it down to Poliziano and the perfect subjectivity of nature in his work:

Quanto giova a mirar pender da un'erta
la capra, e pascer questo o quel virgulto[;]

(How good it is to watch the goat hang
from a slope and graze on this or that sapling);

and we can even frog-leap the centuries to Leopardi, where the distant frog in the countryside keeps far from the poet so as to echo and resonate within, like the train-whistles in Proust, enclosed inside the subject's state of mind; whereas for Dante, forever tensed in motion, the state of mind flashes for an instant but does not congeal.

These epigrams of nature, moreover, which sweep us up in their commanding definition, possess no formal autonomy of their own. Firefly, bachelor, surveyor, and so on, are all similes or metaphors ("Quale...," "Quanto...," "Come..."). Not content with sitting on the page as a function of something else, they are stuffed with parenthetical and incidental clauses like so many Chinese boxes, not all of them lyrically relevant. Inside the image of the peasant contemplating the fireflies is wedged, past the indication of the hour ("come la mosca..."), a less directly fruitful periphrasis of the season (*Inf.* XXVI, 25-27):

> Quante il villan ch'al poggio si riposa,
> nel tempo che colui che 'l mondo schiara
> la faccia sua a noi tien meno ascosa...;
>
> (As many [fireflies] as the peasant resting
> at a time when he who lights the world
> hides his face least from us...;)

in order to isolate the metaphor, we would have to clean it up not only from without, but also from within. But the instance where we might manage to separate things spatially is relatively simple. First petrified, then melting into tears at Beatrice's reproaches, Dante compares himself to a forest first frozen, then thawed by warm winds (*Purg.* XXX, 85-90):

> Sí come neve tra le vive travi
> per lo dosso d'Italia si congela
> soffiata e stretta da li venti schiavi,
>   poi, liquefatta, in se stessa trapela,
> pur che la terra che perde ombra spiri,
> sì che par foco fonder la candela...
>
> (Just as the snow between the living beams
> across the spine of Italy freezes,
> blown and packed by Slavic winds,
>   then, upon melting, seeps through itself
> so long as the land losing shadow breathes,
> so that it looks as when a flame melts a candle...)

The same thing happens here as in the prior example: the landscape exists, syntactically, as a function of something else; it is perceived through personal experience (*per lo dosso d'Italia*); it produces in turn a subsidiary image (the candle). But more than this, the landscape encompasses, especially through the periphrasis of *la terra che perde ombra*, secondary cultural suggestions that cannot be removed to purify the context—which, aside from such veneers, penetrates the imagination by means of direct metaphors (*vive travi*). In an extreme case, a beautiful line of direct imagery such as

> La divina foresta spessa e viva[41]

---

[41] "The divine forest dense and alive" (*Purg.* XXVIII, 2).

does not illustrate, in the reality of the sublime context, a joy of nature, but rather a miraculous, "divine" entity. Just above it, in fact, is a celebration of the vegetation "che qui la terra *sol da sé* produce" ("that the earth here produces *all by itself*"); then, further on, the limpid river flows past "l'acque che son *di qua* piú monde" ("the waters that are cleaner *on this side*"); and flowers bloom "sanza seme" ("without seeds"). Added to this are the continual mythological references: to Proserpina, Venus, Leander, in confirmation of the role mythology plays as reservoir of symbols. The sacred world and the Classical world indeed correspond and merge, in accordance with the tradition actually handed down from school textbooks (Theodulus),[42] to the point of rhyming MANIBUS O DATE LILIA PLENIS with BENEDICTUS QUI VENIS.[43] To remove any bulkhead between the two sources of learning, the lizard and the phoenix, the country boy terrorized by the sea and the prophet Elisha, who witnessed the rise of Elijah, are placed on the same structural level.

Reality, which is predominant but generic in Petrarch, is, in Dante, precise but subordinate. When it appears, it is miraculous, and thus its indirect character grants it no free pass. Landscape as an end in itself gives way, clearly, to aestheticism. In a great author, it must become restrained; or, as in Dante, incidental or heteronomous: the essential otherness, the continual didactic interruptions are, in him, equivalent to what, in others, is the internal limit. The fabric of the heteronomous "libretto," in which the author's inexhaustible representational ability is made to serve doctrine or figurative narration, guarantees true independence to each scene, so that they each can have meaning, for posterity, on their own. *Here* lies the crux of the relationship between "structure" and poetry; but this situation needs to be considered in the context of the particular condition of freedom in the Middle Ages. In contrast to the modern world, it is realized with extraordinary elasticity within a perimeter of total security, authority, and faith. The religious orthodoxy, like the political orthodoxy, produced a literary and critical latitude that surprises modern observers accustomed to the Counter-Reformation and absolutism. Similarly a rigorously theocentric cosmology ordered around an infinitely remote nucleus grants extraordinary freedom to construc-

---

[42] The Eclogue of Theodulus (*Eclogi Teoduli*) was a standard school text in the Middle Ages, consisting of an argument in Latin between Alithia (truth) and Pseustis (falsity), with Phronesis (reason) acting as arbiter. The origins of the text, once thought to be Greek, have been disputed by modern scholars.

[43] In *Purg.* XXX, 19-21, where Dante rhymes the Benedictus with Virgil ("Manibus..."). (GC)

tions of the human intelligence and imagination, allowing doctrinal texts (including Dante's) to ignore, in their open structures, the geometrical rigor that has become the custom for us since the Enlightenment, and thus leaving works of the imagination immune to the regularity prescribed by the Humanists, even if they can sometimes take on a rather strict *"fren de l'arte"* (a "brake on art") that is nevertheless not predictable *a priori*. Neither enlightened nor Humanistic, the world can therefore continue to open itself up to reality; but I am not sure one can speak, as one does in art history, of a "realism of details," since there is no literary Masaccio around to eclipse Dante—and since, moreover, these details refer to a whole that is certainly not realistic (that is, selected and anthologized), but real like reality itself, which is not realistic but revelatory at high frequencies.

Though never mentioned, the *tranche de vie* staged by Dante is also of a sort that can be integrated into comprehensive series, in order to homogenize it with a totalizing and, as one trivially says, encyclopedic culture. From cumulative effects, as in the catalogues of reptiles and the sick (for the thieves and counterfeiters), we arrive at pure lists,

> Oro e argento fine, cocco e biacca...,[44]

which, with their fleshly emphasis, end up informing, in more bloodless, more melodic guise, the lists of Petrarch and his descenents. Dante's secret—in some ways his *biological* secret—lies in his equally intense participation, and actually his subsequent identification, with objects, an engagement of which he is clearly conscious (*Par.* V, 98-99):

> qual mi fec'io che pur da mia natura
> trasmutabile son per tutte guise!
>
> (what did I become, who by my nature
> can assume all guises?)

This sort of disposition to metamorphosis explains the competition with Ovid—which is even explicit ("Taccia di Cadmo e d'Aretusa Ovidio"; *Inf.* XXV, 97; "Let Ovid be silent on Cadmus and Arethusa"), but only when projected onto a more modest descriptive level. It is surprising to note the progression from the

---

[44] "Gold and fine silver, cochineal and ceruse"; *Purg.* VII, 73.

Vita Nuova, which is, here too, a necessary precedent to Petrarch: the Petrarch of the canzone *Nel dolce tempo*, which takes as its subject "la trasfigurata mia persona" ("my transfigured person"). The word itself reveals the poem's origin in the "trasfigurazione" or "trasfiguramento" that Dante undergoes for Beatrice at the wedding banquet in the episode of the *gabbo* (hoax), when, as told in the sonnet, *Con l'altre donne*, he'd taken on a "figura nova": "mi cangio in figura d'altrui" ("I change myself into the shape of another"). Another transfiguration, through weeping, occurs at the news of Beatrice being aggrieved by the death of her father ("ma la figura ne par d'altra gente," in the sonnet *Se' tu colui*). If the *Vita Nuova* could literally be the novel of these transformations, the *Commedia* is the hyperbole, driven beyond the usual human boundaries:

> Trasumanar significar *per verba*
> non si poria...[45]

(and this is even hinted at with one of his customary Ovidian metamorphoses, that of Glaucus "nel gustar de l'erba" ["upon tasting of the grass," *Par.* I, 68]). Transhumanization is boldly proclaimed, but from without, and yet Dante is able, in defining himself through metaphor, to bring the metaphor to a metamorphosis actually lived from within. And here he is, at the final crag in Purgatory, held back with Virgil and Statius by the nocturnal law of the mountain:

> Quali si stanno ruminando manse
> le capre [...]
> guardate dal pastor [...]
>   e quale il mandrian che fori alberga,
> lungo il peculio suo questo pernotta [...];
>   tali eravam noi tutti e tre allotta,
> *io come capra*, ed ei come pastori [...].
>   Sí *ruminando* e sí mirando in quelle [stelle]
> mi prese il sonno [...].[46]

> (Like goats as they gently
> ruminate [...]
> before the shepherd's watchful eyes [...]
>   and like the herdsman who lodging outside
> spends the night beside his flock [...];

---

[45] "Surpassing the human cannot be put *into words*," *Par.* I, 70.
[46] *Par.* XXVI, 76-92, *passim*. Italics are Contini's.

> so were the three of us just then,
> *I like a goat*, and they like shepherds [...].
> Thus *ruminating*, and thus gazing at [the stars],
> sleep came over me [...])

The goal is a kind of sublime, visionary bestiality.

The reality upon which Dante's versatility and openness hurls itself is historically felt even when it is eternal and repeatable; and its concreteness becomes all the more manifest as one descends towards the individually determined entities. Geographical reality, for example, is inferred with such richness and freshness that it transforms the *Commedia* into a kind of honor roll of Italian locales such as one won't find again until the appearance of the *History of Italy* by Guicciardini, another man devoted to reality. The roar of the waterfall at San Benedetto dell'Alpe, the rustling of the pine grove at Classe were clearly familiar sounds to Dante's ear; and yet the representation is always so lively that, even for much remoter sites—as far away as the rocks at Noli or indeed the dykes of Flanders—it justifies Bassermann's suspicion that we are dealing with lived memories.

It is true that the general use of experience does not, however, make it possible to distinguish, as a general principle, between direct and indirect knowledge, and even knowledge gained from books. A dictionary is thus a reservoir of discoveries, and Uguccione da Pisa's *Derivationes Magnae* serves the same heuristic function for Dante as the Tommaseo-Bellini dictionary did for D'Annunzio. *Distingue frequenter*, however. We ourselves can sample the Vercelli and the Marcabò, the Cianghelle and the Lapi Salterelli, the many names of people and places constellating the immense machine of the *Commedia*, but their function is not ornamental, their physicality hardly reassuring. Their nature remains instead sketchy, more reminiscent of Homeric granularity— Πηληϊάδεω ’Αχιλῆος —than of alexandrine balm. An alexandrine functions through "*bibelot[s] d'inanité sonore*":[47]

> [...] Il Maturanzio
> Sogna Achille Pelíde e il Telamonio.[48]

---

[47] A phrase from Stéphane Mallarmé's famous "Sonnet en Yx": "...trinket(s) of sonorous emptiness."

[48] D'Annunzio, from *Le città del silenzio* (1904).

And here is Dante's rougher onomastic reality:

> del villan d'Aguglion, di quel da Signa.

Let me add a drastic demonstration:

> Vieni a veder Montecchi e Cappelletti,
> Monaldi e Filippeschi, uom sanza cura.[49]

The versifier seeking evocative flow would certainly have avoided the harsh synalepha between *Filippeschi* and *uom*, which practically straddles the pause. This calls to mind, no doubt, a very general characteristic of Dante: either one aims, to assert oneself and survive, at selection and eternity, as Petrarch does, or one takes aim, like Dante, at everything, blending even the ephemeral and contingent into the mix. More than anyone else, therefore, the comic author needs commentary, and Dante does not escape this fate.

The lack of distinction between experience and culture manifests itself quite strikingly in the equalization of the historical characters, all of them summoned—appearing before our consciousness representing the *status animarum post mortem*—into the present, contemporary moment, and therefore not gradated by perspective. Even within the framework of the medieval mind, the placement of contemporary characters, perhaps guilty of violent crimes or frequenters of homosexual orgies, on the same level as figures covered with glory over the centuries; the equal treatment of historical fact and fiction, and of Biblical and mythological and merely literary themes from any cultural stratum ("Vidi París, Tristano..." ["I saw Paris, Tristan..."]), and even more so, of the real and the symbolic; constitutes a novelty of striking importance. What matters, essentially, is not such characters' historical existence, but what they have in common, and the exemplary manner in which the catharsis is enacted. Cacciaguida says it clearly, even if he exaggerates the characters' celebrity fittingly only for the highest levels of Paradise:

> Però ti son mostrate in queste rote,
> nel monte e ne la valle dolorosa
> pur l'anime che son di fama note,

---

[49] *Purg.* VI, 106-107. ("Come and see Montecchi and Cappelletti, / Monaldi and Filippeschi, man without care.")

> ché l'animo di quel ch'ode, non posa
> né ferma fede per essemplo ch'aia
> la sua radice incognita e nascosa,
>
> né per altro argomento che non paia.[50]
>
> (Therefore, within these spheres, upon the mountain,
> and in the dismal valley, you were shown
> only those souls that unto fame are known—
>
> because the mind of one who hears will not
> put doubt to rest, put trust in you, if given
> examples with their roots unknown and hidden,
>
> or arguments too dim, too unapparent.)[51]

And the characters are no more the free protagonists of individual dramas than Dante's nature is the object of unrestricted, interjective lyrical contemplation.

Mediating this situation is the twofold aspect of the protagonist, which arises from the realistic impossibility of having a regular man act things out. The name "here recorded of necessity" ("che di necessità qui si registra"; *Purg.* XXX, 63) leads us back to a prior moment, that of the *Roman de la Rose*, where the character who says "I" (even in the part written by Jean de Meung) is named Guillaume (de Lorris). The master of *Il Fiore*, an important link in this chain (even for those who might contest his identity), replaces this character with Ser Durante. One more step: in the *Tesoretto*, the protagonist not only confesses that he is Brunetto, but he grafts vision and indoctrination into a historical context, just as the corps of teachers can be recruited without distinction from among masters of ancient science and sketchy edifying personifications. Dante surpassed these rough, generic canvases above all by developing a worthy deuteragonist: and the human being who serves as the occasion, in love and in death, for the supreme internal experience assumes a duality of function comparable to that of the I. The metaphorical plain of the Dolce Stile, which is essentially still intact in Petrarch, is abandoned here, an abandonment already hinted at in the *Vita Nuova* through transfiguration ("io vidi la speranza de' beati" ["I witnessed the hope of the blessèd"]); and it is the possible root of the dispute

---

[50] *Par.* XVII, 136-142.
[51] Mandelbaum translation (cf. *Paradiso* 17 – Digital Dante (columbia.edu)).

with Cavalcanti. Scattered about Beatrice is a small court of nominally historical beings, replacing (in one instance we've noted an overlapping) the allegorical constellations of the *Roman de la rose* and *Il Fiore* (whose manner serves, in a kind of ironic *déclassement*, to inspire only the names of the decury of demons in Malebolge). Then the lists, so meagerly and painstakingly begun in traditional fashion, become suddenly specific and come alive once we reach Francesca, and the population of the beyond starts to file before us. The poet's hybridism comes to perfect maturity in the dispute between Maestro Adamo and Sinon, which is a clash between historical chronicle and culture, and polyvalent culture at that, considering that the counterfeiter's story stretches between Virgil's appearance and that of the Biblical Potiphar's wife. I don't mean to deny that those mutual reproaches do not possess a genuine stridency, one revealing a proper mannerism on Dante's part. This we see in the grotesqueness of the trick played on the capering Minotaur, with the joke about the "Duke of Athens," or the negotiations with the giants ("Do not make us go to Tityus or Typhon"; "Non ci fare ire a Tizio né a Tifo"; *Inf.* XXXI, 124). Such is the price to be paid for the eschatological levelling of humanity, based on the assumption that the past has no objective substance. In this regard it is clear why we cannot call the *Commedia* a narrative work. Narrative would presuppose either the chance unpredictability of what happens, or an examination of deterministic condemnation with all hope extinguished. For Dante the dice have already been thrown, and one can apply to him what one great convert of our time once said to me: "the most is done; the head of the mystical body is in the heavens."

The commingling of crowned heads and individuals of little pedigree is truly anti-tragic; it is comic. And this reveals another break by Dante from his culture, because the historical levelling is an extension of the "burlesque-realistic" style of caricature. Not for nothing is the extreme case of this the verbal tussle between Fra Sinon and Maestro Adamo, which transposes the *tenzone* between Dante and Forese to the beyond. Virgil condemns the poet's "base desire" ("bassa voglia") to listen to such things—that is, the pure state of the derision of caricatured contemporaries, such as it was practiced by the Sienese friends and correspondents of Dante, Cecco, and Meo (the Sienese having been skewered in the prior canto), never to be redeemed in the vast polytonal machine.

Dante does not arrive at this full recognition of the comic condition until he is near the bottom of the funnel. It is no accident that the first time the "*comedía*" is named is just before the descent into Malebolge; and only in the bolgia of the soothsayers, with Eurypylus as his pretext, does Virgil mention "*his* lofty tragedy" ("l'alta mia tragedía; *Inf.* XX, 113): "you know it well, you who know the whole story" ("ben lo sai tu che la sai tutta quanta"; line 114)—apparently because, just a few lines later, past the rubric of the next canto, Dante cites, by way of contrast, *his* comedy ("che la mia comedía cantar non cura"; *Inf.* XXI, 2). And it is shortly past the end of Malebolge, in the scene of the critical *conflictus* between the two counterfeiters, that Dante invokes "harsh and raucous rhymes" ("le rime aspre e chiocce"; *Inf.* XXXII, 1). In these same precincts we note some very precise linguistic features, and Guido da Montefeltro catches Virgil using Lombard speech just as he is taking leave of the Greek Ulysses—thus not in *"gramatica"* or *"locutio secundaria,"* but indeed in *"locutio vulgaris."* In sum, the comical *cantica* ends in a harsh and raucous style, amid horrors and practically royal misadventures, with the cannibalism whose victims are the Archbishop Ruggeri and Brutus and his associates. It is a true anti-tragedy, an *Aeneid* or *Thebeiad* a bit straightforward and a bit upside down.

Competing with the *Aeneid* (or the *Thebaid*, or the *Pharsalia*), competing with the *Metamorphoses*, having progressed beyond the *Rose* and the *Tesoretto*, not to mention the progeny of Rustico Filippi, and emulating not only Virgil and Ovid, but even the Scriptures in its overall polysemic design, Dante's synthesis appears as an unprecedented novelty, in keeping with his recurrent topos of the new: the proposition, at the end of the *Vita Nuova*, "to say of her what has never before been said of any woman" ("di dicer di lei quello che mai non fue detto d'alcuna"); "the novelty that through your form shines, / which never was conceived in any time" ("la novità che per tua forma luce, / che non fu mai pensato in alcun tempo"), in the double sestina; "something new and previously unattempted in the art" (*"novùm aliquid atque intentatum artis"*) in the *De vulgari*, which in turn opens by boasting of its own unprecedented contents ("Since I find that no one, before myself, has dealt in any way with the theory of eloquence in the vernacular" [*"Cum neminem ante nos de vulgaris eloquentiae doctrina quicquam inveniamus tractasse"*]); "deeply obscure" (*"maxime latens"*) and "never tried by anyone" (*"ab omnibus intentata"*) is the material of *De Monarchia*, whose author will obtain "the palm of so great a prize for my own glory"[52] (*"palmam tantii bravii primus in suam gloriam"*). In this locus that

---

[52] Translation by Aurelia Henry, Houghton & Mifflin, Boston and New York: 1904 (*"solet dici quod intellectus speculativus extensione fit praticus, cuius finis est agere atque facere. Quod dico propter agibilia, quae politica prudentia regulantur, et propter factibilia, quae regulantur arte."*) All subsequent English quotes from *DeMonarchia* are from this translation.

is the summation of all traditions, in this extraordinary project blending themes and tones (after all, the *De vulgari* breaks off not long after the statement that "it is the mingling of harsh and gentle rhymes that gives tragedy its splendor" ("*lenium asperorumque rithimorum mixtura ipsa tragedia nitescit*"), the stroke of intellectual genius was to declare himself at the lowest level, almost as a sign and measure of maximum range, just as in the traditional metaphysics of the *De vulgari* (though in reverse), all royal personages are measured by their simplest individuality, all numbers by one, all colors by white, all being by God—and thus the vernacular by the illustrious vernacular.

Declaring oneself at the bottommost level is a proclamation of freedom. The linguistic pluralism of the *comedía* is not in fact always tending towards expressiveness, but contains it as its limit. The outermost extensions of such pluralism, in the sublime and the grotesque, can be easily documented; they, and their co-existence, stand in opposition to the sovereign evenness of tone—only lightly ruffled here and there—which we find in that other, contrary genius, Petrarch, who carried out the full realization of Dante's *stilnovismo*. It is of greater importance to highlight the clear, sharp distinction of Dante from the Petrarchian tone, even in the middle ranges, particularly those sequences which, by means of enjambments and breaks from the confines of the hendecasyllabic line, unfold in quasi-prose, in a *recitativo* which, if anything, anticipates the looseness of Manzoni's tragedies. No passage is more decisive than the dialogue—which one could almost call Monteverdian—between Trajan and the widow (about halfway through the poem)[53]:

> …"Or aspetta
> tanto ch'i' torni." E quella: "Segnor mio,"
> come persona in cui dolor s'affretta,
>   "se tu non torni?" Ed ei: "Chi fia dov'io
> la ti farà…"

> (…"Now wait
> till I return. And she: "My lord,"
> like one compelled by grief,
>   "And if you don't return?" And he: "Whoever
> is in my place will do it for you"…)

---

[53] *Purg.* X, 85-89.

It's an enchanting *grisaille*, white on white or grey on grey, in keeping with the nature of these words, which are not spoken or heard but suggested by divine inlay, against a monochrome background ("...on a plain, / more lonely than a desert road"; "...in su un piano, / solingo piú che strade per diserti"), with the resulting dislocation of sensations ("...my eyes and nose / in discord said both yes and no"; "...li occhi e 'l naso / al sí e al no discordi fensi"), with the verb *parere* ("to seem, to appear") long remaining implicit or reappearing here and there. Novelty is reaffirmed as such and proclaimed in the paradox of the oxymoron (ll. 94-96):

> Colui che mai non vide cosa nova
> produsse esto visibile parlare,
> novello a noi perché qui non si trova.
>
> (He for whom no thing is new
> created this visible speech,
> new to us as it is not found here.)

The refinement of the dialogue in this region of Purgatory becomes such that it even penetrates Sapia's blindness ("so that I lifted up my face in boldness"; "tanto ch'io volsi in su l'ardita faccia"; *Purg.* XIII, 121), or above all that of Guido del Duca and Rinieri da Calboni, who are conversing in whispers as the canto opens, until we reach the line

> Non so chi sia, ma so che non è solo,[54]

which is utterly identical to the way we would say it today.

To return, however, to the divergence between the pace of the *terzina* and that of the argument, this ever so subtle break, which perhaps becomes most truly exquisite in the *Purgatorio*, as in the Virgin Mary's gentle reproach to Christ:

> ..."Figliuol mio,
> perché hai tu verso noi cosí fatto?
> Ecco, dolenti, lo tuo padre e io
> ti cercavamo...."[55]

---

[54] "I don't know who he is, but he is not alone" (*Purg.* XIV, 4).
[55] *Purg.* XV, 89-92.

..."My son,
why have you done this to us?
  Behold us in our grief, your father
and I; we were looking for you..."

remains nevertheless possible and kept in reserve for every canticle, in opposition to the careful symmetry caging even dense, Socratic exchanges such as the conversation with Charles Martel.

Dante's "comic" novelty lies also in the elasticity of this relation between prosody and syntax, and is therefore tied to the invention of its meter. Is it a narrative meter? The first thing the *Commedia* wishes to be is, of course, a prophecy, to the point that it ostentatiously retraces Isaiah: "*Ego dixi: In dimidio dierum meorum fadam ad portas inferi*,"[56] and immediately afterwards lifts from Jeremiah the association of "*leo*," "*lupus*," and "*pardus*." But the certainty of final salvation is solid and constant, and no surprise—that without which the narrative is inconceivable—is admissible as concerns the outcome of the journey, the general frame of the work. Freedom (freedom as divine prerogative, here boldly usurped by the poet-demiurge) is reserved for inscription into the two lists: the chosen (*eletti*) and the reprobates. Whence the paralipomena, concealed from the temporal world ("if the pastor of Cosenza ... had read this face in God"; ["se il pastor di Cosenza... avesse in Dio ben letta questa faccia"; *Purg*. III, 124, 126]; "if the world knew what heart he had..."; ["e se 'l mondo sapesse il cor ch'egli ebbe..."; *Par*. VI, 140]), of Guido da Montefeltro, Manfredi, Ulysses, and Piccarda Donati. Maximum constraint on the outside, maximum freedom on the inside: here too we find the same fundamental approach on Dante's part, and the meter must allow an easy transition from one speed to another, from one state to another, from the eternal, permanent and universal, to the momentary, unpredictable, and fanciful.

Dante did not have adequate vernacular narrative tools available: the distich of *octosyllabes* (reproduced or copied also in Tuscany) had never shown a great deal of latitude, not even in the most expert hands, such as those of Chrétien de Troyes and the versifiers of the Tristan saga. That cousin of the hendecasyllable, the *décasyllabe* of the *chansons de geste,* lends itself, when isolated, to remarkable effects, such as those achieved in the *Chanson de Roland*, but

---

[56] Isaiah, 38, 10-11: "I said, in the noontide of my days I must depart; I am consigned to the gates of Sheol..."; New Oxford Annotated Bible.

the laisse, instead of the rigor he needs, grants the poet as much license as a street-singer. In analyzing the components of Dantean terza rima, whose continuity affords a link each time to the prior verses and an innovation each time to those forthcoming, is adaptable to accelerations and slowdowns, to readings of the general frame and readings of specific phrasings, Tommaso Casini recognized the interlinking of a certain kind of *sirventès*, in Sapphic stanzas, where the short line, changing the rhyme from the hendecasyllabic lines, foreshadowed it for the lines of the subsequent strophe. Using this suggestive working hyposthesis, Casini pushed forward, assuming that Dante had composed the lost *serventese* enumerating the most beautiful women in Florence: if true, this would be another vein of continuity in Dante's career, one further degrading of the prior stages of his experience to pure material. But if such is the order of transmission, where does the vehicle of the tercets come from? There are no prior sequences in terza rima in Dante; but clearly there are tercets imbricated inside other forms: in the sonnet, in the lyrical meter, which is also—in keeping with the precept of the *De vulgari* that assigns for comic use "*quandoque mediocre, quandoque humile vulgare*"[57]—the sole meter of the crude realists (those realists whom Dante does not name, but sort of rejects, passing over many in silence, as pure "moralists," to whose number nevertheless belong his adversary Forese Donati and the master of *Il Fiore*). And indeed *Il Fiore*, as well as the little treatise on amorous case histories of that friend of Dante's in whom Salvadori's Cavalcanti is no longer recognized, uses the sonnet as a strophe, according to the decisive study by Pio Rajna—who in this way allows us to find this ancient stage along our itinerary.

It is an inclusion into the supremely comic Dante, in which the stages left behind (but preserved) can be read as clearly as a scarab in amber. A retrospective examination of Dante without the *Commedia*—nevertheless a man of letters of decisive importance—must involve not just the "artist" within the "poet," but also the man of culture. Well, corresponding in equal measure to the recognized versatility of the artificer is the experimentality of the philosopher. As we've seen previously in the two Guidos, the frequentation of the halls of Scholasticism will have an overriding significance more in terms of (eclectic) linguistic heuristics than of any faithfulness to one sect or another, or any unilateral adherence to a thesis. And what is the radical divergence between the greater nobility of the vernacular and that of Latin, as we pass, over a certainly short span of

---

[57] "…sometimes the middle range of the vernacular, sometimes the lowly…"

time, from the *De vulgari* to the *Convivio*? or that between the invariability or variability of Hebrew, from the *De vulgari* to the *Paradiso*? or even the palinode on the moon's spots or the lands above sea-level from one work to the next? The contradiction reveals a preponderance of the subject over the thesis, which is rather similar to the prevalence of phonetic or rhythmic values over meaning, and seems to confer a formal aspect even to clearly mental data. *Habemus confitentem reum* ("We have a crime to confess"). Such is proclaimed, in speaking of the *Commedia*, by the letter to Cangrande, the authenticity of which was understandably questioned, though reconfirmed by the latest studies: "The genus of philosophy under which we proceed here in the whole and in the part is the business of morals or ethics, since both the part and the whole are composed for practice rather than theory. But if in some place or passage things are lengthened out in the manner of theory, this is not for the purpose of theory, but of practice; for, as the Philosopher says in the second book of Metaphysics: 'practical men theorize now and again.'"[58]

Even more precise is a passage at the start of *De monarchia*, one which, moreover, could be adduced, where necessary, to testify to the identity of the author with the prior text: "…it is a common saying that the speculative intellect becomes by extension the practical, whose end is to do and to make. I speak of things to be done, which are controlled by political sagacity, and things to be made, which are controlled by art."[59] What follows here, solemnly signaled by the *cursus* (and particularly by the *velox*), is an act of homage to the speculative intellect and the absolute and still Platonic priority of the philosopher: "… because they are all handmaids of speculation, that supreme end for which the Primal Good brought into being the human race. From this now grows clear the saying in the *Politics* that 'the vigorous in intellect naturally govern other men.'"[60]

---

[58] Translation by James Marchand: Dante to Cangrande: English (georgetown.edu) (*"Genus vero phylosophiae sub quo hic in toto et parte proceditur, est morale negotium, sive ethica; quia non ad speculandum, sed ad opus inventum est totum et pars. Nam si in aliquo loco vel passu pertractatur ad modum speculativi negotii, hoc non est gratia speculativi negotii, sed gratia operis; quia, ut ait Phylosophus in secundo Metaphysicorum, 'ad aliquid et nunc speculantur pratici aliquando."*)

[59] Translation by Aurelia Henry, *op. cit.* (…"*solet dici quod intellectus speculativus extensione fit praticus, cuius finis est agere atque facere. Quod dico propter agibilia, quae politica prudentia regulantur, et propter factibilia, quae regulantur arte."*)

[60] Idem. ". . . *quae omnia speculationi ancillantur tanquam optimo ad quod humanum genus Prima Bonitas in ésse prodúxit; et quia iam innotescit illud Politicae, 'intellectu scilicet vigentes aliis naturáliter príncipári.'"*

But this is sort of the circus maximus of certainty for theoretical philosophy, within which a freedom not only of practical action, but of poetic action, is being developed—"*agere atque facere*"[61]—with both concepts wisely (however traditionally) placed together in parallel, with the specific spheres of the concrete ends pursued by Dante and the precise effects he puts into play—political reality and expressive reality—being subject to discretion.

And we haven't even quoted the most decisive passage yet, one nevertheless insufficiently appreciated as a key passage for displaying Dante's intelligence. This is the eulogy of Solomon, not by accident attributed to Saint Thomas: "a veder tanto non surse il secondo" ("having seen so much, a second never arose"; *Par.* X, 114)—a second *king*, he specifies. But by whom is he surpassed in the absolute, if not by Adam and Jesus, and not by any philosopher? Solomon thus

> ...chiese senno
> acciò che re sufficïente fosse;
>   non per sapere il numero in che enno
> li motor di qua su, o se *necesse*
> con contingente mai *necesse* fenno;
>   non, *si est dare primum motum esse*,
> o se del mezzo cerchio far si puote
> triangol sí ch'un retto non avesse.[62]

> (...asked for wisdom
> that he might be a worthy king;
>   not that he might know how many
> angels move the heavens, nor if *necesse*
> with contingent ever made *necesse*;
>   nor *si est dare primum motum esse*,
> nor if a semicircle could be made to form
> a triangle that would have no right angle.)

Here the wisdom of geometry, dialectics, metaphysics, theology, the very same whose many fruits are presented—I was about to say "flaunted"—in the *Paradiso*, is parodied in its own language and tone, and the parody is put in the mouth of the foremost philosopher of the age (Thomas Aquinas). Just as burlesque poetry is condemned by Virgil ("to wish to hear such things is base desire"; "ché

---

[61] "to act as well as to make"
[62] *Par.* XIII, 95-102.

voler ciò udire è bassa voglia"; *Inf.* XXX, 138), yet not before it has been voiced in the dispute between Sinon and Maestro Adamo, so here the scientific theorems that so fill the *Commedia* are articulated in homogeneous form, but only to be scaled back and limited with respect to a higher wisdom.

And I do not wish to insist unilaterally on the literary aspect of the comic style, concerning which it may be legitimate to wonder whether it is not perhaps necessarily linked to the author's operative aim. Such author being not an ascetic, but a wordly, secular man. For the cantos of the earthly Paradise, the *Commedia*, as Parodi has correctly noted, becomes a parallel of *De monarchia*. The world beyond the grave paradoxically teaches Dante not how to die a good death, but how to live a good life. Worldliness is bodiliness: the reason why Dante, who cannot touch Brunetto Latini and is prevented from embracing Casella, physically abuses Bocca degli Abati and Filippo Argenti (or causes them to be physically abused), the sound of which echoes "as if it were a drum" ("come fosse un taburo," *Inf.* XXX, 103), as when Maestro Adamo's paunch is struck. And such bodiliness finds its reflection precisely in the comic style: the moral interpretation joins the stylistic one.

The continual, gradual sedimentation of ends towards the ultimate integrated goal legitimates the multiplicity of exegeses applied to Dante and provides a justification for each of them. Every one of these appropriations has something in its favor. First, however, it is necessary to point out that a choice must be made: the totality of Dante stems from his method, and it can be reconstructed with historical fidelity and cold intellection, but it cannot be viably or acceptably reproduced outside of his culture. What we can legitimately say, on the other hand, is that there is a Dante, so to speak, of the right, a Dante of the center, and a Dante of the left. There is the symbolic, allusive Dante, the allegorical, multi-meaningful Dante, in keeping with his poetics, and even a prophetic, enigmatic, initiatic Dante, not infrequently connected with the pre-Raphaelite Dante,[63] almost as if that presumed draughtsman of bloodless, exquisite apparitions did not have enough reality not to need transfusions of secret matter. And there is also a Dante adjusted to sentimental values, a lyrical-melodic Dante, or even a dramatic-pathetic Dante in the Romantic mould.

---

[63] A direct reference to Dante Gabriel Rossetti, but also an indirect implication of the esoteric Dante whom the Pre-Raphaelites "created," so to speak, through their projections.

It seems to me that our Dante can only be the Dante of reality and continuous experimentation, though not strictly a naturalistic Dante. One presupposition of this representation is that his language remains more "on this side" of his culture and is his true forwardmost point. The "miracle" by virtue of which the *Commedia* is the sole literary masterpiece of the Middle Ages in an accessible language—and not just an accessible but a surviving language, not, as with the *Chanson de Roland* or the *Cid*, or the *Niebelungen* or the Eddas, an object of merely specialized archaeological study—can be rationally explained by the opposing recipes of Italy's lateness in gaining national unity, and, first and foremost, the extreme precociousness of the Tuscan bourgeoisie. But the linguistic fixing effected personally by Dante makes it so that not only does the language remain stationary, but, within certain limits, so does the historical content, thus preserving for Italians a thoroughgoing knowledge, otherwise unthinkable, of his times, without parallel in other modern civilizations.

Dante's anachronism and untimeliness become clear in a twofold manner. At the starting point: as a representative of the former ruling class that had adjusted to "taking a membership card" and never surpassing the limits of power. *Laudator temporis acti*,[64] nostalgic for the small city of landowners of the time of Cacciaguida, averse to urban development, to finance (called *usura*), to industrial and commercial activity and the *"confusion de le persone,"* he comes across as one truly defeated by history. Yet it would be reckless to claim that its winners have really survived their success *pro tempore*. And at the finish line: his popularization through the vehicle of mercantile culture, and the propagandistic annexation of his doctrine (after initial suspicions of heterodoxy) by the mendicant orders, in no way limit him to these mortifying reductions; and, to top it off, avid Danteism itself leaves him unscathed. The vital contradiction of Dante is that his culture—Scholastic, Thomist, universalist, encyclopedic—was fitted into a particular national vehicle belonging as well to the *"mulierculae"*.[65] It is precisely the inclusivity of his remote culture that always leaves a margin allowing one to circumvent the obstacles of contingent antitheses. His great distance from us is at once a confirmation and guarantee of his vital closeness. Posterity's genuine impression, when encountering Dante, is

---

[64] "Praiser of times past." Horace, *Ars Poetica*, 173.
[65] "little women"

not that of coming upon a tenacious, well-preserved survivor, but of reaching someone who arrived before we did.[66]

[Originally printed in *Paragone*, October 1965, with a dedication to Anna Banti. A revised variant of the first part, under the title of "Dante come poeta popolare e come autore classico," was published in *Acta Litteraria Academiae Scientarium Hungaricae*, t. 8 (1-2), pp. 155-168 (1966), and had been presented the previous year at the celebrations organized by the same Academy at Budapest].

---

[66] These pages are the target of an interesting and very often concretely suggestive essay by Lucia Ricci Battaglia, "Dall'Antico Testamento alla 'Commedia'. Indagini su lessico e stile,' in *Rivista di storia e letteratura religiosa*, VII (1971), No. 2, pp. 252-277. The essay is based on the presupposition that Dante's "realism" is often not direct but filtered through the *sermo humilis* (with a clear reference to Auerbach's studies) of sacred texts. Signora Ricci Battaglia reproaches Dantean critics for having neglected this premise (which is acceptable in a subordinate but nevertheless important role, and one not unilaterally exclusive), and on this basis attacks the comedy thesis dictated by the poet's lowest level of discourse and involuntary memory. The necessity of such condemnation is only judged by a cultural "fundamentalism," since what must seem to it "secularist" will take its merit where it finds it, in this case, for example, in the contribution of an adversary. Taking the present essay as its starting point, on the other hand, is that by Gian Luigi Beccaria, "L'autonomia del significante. Figure dantesche," now chapter II of the volume *L'autonomia del significante, Figure del ritmo e della sintassi. Dante, Pascoli, D'Annunzio* (Turin 1975). (GC)

Philology and Dantean Exegesis

The natural, indeed proper hesitation of anyone who comes to speak on so solemn an occasion as this, and among such illustrious figures,[1] is today augmented by such a special celebration. It is not possible to be lighthearted when adding a few more drops to the torrents of eloquence requested or extorted from critics, much less to the oceans of centuries of exegesis. Such an occasion can only elicit an admission of the fear, and indeed vexation, aroused by the endless and growing mass of hermeneutics on the great poem—a vexation aroused in those who, in settling down to read it, sense an imposition of the need, before even starting, to interpolate an unquestionable technical certification of the meaning; and a vexation, too, in the involuntary interpreter, who, stimulated by the text itself to form his own philological image of it, finds imposed on him a disheartening screen of exhaustive verification in what we call the bibliography on the subject. The fact remains, however, that the reader and interpreter must then recognize, even if only in surprise and wonder, the always in some ways useful, pertitent, and almost never wholly inane aspect of prior interventions—especially the most recent ones, at least in cases where new connections between textual elements or concerning concrete facts about the cultural context are brought to our attention. Where lies the root of such a contradiction?

My present intention is not to resolve the aporia, but, if anything, to break it open. Formulated crudely, it goes as follows: that at a given moment, one either enjoys the poetry, or one judges it and establishes its cultural connections. The demand for a systematic, complete body of information is not, perhaps, impossible to fulfill; except that for all this time—and we're not talking about a brief interval—pleasure is suspended or, as one says, bracketed in parentheses. And yet the temptation to understand as best one can rises inevitably up in the

---

[1] The centenary celebration of the Accademia dei Lincei, Rome, June 18, 1965.

lover of poetry. Clearly Benedetto Croce let the philological operations recede to a merely practical precedent. And yet (if I may be allowed to recall a personal memory), I happened to find him one day extremely concerned with determining the exact meaning of a phrase in Baudelaire (who for him was the last great poet he actually accepted). What exactly, Croce asked me, are the "*seins stigmatisées*" (those, that is, in the poem, *Femmes damnées*)? Did I think they could be breasts marked by suckling? Croce, for his part, had never embraced the illusion of so-called total reading, which risked losing track of the text in an irremediable transcendence; on the other hand, any reading that was not founded on the text grammatically reconstituted in one's mind was inconceivable. It is useful, for the reader of Dante, or of any other author, to recognize the gap between one's surrender to the charm of the execution and the penetrating clarification of the literal meaning. Most striking is that the discontinuity between the two moments is implicit in the very doctrine of the *tinta neutra*, the "neutral tint," which finds its perhaps not sufficiently remembered place in Croce's introduction to *Poesia di Dante*. "The analytical moment preceding the synthetic moment," he writes there, "this I would call the *explanatio verborum*, the interpretation, as broadly intended, of the meaning of the words." Where this does not succeed, for the obscure passages, he suggests that we stick to "one of the two following approaches: either treat them as we treat the lost or unrestorable parts of a painting, over which one applies a neutral tint; or restore them, by adopting, from the various possible interpretations, the most fitting and beautiful."

I am reluctant to hide my perplexity as to the second method, that of restoration, whose expression in subjective terms (*iudicium*, as we practitioners of textual criticism would say) seems to me to slander Croce's true practice, which the philosopher then exemplifies by applying it to some celebrated lines, first: "Poscia, piú che 'l dolor, poté 'l digiuno" ("Then, more than grief could do, hunger did"; *Inf.* XXXIII, 75). About this line, he states that the currently widespread interpretation is "certainly the preferable one"; while adding, however, "but this does not rule out in any exclusive manner" that Dante's intention might have been to echo the rumor of cannibalism that had circulated in parts of Italy. But what does he mean by "this does not rule out," if not that the definitive conclusion is still up in the air and that, whatever one's personal leanings, the "neutral tint" has been ideally applied to the passage? The "neutral tint" method allows for the possiblity—which should be firmly asserted (and from which we must not exclude, by some sort of backward-looking privilege, putatively obscure modern poetry from Symbolism to the present)—of reading and enjoying before having understood everything (it would be a very bad sign, I think, if the brilliance of the poetry, even in a foreign language, even our own, weren't perceptible from the start); whereas "restoration" is the recurrent, necessary temptation not only to choose from among several available translations of one same manifestly univocal verbal sequence, but also in general to reestablish, through a fortunately conjectural and therefore not irreversible procedure, legitimate lines and color tones instead of the "neutral tint."

Let it indeed be settled that the paraphrasings of Dante, which are obscure but not dubious, imply a modality, and only one, of Ugolino's end as of any other circumlocution or reticence concerning reality. Here we cannot romantically agree with De Sanctis that the line is "dense with darkness and full of insinuations [...] due to all the instances of *forse* ("perhaps") teeming within it, which are so poetic" (one such "perhaps" also concerns whether nature drove "i denti nelle misere carni" ("[her] teeth into wretched flesh"). It is one thing to say that Dante, here and often elsewhere, refrains, like a Greek tragedian, from displaying atrocities on stage; it is another thing entirely to say that he nuances or interrupts the representation, and still another that he allows for a plurality of contradictory hypotheses. If, then, a choice must be made, it is not, perhaps, so scholarly to adopt the "most beautiful" of these (as publishers used to do between the variants for teaching, even specifically for the *Commedia*), as it is indeed to choose the "most fitting," if by such expression we mean the most economic solution within the range of known, interrelated realities.

On the other hand, the alternative of "either one reads or one comments" does not constitute a troubling or anguishing fate. It is not clear why the fact that observation influences the object of observation should be more scandalous in the so-called human sciences than it is in the natural sciences. The lamentable ignorance of "humanists" (a word in which we should be able to hear, like Proust, the *guillemets*) in the area of the natural sciences is not so great that they will not have heard tell that a major principle of modern physics dictates that either one measures the speed of elementary particles or one determines their position. Now the epistemology of the first branch of science is not in the end so remote from that of the other branch. Even modern linguistics, for example, are based on a sort of principle of indeterminacy: Saussure's postulate whereby a proposition of linguistics either belongs to diachronic linguistics (the evolution of the isolated facts of a language) or to synchronic linguistics (the systematic consideration of all the facts of a language simultaneously). The above alternative, moreover, is formulated in a similar manner. A specific critical act either involves the sphere of pure expression, or it concerns the entire scope of linguistic relationships.

The analogy goes even further. Just as a linguist cannot so easily take actions that concern purely diachronic linguistics or purely synchronic linguistics; and just as the central effort of modern linguistics (leaving aside the much-debated question of how many kinds of Saussurian linguistics there actually are) does not manifest itself exclusively in alternation ("Growth AND Structure"), but rather in connecting the two levels, interpreting the terms of the one in the light of the other; so there is no doubt that the most modern Dantean criticism consists of bringing closer together the expressive and, so to speak, executive line, and the exegetical and systematic line, interrupting the former to establish connections of the latter order and returning to a direct reading with this background of experience. Unlike the exercises of puzzle-solving or the search for "keys" typical of traditional Dante scholarship, the approaches of modern Dante scholarship are: precise verification of the rhetorical canons, to fit them in with the continuing classical tradition; discovering specific connections in which data of the overall structure are reflected, like the macrocosm in the monad; gnoseological interpretations on the same level as the grammatical rendering; new and intense auscultations of the literal meaning until it should give rise to an unprecedented translation; and, in the best of cases, an analysis of the phonetico-symbolic values. These kinds of interventions are quite various in their morphology and cannot have correctly applied to them such terms as stylistic or structural criticism, or others still, which would only be strictly valid for individual parts. I would propose bringing them all together under the label of "verbal criticism," now that this term has entirely fallen out of the sphere of textual criticism and seems therefore available to use without misunderstanding. The masters as well as the artisans of verbal criticism—"*quorum nomina*," I repeat, with the Astonomer of the Limousin, "*quia vulgata sunt, dicere supersedi*"[2]—all display something akin to that "taste for signs," that "*Geschmack an Zeichen*," that so thrilled Hegel in Hamann. Without forcing things so much, I would venture ideally, in spite of everything, to place at its head, and as its motto, an assertion by Croce himself, drawn from the same page quoted just above and worthy of being inscribed in gold: "Philosophical propositions, names of persons, references to historical instances, moral judgements, and so on, are, in poetry, nothing but

---

[2] "...that which is known by all, I won't mention" (from the *Gesta Francorum*).

words, essentially identical to all other words, and should be interpreted within these limits."

While it would certainly be an exaggeration to posit the end of all ideological exegesis, it is clear that the best of it takes place entirely upon solid verbal foundations. The twofold nature of the *Commedia*'s protagonist, for example, the historical individual and the representative of humanity, has been asserted by one of the last of the serious ideological interpreters, Charles Singleton (and here it is of less concern to chart exactly how far one can follow his developments), who bases his position on a creak he hears in the poem's opening lines. It is often currently and commonly observed that lines such as those that open the *Commedia* could, for the persistent familiarity of their vocabulary and grammar, have been written today. Some benefit of inventory, of course, would be in order, were we to repeat such an observation. Our worthy American friend has given form to the slight discomfort felt by anyone who reads with naïve eyes,

> Nel mezzo del cammin di nostra vita
> mi ritrovai per una selva oscura.

The "squeak" is in the split—not easily adapted to modern expression—between the first person plural (*nostra*) and the first person singular (*mi ritrovai*). Singleton is justified in his claim of drawing a conceptual interpretation from a linguistic clue.

Without going back down the road of extra-textual inferences in this instance, we can nevertheless return to the first line to highlight how the commentaries usually shed light on the literal meaning in two distinct frameworks, or two which should in any case be kept carefully separate from each other. One the one hand, people cite the passage from the *Convivio* in which the "punto sommo" ("highest point") in the arc of life for those who are "perfettamente naturati" ("perfectly created") is at the "thirty-fifth year". "And I believe it," says Dante ("e io credo"), though he is also corroborated by well-known Aristotelian and Scholastic sources duly studied by the incomparably erudite Bruno Nardi, which are consistent with the line from the Mosaic sermon in the Vulgate (Psalms 89, 10), *"Dies annorum nostrorum in ipsis, septuaginta anni"* ("The days of our years in them are seventy years."). On the other hand some have cited in this connection, no less obviously, Ezechiel's proclamation to Isaiah invoking the Gates of Hell (Isaiah 38, 10-11): *"Ego dixi: In dimidio dierum meorum vadam ad portas inferi*."³ (It should, however, be pointed out that, in the context, this is a hymn of salvation, one that reaches beyond great bitterness: "*Ecce in pace amaritudo mea amarissima. Tu autem eruisti animam meam ut non periret, proiecisti post tergum tuum omnia peccata mea*"⁴; and similarly beyond any connection with hope, morning light, the menacing lion: "*Sperabam usque ad mane, quasi leo sic contrivit omnia ossa mea.*"⁵ Such elements are added as secondary flavors to the much-cited Scriptural passages on bitter death and the three beasts.)

Now, these two echoes, both quite clear, do not form an equation, but rather add together to form a sum. They are not at all contradictory—as would instead be the case with the obtuse ancient interpretation whereby the "mezzo de la vita" is one of the two (discontinuous) halves of human existence, that spent in sleep and dream. Either the "mezzo" is *one* half, or it is *the* middle point: there is no possibility of compromise on the literal meaning. And thus there is no reconciliation, however hard one might try, in Saint Francis's "Laudato si' [. . .] per sora luna" and similar lines, between the "a causa di" version and the "per mezzo di" and "…da" versions; just as there is none, taking the line "che paia il giorno che si more" (*Purg.* VIII, 6), between the version with *giorno* as object—the only tolerable one, in any case—and the version with *giorno* as subject, although one commentator, to whom one often defers, valiantly deems it "possible that Dante, in formulating the verse in this fashion, meant to suggest both meanings."⁶ Like Goldoni's miser with his famous ring for measuring eggs—"*questo passa, questo non passa*"—the grammar seems to let a very great deal of stuff pass through, but in the end it's all rather fantastical merchandise, such as "this round table is square." When solidly rooted on its own ground, grammar is quite rigid and doesn't allow for ambiguity.

---

³ "I said, in the noontide of my days I must depart; I am consigned to the gates of Sheol…" (i.e., Hell); *New Oxford Annotated Bible*, p. 868.

⁴ Isaiah 38, 17. ("Lo, it was for my welfare / that I had great bitterness; / but thou hast held back my life / from the pit of destruction, / for thou hast cast all my sins / behind thy back." *New Oxford Annotated Bible*, p. 868)

⁵ Isaiah 38, 13. ("I cry for help until morning; like a lion he breaks all my bones;…" *New Oxford Annotated Bible*, p. 868)

⁶ This was Daniele Mattalia, in his commentary on the *Divina Commedia*, Milan, Rizzoli, 1960 (reference cited in *Dante Studies, with the Annual Report of the Dante Society*, No. 87 (1969), Johns Hopkins University Press, p. 30).

With this starting point well-established, it is nevertheless legitimate, indeed obligatory, to note the broadening of meanings. Taking "*il* punto medio" as the only acceptable equivalency (even though Isaiah no doubt was talking about a life cut short—without any intention of geometrical division, of course—in full flower and vigor), we can see that an arithmetical reading can easily be applied, for which a whole other series of sources comes into play. At first Dante shapes his opening in *imitation* of a prophetic passage, but its literal interpretation in turn implies other, physiological allusions. In spite of this, what we have here is not polysemy in any strict sense, or any specifically Dantean sense—that is, we are not in the presence of one or more meanings beyond the literal one—but another polysemy (one which those less zealously inclined to allegory may well find more enticing), one which unfolds entirely within the literal meaning, through a multiplicity of internal echoes and cultural allusions. While I'm not so sure about polysemy in the strict sense, this Dantean polysemy is an absolutely exceptional procedure—at least in this respect—in the annals of literary expression, due to the dazzling richness of the author's memory, in which his experiences and readings accumulate and stratify, so that proximate elements, and oftentimes the same elements, become single points of multiple networks and systems that are usually implied and not worked out and should thus be approached with an appropriately light touch. It is the commentator's task to magnify these hints and each time retrace the entire system of points, without, however, letting it imprison the author, to whose prodigiously retentive mind that system not infrequently proved to be merely tangential.

This wealth of associations is fed by what culturally is Dante's dual nature: precious and "comic." As a poet of the scholarly sort, educated in the *auctores*, well-trained in all the practices of rhetorical refinement, and steeped, moreover, in every vat of the knowable, Dante elicits the same abundance of illustration and explication as any Alexandrian or Parnassian. As a "comic" poet, wide open to the full gamut of everyday reality, even the most perishable and transitory, of the very sort that would have been lost had he not crystallized it in verse—indeed a considerable body of knowledge of the names and facts, and of the concrete history, of the Italian thirteenth and fourteenth centuries has been hammered tight with the nails of the *Commedia* into our national schooling—he demands that further detail of commentary without which it is impossible to grasp a "comic" writer the moment he is a little *engagé* (say, Aristophanes or Petronius). But the contemporary world of the classical and popular poet, already rather astonishing and probably unique, comes alive above all, as bears repeating, in an inexorble memory of life and book knowledge, which enriches it with implied allusions and background harmonies, without altering the extraordinary contextual and imaginative precision of the discourse.

Leaving aside the hidden meanings—which are not our concern here, at least not today—the commentary (on the literal meaning) has traditionally unfolded along lines of strict erudition as concerns both the "precious" and "comic" aspects, in addition to the equally strict ascertainment of the grammatical meaning. Verbal criticism has come to augment the interplay of references, availing itself of two procedures: the recomposition of Dante's readings, in order to determine his secondary allusions; and a reconnaissance of the lexical and phonetic material used by him, to establish connections of a formal nature. Articulating a plan of this sort is not the same as mapping out a systematic working plan. As there are famously no *a priori* categories in stylistic criticism (in truth there are none for grammar either, since even the noun/verb opposition is not universal, though it doesn't even seem possible to speak of "general" stylistic criticism the way we speak of *grammaire générale*), the interpreter can only usefully rely on his own memory, when reading texts by Dante or others, in order to succeed, with a bit of luck, in reproducing some of the original mnemonic connections. And in order to enjoy Dante's poetry, we need not wait, I repeat, until the whole catalogue of readings is exhausted; we may let ourselves, on the contrary, be stimulated by that same poetry in order to rediscover it in its less frequented regions when we return to it.

Not, however, that we can't chart some kind of plan of approach. There is no want of people, for example, who for heuristic ends (met or unmet, I can't say) undertake to read the entire *Patrologia Latina*. Then there are those who, more modestly, knowing Dante's debt to lexicography, plow through the so-to-speak etymological dictionaries of the time, from Isidoro to Papia to Giovanni da Genova, but showing perhaps a preference for Uguccione da Pisa, thus following in the illustrious footsteps of Paget Toynbee and Pio Rajna by concentrating on the only one still unpublished. The codices of Uguccione's *Derivationes Magnae*, diligently perused by Giovanni Nencioni, have rewarded the latter with some of the finest discoveries of recent date, such as that of the *cuncta* "delay" (presumed in the *Disticha Catonis*, or the *Distichs of Cato*) as a precedent for the alleged *hapax* "sanza cunta" in *Purgatorio*, XXXI, 4. Overall, however, commentators of the sort here described operate *a posteriori*, not *a priori*, assisted in their free-reading adventures by a few fantasies from their associative memories—in the same way, truth be told, as correct etymologies are found, not sought. In order to restore the balance, it may not be a bad idea for such positivistic and technical procedures to be presided over, once and for all, by what the Romantics would have called "inspiration"— "boogeyman inspiration" (*il baubau ispirazione*), as an excellent contemporary poet disparagingly caricatured it on his own behalf.

This appendix, indeed "addition" (in the same sense as Ferrara's Erculean Addition), which verbal criticism has affixed to the map of traditional exegesis—an unnecessary addition nurtured on an already substantial familiarity, but still able to mystify and reaffirm it—thus has the advantage, or disadvantage, if you will, of resisting any systematic planning. Corresponding to this is the limitation, or merit, that it cannot be turned into a key. It must be the pretense to consequentiality that distorts so many propositions that are basically legitimate when advanced with a light touch, and which turns us away from many substantial entries in the recent bibliography like so many aberrant solipsisms, which they do, in the end, actually turn out to be. But on what basis do we recognize the "truth" of any proposition? On the same basis as any scholarly "truth"—that is, on the firmness of the relationship asserted; or, if we're not dealing with a multiple relationship, then on its "certainty," in the Viconian sense of the term, on its factual nature, which will then mean greater economy in interpreting that relationship as not random.

Criticism working with formal elements works with elements that are not necessarily all significant or, as one says in more technical fashion, not pertinent or relevant. A book like the *Commedia* will contain a fixed number of lines, as well as words and constituent phonemes (if it's a definitively established text), and these will be distributed in forms and patterns from which certain series will assuredly be excerpted. Just how much of this quantitative and qualitative data is random and how much meaningful is certainly a question of judgment. Similarly, whether the verified connections stand on their own, with their own pure, original formal value, or whether they instead function in ancillary fashion to the representation, will also have to be determined on a case-by-case basis. We must take great care to prevent wondrous symmetries and numerical combinations, alliterative figures and embroideries of dentals and labials from slandering the legitimacy of structural research, transforming accident into necessity and pursuing its application across the entire range of the mass of expression. When an interpreter's initial observation is well-founded, we regret that he didn't stop while he was ahead.[7] It is not, however, a question of quantity, but of quality. All things considered, the hardest part is perhaps verifying that structural allusions also exist, developed by the author just enough to suggest the organicity of the whole, without falling into the slavishness of an all-encompassing ritual or pharasaic plan, which, as a hidden meaning of a novel nature (a pathological form of verbal criticism indeed has something about it similar to allegorism or puzzle-solving beyond allegory) would be associated, in a secondary or more remote respect, with the literal level alone. An example will help to clarify what I mean here.

To note that each book or *cantica* of the *Commedia* finishes with the word *stelle* (accompanied by the definite article)[8] and that the start of each *cantica* features *stelle* in rhymes ("con quelle stelle / ch'eran con lui"; "e vidi quattro stelle"; "con migliore stella"),[9] is as banal as it is incontestable. Equally obvious is the inference of Dante's optimism by pointing out his itinerary of ascension, considering that the first stars seen after the protasis[10] are the private ones seen just inside the secret realm, "l'aere sanza stelle" (*Inf.* III, 23). And bearing in mind an important point near the end of the *Paradiso*, which I will further discuss below—"e come stella in cielo il ver si vide" ("and like a star in the sky the truth was seen"; *Par.* XXVIII, 87)—we may add that the star is an emblem of unveiled consciousness made visible, as indeed in the phrase "riveder le stelle." But what is the formal value of the cross-reference? It can only be likened, I think, to the rhetorical norms of lyric poetry, such as the refrain or ritornello in a *ballata* or similar genre—or even, if you will, the repetition of the end-word in a sestina. If this birth certificate is valid, some kind of proof is needed. And such proof appears to be found in the reverberation of the word *vero* in the closing words of *Paradiso* XXVII ("e vero frutto verrà dopo 'l fiore") in the first tercet of the following canto ("...aperse 'l vero") as well as in its own closing words ("con altro assai del ver di questi giri"), in keeping with the canto's insistence on

---

[7] Such would be the springboard for Gian Luigi Beccaria, in his *Allitterazioni dantesche* (now the second chapter of the abovecited volume, *L'autonomia del significante*). (GC)

[8] The end of the *Inferno* is foreshadowed around the middle of the *cantica* with the words "e torni a riveder le belle stelle" (*Inf.* XVI, 83). (GC)

[9] *Inf.* I, 38; *Purg.* I, 23; *Par.* I, 40, respectively.

[10] I am of course leaving out the famous line for Beatrice, "Lucevan li occhi suoi piú che la stella" (whereas in other places in Dante, *stella* seems to have a collective meaning); I believe I may in the past have conjectured, concerning this line, an involuntary mnemonic echo of Cavalcanti's "piú che la stella –bella, al mi' parere" in *In un boschetto*. (GC)

the truth ("il vero"). For it is scarcely an accident that any echoing of "il vero" is elsewhere limited—in a reply by Maestro Adamo—to the tight frame of a single tercet. *Paradiso* XXVII thus swallows its own tail and functions like a *cobla capfinida* of troubadour craft with respect to the prior canto, using an artifice that brings together eminent models of *trobar* first from the Provençal, then the Sicilian, and even the stilnovista schools. We find this procedure—if we want to aim high— in the great, groundbreaking poem, *Al cor gentil*, by "founding father" Guinizzelli ("come calore in clarità du foco. // Foco d'amore..."), and it reappears, but with significant discontinuity, in the young Dante.

Take, for example, the canzone *E' m'incresce di me*. Three of its stanzas—that is, half of the composition—are linked as follows: "...Nostro lume porta pace." // "Noi darem pace al core..." Or take the poem that follows this one, *Lo doloroso amor*, where a similar interlinking marks the first two stanzas: "Per quella moro c'ha nome Beatrice." // Quel dolce nome ..."). In other words, Dante was content merely to hint at the structure and unity of his poems, without rigidifying them with constant repetitions. Even looser is the relationship between the first line of the *Paradiso* ("la gloria di Colui che tutto move") to another ("la gloria di Colui che la innamora"), which doesn't appear until near the end (XXXI, 5), integrated with an offhandedness that is actually the soul of discretion.

And if we're talking about canzoni, we can even include the *Commedia*. The term now used for each of its three major subdivisions is *cantica*, in keeping with the line in the *Purgatorio* ("le carte / ordite a questa cantica seconda"; XXXIII, 140), and particularly with the theoretical argument in the Letter to Cangrande. It is a term whose origin is anything but clear (especially if one wishes to link it to the mysterious Iberian *cantiga*); all we really know is that before Dante we have only the Church Latin word *cantica* for a "book of hymns." In the *Inferno*, however, the same subdivision is called a canzone ("de la prima canzon, ch'è de' sommersi"; XX, 3), but this may serve as a useful terminological bridge to the category presently under examination. (Canzoni, the now remote *De vulgari* taught us, are only so-called "because of their pre-eminence" ["*per superexcellentiam*"], since the term generally applies to "all arrangements of words, of whatever kind, that are based on harmony, whether in the vernacular or in the regulated language" ["*omnia cuiuscunquemodi verba scilicet armonizata vulgariter et regulariter.*"]) It would be absurd to set out looking for similar systematic artifices throughout the great poem. By limiting himself to placing these mentions in the most obvious rhythmic position (the very end of a *cantica*), and then at a highly delicate point, where, getting ready to tie up the loose ends, he sings on the theme of truth, Dante justifies, in this regard, a conclusion of simple stuctural allusion (since the mystical meanings, moreover, are hardly everywhere present). And with such discretion he provides a paradigm for the discretion of the commentators.

Those commentators inspired to similar discretion will also be the first to gauge the risks we take in asserting the substantiality and relevance of echoes that are hardly major, and indeed marginal. This is the "calculated risk" with which I will venture below to illustrate the typology of verbal criticism, using excerpts from prior scholarship and a few new (within the scope of my knowledge) propositions, from a gradated perspective ranging from positions taken with respect to an outside point view to those entirely internal to Dante's own system. It is, however, a risk that must be taken if we do not wish to sail into that other dangerous reef that strikes fear in the heart of any good nominalist, that of a methodology divorced from application and spilling over, as it can, into metaphysics. But so it is.

One extreme of the question is therefore represented by the external points of reference, which sometimes allow for additions to be made, even to thoroughly investigated points. I will advance one, of a thematic nature, concerning Ugolino; then I shall recall another, of a linguistic nature, concerning Francesca.

It would be overstating the case to say that everything in the Ugolino episode is settled—even if we refrain from reconsidering the man-eating interpretation that Croce was unable to dismiss entirely, and which, reading between the lines, would cast a very particular shade upon the whole episode, one of horror, perhaps, but certainly not of the poetry of horror. If this were somehow on the mark, the verse would display some sort of lump of reticence in the throat, a psychological *coup de glotte* along the lines of "Quel giorno piú non vi leggemmo avante," or "Iddio si sa qual poi mia vita fusi"; or even, to turn to another eminence never suspected of being under Dante's sway: "La sventurata rispose."[11] I do confess, however—let it be said in passing—that such a reading, which always has Dante scholars shaking their heads, seems to me the most fitting to the cultural situation. Central to this, yet again, are Uguccione's *Derivationes*, for their definition of tragedy, which was already quite usefully probed by Toynbee and Rajna:

---

[11] Manzoni, *I promessi sposi*. See prior chapter, p. 108.

> '*oda*' [...] *componitur cum '*tragos,*' quod est hircus, et dicitur '*haec tragoedia –ae,*' idest hircina laus, vel hircinus cantus, idest foetidus;* EST ENIM DE CRUDELISSIMIS REBUS, SICUT QUI *patrem interfcicit, vel* COMEDIT FILIUM*, vel e contrario, et huiusmodi.*[12] (my emphasis)

Dante repeats words similar to these, with different examples, in his letter to Cangrande. If the *Inferno* is thematically the tragic part of the *Commedia*—and the letter states "*inchoat asperitatem alicuius rei*," and "*a principio horribilis et foetida est*"[13]—there is nothing more hircine and fetid than the pit of the traitors, at whose inverted summit we find in fact another subject "eaten up": Brutus the parricide. (Also a parricide of sorts is Judas, at the same depth.) And so it seems quite fitting that the scene should be preceded by one who "*comedit filium*" ("ate his son"). To the Thebes of Statius's Tydeus and Melanippus in Dante's explicit metaphor of Pisa (*Inf.* XXXIII, 89) we can add the Argos (possibly suggested by the Virglianizing "gente argolica" in *Inf.* XXVIII, 84) of Atreus and Thyestes. The fact remains that in the passage from Horace's *Ars Poetica* generously tapped by Dante in his letter, in which he posits the distinction between comedy and tragedy, it is precisely Thyestes's dinner that is used to illustrate the tragic situation:

> Versibus exponi tragica res comica non vult:
> Indignatur item privatis ac prope socco
> Dignis carminibus narrari coena Thyestae.[14]
> (ll. 89-91)

Drawing on Uguccione for his definition of tradegy, Dante, it used to be said, forgoes giving examples. In compensation he adds: "*ut patet per Senecam in suis tragoediis*" ("as is clear from Seneca's tragedies").[15] One such tragedy is in-

---

[12] "'...so the root 'ode' placed next to the root 'tragos,' meaning goat-smell,...that is called 'tragedy': as a matter of fact, the praise of the billy goat, the song of the billy goat, with its fetid odor, are very cruel subjects! Quite comparable to he who kills his father, or to the one who devours his son, or the other way around." (Translation by Loyse Paradiso)

[13] "[comedy] begins with harshness in some things... "; "in the beginning it is horrible and smelly..."

[14] "A comic subject does not want to be expressed in tragic verses; the threads of daily life that may well fit the comic sock, are scorned by the dinner of Thyestes ..." (*Ars Poetica*, ll. 89-91)

[15] It behooves me to note that an opinion contrary to the inference of Dante's knowledge of the tragedic Seneca was voiced by Ettore Paratore, now in *Tradizione e struttura in Dante* (Florence 1968), pp. 108 ff. and 134 ff., although a note in the volume (p. 136, no. 18) seems to hint at a retraction. (GC)

deed the *Thyestes*, whose protagonist, upon learning of the inconceivable crime, also apostrophizes (and I am not insinuating, in so obvious a development, any *post hoc ergo propter hoc*) the "raw earth":

> Agnosco fratrem. Sustines tantum nefas
> Gestare, Tellus? non ad infernam Styga
> Te nosque mergis? [...]
> Immota Tellus, pondus ignavum iaces;[16]

and he asks why the innocent are put "to such torture":

> Quid liberi meruere? [17]

Thyestes, but also Count Ugolino, belong to the ranks of those "*reges et magnates*" whose deeds, still according to Uguccione's definition, are fit for tragedy.[18]

Read in this light, Count Ugolino's story grows in horror, as the teller of his story grows in restraint. In the *cantica* that follows, of a rather different character touched upon only in passing, Dante will say that she "nel figlio diè di becco" ("stuck her beak in him"; *Purg.* XXIII, 30). But this is not the point to which I would venture to add a suggestion. The trope of children offering themselves as food to the father (which Dante presents with an *agudeza* of taste quite worthy of Seneca: "[...] tu ne vestisti / queste misere carni, e tu le spoglia"),[19] comes across to us as too contrived and melodramatic. "An ugly thing, an act beyond nature and realism," as De Sanctis said when reproaching Cesari for thinking so, adding a mistaken interpretation of his own. But what if the heroism of the children was a pre-existing topos, one inserted and as though inlaid as a borderline case within a proverbially extreme affair, a supreme self-abnegation in the face of supreme wickedness?

---

[16] "I recognize my brother; Can you bear, O Earth, a crime so monstrous? Why do you not burst apart and cast yourself down to the infernal Styx? [...] Earth [is] unmoved, lies like an inert mass." (ll. 106-108; 1020)

[17] "What was my children's sin?" (l. 1100)

[18] It is extremely interesting that in the *Aeneid* even Dido (who not many lines earlier had been compared, and not by accident, to such tragic characters as the Pentheus the Theban and the "scaenis agitatus" Orestes) regrets not having inflicted an "Atridian" form of atrocity upon her deserter: "non [potui] ipsum absumere ferro / Ascanium patriisque epulandum ponere mensis?" (*Aeneid*, ll. 601-602). (GC)

[19] "... you clothed us / in this wretched flesh, and now you strip it away." (*Inf.* XXIII, 62-63)

This would seem to be the case, since a surprisingly analogous situation appears in a thirteenth-century *chanson de geste, Ami et Amile*. I won't summarize the saga, which was also well known in medieval Italy[20] (and authoritatively studied by, among others, Angelo Monteverdi). I shall merely limit myself to saying that at the climax of the story, it is revealed to Ami, struck with leprosy as divine punishment, that he could be cured by a bath in blood still warm. Let me add, incidentally, that the problems of recovering from leprosy were also a concern of Dante's. Indeed they drive the episode of Constantine and Sylvester, which itself is an analogue to that of Guido da Montefeltro. But the angel adds an extra burden to Ami's task: the blood required has to be that of the two children of his dear friend, stand-in, and beneficiary, Amile, and they can only be beheaded by their own father. I hasten to reassure those unfamiliar with what happens next: Amile, informed of the revelation by a hesitant Ami, though torn, à la Corneille, between gratitude and paternal love, is willing to carry out the pious misdeed, allowing Ami to recover his health in the cleansing; but the children will be miraculously brought back to life.

Thus reassured as to the happy ending, let us return to the details. Amile, having made the horrific decision, grabs the tools necessary—sword and basin—and goes into the sleeping children's bedroom. A noise he (luckily) makes in his hesitation wakes the older boy, who then questions the parent as to his sinister intentions, whereupon he is thoroughly informed. "If that's the way it is," the child immediately (*"errament"*) replies:

> Noz sommes vostre de vostre engendrement,
> Faire en poez del tout a vo talent.
> Or noz copes les chiés isnellement [...].[21]

Would Dante have known this edifying *chanson*? I tend to conjecture that he would, in as much as the term for the desquamation of a leper is here identical to a famous *hapax legomenon* in Dante:[22]

---

[20] As it is well known in modern culture thanks to an essay by Walter Pater ("Two Early French Stories," published first in *The Renaissance. Studies in Art and Poetry*), though based on a version not of interest to us here. (GC)

[21] "We are yours by your siring, / You may do all that you desire. / Now cut our heads off quickly [...]"

[22] *Par.* XXVIII, 82: "par che si purga e risolve la roffia..."

Li chiet la roiffe dont il estoit sozprins.[23]

Frankly I do not see how the *roffia* clouding the heavens, and of which they are purged by the Mistral wind (at least in the Romagna province, where the end of the *Paradiso* was probably written and where they call the wind *il serenaro*), can be compared to any technical meanings that *pellicola* or *squama* ("flake, scale") assume in Tuscan rules. E.G. Parodi, well versed in that vernacular, refers it to the "cleaning and trimming of tanned hides." It could, however, and only, be compared—as Torraca has already realized—to the northern Italian and French meaning of "crust, dandruff" and the like. So much the better if honorable literary precedents are found, such as in the present and other instances; the problem is that they are all in the *langue d'oïl*.

Another external point of reference, this time linguistic, has already once made it possible to get a better sense of a point in another highly popular Dantean passage, that of Francesca da Rimini. Still, a further perusal will not be time wasted, as it will allow us to distinguish the results from those produced by a purely internal analysis. An ancient, medieval *parlamento* (discussion, parley, conference), no matter the direness of the circumstances, was always pompous and shrewd. Such is the *parlamento* of Ugolino's sons, despite their tender age; and such, as is widely recognized, is that of Francesca, a well-read provincial lady:

> "O animal grazïoso e benigno
> che visitando vai per l'aere perso
> noi che tignemmo il mondo di sanguigno [...]"[24]

Suffice it to dwell for a moment on this opening, specifically on the play between *perso* and *sanguigno*. *Perso*, as in French (Eng. "perse"), would probably also have meant a distinct color (it has sometimes been translated as "violet"). But even as Dante points this out in a famous passage in the *Convivio* (IV, xx, 2), when explaining the line "Dunque verrà, come dal nero il perso," saying that "Perso is a color blended from purple and black, but the black wins out, thus giving the color its name" ("Lo perso è uno colore misto di purpureo e di nero, ma vince lo nero, e da lui si denomina"), he is, in fact, adding a popular etymology to the formulation—that is, a connection with the verb *perdere*. And it applies

---

[23] "The scales on his head of which he was surprised...".

[24] *Inf.* V. 88-90. ("O living creature, gracious and benign, that go through the black air visiting us who stained the world with blood..."; Singleton trans.)

not only to this reflection, but is further mirrored in his praxis, representing a semantic expansion and leavening that is striking in the ever so realistic and proper Dante. While not immediately visible, this becomes quite clear when we are able, through concordances, to line up all the instances. And this shows how *perso*, used quite precisely in the abovecited verse line, generally represents an axiomatic summation of darkness, applied to a non-transparent medium ("l'aere") and, further, to the water, which is "buia assai piú che persa" (*Inf.* VII, 103)—and synonymous with "onde bige" (the "murky stream" in l. 104)—and in the "fondi" not "persi" of waters that are not "profonde" (*Par.* III, 12). As for solid mediums, we have the "scaglion" ("terraced step") that is "tinto piú che perso" (*Purg.* IX, 97), not to mention the "bianchi fiori" which turn "persi" in the canzone, *Tre donne*.

The "aere perso" is therefore perfectly synonymous with the *Inferno*'s (III, 29) "aura sanza tempo tinta" (that is, eternally gloomy), whose hue is cast upon it by the "colore oscuro" in line 10 of the same canto (I abide by the reading attributing "di colore oscure" not to *parole*, but to *scritte*). *Perso* is indeed literally contiguous with *tinto* ("tinto piú che perso") and lines up with it in the non-technical definition (which survives to this day in Italy and elsewhere) of "dirty, turbid, blackening or reddening," as in the "acqua tinta" of the gluttons (*Inf.* XI, 10) and the water of the Phlegethon (*Inf.* XVI, 104), where it is synonymous with "acqua rossa"; or, farther ahead, in the "impetrato tinto" (*Purg.* XXXIII, 74), where *tinto* describes the stain made by the blood of Pyramis (l. 69), which then takes us back to the Furies "di sangue tinte."[25] (*Inf.* IX, 38)

Sticking to a strict internal analysis—a little more black, a little less black, a little more red, a little less red—*perso* and *sanguigno* are almost the same thing, sharing a corresponding homogeneity if not an anticipatory *contrappasso*,[26] while *tinto* comes in third, so to speak, but in active form, almost as if to signify the sinners' participation and responsibility in the creation of Erebus. The "taint" has spread universally over the entire world, including the heavens beyond: again we have the same process of expansion. The reasoning tallies, but why *sanguigno* and not *sangue*? Why the color and not the substance? Here too we note another one of those creaks that demand a precise explanation, one that might be provided, if formulated *a priori*, by the fact—discovered by

---

[25] The "tinto aspetto" of Jacopo Rusticucci is the same as the "cotto" of Brunetto. (GC)

[26] In the specific context of the *Divine Comedy*, *contrappasso* is the correspondence, either through similarity or contrast, of respective punishments of the sinners with the sins committed.

Torraca, one of the most diligent commentators in exploring parallel loci from the great mass of interpretations—that the Statuto dell'Università ed Arte della Lana di Siena, drafted right at the turn of the 13th to the 14th century, specifically forbade dyers to "tégnare neuna lana né in nero né in sanguegno,"[27] except in specific circumstances. In jumping from *perso* to *sanguigno*, the poet ties semantically together the endings of the two lines that follow (which necessarily do not rhyme), imbricating them within the play of rhymes by means of a metaphor borrowed from the language of commerce (as with the Arbia "colorata in rosso" in *Inf.* X, 86), one that injects a tinge of dark humor into Francesca's speech (if we can imagine a rhetoric of Francesca's distinct from Dante's own) and confirms, with this touch, the already mentioned composite, plurilinguistic, open-minded character of this *ars dictandi*.

A particular case of external referencing is the use of quotations, although it is not always easy to gauge the degree of *intentionality* in their use. I shall limit myself here to echoes of other vernacular poetry, since there are not many in the *Commedia*. While expounding on generation, Virgil, with due respect, criticizes Averroes for having sundered "da l'anima il possibile intelletto" ("the possible intellect from the soul"; *Purg.* XXV, 65). The setting of the philosophical technicality in rhyme—including the syntactical inversion being compelled by the rhythm—irresistibly evokes Guido Cavalcanti's most celebrated canzone, so admired by Dante, *Donna mi prega*:

> Ven da veduta forma che s'intende,
> che prende—nel possibile intelletto,
> come in subietto,—loco e dimoranza,

Thus does Dante implicate and parade his first friend's Averroism. Elsewhere the gesture may simply be implied. In the line

> come di neve in alpe sanza vento

we find, for example, a well known echo (and perfecting) of the hendecasyllable from Cavalcanti's *plazer*, *Biltà di donna*:

> e bianca neve scender senza venti.

---

[27] "to die no wool in either black or sanguine"

The contextual signficance of the borrowing is inverted from the list of the beloved's delights to the terrifying spectacle of the rain of fire; and yet we can, indeed we are compelled—by virtue of the author's typical bivalence between contextual meaning and isolated images—to read Dante's line as an enchanting little excerpt. The homage would be that much more intense if it operated below the threshhold of awareness, since any investigation of structure must preclude the neoclassical myth of conscious clarity as the supposed ideal in literature. Limiting ourselves to cases of blatant intentionality (as can be likely surmised in the prior example) would arbitrarily restrict the selection to a great extent, since the processes of association, assimilation and dissimilation unfold at a speed that, like a driver's reflexes, elude consciousness, whereas their solidity is objectively proved by the repetition and firmness of the relationships. The homage to Cavalcanti's sonnet, for example, is confirmed (in the *Commedia*, that is, leaving aside the conjunctions with the sonnet, *Guido, i' vorrei*) by the taste for enumeration informing the opening tercets of the canto:

> Io vidi già cavalier muover campo...[28]

(This *incipit* troubles many interpreters, and yet it enjoys a considerable contemplative independence, thanks to its position.) Elsewhere (*Purg.* VII, 73), in another enumerative instance, we have:

> Oro e argento fine, cocco e biacca,

which is surely inspired (as Sapegno correctly assumed) by

> oro e argento, azzuro 'n ornamenti.[29]

Such convergence precludes pure chance, just as the echo of Guinizzelli's line,

> Tutti color' di fior', giano e vermiglio,[30]

which Mattalia likens to the moment when Matelda

---

[28] *Inf.* XXII.
[29] Cavalcanti, *Biltà di donna*, line 8.
[30] Guinizzelli, *Io voglio del ver*, line 6. ["All the flowers' colors, yellow and vermillion..."]

> volsesi in su i vermigli e in su i gialli
> fioretti [...],[31]

becomes unquestionable when we realize that Guinizzelli's sonnet, *Io vogli' del ver* (a *plazer* that for its own part influenced the Cavalcanti poem, echoing even the detail of "oro ed azzurro e ricche gioi per dare"), was continually echoed in the *Vita Nuova* canzone, *Donne ch'avete* (as well as the sonnet *Di donne io vidi*).

So far we have been dealing with poetry that we could not call "noble," since the sonnet never reaches beyond a "middling" style. It is, rather, stilnovistic poetry. All the same, it is hardly an accident that the standard of the so-called *ignavi* (sloths, cowards) of Canto III of the *Inferno*,

> [q]uesti sciaurati, che mai non fur vivi, [32]
>
> (these wretches who were never even alive)

reminded a commentator of the *poeti giocosi*,[33] Mario Marti, of another similar banner, the one that Meuccio Tolomei, in one of his less chaste sonnets, applies to his brother, Min Zeppa:

> Tu porti 'l gonfalon degli sciaurati[.]
>
> (You bear the standard of the wretched.)[34]

We note that the term *sciaurati* ("wretched") is by this point typical of the "comic" repertoire. As in Rustico Filippi's "Dio, com' bene le stette a le sciaurate" ("God, how fitting it was for the wretched women").[35] But we can dispense with Marti's reserve and more generally connect this "burlesque/realistic" echo to stilnovismo, as it puts the two vernacular matrices of the *Commedia* on the same level.

---

[31] *Purg.* XXVIII, 55, 56. ([when she] "turned, over the little vermilion and yellow / flowers ...")

[32] Line 64.

[33] The "playful poets," a general term indicating versifiers such as Cecco Angiolieri, Rustico Filippi and other poets of the "low" and comic vein in late-medieval Italy.

[34] From the sonnet, *Per Die, Min Zeppa*, line 12. Cf. *Poeti giocosi del tempo di Dante*, Mario Marti, ed., Milan: Rizzoli, 1956. (Cited in the A.L. Pellegrini translation of this same article, "Philology and Dante Exegesis," *Dante Studies*, no. 87, 1968, note 29, p. 31.)

[35] From the sonnet, *Volete udir vendetta*, line 5.

Let it be added that this sort of research, once called "source research," is supposed to bypass the superfluous aspects of tonal reading in order to arrive at the necessary literal comprehension. What, exactly, does "I' mi sobbarco" (*Purg.* VI, 135) mean? (It should, I hasten to add, be read in context, rhymed with *incarco*, here intended as "weight" or "burden," and not as *incarico*, "charge, responsibility.") Translating it as "I boldly offer myself, without being strictly beholden, to a weighty purpose," is to yield to an odd *petitio principii*: it explains our own method—our Danteanism by now unconscious—instead of the poet's own valid metaphor, now settled and packed away. In a *motetto* of his—a genre even more lowly than "middling"—Cavalcanti expresses his readiness (*pronto*) as an "archer" (*arciere*) with the related *sobarcolato*, which follows *apparecchiato* ("ready," "set"). In the *Ovidio Maggiore*, the Italian Renaissance version of the *Metamorphoses*, such will be a frequent rendering of *subcinctus*. In Dante himself—if he is indeed the Durante who authored *Il Fiore*, as I do not doubt—there is a woman who, to ensnare an enemy, "s'era molto ben sobarcolata."[36] The equivalence of *sobbarcarsi* and *sobbarcolarsi*—if we rule out the links with *barca* and *brachium* that have been suggested—evokes, at its foundation, the word *arcus*, whose plural is *arcora* (from which we obtain, for example, *arcolaio*, or "skein-winder"). Cavalcanti's image therefore appears to be etymologically grounded; what matters to us here, however, is what it means in the present context, that of the *Purgatorio*, where it is equivalent, more or less to the present-day, to "I'll roll up my sleeves" (the better to pull the bow or to wage an act of war or to bear a burden). It is an idiom, therefore, belonging to the same crude category as the itch to be scratched ("grattar dov'è la rogna," *Par.* XVII, 129), the grass kept far from the goat ("...ma lungi fia dal becco l'erba"; *Inf.* XV, 72), and the mutant *bozzacchioni* formed by plums from too much rain (*Par.* XXVII, 126), in keeping with the crude *auctoritates* that Dante does not hesitate to put on the noblest of lips.

And among the stilnovistic echoes there are still those from Dante's own time working in the style. I won't bother to review the fact that, between the "attendite et videte" of the Vulgate Lamentations (I:12) and "guardate e attendete (in what one might call Maestro Adamo's "jeremiad" in *Inf.* XXX, 60), we have "attendete e guardate" in the *Vita Nuova* (VII, line 2). I would rather point out the advantage gained from linking his "peregrini" (in the *Vita*) with the "novo peregrin" (*Purg.* VIII, 4) from the canto that begins *Era già l'ora...*, which,

---

[36] *Il Fiore*, CXXXVI, 10.

appearing at the start of the canto, as with *Io vidi già*, evokes a relatively autonomous scene to be witnessed. And what indeed is this "disio" ("desire") that ends this great opening line? What love is this? It should be read in conjunction with the "dolci amici" of line 3. We see this more clearly, in a general sense, in the sonnet *Deh peregini*, which calls them "pensosi [...] / forse di cosa che non v'è presente" (with *cosa* meaning "*creature*"; line 2); they become explicit in the prose explication to the poem, where Dante writes: "for they perhaps are thinking of their faraway friends, whom we do not know." Given this prose translation, we can see already how the poem in the *Vita Nuova* nuances it; and then the *Commedia* intensifies the dissolve. We must recognize how, by shifting the reference to "faraway friends," then suppressing it altogether in "disio" and "amore," Dante has objectively sidetracked both towards the by now commonplace—and in itself anachronistic—implication of "nostaglia," just as the elision of the object turns the verb from transitive into intransitive.

As the hotbed of future cultural positions that he is, Dante here actually appears dedicated to that creatively suggestive linguistic approach where the general allows the imagination to spread out, ultimately to infinity. It is a procedure that Romanticism famously exploited, to the point that the best description we have of it is in Leopardi. De Sanctis himself leans on it in his exegesis of Dante. (And it is in fact what gives us a handle on the "downside" of the Preraphaelites and on literary mysticism in general, all the way down to D'Annunzio and beyond.) The method for arriving at this theorem is diachronic; and yet with the tonal description, we are entirely in the synchronic sphere. And thus we recognize that the metaphor of the two linguistics (if indeed there are only two) was not at all heterogeneous. An act of hermeneutic erudition influences an act of present-day reading. I do not deny the break in continuity, but merely find it reduced to a minimum: to that measure of variation within which even modern evolutionary science, I suppose, recognized the "freedom" of nature. The interaction of commentary and reading has become increasingly dense.

So here we are in an area of research with exclusively internal parameters—where, were an external point of reference to intervene, its import would be purely didactic and negative. For example, Saint Francis's line

> Tue so' le laude, la gloria e l'honore[37]

---

[37] Compare also Virgil's "HONOS NOMENque tuum LAUDESque manebunt." (My emphasis.) The spontaneous orderiing of the three nouns can also be found in the Vulgate Revelations: "*gloriam*

is clearly inspired by the *"omnis honor et gloria"* which *Per ipsum* doxology pays to the Almighty, and by the end of the Canon of Consecration, and even moreso by the hexameter line that opens the hymn of triumph for Palm Sanday, *Gloria, laus et honor tibi sit, rex Christe redemptor"*. Thus in that one line we have an entire fluvial system whose tributaries, so to speak, Dante has reconstituted and separated, assigning *gloria* to God, *onore* to humanity, the *lode* (praise) to the mediation towards God. In the face of Francis's theological fundamentalism—if I may be allowed the qualification—we have the discerning worldliness of the Dante of the *Commedia*: *"unicuique suum."* The *gloria* is precisely "la gloria de Colui che tutto move" ("the glory of Him who moves all"; *Par.* I, 1)—leaving aside those cases where *gloria* is the substantive corresponding to the verb *gloriarsi* ("to glory, to be proud, to boast"): "ch'alcuna gloria i rei avrebber d'elli" ("as the wicked would have glory over them"; *Inf.* III, 42). The *onore* is so-called worldly glory, though we might better speak here of fame— "la fama, che la vostra casa onora" ("the fame that honors your house"; *Purg.* VIII, 124); "l'onrata nominanza" ("honored renown," *Inf.* IV, 76)—especially that conferred upon artists. The poet's is the "nome che piú dura e piú onora" ("the name most lasting and most honored"; *Purg.* XXI, 85); "Onorate l'altissimo poeta" ("Honor the loftiest of poets"; *Inf.* IV, 80), proclaims the voice that greets Virgil, whereupon the latter admits: "fannomi onore, e di ciò fanno bene" ("they do me honor, and they are right to do so"; line 93). He will, of course, later suggest to the souls in Purgatory, in regard to Dante, "faccianli onore, ed esser può lor caro" ("let them do him honor, as this may benefit them"; *Purg.* V, 36), since of course Dante is a poet too.[38] Note the point of junction in the "vana gloria de l'umane posse" ("vain glory of human powers"; *Purg.* XI, 91), that precarious and therefore contradictory, almost ironic "gloria della lingua" (ll. 98-99) that one Guido (Cavalcanti) took from another Guido (Guinizzelli), a glory which, in the latter, is even fleeting and therefore rather a "fama [...] oscura" (line 96), like that of Cimabue. There follows a wondrous, iridescent

---

et honorem et benedictionem" (IV, 9), cited here because of Francis's later "benedictione," in more extended series in V, 12 ff.), "gloriam et honorem et virtutem." (IV 11) (GC)

[38] The lines here cited are only mild samples of the honor reserved for Virgil at the start of the great poem: "O de li altri poeti onore e lume," wellspring of the *bello stile* that "ha fatto onore" to Dante, "parlare onesto / ch'onora te e quei ch'udito l'hanno" (the reflection on Dante's colleagues is comparable to that of beauty on other women), "tutti onor li fanno" (which follows the series of "orrevol gente," "onori scienzia ed arte," "cotanta onranza," etc.) Whereby "e piú d'onore [...] mi fenno" to Dante too. (GC)

cascade of synonyms: "il mondan romore" (line 100); the "voce" (line 103); "la vostra nominanza" (line 115).

As for the *lode* (praise), Beatrice is "loda di Dio vera" ("true praise of God"; *Inf.* II, 103). Beatrice here is brought unto her true purpose, as one who surpasses and bears the truth, she who was the object of the lyrics of praise in the theologico-hagiographical parody that is the *Vita Nuova* (according to the excellent thesis of Alfredo Schiaffini). A quick glance at the rhyme indexes confirms the spread of this notion across the whole schema: *gloria* figures in several rhymes in the *Paradiso*; in the *Purgatorio* (X, 74) we find "l'alta gloria / del roman principato" ("the lofty glory / of the Roman prince") paying homage to Trajan, *naturaliter Christianus*. One should even "dar lode" ("give praise"; *Inf.* VII, 92) to Fortune, God's "general ministra" (l. 78). Such, roughly sketched, is the picture we gain from the Concordances. A line such as Petrarch's "Stiamo, Amor, a veder la gloria nostra" ("So, Love, do we gaze upon our glory"; *Canzoniere*, CXCII), is an un-Dantean as one could possibly imagine.

The constants followed when one sets out to "explain Dante through Dante" may also lead to better verification of the literal meaning. I will cite one instance of punctuation—that is, of the intonation and separation of clauses—in another famous passage, the one featuring Cavalcante de' Cavalacanti's shock, which in the standard version of the text goes as follows:

> Di subito drizzato gridò: "Come
> dicesti? elli ebbe? non viv'elli ancora?
> non fiere li occhi suoi il dolce lume?"[39]

(Here I read *lume* instead of the late and erroneous *lome*, which I am happy to say has finally been firmly corrected by Natalino Sapegno.) *Come dicesti*, when read together without a pause, reads not unlike "Come degnasti d'accedere al monte?" (*Purg.* XXX, 74). In other connections as well, *come* is highly susceptible to enjambment, hardly surprising when we consider, for example, the way the poet breaks up *Ave / Maria* at the end of a line (*Par.* III, 121-122), or the way *Quando* is severed at the line break at the start of a speech ("Quando / mi diparti' da Circe..."; *Inf.* XXVI, 91) once in each *cantica*. Yet the other two times that

---

[39] *Inf.* X, 67-69. With the punctuation as presented here, it translates as: "Suddenly straightening, he cried: 'What / did you say? 'he had?' does he live no more? / does the sweet light no longer strike his eyes?" The Singleton translation, for example (Princeton U. Press, 1970), uses the punctuation preferred by Contini.

come appears in rhyme as an interrogative adverb, it is syntactically autonomous. If we set aside the exception of "[...] e se volesse alcun dire 'Come?'" (*Purg.* XIII, 101), Virgil's exhortation before wall of fire (*Purg.* XXVII, 43-44) becomes decisive:

> Ond'ei crollò la fronte e disse: "Come!
> volenci star di qua?" [...][40]

The parallel between the two passages is entirely homologous to the movement likening Virgil's "Volgiti: che fai?" ("Turn round: what are you doing?") in this same Farinata canto (*Inf.* X, 31) to Matelda's "Surgi: che fai?" ("Arise: what are you doing?"; *Purg.* XXXII, 72). This leads us—of necessity, I would say—to read the first *Come* also as an exclamation, and thus to insert punctuation after it, basically in keeping with Mario Casella's reading:[41]

> [...] "Come?
> dicesti 'elli ebbe': non viv'elli ancora?"[42]

Cavalcante has understood perfectly. He merely hesitates, and not for very long, before the inference to be drawn.

Naturally, however, explicating Dante with Dante involves primarily word choices and syntagmata. *Atro*, for example, carries no connotation of blackness or darkness, but only grimness and filth: Dante's cheeks become *atre* with tears, as opposed to "nette di rugiada" ("clean with dew"; *Purg.* XXX, 54); Cerberus's "barba unta e atra" ("oily, dirty beard"; *Inf.* VI, 16) is made colorless (i.e., not black) by virtue of the fact that it follows "occhi vermigli" in the same line. The word's semantic range should be identified with that implied in Cleopatra's "subitana e atra" death, which we find prefigured (for the most part featuring the same rhymes, of course) in the *petrosa* canzone *Così nel mio parlar*: "[...] poi non mi sarebb' atra / la morte [...]." If all these meanings could be summed up by translating the term as "regrettable," it might justify the use of a word in a manner more suggestive than representative, since on the one hand it carries a Latinizing preciosity—in Horace death is *atra*, poison is *atrum*, the "Cura" is *atra*)—and on other, it is phonetically evocative.

---

[40] "Whereupon he frowned and said: What! / do we wish to stay on this side?"

[41] And now Petrocchi as well (who also reads *lume*). (GC)

[42] Thus: "What? / you said: 'he had': does he live no more?"

Only Dante's echoes of himself avail in coaxing forth the precise implications of a particularly pregnant locution. In a commentary by Daniele Mattalia, which I praised above, the overlapping of the "mente che non erra" (*Inf.* II, 6) with Livy "che non erra" (*Inf.* XXVIII, 12),[43] implies that the phrase *non erra* is, so to speak, Dante's privately technical formula for indicating historical precision. That is, he declares through linguistic inference his own attributes as not only a prophetic visionary but indeed as a historian. And when the bearing of Rizzardo da Camino, who "va con la testa alta" ("walks with head held high"; *Par.* IX, 50, in rhyme), repeats that of the lion, who comes "con la testa alta" (*Inf.* I, 47) (at the start of a line—that is, at a rhythmically differerent "demarcating" juncture), it highlights an analogy epitomizing pride. Nor can I say, really, whether there is any implication, in the first line of the tercet on the Veltro (the "Hound"), as to its identity in the assertion that the animal "non ciberà terra né peltro" ("will eat neither earth nor pelf"; *Inf.* I, 103), as this line anticipates "non curar d'argento né d'affanni" ("caring neither for silver nor for troubles"; *Par.* XVII, 84), which is said in regard to Cangrande. I would add that in all of its behavior, from beginning to end, the Veltro proves curiously quite similar to the Phoenix, which "erba né biada in sua vita non pasce" ("feeds on neither grass nor grain"; *Inf.* XXIV, 109).

It is strange, on the other hand, that the interpretation of "miser" has prevailed, from Francesco Buti[44] down to the moderns, for "quei che volentieri acquista, / e giugne 'l tempo che perder lo face" ("he who so delights in winning, / then the time comes for him to lose"; *Inf.* I, 55-56). This is utterly unlike the representation of the miser in Dante, from *Doglia mi reca* to the *Commedia*; the language, in fact, alludes to the gambler. We are reminded of "colui che perde," (*Purg.* VI, 2), the man who loses at *zara*[45] and how he behaves. (Coming at the start of a line, the words "colui che perde" here stand in contrast with another simile of competition, if not gaming, that concerning the Palio of Verona, at *Inf.* XV, 124.) Dante is the man who has "gambled" his salvation, or suddenly sees it at stake.

The aura surrounding the semantic grid concerns specifically the question of the polysemy mentioned above. We see it in action in one of Dante's most leg-

---

[43] Same in the *Fiore* (CXII 4), also at the end of a line: "se·llo scritto [i.e., Scripture] non erra"; also, Rose 2989, "*se la lettre ne ment*." (GC)

[44] L'Ottimo Fiorentino has no doubts: "Questa similitudine è chiara." (GC)

[45] A medieval game of chance played with three dice.

endarily enigmatic lines, that of the "pie' fermo" (the "firm foot"; *Inf.* I, 30). The young Italian-American scholar, John Freccero, has come up with an excellent twofold discovery in this regard, as presented in a prestigious theological publication, *The Harvard Theological Review*.[46] In a compendium of Aristotelian physiology, Albertus Magnus writes that "*pes* [...] *sinister stabilior et firmior est*";[47] Patristic doctrine, moreover, concerning "*pedes interiores*" (thus Saint Ambrose), specifies that "*Duos pedes habet anima, intellectum, scilicet et affectum.*"[48] These and other highly relevant quotations lead Freccero to formulate a pointed hypothesis, one which moreover assumes the absurdity of the literal meaning and exclusively favors the allegorical one. To say it with Croce: "One finds oneself in a wood that is not a wood, one sees a hill that is not a hill, one gazes at a sun that is not the sun, and one encounters three wild beasts that are and are not wild beasts." And to this list one could add the feet that are not feet. Yet what combinations of words and images in Dante are associated with feet and walking? Freccero cites *Paradiso* V, 5-6, where the

> perfetto veder, che, come apprende,
> cosí nel bene appreso move il piede[.][49]

This image rather closely follows the oft-quoted one in Bonaventure: "*Unus pes animae est motus apprehensivus, alter motus appetitivus.*"[50] Yet two other passages say considerably more. First we have the analogous slowing down of the vision whereby Mahomet (*Inf.* XXVII, 61, 63):

> l'un piè per girsene sospese,
> [...]
> indi a partirsi in terra lo distese;[51]

---

[46] "Dante's firm foot and the Journey without a Guide," by John Freccero, *Harvard Theological Review*, LII, 1959, pp. 245-281.

[47] "...the left foot ... is firmer and stabler..."

[48] "...inner feet..."; "The soul has two feet, intellect, of course, and emotion."

[49] ("[P]erfect sight, which as it learns, / moves the foot into the goodness learned".) Compare this, I would add, to "Là su non eran mossi i piè nostri anco" ("Neither had our feet yet moved on it"; *Purg.* X, 28). (GC)

[50] "One foot of the soul is the movement of learning for the other..."

[51] "he raised one foot to go / [...] / then set it on the ground to leave."

then we have the advice Virgil gives in *Purgatorio* (IV, 37-38) when asked "che via faremo" ("what road shall we take"):

> "Nessun tuo passo caggia:
> pur su al monte dietro a me acquista [...]"

> ("No step of yours must descend:
> but up the hill behind me win its way [...]")

When applied to our passage, which features many of them, these constants of language and image show us that Dante breaks up the representation of walking and is concerned with its purpose, whether or not one advances along the road. Dante here sets out on his way again ("ripresi via", *Inf.* I, 29), without proceeding upwards yet without descending either, finding himself more or less on level ground, on the "piaggia" ("shore, strand") that lies before the "cominciar de l'erta" ("beginning of the slope"; line 31), where Isaiah's other beasts await him. (We might recall here what the bestiaries say about the lion, as in one Tuscan edition: that "the other nature the lion posesses is that when he is at the top of the mountain, he may descend into the valley with great force."[52]) That such a declaration by Dante is, for Freccero, "a tautology if not an absurdity," seems all the less necessary as it does not compromise the allegorical equation presented, that *affectus* is not proportionate to *intellectus*. Dante, in other words, is taking a cautious step towards approaching the foot of the hill.

At the other extreme, our examination concerns the literal meaning in and of itself. I am referring to those points, of which we've already encountered several, that break up the smooth surface of Dante's text and make it appear as though non-exhaustive, ceding to suggestions I am quick to call irrational, just as the "creak" in the literal meaning alerted us to the presence of another meaning lurking behind it.

Here is another famous line (*Inf.* V, 126), not unlike the one still on Francesca's lips:

> dirò come colui che piange e dice.[53]

> (I will tell as one who weeps and tells.)

---

[52] M.S. Garver, K. McKenzie, eds., "Il bestiario toscano secondo la lezione dei codici di Parigi e di Londra," in *Studi romanzi* VIII, 1912, 1-100, p. 33. (Footnote in *Dante Studies*, cit.)

[53] One variant has (the easier) *farò* in the place of *dirò*. (GC) [The translation is Singleton's.]

Clearly lying at the center of the process is a binomial related to a single verb, as in Ugolino's frank zeugma: "parlare e lacrimar vedrai insieme"[54] ("you'll see speaking and weeping together"; *Inf.* XXXIII, 9). At the far end of the series of such cases—featuring among others the even more heterogeneous binomial (also marked by the word *inseme*) of Pier della Vigna: "usciva inseme / parole e sangue" ("there issued, together / words and blood"; *Inf.* XIII, 43-44), where *usciva*, coming as it does at the start of the statement, and since it is singular, becomes impersonal, like *pluit sanguine* or *sanguinem*—we find anomalous articulations of speech with irregular pneuma, such as in the case of the splintered tree trunk ("per vento che va via"; line 42), and at the tip of Ulysses's flame ("cui vento affatica"; *Inf.* XXVI, 87).[55] Here, at least, the binomial in no way serves the basically ornamental function, however emphatic, of the customary iteration of synonyms such as we find in abundance in manuals of style; rather, it designates a critical state. Think, for example—though the wording here is far less paradoxical— of the apparition of a reproachful Beatrice (*Purg.* XXX, 72):

> continuò come colui che dice
> e 'l piú caldo del parlar dietro riserva;

> (she continued as one who speaks
> but holds the hottest speech in reserve;)

We also have, moreover, the instance of "stetti come l'uom che teme" ("I stood there like the man who fears"; *Inf.* XIII, 45). Caught in this web of morphological comparisons, Francesca's line better reveals the rarity, in Dante, of his formula of "fare come chi fa [in variant A] ("to do as one who does"); and *fa'* [variant B], where *fare* is an algebraic symbol of the concrete verb, though substituted even in its initial and summary variant by variant B. In other words, Francesca keeps a distance from direct expression ("piangerò e dirò," *at the same time*, in other words) in order to recompose the act in a paradigm. It is a semantically "empty" procedure that D'Annunzio surely recalled, while more visibly "filling it up," when he wrote:

---

[54] The normal, non-paradoxical behavior would be that of Guido del Duca in *Purg.* XIV, 124-125: "Ma va via, Tosco, omai; ch'or mi diletta / troppo di pianger piú che di parlare." ["But go away now, Tosco, for I enjoy / weeping too much more than speaking."] (GC)

[55] Similary not too remote from this is the phenomenology of Dante's pained reply to Beatrice (*Purg.* XXX, 85-99; XXXI, 13-15). (GC)

> ti loderò come si loda il volto
> di colei che sul nostro cuor s'inclina.[56]
>
> ("I will praise you as one praises the face
> of her o'er whom our hearts bow down.")

In Francesca's case, a description of the verbal field still served to bring out the oddity of the example. Shortly before Beatrice continues her statement of reproach, we find, among her first words, the following (*Purg.* XXX, 56):

> non pianger anco, non pianger ancora;

The line oozes with grammatical nonsense. And its daring, possibly mistaken for awkwardness, explains why it has never become one of the better known lines. Might it be a threat? The line that follows runs "ché pianger ti conven per altra spada."[57] Yet it's a cry of affection, and it begins with her calling him by name: Dante, a name "che di necessità qui si registra" (line 63).[58] The phonic structure already speaks volumes: *anco* and *ancora* are synonyms too obvious, too close to being identical, for their juxtaposition—halfway between repetition and variation—not to appear extremely strange, with only the slightest alteration of the syllabic and accentual mass allowing the uneven verse line to be broken into two halves as equally as possible. It is a phonosymbolically arranged sob, expressing sympathy with the person being reproached while persisting in, and insisting on, the necessity of the reproach.

And so our typological excursion comes up against a boundary wall, where verbal criticism is no longer distinct from what was once called "aesthetic analysis" and which is, perhaps, just plain criticism with no qualifying adjective. If the road leading us to this point has seemed a bit long, the essence of this commentator's apologia will always be that the immense scope of Dantean hermeneutics are a candid homage rendered in kind to the fertility of the material commented upon. To the object glossed goes all the merit of invention, when there is any; but since its effect is not exactly to clip the wings of the imagination, in all fairness we must also lay some responsibility for some of

---

[56] Quote from "Ferrara, Pisa, Ravenna," ll. 2-3, in *Le città del silenzio*.

[57] Together they translate, more or less, as "Weep not now, weep not yet; / for you would better weep for another sword."

[58] A name "that is recorded here of necessity."

the glossatory excess on it, too. Reversing the well-known adage, we can well say that "*quidquid recipitur*" inflicts some of its form upon the "*recipiens*."[59] Though sometimes distorted and aberrant, even the least vigilant hermeneutics attest, through a kind of analogy, not, alas, to the brilliance of the object, but to its richness.

[From *Rendiconti delle Adunanze solenni*, of the Accademia dei Lincei, volume VII, fascicle I.]

---

[59] Aquinas: *Quidquid recipitur ad modum recipientis recipitur*: "Whatever is received is received in the manner of the receiver."

Cavalcanti in Dante

Giovanni Mardersteig[1] has chosen to honor the Dante centennial with an edition of Guido Cavalcanti. As a kind of proxy for him, I have assumed the role, in this brief appearance, of justifying his undertaking.

If Dante's so-called stilnovistic phase is indeed primarily of Cavalcantian derivation, the shadow and thought of Cavalcanti accompany him to the very end of a career not only inseparable from its origins, but during which he continued to resettle his accounts with the patron of his first years as a poet. (I say *re*-settle because, as peremptory as the author customarily is, they had already been, or seemed, definitively settled.) Cavalcanti's presence hovers over the *Commedia* in a manner all the more disturbing as it is indirect: disturbing for posterity, that is, not for the writer, whose silences, reticences, obscurities and ambiguities are as ironclad as everything else. Having passed away in the dead zone (less than five months) after the start of the imaginary journey, Guido misses the final verdict, and misses the prophecies as well; and there is not even any need to point out that it all seems prearranged (not the exact date, of course, but the idea of the damned being farsighted) so that the younger poet would not have to judge him explicitly. This, in itself, is a revealing clue as to the importance Dante assigns to his former "first friend." There is no point in speculating (even though he did, after all, pose the question of Guido's salvation) whether Dante would have let him benefit from grace (but then why so much evasiveness?) and in which circle, of Hell or Purgatory, he would have placed him. Where indeed to put Guido, the contemplator of death by metaphor, the pessimistic, saturnine poet of loves half-alive, in a gap or limbo suspending the great rapport with the afterlife revolving around his avoided earthly end?

---

[1] Giovanni Mardersteig (1892-1977) was a German-born naturalized Italian publisher, printer, and author.

(While the naïve reader's impression is that the Epicurianism of Cavalcante de' Cavalcanti fades away in the son, about whom similar references circulate, reliable testimonies exist as to Guido's irascibility and, more authoritatively, his taste for sodomy, another apanage of the "litterati grandi e di gran fama" (*Inf.* XV, 107). Almost all of the leading figures of the Florentine ruling class before Dante—men he admired in any case: Farinata, Cavalcante, Jacopo Rusticucci, il Tegghiaio, Brunetto Latini, et al.—were worldly men, *esprits forts*, "libertines" in the seventeenth-century sense of the word.)

Both Cavalcantian passages in the *Commedia*—and not only the tortured, well-known one—enclose a temporal crux. When Odirisi says "ha tolto" (*Purg.* X1, 97), referring to Cavalcanti's borrowing from Guinizzelli (nuancing the prior stanza, beginning "Cimabue credette," where the latter, believing he "held the field," Giotto "ora ha il grido"), he implies that, at the moment in time when the speech concludes—that is, during Cavalcanti's lifetime, most probably still during the drafting of the *Purgatorio*—the latter Guido's supremacy is still in effect (a supremacy, therefore, extending at the very least to the stilnovistic Dante as well and to the *Vita Nuova*). A courteous *forse* qualifies the assertion that "è nato / chi l'uno e l'altro caccerà dal nido" ("is born / the one who will drive both [Guidos] from the nest"; ll. 98-99); and *caccerà* to all appearances seems to be alluding to the *Commedia*, not to Dante's *canzoni morali*.

It is scarcely negligible that the *Commedia* contains no other praise of Cavalcanti, as the recognition of "paternity" is renewed for Guinizzelli—in the latter's vocative (*Purg.* XXVI, 115) to a Guittone mistreated by both Cavalcanti and Dante—having the "nove rime" begin with *Donne ch'avete*, further citing *Amor che ne la mente* (possibly for merely personal reasons). Cavalcanti, also a "son," is anonymously implied among the "others" of Dante's "betters."[2]

What, furthermore, is concretely meant by the "gloria della lingua" (*Purg.* XI, 98), in as much as it tabs Cavalcanti over Guinizzelli, can be found in the facts. One need only compare, in their similar parts, Cavalcanti's sonnets *Avete 'n vo'*, *Biltà di donna*, *Chi è questa*, *L'anima mia*, *Tu m'hai si piena*, with Guinizzelli's *Io vogli' del ver*, *Lo vostro bel saluto*, and even *Dolente, lasso*. Guinizzelli:

---

[2] The passage here alluded to contains, among other things, the famous phrase "il miglior fabbro" ("the better craftsman"), made famous to English-speaking readers by T.S. Eliot in his dedication of *The Waste Land* to Pound.

> e ciò ch'é lassú bello a lei somiglio.
>
> Verde river' a lei rasembro e l'âre,
> tutti color' di fior', giano e vermiglio,
> oro e azzurro e ricche gioi per dare.

Cavalcanti:

> Avete 'n vo' li fior' e la verdura
> e ciò che luce ed è bello a vedere;

and:

> rivera d'acqua e prato d'ogni fiore;
> oro, argento, azzurro 'n ornamenti[.]   [variant: oro *e* argento]

Guinizzelli:

> Per li occhi passa come fa lo trono,
> che [...]
> ciò che dentro trova spezza e fende:
>
> remagno come statüa d'otono,
> ove vita né spirito non ricorre,
> se non che la figura d'omo rende.

Cavalcanti:

> Per li occhi venne la battaglia in pria,
> che ruppe ogni valore immantenente[;]

and:

> I' vo come colui ch'è fuor di vita,
> che pare, a chi lo sguarda, ch'omo sia
> fatto di rame o di pietra o di legno.³

---

³ Basic translations of the above poetry quotes are as follows: Guinizzelli: "To the beauty up above I will liken you. / To the green riverbanks and air I compare you, / and to the colors of all flowers, yellow and vermilion, / gold and azure and fine jewels to bestow." Cavalcanti: "You have in you flowers and verdure / and all that shines and is lovely to behold"; and: "watery streams and meadows blooming with every flower; gold, silver, azure for ornament." Guinizzelli: "Through the

The brilliant analogical method of the founder ("somiglio," "rasembro") maintains the two poles around an implied simile, whereas Cavalcanti merges and unifies ("Avete 'n vo'"); and there remains in the former a rough, external reality ("statüa d'otono"), which recedes and inverts into Cavalcanti's equalization of realities ("di rame o di pietra o di legno"). Cavalcanti encloses and perfects things within the limitations of internal analysis alone, conveying movement and drama like Chinese shadows of hypostasis (he was in fact praised as a natural philosopher—in other words, a psychologist). The perfecting and enclosing occur on the level of conventional terminology as well.

The Guinizzelli-Cavalcanti connection is thus established as a target re-echoed twice in the *Commedia*. Indeed the opening of one of its enumerative verses (which then wondrously takes off tangentially)—"Oro e argento fine, cocco e biacca" ("Gold and fine silver, cochineal and ceruse"; *Purg.* VII, 73)—stays fairly close to the Cavalcantian version, and from one entirely new entry in the same *Biltà di donna* ("e bianca neve scender senza venti") ["and white snow falling windless"], Dante in fact derives his own "come di neve in alpe sanza vento" ["like snow upon windless mountains"; *Inf.* XIV, 30]. Let us pause here for a moment, traumatized by the effect of the transformation. Just as "cocco e biacca," the first of a series of new brushstrokes, earlier erupted from the plain of reminiscences in Fauvist smudges, so here the spectacle is attenuated and softened, all but the most succinct elements dismissed—"bianca" and "scender," which are implicit in "neve"—as the pregnant (and enclosing) circumstance, "in alpe," is added. But the most important addition—for the purposes of softening, of quieting (even the first accent in the line is dampened), so that even so little as an echo cannot escape the mountainous isolation—is the word "come"; which, if we bring it back from its rhythmic function to its semantic literalness, reintroduces the customary paradoxical autonomy of Dantean reality through analogy. Never mind that, in the face of Cavalcanti's intellectualism, so rigorous in its abstract equalization of natural data, one may speak here of a return to Guinizzelli. The fact certainly remains that Dante, as we have observed, does go back to Guinizzelli, indeed concretely rebutting his incipient abstraction through "i

---

eyes it [your greeting] passes as does the thunder / that [...] / splits and shatters what is inside; / I am left as a statue of brass / through which passes no life or spirit / but renders an image of the man." Cavalcanti: "Through the eyes came the battle like a pyre, / shattering all valor forthwith"; and: "I go as one outside of life, / who seems, to those who look upon him, to be a man / made of copper or stone or wood."

vermigli" and "gialli / fioretti" of Matelda (*Purg.* XXVIII, 55-56). (Those who have read Charles Bally will recall the linguistic contrast of the realistic "*colonnes blanches*" with the Impressionistic, Symbolist "*blancheur de colonnes.*")

But Dante, moreover, did not wait until the *Commedia* to take this course. Lining up nicely with *Io vogli' del ver* is Cavalcanti's essential *Chi è questa che vèn*—essential not only because in it we glimpse a summit of "pre-Raphaelitesque" visualization ("fa tremar di chiaritate l'âre"; "…makes the air quiver with brightness"),[4] but also ideologically essential, because it reconsolidated, somewhat ritually and religiously, the doctrine of feminine sublimation through the imitation of biblical language. The emulation displays itself in the periodically regular assumption of rhymes and words in rhyme from the model used. Such, indeed, is the template for Dante's sonnet *Di donne io vidi*: for its weave of alternating rhymes (Cavalcanti uses twice *abba*, then *cde edc*), and even more so for the conceit of the tercets, which borrow some of the latter's rhyme words, but with a clear Guinizzellian inclination (Dante's "A chi … donava salute" comes from Guinizzelli's "a cui dona salute"). And on the trail of *Io vogli' del ver* we enter into the very heart of the *Vita Nuova* through the canzone *Donne ch'avete*, which is threaded with the counterpoint of *gentile / vile* (and at the center is the woman who goes "per via") and preeminently heads the list of the lyric poems of praise (*la lode*). Note that Guinizzelli's opening line concludes with "la mia donna laudare," whereas neither *laudare* nor any of its close relatives (except for an insignificant *ragione laudata*) appear in Cavalcanti's lexicon. The same is true for the drastic *trono*, which is excluded from Cavalcanti; indeed the simile "come (fa) lo trono" ["as (does) the thunder"] (which "fere" ["harms"] in *Lo vostro bel saluto* and in *Dolente, lasso*, and in the former also "spezza e fende" ["shatters and splits"]), bursts out again, no less, in *Amor che ne la mente* ("e rompon come trono"; "and [they] break like thunder"). And of course we know how the *Commedia* will then overflow with *loda* and *trono*. Following directly on the heels of *Donne ch'Avete* in the *Vita Nuova* is *Amore e 'l cor gentil*, with its famous evocation of the "saggio" and "suo dittare."[5] Dante's own homage to Guinizzelli's "paternity" thus never suffered any eclipse or intermittences.

---

[4] Giorgio Petrocchi now believes he has found the imprint of this in "l'aere ne tremesse" (*Inf.* I, 48) (but linked of course with even the classical *tremere* "temere"—of Salimbene, for example: "*ita tremebant eum* [Ezzelino] *omnes, sicut tremit iuncus in aqua.*") (GC)

[5] The title of the latter poem alone invokes the precedent of Guinizzelli's *Al cor gentil rempaira sempre amore*.

But now, from the crystal-clear Oderisi episode, we backtrack to the shadowy Cavalcante de' Cavalcanti encounter (*Inf.* X, 52-72), whose arduousness is in no way alleviated by its popularization (which, if anything, is limited to clouding with a light veiling whatever polemical and sentimental content there is in the invention: i.e., that, unlike the unflappable Farinata degli Uberti, father-in-law of his son Guido, Cavalcante is afflicted, and punished for weakness and fatherly blindness; he's a Cacciaguida gone bad.) Not alleviated, and certainly not set to rest by the commentators. Let it suffice, on the matter of this disputed passage, for the present author to refer to the preselected propositions: *cui* as a direct object of *ebbe a disdegno* (line 63), with no implied infinitive; *cui* as not only a relative pronoun (that is, referring to *colui*, Virgil), but also as containing within itself "one who" (meaning, in the context, that it refers to Beatrice, not to God, where the first guide cannot go); *forse* (same line), as in the previous illustration, as a mere attenuation for the sake of courtesy (comparable to *quasi*, "more or less, if I may say so") to be linked not with *mena* (line 62) but with *ebbe*. And the Beatrice under discussion here is not the living one (whereby any form of support would be missing), but the dead one, hailed in glory and bearing hidden meanings—in other words, conforming to the metaphorical poetics reflected in the *Vita Nuova*, which at the time Dante and Cavalcanti were still in agreement about: "and yet what great shame would come to one who poetized on matters under the garments of metaphor [*figura*] or rhetorical color, and then, when asked, might not know how to strip his words of such garments, on the assumption that they bore true meaning. And this first friend and I know well who are those that poetize so inanely."[6]

Dante is making this declaration in reference to the representation of Amore in the sonnet *Io mi senti' svegliar*, which confirms not only the solidarity between Guido and Dante, but also that between "monna Vanna and monna Bice," who are promoted to Spring and Love, respectively. "Amore non è per sé sí come sustanzia, ma è uno accidente in sustanzia" ("Love is not in itself as like a substance, but is an accident in substance.") So saying, Dante is echoing—no doubt intentionally, the initial definition given in Cavalcanti's *Donna me prega*: "un accidente – che sovente – è fero" ("an accident – that often – is fierce"). To say that the *Vita Nuova*, that sort of letter or memorial to Guido, is already already straying from Cavalcantian orthodoxy, would not be easy to justify.

---

[6] From *Vita Nuova*, XXV, 10.

The hagiographic transformation is a perfect corollary to the religious, and thus metaphorical, mimesis instituted by Cavalcanti (since Guinizzelli's undertaking stopped at the notion of the lady who brings salvation, upon which Cavalcanti, after having further explored, in *Chi è questa*, the question of *"salute"* ["salvation," "well-being"] in its connection with that of insufficient *"canoscenza"* ["knowledge"], himself ceases to insist). In all probability, with Beatrice's death and inchoate life *post mortem*, the *Vita Nuova* had reached its limit (for his part Cavalcanti, unlike almost all of his confrères, speaks of death only in tropes and, more generally, speaks of his own imagined death): Dante does not write "de la sua partita da noi" ("of her departure from us"; *VN* XXVIII), because "ciò non è del presente proposito" ("that is not part of the present purpose"). The "mirabile visione" dictates that further treatment of the matter be postponed to a hoped-for better time. The limit is marked by the double meaning of the "senso allegorico," such as it is invoked in the *Convivio*, in keeping with "lo modo de li poeti," by which this critical work abides, and in keeping with that of the theologians as well—which is no longer the case in the letter to Cangrande.

If my conjecture is well-founded, if the divorce from Cavalcanti is tied to the transferral of Beatrice from poetry to theology, the essence of the polemic—which is gnoseological as much as it is literary—would nevertheless not change, no matter how we translated *cui*: whether Virgil, or even God. Concerning Cavalcanti's "disdegno" for Virgil, even on literary terms, many correct things were said a while back that maintain their value even today, now that such a grammatical interpretation has lost its currency. They merely deserve to be refreshed, like all correct things said a while back. In the *Vita Nuova*, Dante does not transcribe his (naturally Latin) epistle to the "princes of the earth" over the death of Beatrice, because his plan was to write only in Italian. "And I know that my first friend, to whom I dedicate this writing, had the same intention, that is, that I write them only in the vernacular." ("E simile intenzione so ch'ebbe questo mio primo amico a cui io ciò scrivo, cioè ch'io li scrivessi solamente volgare" [*VN*, XXX].)

Cavalcanti therefore encouraged this unprecedented experiment of *prosimetrum* in the Italian language, but he also displayed a stylistic hostility to Latin that is flagrant in his work, at least in the sense that the ancient tongue is totally extraneous to it. On his bookshelf, aside from the *canzonieri* of prior vernacular poets, a psaltery, and Andreas Cappellanus (Cavalcanti seems to take even Ovid rather lightly, to judge from a sonnet to Guido Orlandi), we find only a few manuals of philosophy with all their excessive jargon, which nevertheless remains on this side (or that) of style and hence a tool befitting an ironic muse. Well, Dante, at his apex, had to reconcile the melodiousness of Guido's even, sober, everyday language (however much the latter was, it must be said, also prone to technicalisms and to insertion into elliptical contexts) with the violence of "realism" (one not lacking the endorsement of some minor participation on the part of Cavalcanti and Guinizzelli as well) and above all with the density of meaning, mass, and volume (which one might even call "cubist") of Latin verse, especially that of Virgil. (At this point one can only fantasize what a meeting of a reader of Persius Flaccus and Juvenal with Lucretius would have been like.) Dante's emulative condensation is greatest in the *auctoritates* he translates ("torna Giustizia e primo tempo umano"[7]; *Purg.* XXII, 71); and Cavalcanti, in an exceptional case, undoubtedly gains a similar decisiveness in his grand canzone, *Donna me prega*:

> Non già selvagge – le bieltà son dardo,
> ché tal volere – per temere – è sperto.
> [...]
> For di colore, d'essere diviso,
> Assiso – 'n mezzo scuro, luce rade[8]

Indeed the poem earns a prominent spot in the catalogue of the most intensely "Cézannian" compositions from Homer to Pasternak or Garcia Lorca. Examined more closely, however, *Donna me prega*, beyond its apparent formalistic power (which in Cavalcanti seems alternatively to break out in certainly spontaneous alliterative sequences such as "piacente primavera, / per prata e per rivera"; "chi vo' non vede, ma' non po' valere"; "di grande sua pietate piangeria" and other countless instances), displays something rather different from Dante's linear concentration ("mestier non era parturir Maria"; *Purg.* III, 29) or even Virgil's (*"Novus ab integro saeclorum nascitur ordo"*). These examples, due to their internal rhymes—the *"rithimorum repercussio"* that Dante himself indicates, in *Poscia ch'Amor*, as having been derived from his "first friend," though in more sober fashion—are clustered tollings, collages of cut-up sounds, and a wager surely won, but one which harks back to the former competitions of the

---

[7] A translated paraphrase of Virgil, *Eclogue* IV, 5-7.

[8] These lines are rendered by Ezra Pound as: "Not yet wild-cruel as darts, / So hath man craft from fear / in such his desire [...] There, beyond colour, essence set apart, / In midst of darkness light light giveth forth [...]"

so-called Sicilian-Tuscan literary culture and those in Latin in certain medieval uses of rhythm (a strophe of the *Stabat Mater* comes to mind: "*Tui nati – vulnerati, / tam dignati – pro me pati, / poenas mecum divide*"). This is the ideal of compactness aimed at in the *De Vulgari*, when Dante elaborates the category of "*gradus constructioniis excellentissimus*," though it is more apparent in the fictitious Latin example he gives than in actual vernacular ones—among which we may count that of Dante and that of Cavalcanti, who is linked to some of the others cited (such as "*Trinacriam Totila*," Arnaut Daniel's "*Sols sui*," etc.) though only through the usual alliterative strategies, whether at the start ("*Poi che di doglia cor conven ch'i' porti*") or later ("virtú... vil"; "di pietà pianger"; "porta ... possanza"). Dante apologizes for the excess of examples as the only manner capable of illustrating what he means, but it is, as often happens, an abundance that misses the mark. It is best to read the passage as an allusion struggling towards something not yet realized, but which would come to fruition in the magnum opus.

The *Inferno*'s passage on Cavalcanti *père* contains other details rich in obscure meaning, which only a familiarity on the reader's part can prevent him or her from stopping in surprise to consider. One is the "altezza d'ingegno" (line 59) in which the father surmises the reason for Dante's voyage and asks, Why isn't his son there with him? And such "lofty genius" is literally in proportion to the blindess of the prison ("per questo cieco / carcere"); in other words, it attests to an extraordinary visual acuity. That is, a literary activity is the pre-condition, the basic given for this genre and event, the journey that is also a vision. Such a condition is necessary, but not sufficient—a fact that does not escape Cavalcante de' Cavalcanti, who still thinks within the parameters of Epicureanism and is thus an automatic partisan for art for art's sake. What would the poet of death be doing in the kingdom of the dead? The νέχυια,[9] for Dante, is a form of *certification*. (In the same respect, the fact that Guido's noble villany lay, according to the well-known anecdote in the *Decameron*, in bringing death to others takes on a less light-hearted flavor.) Nevertheless, the fact that a starting point and a finishing point extraneous to Guido, Virgil, and the transfigured Beatrice are needed, does not rule out, and indeed implies, that the essential root of Dante's eternal salvation (like that of Statius earlier) is a "lungo studio" and a "grande

---

[9] That is, the Underworld.

amore" (*Inf.* I, 83) for poetry. "*Sic vos non vobis*,"[10] as the theme of the Virgilian legend goes.

The other mysterious word in the passage is the simple past *ebbe*, indeed the key to the misunderstanding, but whose singularity here has only been pointed out by attentive modern critics. In the historic, not continuous, past tense, it indicates that Guido's aversion or refusal wasn't a mere state of mind, but a specific act or gesture: a critical process now distant because completed. In the framework of the suggestions present, the use of *ebbe* can only be intereperted as a definitive break between Dante and Guido. In so saying, Dante is shaking the dust from his shoes. If Cavalcanti's sonnet *Io vengo 'l giorno* could be linked, as Michele Barbi maintains, to Guido's attitude towards a Dante afflicted by the death of Beatrice, we would have one of those confirmations we call priceless—but priceless in the same way we call those treasures of coins no longer in circulation sometimes discovered in attics and basements, since it would be impossible to reconstruct the context in which the *viltà* evoked in the second and ninth lines of Guido's poem ("trovoti troppo pensar vilmente"; "la tua vil vita"), so multiple in meanings in the abstract, might regain its univocal signification. (A somewhat less polysemic key might be the "annoiosa gente" in line 6, where not everyone will agree on seeing an evocation of theologizing friars; might they not instead be comrades in the style of Forese and Cecco, and might this not be in keeping with "burlesco-realistic" excess?) But we can give up on the out-of-use currency: *ebbe*, whatever the true meaning of Dante's tercet, remains a sufficiently decisive indication.

The strangest thing is that, in order to realize the process of transfiguration in which his detachment from Cavalcanti is confirmed, Dante uses Cavalcantian fantastical-linguistic ingredients. One of the key words, or more precisely, one of the key words of Guido's psycho-physiological hypostases, is indeed *figura* (except for the apparently early texts, where only *volto* avails). *Figura*: that is, the outward representation (or the sign, the demonstration) of one's state of mind—which is, much more so than the famous motory images that are the *spiriti*, a Cavalcantian magnification of Guinizzellian extraction. And thus in one sonnet (*Certe mie rime*), perhaps sent to Dante, we have: "Amor aparve a me in figura morta" ("Love appeared to me in a figure of death"; line 3); after which

---

[10] "For you, but not yours." These were the words that, according to legend, Virgil wrote on the wall after Bathyllus, a lesser poet, plagiarized his work.

Guido (line 13) leaves the addressee his own "semblance" (*sembianza*)—in other words the very pallor of the man (indeed the *poeta*) said to be *smorto* ("wan, lifeless") in *Inferno*, IV, 14. In a similar vein, we have: "Questi [spiriti] sono in figura / d'un che si more..." (in the last two lines of the ballata, *Io non pensava*); or "che Morte non ti ponga 'n sua figura" (in the sonnet *Io temo*).[11] Elsewhere we have: "fatta di gioco in figura d'amore" (in the ballata, *Era in penser*).[12]

A grafting of Cavalcanti with Ovid—that is, of his competition with the *Metamorphoses*, with its natural mutability "per tutte guise"—could serve as a not entirely inappropriate genealogical epigram for the cognitive leap Dante makes. Similar studies could be tailored around the traces of such words as *imaginare* or *parere* or even *piovere* (metaphorically intended, that is—to the point of "Poi piovve dentro a l'alta fantasia").[13] One could say that Dante took Cavalcanti at his word—such that the last part of the *Vita Nuova*, plus the canzone *Amor che ne la mente*, seems a mere working hypothesis, as if the death of Beatrice was an imaginary hypothesis to be applied, a simple narrative projection of his lyrical attitude—precisely in those places where Guido experiments in the extreme with multiplications of entities connected to the advent of salvation and the sublimation of the beloved in heaven. In the ballata *Veggio negli occhi*, with its openly admitted irrational unfolding ("Cosa... / ch'i' no la posso a lo 'ntelletto dire"; "What [happens to me]... I cannot tell my mind"), there emerges from the real, visible woman ("la sua labbia") an image similarly eluding reason ("una sí bella donna, che la mente / comprender no la può"; "a woman so lovely, that the mind / cannot grasp her"; might this be the "nova persona" of *Quando di morte*?); then, "un'altra di bellezza nova," whom we may even call the ideal woman fit to save the man ("La salute tua è apparita"; "Your salvation has appeared," she says) and to transcend the worldly sphere ("vedrà' la sua vertú nel ciel salita"; "you shall see her virtue risen to the heavens").

Cavalcanti's recourse (and, in his wake, that of the young Dante as well) to the culture not of today but of yesterday (to say nothing of phenomena like Pre-Raphaelitism, which is of the day before yesterday), in my opinion restores him, beyond theology, to the confines of pure literature. This approach occurs in fact in a late manifestation of symbolism, one carefully separate from that of

---

[11] "These [spirits] are the image / of one who is dying"; "lest Death put you in his image".

[12] "[she was] made of play in the image of love"

[13] "Then rained down within the fantasy..."; *Purg.* XVII, 25

the devotees of the supposed hidden meaning of the *Fedeli d'Amore*, which is thought to be exclusively political in import.[14]

In spite of this polemic, or perhaps by virtue of it, Dante's homage to Cavalcanti never ended. An homage to a career that must have been at once intense and brief, as we can already infer from a *canzoniere* of less than vast proportions, but with an almost invariable consistency (except for a few poems of correspondence, of course) of language and tone. Dante advanced by leaps and bounds, but chronologically speaking, the poems included in the *Vita Nuova*, and the romance itself, and then those illustrated in the *Convivio*, must be considered close to the Cavalcantian originals. (It has been determined by indirect calculation that Cavalcanti was at least six years older than Dante, and there is nothing that might prompt us to increase by much this minimum difference in age.) Among these originals, one of the most distinct is certainly the ballata *Fresca rosa novella*, still quite clearly derived from Bonagiunta. And yet it is already tied to Dante by a double bond: an external one, because in the oldest songbook containing it, the Palatino, the annotator attributed it to Dante, an error that is usually explained by the customary confusion between sender and recipient; and an internal one, because by giving monna Vanna the *senhal* of "Primavera" (in the sonnet *Io mi senti' svegliar*), Dante, by making her the counterpart to monna Bice (i.e., Beatrice), may simply be quoting Cavalcanti's "piacente primavera," as the word does not appear otherwise in Guido's work.

Naturally, Dante's homage to Cavalcanti makes livelier sense outside the obvious stilnovistic sphere—that is, in the thoroughly "comic" sphere on the one hand, and in the *Commedia* on the other. In the former category, important evidence can be found in the *Fiore*, now that stylistic analyses have borne out the already well-founded thesis of Dante's authorship of that text. The first sonnet in the *Fiore*, where the arrow called Bieltà (Beauty) "per li occhi il core / mi

---

[14] The Fedeli d'Amore ("Love's Faithful") are said to have been a secret initiatory sect to which Dante and Cavalcanti belonged. The *Fedeli* are mentioned in the *Vita Nuova* (I, 20), as those "trovatori" at whom his poems are directed (..."propuosi di fare uno sonetto, nel quale io salutasse tutti li *fedeli d'Amore*"). While there is no historical documentation of the group ever having existed, some modern scholars, such as Luigi Valli and Renzo Manetti, have developed the thesis on the basis of certain spiritual/intellectual similarities between Dante's ideas and those of esoteric religionists such as the Knights Templar and the Sufis. French esoteric philosopher René Guénon explored these putative connections in his book, *L'esotérisme de Dante* (1925), whose aim was to decipher the hidden messages behind the verses of the *Divine Comedy*.

passò," offers a clear verbal memory of Cavalcanti's *Voi che per li occhi mi passaste il core*, indeed further confirming this position, which one part of tradition counters with a reading of "*al core.*" (We must at any rate refrain from comparing it with the cry, "Dentro, Biltà, ch'e' more," at the end of Cavalcanti's ballata, *Vedete ch'i' son un*, since the concept might simply be a *cheval de retour* of the *Roman de la Rose*.) And we would be tempted to see, in this liminal remembrance, not exactly a call to an accomplice (we know how much both *Rose* and *Fiore* lean towards the tenets of the so-called Latin Averroists), but rather a patent self-positioning under Cavalcantian patronage, if not for the fact that that the original phrase thus echoed is indeed an opening line, like those we will be displaying shortly, and the phenomenal sameness provides another argument, however supererogatory, to the Dantean attribution—that is, it attests to an acrophonic specialization of rhythmic memory.

And other rebounds are not lacking, either: such as (*Fiore*, sonnet CLI): "cuore umano / non penserebbe il gran dolor ch'i' sento" (the phrase "dolor ch'i' sento" also reappears in Dante's canzone, *Li occhi dolenti*), which echoes the lines from Cavalcanti's ballata *I' prego voi*: "ch'altro cor non poria pensar né dire / quant'è 'l dolor che mi convien soffrire"—which, however enriched in Cavalcantian fashion with the word *dolor*, echo in turn Lentini's "cor lo lo penseria né diria lingua," from *Madonna, dir vo voglio*.

The words of Cavalcantian descent that appear in the *Fiore* are: *cassero* (XXVIII, 5, CXXXVI), which includes, in Cavalcanti's *Vedeste, al mio parere*, the famous line "cassar de la mente," addressed directly to Dante (and lifted verbatim by Lapo Gianni); *sobarcolato* (CXXXVI, 10), from the mottetto to Gianni Alfani (likewise the ancestor of "I' mi sobbarco!" *Purg.* VI, 135). Another, subtler point of contact is when Malabocca (XXXII, 10) shouts "a suon di corno" in an internal rhyme with *giorno* and *(i)ntorno*, which might seem involuntary and random if the rhymed words weren't all, this time, at the proper ends of lines. The first time they appear in an opening line of a poem not by Cavalcanti but by Guido Orlandi, addressed to Cavalcanti: *A suon di trombe, anzi che di corno*, rhyming with *giorno* and *girle intorno*. That the drafting of the *Fiore* coincides chronologically with a frequentation of Cavalcanti emerges, finally, from the many syntagmatic correspondences between another of its first poems (X) and indeed the sonnet, *Io mi senti'*, in which Dante associates monna Vanna with monna Bice and remembers her as Primavera.

The Cavalcantian clues in the *Commedia* are, on the other hand, a bit more substantial, compared to the paucity of echoes of other vernacular poets.

But these, significantly, do not include the Cavalcanti compositions praised in the *De vulgari*: the stanza *Poi che di doglia* and the great canzone, *Donna me prega*, in which the line, "imaginar nol pote om che nol prova," together with the previously mentioned "...che la mente / comprender no la può" (compare, morever, with "ciò che lo mio intelletto non comprender" in Dante's *Amor che ne la mente*), is the origin of "che 'ntender no la può chi no la prova" in *Tanto gentil e tanto onesta pare*, one of Dante's most famous lines of lyric poetry. And, just to be thorough, from it is also derived the clause, at the moment in which Averroism is refuted, about the "possibile intelletto" (*Purg.* XXV, 65), the last polemical reference—yet how very discreet—to Guido in the great poem.

Quite different, on the other hand, are the unintentional traces, which for their involuntariness are all the more probative—particularly those appearing in series, attesting to the already acrophonic impression we have noted. The opening of Cavalcanti's *Vedete ch'i' son un che vo piangendo* is retraced in the words spoken (*Inf.* VIII, 36) by Filippo Argenti: "Vedi che [also variant: *ch'i(o)*] son un che piango"; another opening of Guido's, *Se Mercé fosse amica a' miei disiri*, inspires Francesca's line "Se fosse amico il re de l'universo" (*Inf.* V, 91). This also happens outside the *Commedia*, though sometimes in circumstances still connected to it. Certainly the conceit of the epigram for la Garisenda, *Non mi poriano*, harks back (with perhaps an echo of *Li mie' foll'occhi* in the word "scanoscenti") to the start of Guido's *Perché non fuoro a me gli occhi dispenti* (the finale of which we see imprinted on the first sonnet of the *Vita Nuova*); we even find *veduta* rhymed in Dante's lyric, as in the first stophe of *Perché non fuoro*. And the "paura di novi tormenti" in the latter poem's second strophe is probably reflected in the "novi tormenti and novi tormentati" (*Inf.* VI, 4) in the Canto on Cerberus (complemented, in the first bolgia, by "novo tormento[15] e novi frustatori"; *Inf.* XVIII, 23). Some readers have seen in the *Fiore* a trace of Guido's *Voi che per li occhi mi passaste 'l core*; but if you take in the whole first stanza of the latter (with the line "guardate a l'angosciosa vita mia"), there is no question that you will recognize it in the opening of the famous *sonetto rinterzato* of *Vita Nuova*, VII: "O voi che per la via d'Amor passate, / attendete e guardate ..."— unless the latter is actually following Jeremiah in the Vulgate, with "passate," in particular, corresponding to "*transitis*" and "guardate" to "*videte*."

---

[15] Variant: *novi tormenti*. (GC)

Or is Jeremiah latent in Guido too? (See, for example, his ballata *Quando di morte*, where we find, in line 13, "guardi... e miri," which is quite close to "*attendite et videte*.") And should we go so far as to advance the hypothesis of a more even exchange of experiences between Dante and Guido, as opposed to derivations only in one direction, from the latter to the former? The fact remains that when Maestro Adamo bursts out with his entreaty ("O voi che..., / ... guardate e attendete / a la miseria..."; *Inf.* XXX, 58, 60-61), he seems to be voicing a Cavalcantianism in the same formulation as in the *Vita Nuova*, but he is also echoing Jeremiah.

On the other hand, the acrophonic sensibility of the Dante of the *Commedia* can also function in reverse, where, for example, the opening of a canto might resonate richly with Cavalcanti. "Taciti, soli, sanza compagnia" (*Inf.* XXIII, 1) recalls "e vanno soli, senza compagnia" (in *Io non pensava*), with *compagnia* in both cases rhyming with "*per... via*." Nor would such a similar feature be accidental at the start of a strophe, such as we find in Guido's *Veggio negli occhi* ("Cosa m'aven...")[16] and then again in Dante's *Amor che ne la mente* ("Cose appariscon..."). For this reason, the fact that in a single Dantean opening, *Io sento pianger l'anima nel core*, we find two Cavalcanti references joined together—"I' sento pianger fra li miei sospiri" (*Gli occhi di quella*), "ch'i' sento lo sospir tremar nel core (*ibid*), and "l'anima sento per lo cor tremare" (*Io non pensava*)—might be a fairly convincing argument for settling the contested attribution between Dante and Cino.

As for the *Commedia* itself, other echoes, such as the snowy scene recalled above, are naturally inside the chapters. It has been pointed out elsewhere that "ricevere inganno" (from *Poi che di doglia*), "giacere" used for a wounded man (from *O tu, che porti*, and *La forte e nova*), and "piú che la stella" (from *In un boschetto*) are Cavalcantian words and phrases renewed in the *Commedia*. To this we can add "fare onore," which, already derivative in the lyric poems (*Parole mie*, e.g.), even exceeds, in the *Commedia*, the prominence given it by Cavalcanti in limiting it to the rhyming position. The full meaning of emphases of this sort only emerges when we consider the moderation with which non-Dantean vernacular texts generally resonate within the *Commedia*. I remember the first time I met Emilio Cecchi, and he spoke to me of those books (which for

---

[16] If we complete the quotation, ("Cosa m'aven... / ch'i' no la posso a lo 'ntelletto dire" etc.), a moment from *Poscia ch'Amor* also comes to mind ("veggendo rider cosa / che lo 'ntelletto cieco non la vede"). (GC)

him were Vico's *Scienza Nuova* and Maurice Blondel's *L'action*) that "salt the blood." Let us therefore say, with him in mind, that Cavalcanti had salted Dante's blood, *quod erat demonstrandum*.

[From the Verona edition of the *Rime* of Guido Cavalcanti, Editiones Officinae Bodoni, 1968.]

On Canto XXX of the Inferno

This would scarcely be the time or place to determine to what degree the exegetical tradition that hypostatizes the individual cantos of the *Divina Commedia* is a legitimate one. The clear didactic opportunity is quite enough. But the specific canto proposed here for discussion is an unusual case, framed as it is between the *exempla* of the opening and the proverb or *sententia communis* of the *peroratio* (whereby Father Berthier might elicit the pointed reaction from Bernardo to "*Audire quod turpe est, pudori maximo est*"[1]), while featuring in the middle a lively episodic account from a primary character. And if the canto achieves an outward unity in its obedience to the most authoritative rules of rhetoric[2]—thanks to what, with wondrous conceptual and linguistic inventiveness, we call "structure" in the modern age—it also provides an economical and systematic opportunity for Dante's imagination to burst forth in in all its essential variety and plurality of tone. For this reason—and also, it must be said, for the unprecedented historical flattening to which it has been subject—Canto XXX of the *Inferno* can be read as exemplary of the entire poem.

The canto's opening, quite purposefully marked by an unusually extended syntactical unit,[3] surely stands as an absolute beginning, an autonomous thing, as there is an appropriate break before the sudden, next apparition. And so, in keeping with the *expolitio* that is the principle of the *ornatus difficilis*, an indi-

---

[1] "To hear what is shameful is the greatest shame." From *De ordine vitae*, author unknown.

[2] Cf. E. Faral, *Les arts poétiques du XIIe et du XIIIe siècle* ..., Paris 1923, pp. 58, 201, 266 ff. (first *exemplum* in Geoffrey de Vinsauf and John of Garland); 320 (final proverb in Geoffrey); and for now 63-64 (*expolitio* in Cornificius); 68 (periphrasis). (GC)

[3] The perceptive study was done by Giuseppe Lisio, who actually considers it the longest sentence in the *Commedia*, though he is contradicted in this by Parodi (now in *Lingua e Letteratura*, II, 309 n.), but the dispute ends up revolving around questions of punctuation and whether they should be full stops or semicolons. (GC)

rect light is prefigured by the twofold mythological simile; by preparing, but also culturally filtering and lessening, through the length of the utterance, the occurrence of that beastly alienation. The motives are provided by the immensity of Thebes and Troy's wounded pride ("superbo Ilïon"): two highly specified (that is, already "moralized" with those psychological accents) elements of ancient material which, if Dante doesn't join them together elsewhere, had been running in parallel since Statius, and had, moreover, been brought closer together in French culture by romances from a century and a half earlier, *Thèbes* and *Troie*.

Concretely speaking, however, Dante's point of reference here continues to be Ovid—who, though left behind in the bolgia of the thieves ("Taccia di Cadmo e d'Aretusa Ovidio"; *Inf.* XXV, 97), had still, as recently as the prior canto to the present one, served as mediator for the "ultima chiostra / di Malebolge," cast in the light of the plague of Aegina. In his evocation of the brother of Ixion, I would actually venture to presume that he was not citing from memory, but with the book right before his eyes. Indeed, in the *Metamorphoses* (IV, 513-14) the madman gives the same cry: "*Io, comites, his* RETIA TENDITE *silvis! Hic modo cum gemina visa est hi prole laena*";[4] the killing of the boy is the same (518-19): "*more* ROTAT *fundae, rigidoque infantia* SAXO *Discutit ora*";[5] my emphasis). And in regard to the latter, the word *sasso*, in *Inf.* XXX, 11 ("...e rotollo e percosselo ad un sasso"), sounds not so much like an ill-chosen Latinism as simply out of place (for the sake of contrast, see, the highly appropriate use in the line "sasso di monte Aventino" or in "crudo sasso intra Tevero e Arno"; *Inf.* XXV, 26, *Par.* XI, 106, respectively). Also identical is the paraphrase indicating the unnamed Melicerte, "l'altro carco": "*seque super pontum ... Mittit* ONUS*que suum*";[6] 529-530). But that we are dealing here with an imposed derivation is demonstrated above all by an internal clue—that is, the prosaic pace of the elocution: the shrunken allusion to the reason for the madness; Juno's wrath (although, thus transformed from a cause to a circumstance, it opens the doors to the beautiful and later commonly established formula: "Nel tempo che..."; *Inf.* XXX, 1); the even hastier and more impatient allusion to the previous Ovidian

---

[4] "'Here in this copse, friends, SPREAD THE NETS! / I've seen a lioness with her two cubs!'" Translation A.D. Melville. Oxford University Press, 1986. All subsequent Englishings of Ovid are from this translation, unless otherwise indicated.

[5] "And like a slinger whirled him round and round / and wildly smashed the baby's head against / a granite block;..."

[6] "...and with her burden launched herself..."

anecdote ("una e altra fïata"; line 30); the tired pace of the gloss ("l'un che aveva nome Learco"; line 10), precisely at one of those moments that normally spur Dante's inventiveness: a rare name (even that of Athamas had submissively appeared, just above [in line 4] devoid of resonance), to the point that, practicing a highly significant abstinence, he refuses to exploit the residual onomastic richness of the unhappy little family, Ino and Melicerte (who, in Ovid's original, is subjected to transmutations that proved useless to Dante). It is another matter entirely with Hecuba, whose story is conveyed not summarily but in a figurative foreshortening. Here there is not even any mention of the vendetta against King Polymestor, which would have been a good vehicle for Dante's use and in Ovid's text is presented with skilled simulation (XIII, 550 ff.). The representation of Hecuba reaches its culmination in the three adjectives, "trista, misera e cattiva," (which vaguely recall Ovid's triad, 510, "*exsul, inops, tumulis avulsa meorum*"), and in the excellently placed enjambment, "in su la riva / del mar" (Ovid, 536, says only "*in litore*").

But for whom is this luxuriant catalogue of illustrious memories and kingly misadventures intended? The pilgrim to the afterlife found himself involved in conversations verging on friendly with two chemists from his parts, an unnamed man from Arezzo (Griffolino, according to 14th-century commentaries)[7] and another Tuscan of less certain provenance,[8] Capocchio. Crime stories and romance sheets, gossip heard at the pharmacy, civic defamations, all pertaining no less to so-called "little Tuscany" than to the virile, iron Tuscany of legend (co-eternal entities both tolerated by trivial aesthetes), figure among the crucial ingredients of Dante's vast *contaminatio*. Still, assiduously frequenting his writings should not detract in any way from the freshness of the surprise at seeing blended together, and projected on a single scale, history and local news, sacred mythology and profane mythology, and documented as well as imaginary entities, all outside of historical time (for us), and on one single plain of univocal truth. Leaving aside the degrees of admixture, which Dante carries to extremes, the consciousness dealing with a theological epoch in which history is universal, indistinct representation, and its events all equidistant from the spectator like mansions in a medieval mystery play, must accompany, in the reader's mind, the additional consideration that for the Renaissance tradition from which Italian

---

[7] This identification now seems to be generally accepted.

[8] Of course, as per Jacopo and Pietro di Dante, Benvenuto, l'Ottimo and other authorities; but Florentine, not Sienese. (GC)

scholastic education derives, modernity holds sway only in the embalmed precincts of apotheosis. Such is the mentality that posits the premises of the radical divorce between history and invention (at that moment when the crisis of realism becomes acute and so great an obsession for Cesare De Lollis). What criterion, then, will help one to gradate the conglomeration in which such disparate "histories" are cemented together? The ordering of the realms of the afterlife, especially Hell, for which the natural morality of Aristotle suffices, is founded on a classificatory, intellectualizing ethics.

Thus the "ultima bolgia de le diece" (*Inf.* XXIX, 118), this "last circle of the ten." Assigned to inhabit it are the falsifiers—who are, as punishment, overwhelmed by infirmities in their physical appearance, whether the object of their cheating in life were the chemical elements, human beings, coins, or historical truth. In this way, to the first medley bringing together a chemist and a waggish cheat, both recently deceased, a walk-on from the *Aeneid*, an incestuous adulteress of ancient myth, and a character from the Old Testament (a logical cohabitation, to be sure, but one which pushes the limit by degenerating into physical contact, into fisticuffs and so on, Virgilian Sinon's punch to the belly of a counterfeiter not long out of the morgue), is added a second mishmash combining, in the shadow of a simple verbal label and beyond all recognized theological and juridical canons—as demonstrated by an accredited specialist[9]—an alchemist *naturae simia* (though clearly in bad faith, otherwise he would presumably be among the sodomites and usurers),[10] a slandering woman, an impostor, a counterfeiter, and an impersonator. (Such is how Myrrha figures here, otherwise her forbidden libido would have consigned her merely to the second circle of the lustful; as for Gianni Schicchi *de Cavalcantibus*, we don't really have a history, moreover, but merely a tall tale, which Dante egregiously treats as history.) Such a manufactured association, moreover, fails to differentiate clearly into distinct, separate punishments, which flusters the industriousness of the exegetes, for it

---

[9] M. Finzi, in GD, XXVIII, 216-37, contrary to the theses of Filomusi Guelfi and del Kohler. (GC)

[10] That Dante admitted, in theory, along with Thomas Aquinas, the possibility of a legitimate alchemy alongside the illicit one, has been asserted on the strength of 14th-century commentaries, but they are baseless interpolations on the texts. Around that time (1317?) a papal bull by John XXII indiscriminately struck at alchemists as being guilty "de crimini falsi" (L. Thorndike, *A History of Magic and Experimental Science*, III, New York 1934, pp. 33-34); for once Dante was in agreement with the pope from Cahors and not with the jurists (idem, pp. 48-51); otherwise cf. Finzi, *loc. cit.* (GC)

is quite something that the impersonators are in fact degraded to the status of enraged brutes, swine let loose from their pen and setting upon their fellow sufferers. But might there not be *ad personam* justifications to invoke here? In the usual Ovid (*"Hic amor est odio maius scelus,"*[11] *Met.* X, 315), from whom she is snatched and then given a stiffening epithet (the "scellerata" is *"scelestis"* even in the Epistle to Arrigo VII), Myrrha envies the happy animals—heifer, mare, nanny goat, bird—for whom a passion like her own[12] is legitimate. Schicchi, for his part, had taken the place of the deceased rich man Buoso Donati and drawn up a will (it is no accident that Dante says nothing about Donati's nephew Simone, the will's benefiary) to win "la donna de la torma"[13] ("the lady of the herd"; line 43): the mare "that certainly was good for CC gold florins" (Lana) and *"valebat bene mille libras"* (Benvenuto). Explications of this sort do not seem exaggerated for this second moment of the canto—a moment indeed acquainted with the imagination, by virtue of which only one of the interlocutors, Capocchio, succumbs to the fury of the goblin (the *folletto*, i.e., Schicchi), since the other, unharmed for the nonce, is able to remain to inform the exceptional wayfarer.

And here begins the chief episode, in the middle of the canto, as with Francesca or Ulysses earlier. The solemn formula "Io vidi un…" ("I saw one…"; line 49), seen elsewhere as an opening (*Inf.* XXII), marks the interval. And the break is accompanied by two noun-rhymes, unique occurrences which through their heterogenous contact alone allow the image to burst forth, less grotesque than pathetic: *leuto, anguinaia*. Out of this abnormal contact grows a series of precisely pathological images—*idropesí, etico*—to the first of which is attached the boldly metaphorical verb *dispaia* ("make disproportionate"), and to the second the exquisite, almost Latin *rinverte*; and dominating the accumulation of rhymes is the more ignoble, load-bearing, *ventraia*. Anatomy is the *Leitmotiv*, returning as "l'epa croia," "l'epa" ("enfiata"), "il ventre," all crowding before our eyes (and on Sinon's lips); whereas the speaker, Adamo, prudishly laments only "le membra legate," "le membra che son gravi" (81, 107). They arise gro-

---

[11] "This love is a greater crime than hate."

[12] I.e., of a daughter for her father,

[13] Francesco Torraca (BSDI, n.s., II, 156) suggests an interpretation that was rejected by Bruschi (in GSLI, XLU, 456-457. Simone (father of Corso) was the nephew, not the son, and must have known about mares, not mules: for the whole story cf. Barbi, now in *Problemi di critica dantesca*, 1a serie, pp. 305-322. The thesis that the subject was drawn from fiction comes mostly from Altrocchi (cf. also E.G. Parodi, in BSDI, n.s., XXIV, 187-188; A.H. Krappe, in AR, VI, 382-383). (GC)

tesquely, preciously, as in any normal phenomenology, from one same source, but the second predicate dominates: the deformed man is authoritative. And as such, his language meanwhile becomes clearer. A few commentators have availed themselves of the obscurity of his biography to define him as a humble craftsman, a subordinate serf of the Conti Guidi. Aside from the fact that the imputation of accomplices is a common tactic among fraudsters (doesn't Guido da Montefeltro unload in identical fashion upon the "gran Prete"; *Inf.* XXVII, 70?), these same glossers haven't, like Fassò, given any consideration to the fact that the speaker in question, who on top of everything else is a foreigner from a distant land,[14] declares himself to be "Maestro Adamo." And on the basis of this emphasis, *maestro* appears to be a technical term from the university world, a rank equivalent to *dottore*; and his faculty, more than medical, is much more likely that of the *Artes*, among which the so-called natural sciences were also classified.[15] So much for the craftsman! Like Griffolino (assuming Lana and

---

[14] Since 1889 (Palmieri) he has been identified in the "magistro Adam de Anglia familiare comitum de Romena" in a Bolognese legal document from 1277. That this man should be seen, as Zaccagnini states (GSLI, LXIV, 2-8), as the same man as the "magister Adam de Anguila" and the "Adam anglicus" of other Bolognese documents from 1270 (which speak of coins) and 1273 is not guaranteed, since there are no fewer than four Adams with the title of *magister* in those documents (pp. 5-6); there is, moreover, a "Guilielmus quondam Adam de Anglia" who appears in 1275; to crown the parade of homonymy, suffice it to say that Giovanni Livi (in GD, XXIV, 265-270, and later in *Dante e Bologna*, Bologna 1921) found a "magister Adam de Carliolo provinciae Anglianae," arrested in 1304 along with other "falsatores monetae et expenditores falsae monetae," who during the investigation delcared that he'd come to Bologna "causa studendi." Downright reckless, on the other hand, is the identification—excogitated by Zaccagnini in deference to Benvenuto—of Dante's Adamo with an Adamo da Brescia (or simply originally from Brescia), who in none of the three cases in which he is named (1274-1276) is ever called *magister*. Benvenuto's mistake can be explained through the origin of the podestà of Florence in 1281, Matteo de' Maggi, under whose rule the steward of the Conti Guidi was burned (in Paolino Pieri: cf. BSDI, n.s., VI, 204); Livi, though still relying on Maggi, thinks otherwise (cf. also A. Bassermann, in DDJ, n. F., V, 179-181). There is hardly any need to mention the hypothesis of Padre Palmieri (cf. BSDI, n. 4, Dec. 1890, p. 30), that Brescia was a mistaken writing for *Brestia* (Brest); or the conjectural correlations concerning *Anglia* by: Torraca (BSDI, n.s., XI, 100, note 1), who relates it to *Angna* (that is Agna near Poppi), and this because ser Graziolo says Adam is from the Casentino; Vittorio Rossi (in his commentary), *Angleria* (Angera); the anonymous oral source cited by Livi (p. 266, note 2), *Angulo* (in Val Camonica). (GC)

[15] On the synonymy of *magister* and *doctor* in this epoch, cf. C.H. Haskins, *The Rise of Universities*, New York, 1923, p. 17; H. Rashdall, *The Universities of Europe in the Middle Ages*, ed. Powicke-Emden, Oxford 1936, I, 19-20. *Magister* prevailed in Paris for the arts, medicine, and theology (*id.*), and in Bologna for medecine (id., I, 235). In Italy the words *medici* and *artistae* went sometimes together, sometimes apart (id. I, 241 and note 4), but there is no doubt that natural

Buti are correct in calling him "maestro Griffolino"), like Capocchio (assuming Benvenuto, Buti, and the Anonymous Florentine are correct in identifying him as an acquaintance and fellow-student of Dante's), Adamo is a scholar, trained for every manner of function, and retains the eloquence of the pithy rhetorician: "saputa persona e studioso de' poeti" ("a knowledgable person and scholar of the poets"), as Buti describes Griffolino (quite naturalistically, moreover), to explain why it is precisely he who is citing Myrrha.

Adamo's apostrophe opens (line 58) by profanely parodying the words of Jeremiah (*Lam*. I, 12) for the Redeemer in the Vulgate: "*O vos omnes qui transitis per viam, attendite et videte si est dolor sicut dolor meus.*"[16] (Before Adamo, of course, the second sonnet of the *Vita Nuova* had also notoriously paraphrased this same Biblical verse, not to mention that, just two cantos earlier [XXVIII, 132], no less a figure than Bertran de Born had done the same.) Immediately afterwards, as Father Cesari was keen to note, the "gocciol d'acqua" so desired by Adamo is the same as that which the rich man implored from Lazarus (Luke 16, 24); this "drop of water," in turn, contrasts with the well-fed life the patient enjoyed on earth, and antithesis is indeed the central figure in the rhetoric of Maestro Adamo.

In proceeding down this path—that is, in bringing to light new information as to his linguistic personality, we must be cautious. It would be a strange fate inteed to have wished to wash away the criticial psychologism only to let it crop back up on stylistic foundations. (Besides, the stylistic personality of Pier della Vigna is simply an invention of De Sanctis.) Dante's protagonists and supporting actors speak in Dante's own eloquence. For example, Vanni Fucci, "the Beast", knows how to maneuver the subtleties of the antithesis or *rejet*, and does not deny himself the elegance of a good metaphor (among others: "Io

---

philosophy in the thirteenth century was introduced among the *Artes*: cf. H. Denifle, *Die Enstehung der Universitäten des Mittelalters bis 1400*, I (sole volume), Berlin 1885, p. 205 (for Bologna); S. D'Irsay, *Histoire des Universités françaises et étrangères des origines à nos jours*, I (Paris 1933), p. 165; Rashdall, I 444, and II, 153; E. Gilson, *La philosophie au moyen âge*, 2nd ed., Paris 1944, p. 393. Out of respect for hierarchy experimental chemistry would not be admitted into the "theorica i. speculativa" part of *philosophia* or *sapientia* (where *phisica* resided), but rather into the "mechanica i. adulterina", which only featured "artes illiberales", as it corresponded with neither the "opus Dei" nor the "opus naturae," but with the "opus hominis artificis imitantis naturam." Cf. on this matter, the *Didascalicon* of Hugh of Saint Victor, l. I, c. X (in *P.L.*, CLXXVI, 747); M. Grabmann, *Die Geschichte der scholastischen Methode*, Freiburg im Breisgau 1909 ff, I 246 ff., II 37 ff. and 235 ff. (GC)

[16] "O all of you who pass this way, wait and see if there is any sorrow like my sorrow."

piovvi... in questa gola fera"; *Inf.* XXIV, 122-123; just like Adamo "piovvi in questo greppo"; XXX, 95)[17], and even rises to the apocalyptic dignity of prophecy. In this way even Griffolino uses well-measured refinements: "fuor del dritto amore amica"; "falsificando sé in..."; "falsificare in sé..."; "testando e dando al testamento norma" (ll. 39, 41, 43, 44). And aren't Count Ugolino's sons rather concise and witty in inviting their father to divest himself of the flesh with which he clothed them?

Granting this, and dismissing any pretense to overriding information issuing from a person's civil status with inferences drawn from his presumed style, we must nevertheless state that the organization of Adamo's entire speech is far more that of a Humanist engaged in reckless tasks than that of a crude *simia* of the mint. The fractured rhythm of "non ci ha" (line 87), to signify the vastness of the sufferer's ever so restricted space, is almost a daily practice for the Guittonians. And it is precisely on the victorious target, much more than the obstacle, of the rhymed word that Adamo's heuristics unfold: rare or even unique words like *mondiglia* (intended metaphorically), *leppo, rinfarcia*—whose distorted form remains unforgiven by Parodi (who refers to it as "il brutto *rinfarcia*"[18])— and also a metaphorical *si squarcia* (which, while referring in the tormented line to the spate of insults, goes well beyond the psalmlike, Ovidian *dilatare* adopted by the exegetes).[19] It is a violent heuristics that naturally infect even the narration (*croia*, which is alone here, and rhymed; *epa*, also in rhyme and alone, in *Inf.* XXV, 82) and Sinon's speech, which is naturally quite eloquent and from Book II of the *Aeneid* (*marcia, assiepa* used metaphorically). By virtue of Cicero's oft-recommended periphrasis or *circuitio* of "*eandem rem dicere... commutate,*"[20] the notion of drinking water is articulated as "leccar lo specchio di Narcisso" ("licking Narcissus's mirror," another arrow from the Ovidian quiver, though by Dante's time it was already current in vernacualr rhetoric, from *Troie* and *Narcisus* and the *Rose* to Ventadorn and Peirol, to Chiaro and the *Novellino*.) The counterpoint is ever so deft: "L'una è la FALSA...; l'altro è 'l FALSO (my

---

[17] Respectively: "I rained ... into this fell gorge"; "I rained into this ditch."

[18] Now in *Lingua e Letteratura*, II 252. (GC)

[19] Isidore (X 239), quoted by Saint Thomas (II^a II^{ae}, q. XLI): "Rixosus a rictu canino dictus." There appears to be some doubt whether, as Del Luongo and Rossi maintain, the character's mouth is warped by the illness. But the difficulty of interpretation is reflected in the tradition of the manuscripts, which often say *suo mal* (instead of *tuo*) and sometimes *dir* mal, or *mal dir*, or otherwise. (GC)

[20] "...speaking the same thing [but with the words and sentences] changed..."

emphasis: XXX, 97, 98); and thus is the parellel between Bible and mythology subsumed, as confirmed in the wake of Isidore[21] by one of the obligatory texts of the schools, Theodulos); "Tu di' VER....; Ma tu non fosti sí VER; Là 've del VER..."; the contrast between Adamos "membra... gravi" and his arm, which is "sciolto" or "disciolto." And we have the *agudeza* of "Sinon greco di Troia" (also variant: "*da* Troia"), alluding to the citizenship granted him by Priam. In the same vein we have Sinon's retort, "QUANDO...; non l'AVEI...; Ma.... l'AVEI QUANDO..."; "S'io...; e tu..." (and this exactly as in Angiolieri's famous sonnet to Dante); "per un"; "per piú che..."

Most important, however, is that Adamo's speech is stilted: the "mirror of Narcissus" revives an image steeped in culture, but it is prompted by a context entirely tuned to the symptoms of illness tossed before us (and Brunone Bianchi is perhaps right not only to point out that *leccare* "awakens the idea of a dog," but also to read that mirror as an ironic reply to the one who had called him deformed, since, if I've understood correctly, it would have reflected a likeness entirely other than that of the "molto buono e bellissimo cavaliere"). The "lega suggellata del Batista" is a graphic definition of the florin, but within the confession of a counterfeiter; the "fonte Branda," whether the Sienese spring that all the ancient commentators read it to be or the more likely one at Romena (concerning whose name it would be meanwhile useful if the testimonies didn't occur so long past the passage under examination here), is a witty touch of local color, though inserted in an invective against the Counts Guido (II), Alessandro (I) and their brother, whose name is utterly unusable here, Aghinolfo[22] or Ildebrandino. Even the famous passage of the rustling streams of the Casentino cannot be isolated as a fragment without suspending the syntax; one needs to continue with "sempre mi stanno innanzi," since their memory is there like a tantalizing tool of the punishment. There is no lyrical excerpt (and the same goes for images like the one of the steaming hand in winter, a trope perhaps not yet proverbial at the time but having become so) that is not functional, and where the terms don't appear anachronistically insolent; and in all such cases we can say that due to their unrestrainable excess of life force, they burst out of the

---

[21] Cf. E.R. Curtius, *Europaïsche Literatur und Lateinisches Mittelalter*, Bern 1948, pp. 80, 366, 446, but especially 224-225 and 449-450. (GC)

[22] Barbagallo and S.A. Barbi (BSDI, n.s., VII, 147), later corrected by Torraca (*ibid.*, X, 131, note I and XI, 97-108), attributed two sons named Aghinolfo to Guido I. (GC)

structural framework. To say that the structure is set up to produce them would be an axiological interpretation.

More generally speaking, the imagination, when never restricted and gratuitous, grows from concrete culture. It is possible that for the alchemists Dante was thinking of their specific malady, considering that according to Avicenna (as cited by Father Lombardi) the vapor from smelted silver "*facit accidere paralysim.*" But it is clear that the invention concerning Adamo recalls less passages from Scripture (thus Tommaseo, Poletto), than, according to Basserman's illuminating discovery,[23] the theme of the miser tantalized by "hydropica sitis" in Alain de Lille. And the representation of dropsy, including the *epa* and the *tamburo*, derives strictly from the semiotics of the time: Bartholomeus Anglicus, in chapter VII of his *De proprietaribus Rerum*, positing that in dropsy, "*virtus digestiva degeneratur in epate*" (and he repates the term [epate] rather often), singles out a pathological variant, tympanitis, so called "*quod ad modum tympani sonat venter,*" in which "*extenditur venter et sonat sicut tympanum,*" "*collumet extrema efficiuntur gracilia,*"[24] and the subject develops an ardent thirst. The "leppo," the "arsura," the "capo che ti duole," are, for their part, in the mind of the same treatise author, symptoms of "*febris putrida*" (as opposed to "*effimera*" and "*ethica*"): "*dolor capitis, malicia anhelitus, sitis et similia.*" The language is in fact enveloped in timeless cultural harmonics, from the Classical dominant of the beginning to the Biblical tones of the close.

Poletto, for example, sees the "fortuna" that "volse in basso" as the same "*fortuna recessit*" in *Aen*. III, 53, which "receded" for none other than Troy; and all the commentators hear, in "insieme col regno il re," Ovid's "*Troia simul Pri-*

---

[23] *Loc. cit.*, pp. 178-179. In prose: "Iam dives... hydropicae sitis indendiis sitit opes, et in medio ipsarum positus tantalizat." In verse: "Dum stomachum mentis hydropicat ardor habendi, Mens potando sitit, et Tantalus alter in istis Ardet aquis." I would point out that in the same *De planctu Naturae*, Sinon is a paradigm of fraud (in Wright, II 518; the passage is not found in the *P. L.*, CCX, because part of the handwritten translation is missing; such is the case in codex L. 302 of Freiburg in Switzerland, which I presently have before me.) Also figuring in it, moreover (Wright, ed. 463, 473 – *P. L.*, 450, 456), are Myrrha, "in patris dilectione a filiae amore degenerans," and—another falsified, if not falsifier—Narcissus. (GC)

[24] I am citing the Minorite's work from the 1482 incunabulum. The passage was previously cited by V. Cian, in GSLI, Suppl. 5, p. 113, note. Nowadays physicians argue over whether the symptoms indicate, in modern terms, cirrhosis of the liver (cf. BSDI, n.s., XIV, 159-160) or actual dropsy (cf. again BDSI, n.s. xxii, 264)—as though Dante wasn't drawing inspiration from manuals but drafting a hospital file from direct experience. (GC)

amusque recessit" (*Met*. XII 404), and even the bucolic "Hic gelidi fontes, hic mollia prata" (x 42) in the sublime "canali freddi e molli." At the other extreme we have Scartazzini linking "d'ogne trestizia ti disgrava" to "*Tristitiam longe repelle a te*" from the *Ecclesiasticus*; and Poletto seeing the next line's "fa ragion..." as derived from "*Ambula coram me et esto perfectus*" from the Vulgate *Genesis*. Even Dante's echoes of vernacular poetry are not spared his linguistic cultural activities (the most egregious example is the snow "sanza vento" in *Inf*. XIV, 30, a quote from Cavalcanti), especially if we share Bacci's suspicion that the vision of the tantalizing waters gives new life to the idea of a probable correspondent of his being the old Terino da Castelfiorentino. (In the sonnet to Onesto: "Ché maggior pena non si pò avere / che veder l'acque de le chiare fonti / e aver sete e non poterne bere" ["For no greater grief can one have / than to see the waters of the clear springs / and not be able to drink and quench one's thirst."]) And the rhyme of *scimia* with *alchimia*, which closed Canto XXIX, was earlier in a sonnet by Chiaro Davanzati to Pallamidesse. Only in exceptional cases does the language remain passive and repetitive: the "ombre smorte e nude" are a replica, even in the pairing, of the souls that are "lasse e nude," though the latter is rhymed with "crude" (*Inf*. III 100). Dante's apparent search for "sources" seems not to be too wide-ranging, although through it we find—an important theorem—that functionality is complemented by the intense linguistic historicity of the invention.

The quarrel between the dropsical man and the feverish man has been chiseled and refinished in accordance with the required rhetorical embellishements (is the "genre" not precisely that of the *tenzone* with Forese, and in its way "petroso"?[25]), to such a degree that the matter under dispute can be considered exhausted by the time Virgil steps in with one of his most pedagogical and severe interventions. And since the oratorical joust revolved around absolutely nothing—it is pure verbal violence—we might be tempted to ascribe to him the intention of intervening to vindicate representationalism over ornate style. In the reality of the text, his function is no less paradoxical: to graft Dante's moral-aesthetic conscience onto a "bassa voglia" ("base desire") by this point fulfilled to capacity. Rooted as he is to his attachment to the encyclopedia of possibilities, Dante wants to grant an audience to the idle chatter of the slatterns and carters, as well as to banish (without actually renouncing that audience) the sublimity

---

[25] "Petroso": See note 4 to the first essay in this volume.

of the ivory tower: to enjoy the representation, adorn it with every elocutionary frill, and then tack on as coda a sage utterance and thereby attain the poetry of internal events. Since the overall, contradictory intention can be achieved by taking things to the limit, so the internal event will consist of taking things to the limit. Dante's shame at not finding an adequate excuse is, for this reason, an adequate excuse in itself—in the same way that one who in a dream rejects his own vision and desires that his condition be that of dream, already finds himself inside the reality of his desire. The second legendary passage of the canto, "E qual è colui..." ... XXX, 136), is therefore just as functional as the first one, "Li ruscelletti..." (line 64 ff.). But it remains no less worthy of our wonder that two opposite mental modalities, the extroverted and the introverted, provide Dante with entirely equal opportunity, and in equal measure, for poetry.[26]

[From *Letture dantesche, Inferno*, Florence: Sansoni (1955); pre-publication in *Paragone*, August 1953, with only the notes.]

---

[26] In prior footnotes with only the publisher's name in this essay, we specify: Th. Wright, *The Anglo-Latin Satirical Poets and Epigrammatists of the Twelfth Century*, Vol. II (1872); and for the periodicals mentioned, we have adopted the following symbols: AR = *Archivium Romanicum*; BSDI = *Bullettino della Società Dantesca Italiana*; DDJ = Deutsches Dante-Jahrbuch; GD = *Giornale Dantesco*; GSLI = *Giornale storico della Letteratura italiana*. Also P.L. = Migne, *Patrologia Latina*. (GC)

Some Notes on Purgatorio XXVII

If it is not too indecent to recall a personal experience, the much maligned (and I certainly won't say unjustly) traditional practice of the *Lecturae Dantis* has proved not entirely devoid of usefulness. Constrained within the limits of a fictitious autonomy, the extemporaneous interpreter, who apparently cannot rid himself of the inclination to critically surveil his own footsteps, finds himself willy nilly searching through things—that is, in the isolated canto itself—for an objective justification of its conventionally assumed independence. He will thus inevitably find his canto extraordinarily paradigmatic (as happened to me for *Inferno* XXX, as concerns not only the opening *topoi*, but especially the intensely composite, "anachronistic," summary character of the culture therein). Or else he will, as in the present instance, run across rather peculiar, knotty problems in the composition. In both hypothetical cases, the reader, through analogy or through differentiation, finds himself directed, despite, or rather because of, the topographical limits, towards reflections of general import. Each method is, indeed, precisely conditioned. For example, one engaging in "linguistic" criticism begins with highly expressive authors, even expressionistic ones (perhaps deluding himself that their exalted individuality will make them the only specimens conforming to his method), then comes to reduce the area of survey covering his texts and to test the universal applicability of that manner of approximation.

The friend to whom these pages are dedicated[1] is a brilliant contributor to the *"Lecturae"*—and also to the very canto of concern to us here, a fact unfortunately known to us, for now at least, only by oral tradition. Perhaps we should root ourselves in the affinity of our experience and beg his indulgence for this frugal offering.

---

[1] Angelo Monteverdi. Of the bibliography (edited by G. Gerardi Marcuzzo) that closes his fine posthumous volume, *Cento e Duecento* (Rome 1971), only one such "lectura" will end up being printed (1965), on the prior canto of the *Purgatorio*, XXVI. (GC)

The impression one gets in the reading of Canto XXVII of the *Purgatorio*, that it is not a canto like the others, finds rather competent echoes in the critical field. The last appealing commentator on the second *cantica*, Francis Fergusson[2]—my sympathy for whom stems from the sincere virginity of the American exegesis, in his case augmented by the fact that the author is specialized in other areas—makes this (for our purposes) revealing observation: "In this context, 'love' is everyman's." It matters less here that his chapter on the canto in question, whose title is on the sacrifice of love, develops, like the volume in general, a somewhat unfocused thesis—confusing, so to speak, the periphery of the truth with its center. What matters instead is that Fergusson appropriates an exegetical category from Singleton,[3] "everyman," applying it where he distinguishes, in the *Commedia*, an "I" as individual versus an "I" as humanity, calling the latter "everyman," after a famous medieval drama.[4] The return of "everyman" at the conclusion of the review of the expiating souls (or more precisely, of both the damned and expiating souls), in which the historical individuality of both the figures visited and the visitor himself dominates, involves the reappearance of the tale-spinning framework of the journey, where the protagonist is the "I," who is also "we." Even Parodi[5] sees the matter as connected to the first cantos of the *Inferno*; and what matters here is not so much that some details of his interpretation lend themselves to controversy. There is no question[6] that the overall invention of the *Commedia* must be retraced not so much to the Aristotelian thesis, however Christianized, of the "due felicitadi"—such as it is developed in evangelical terms in part XVII of the *Convivio* (l. ff.), in the active life and the contemplative life, as represented by Martha and Mary, to which the moral and intellectual virtues lead us—as much more stringently to the corrected variant at

---

[2] Francis Fergusson, *Dante's Drama of the Mind. A Modern Reading of the 'Purgatorio'*, Princeton 1953, p. 162. (GC)

[3] Charles S. Singleton, *Dante Studies, I. Commedia: Elements of Structure*, Cambridge, MA, 1954, p. 10 ("Everyman as actor"). The corresponding chapter had been previously published in the *Kenyon Review*, 1952. (GC)

[4] *Everyman*, the morality play (from which Hoffmansthal's *Jedermann* is derived). (GC)

[5] That is, in his "lectura Dantis," which was published posthumously under the title *La Divina Commedia, poema della libertà dell'individuo [,] e il canto XXVII del Purgatorio. Raccolta di studi*, Aloizij Res, ed., Gorizia 1921 (though the "final publication date" is 1923), pp. 29-41. (GC)

[6] These are comparisons that would come to Parodi mostly from the school of Adolfo Bartoli, particularly from the widely known thesis of Edoardo Coli, *Il Paradiso terrestre dantesco*, Florence 1897, pp. 208 ff. (GC)

the end of *De Monarchia* (XXX XVI 7 ff.), where, the "*beatitudinem ... huius vitae,*" ["the blessedness of this life"] which "*per paradisum terrestrem figuratur,*" ["was prefigured in the earthly paradise"] can be reached "*per phylosophica documenta*" [through philosophical teaching]; but, it is added, "*dummodo illa sequamur secundum virtutes morales* ET INTELLECTUALES *operando*" [by acting in accordance with the moral and intellectual virtues]; whereas one reaches the happiness of eternal life, consisting of beatific vision for which Grace is needed and which is prefigured "*per paradisum caelestem*" [in the heavenly paradise], through transcendent "*documenta spiritualia*" [spiritual teachings], implementing them in accordance with the theological virtues.

It is also beyond question that if it is the emperor who must lead us to happiness in this life, by seeing to the establishment of the necessary premises, peace and freedom, then Dante is one of the very few who managed to arrive, with other help, "*cum difficultate nimia*" ["with extreme difficulty"], at the stage of "free" will, which is a requirement for entering the earthly Paradise. Rather doubtful, on the other hand, is the split posited by Parodi (for reasons of chronological congruence among Dante's works,[7] among others) between the earthly Paradise of *De Monarchia* and that of the *Commedia*, which prefigures, he asserts, the happiness of the individual (whereas the exceptional means—or, I might say, emergency means—adopted by Dante the individual in the absence of empire take nothing away from the commonality of the ends): corresponding to the former would be the *dilettoso monte* (*Inf.* I, 77), sign of collective social happiness. No less doubtful, on the other hand, is that Matelda (who, between Virgil, "*philosophica documenta,*" and Beatrice, *documenta spiritualia,*" is certainly the happiness attainable within the limits of nature, "*quae in operatione propriae virtutis consistit*" ["which consists in the operation of one's own virtue"]) is foreshadowed not by Leah alone, but by Leah and Rachele together.[8]

---

[7] At least if we accept the date commonly accepted for the *De Monarchia*. The agreement of this third book with the texts of the "anti-erocratic" polemic of 1312-1314 was learnedly elucidated by Michele Maccarrone in *Studi Danteschi*, XXXIII, I (1955), pp. 5-142, especially the note on p. 140. (For an updated exposition of the disputed question of the date, see now pp. x and lx-lxiii, with their notes, of the preface by Francesco Mazzoni to the ERI edition (Turin 1966) of *De Monarchia*). (GC)

[8] A thesis taken up again by Manfredi Porena in "Matelda," (in *Atti dell'Accademia degli Arcadi*, n.s. XIII-XIV [1934-35], 43-65, a p. 49. The main objection derives from the circumstance that Leah's dream (lines 94-96), like the two prior Purgatorial visions (IX 13-15, XIX, 1-6), occurs in the morning, which is said to signify, in keeping with *Inf.* XXVI, 7 and *Purg.* IX 16-18, its truthful character. Now, the opposition between Leah and Rachel (the latter being notoriously close to

But these are fringe concerns that in no way detract from the core of the interpretation.

It remains therefore confirmed that, by the time we reach *Purgatorio* XXVII, one of the guiding structures of the edifice returns to center stage. But does the break precede the canto or open up as the canto evolves? So formulated in the abstract, the question may seem pointless or falsely problematic. In reality the answer lies primarily in Dante's visualization of the suture between Purgatory and Earthly Paradise, and secondly in the culture at work here, whether predominantly theological or predominantly poetical. The wall of fire (and the word *muro* occurs in line 36, but since it stands between Dante and Beatrice, does it not recall indeed the "*paries*" that comes between Pyramus and Thisbe?) is usually understood as the circle that, according to the Church Fathers, surrounds the earthly Paradise, in their interpretation of the "*flammeus gladius*" (Vulgate) or the "*flammea rhomphaea*" (Vetus Latina) of Genesis (3, 24), with an allusion to the baptism by fire of the Gospel as opposed to that of John (Matth. 3, 101-2; Luke 3, 9, and 16-17). This component of Dante's imagination, as studied by Graf and others, was definitively brought into focus in the masterly pag-

---

Beatrice in the second and penultimate cantos of the *Commedia*—*Inf*. II, 102 and *Par*. XXXII, 8— two eminently symmetrical locations) is supposedly belied by their eventual fusion in Matelda. The thesis—which is not necessarily false for being widespread—that there is a neat correspondance between the pairings of Matelda-Beatrice and Leah-Rachel (and both Beatrice, 54, and Rachel, 106, are epitomized by their eyes, a convenient coincidence with "Lia lippis erat oculis" ["Leah was tender-eyed"], Gen. 29, 17) bears probably as much onomastic solidarity for the first as for the second couple: in other words, that whatever Dante's etymon was for the two names (and on Matelda we can only, at present, admit to ignorance), Matelda, like Beatrice, must be gleaned from Dante's private biography. This line of argument of a structural nature clearly supports the opinions of those who tend to identify Matelda as one of Dante's beloved subalterns, likely one of the women from the *Vita Nuova*. Such is the position, most recently (see indications on prior cases on p. 205), of Giulio Natali, in "Il Paradiso terrestre e la sua custode," in *Studi in onore di Salvatore Santangelo* (= *Siculorum Gymnasium*, n.s. VIII, Catania 1955), I, 197-210. More precisely, Natali is thinking of the Donna Gentile, a suggestion to be taken with some sympathy, especially as she too is said, in the *Vita Nuova*, to be "giovane e bella molto (c. XXXV), "bella, giovane e savia" (c. XXXVIII). There would, perhaps, be a confirmation of this in *Purg*. XXXIII 128-129 ("e, come tu se' usa, / la tramortita sua virtú ravviva"), if, as dictated by the deponent (compare *fu nato, morto* as 'nacque, morì') and putting the synonym *soglio* (already a semideponent) in parallel with "ero solito," we interpreted *se' usa* as "you once frequented."There is no commonality, at any rate, with the question of Lucia's name, whatever the solution may be (to be found, perhaps, according to general opinion, only with the help of hagiography and figurative attributes). [On Matelda, see also Friedrich Schneider, in *Deutsches Dante-Jahrbuch*, XXXVI-XXXVII (1958), 72 ff.] (GC)

es of Bruno Nardi,[9] who managed to produce decisive texts by Saint Ambrose and Rupert of Deutz on the return to innocence through the fires of expiation. They're the kind of results one can only return to in order to reconfirm them, whether by underscoring how the angel's invitation, "intrate in esso" (line 11), seems to echo that which, according to Ambrose, the "*Baptista magnus*" addresses to the just, "*Intrate qui praesumitis, qui ignem non timetis*" (then later, "*Intrate in requiem meam*"); or by revealing (without insisting on the hypothesis that the immersion in Lethe and the Eunoe have a similar baptismal implication) how explicitly that fire is likened to water, and how Guido Guinizzelli squirts into it and disappears like a fish into water (XXVI 134-135).

But it doesn't help us much that this fire is a barrier surrounding the earthly Paradise, because the final judgment has already been rendered, by all from Parodi to Fergusson, to which we may add the latest authoritative commentator, Natalino Sapegno. And yet it is precisely because this reading is becoming a commonplace that one should remain energetically reserved—among other reasons, because of the fact that at its indirect, bibliographical point of departure, Graf's valuable essay,[10] that "fiamma viva" becomes part of a phenomenology of the walls of paradise, "talvolta di solida materia," as though they came out of the same bag of tricks as, for example, Giacomino da Verona's walls of the Celestial Jerusalem, made of precious stones with crystal battlements and corridors of fine gold (where, moreover, the angel with the sword of fire stands guard), in the wake of Tobias and the Book of Revelations. However trivial my objection may seem, in the economy of Dante's journey, that barrier is not presented in the least like the wall of Earthly Paradise, but rather as a tool for punishing the lustful (which they are required to traverse because the flame rages from the

---

[9] In the first paragraph of his essay, "Il mito dell'Eden," formerly (under a different title) in the *Giornale Dantesco*, XXV (1922), 289-292, then the last of the *Saggi di filosofia dantesca*, Milan 1930 (and penultimate in the 1967 Florence edition of the same title). The essay might well have been a useful reference, to integrate the documentation, for Singleton's very fine recent essay, "Stars over Eden," in the 75th *Annual Report of the Dante Society*, Cambridge MA, 1957, pp. 1-18 (which cites only texts by the Fathers and doctors of the Church, and, clearly intentionally, not the modern bibliography). (GC)

[10] "Il mito del Paradiso terrestre," the first in the collection *Miti, leggende e superstizioni del medio evo*, I (Turin 1892); cf. p. 18 (at which point it is not Dante speaking). An important comparison can instead be made (cf. note on p. 219) with a short French text describing the journey of Seth, Adam's son, to the earthly Paradise. In the Turin edition of Graf (pp. 219-220), "(Es)purcatoire" is a "gués prilleus" serving to protect Paradise ("Çou est .i. fus qui tous jours art et frit"). (GC)

bank almost all the way to the edge); it is the angel of beatitude exhorting souls to pass through it, for which they must climb several more stairs from the fiery ford, where a new angelic "lume" welcomes them, into the supernal garden.

Initially, and essentially, whatever function may later come to attach to it, that fire, through homeopathic anthithesis, is the purifying pyre of the "*libidinis flamma*" of Gregory (as quoted in a comment by Casini), in conformity with the invitation ("*Lumbos... Flammis adure congruis*") contained in the very hymn in the Breviary chanted by the purging souls (which just about everyone cites[11]). It is a "foco d'amor" (line 96), as stated in a periphrasis that is anything but otiose: a "foco che li affina" (XXVI, 148). Though Dante certainly fed on philosophy and theology, it is perhaps useful here not to forget that his first and primary nourishment is poetry and rhetoric.

If we keep to this unavoidable criterion,[12] we must identify the "foco d'amor" as the same which "in gentil cor s'aprende" at the start of the second stanza of none other than Guinizzelli's great canzone—a line which, its fire now purposefully spent, lies hidden, fused with the *incipit* of that legendary text, in Francesca's pronouncement in *Inf.* V, 100: "Amor ch'al gentil ratto s'apprende." And let us not forget that with Guido and Arnaut, the circle opened by Francesca closes under the same sign of eroticism, a love whose object must be reformed—although "ogni buono operare e 'l suo contrario," ("every good action and its opposite," *Purg.* XVIII, 15) comes down in the end to love. Returning to that periphrasis, it is Cytherea "che di foco d'amor par sempre ardente" ("who seems forever ardent with love's fire"; line 96)—which is a clear foreshadowing of the beginning of *Paradiso* VIII, where from the "terzo epiciclo," "la bella Ciprigna" (Venus is indeed always veiled in periphrasis) radiates "il folle amore" in the pagan religion and her son sits "in grembo a Dido" ("in Dido's lap").

---

[11] Particularly, and not only in the comments, Nunzio Vaccalluzzo, "Un mito del Paradiso terrestre," in *Rassegna critica della letteratura italiana*, VII (1902), 208-211 (reprinted in *Saggi e documenti di letteratura e storia*, Catania 1924). With regard to the "wall" Vaccalluzzo maintains a moderate, common-sense position. But do note that his thesis concerning the doubling (between the "*murus igneus*" and the guardian angel) is already found in Coli, *Il Paradiso terrestre dantesco*, p. 231. (For precedents concerning the contiguity of Purgatory and the earthly Paradise, cf. *ibid*, pp. 144-145 and 151-152.) (GC)

[12] Which I illustrated in the essay "Dante come personaggio-poeta della *Commedia*," reprinted above in this collection. On the *fuoco d'amore* in Guido and in Arnaut, see p. 21 in the excellent "lectura Dantis" of Aurelio Roncaglia, *Il canto XXVI del Purgatorio*, Rome 1951, which unfolds in the context of a generalized interpretation. (GC)

Now, "il folle amore" is technically a gallicism (*l'amour fou*, from the second part of the *Roman de la Rose*) intended to designate carnal love, the love "della schiera ov'è Dido," Francesca's love (no less significantly, a third *Dido* adorns, in rhyme, the *petrosa* canzone, *Cosí nel mio parlar*); and it leads to the Virgilian matrix, in *Aeneid* IV, where we find "*caeco carpitur igni*" (2); "*est mollis flamma medullas*" (66); and especially that "*veteris vestigia flammae*" (23) whose memory and *auctoritas* serve in fact to adorn the reunion with Beatrice (*Purg.* XXX, 47). Thus, lining up right beside "mother" *Aeneid* is the courtly lyric, where Guinizelli's "foco d'amore" has its obvious precedents (particularly in the "amorosa flamma" and the "spirito d'ardore" of the great canzone by another Guido, Guido delle Colonne, *Ancor che l'aigua*); where, in keeping with the Provençaux Peirol and Gaucelm Faidi—as the great Gaspary[13] has shown—the lover is purified in love like gold in fire or the furnace (from Proverbs, 27, 21:

---

[13] I am citing Gaspary's Italian edition (Livorno 1882) of *La scuola poetica siciliana del secolo XIII*, p. 94. The passage of Peirol (*Coras que·m fezes doler*, lines 21-24) in the Aston edition (Cambridge 1953, p. 131), goes as follows: "*Qu ·l flama qu'amors noiris / m'art la nuoich e·l dia, / per qu'ieu devenc tota via / cum fai l'aurs el fuoc plus fis.*" The passage of Gaucelm Faidit (now published by Jean Mouart, Paris 1965) is in the great chanson *Chant e deport* (which De Bartholomeis also wrote on, in *Studi Medievali*, n.s. VII [1934], 65-66 and 70-71, as did Sesini, ibid, XIII [1940], 72-73, not to mention *Musiche trobadoriche* [Naples 1934], pp. 51-53), lines 44-45 ("*aissi for'afinaz / ves leis cum l'aurs s'afin'en la fornaz*": text second G, Bertoni edition, p. 90). The Italian passages adduced by Gaspary are: the beginning (from *V*, a canzoniere similar to the one used by Dante), "Così afino ad amarvi / com'auro a la fornace, / c'afina pur ardendo" (Santangelo ed., in *Siculorum Gymnasium*, n.s. Ix [1956], 4); the canzone by Bartolomeo Mocati (second *V*) *Non penai che distretto*, lines 47-50: "Com l'oro in foco afina, / così mi fa afinare / l'amoroso pensare / de lo suo valimento" (Buzzelli ed., in *Cultura Neolatina*, XII [1952], 253); the *incipit* of the sonnet by ser Bello (in *P*) "Com'auro ch'è affinato a la fornace" (this is supposedly the "statement" by ser Pace, invited to pronounce himself on "un foco c'asembra pennace, / che mi disface – lo core e la mente"); the canzone by Pucciandone Martelli (also in *P*), *Lo fermo intendimento*, line 55 ("E sí n'afinerai com'oro al foco," stated to Amore in that he has entered the "gentil loco" that is "madonna," Zaccagnini ed., *Rimatori siculo-toscani* etc., p. 189); a line from a sonnet preserved in a Bolognese memorial from 1310, "Che pur afino chomo auro in fornace" (Caboni ed., *Antiche rime italiane* etc., p. 88). As for more generic texts on the "fire of love," suffice it to recall the opening of an anonymous canzone (in *P*), "D'uno amoroso foco" (and line 10, "C'ardo in foco amoroso"); and the sonnet by Rustico Filippo, *Similmente la notte* ("E quindi bagno l'amoroso foco", "E nessun foco mai cangia calore, / o che faccia languire o tormentare, / per certo non, com fa il foco d'Amore," etc.), apparently reminiscent of Lentini's *Chi non avesse*. (A number of the texts cited in this note and those that follow are now published by Panvini, *Le rime della scuola siciliana*, I, Florence 1962.) To the above one can add the opening of Italian troubadour Bartolomeo Zorzi (according to the sole canzoniere *A*), "Aissi co'l fuosx consuma totas res, / consuma Amors lo cor o'is degna assire." (GC)

Quomodo probatur... in fornace aurum"; also 17, 3, "*Sicut igne probatur argentum, et aurum camino*" and its derivatives, Book of Wisdom, 3, 6, "*Tamquam aurum in fornace probavit illos*" and Ecclesiasticus 2, 5, "*Quoniam in igne probatur aurum et argentum*").

If such is the topos to which the final word of *Purgatorio* XXVI so pregnantly alludes, Dante never cites the other trope of the lover living inside the "foco amoroso" (Lentini) or the "foco d'amore" (Carnino Ghiberti) like a salamander (a trope that will be revived instead, in a typically "Gothic" recuperation, by Petrarch, CCVII 41)—a metaphor which, as has also been pointed out by Gaspary,[14] dates back to an Occitan troubadour, Peire de Cols, from whence it branched off into Giacomo da Lentini and from there into the Tuscan tradition. And yet the likening of Guinizzelli expiating his sins in Purgatory to a fish in water allows us to read, between the lines, the theme of the elements-as-aliments (fire for the salamander, water for the fish, air for the chameleon, earth for the mole), which is the form the salamander takes in Bondíe Dietaiuti and (aside from the sonnet *La salamandra vive ne lo foco*) in Chiaro Davanzati.[15] But that's

---

[14] The Italian passages cited or referenced in notes by Gaspary, *op. cit.*, p. 105, are: by Lentini, the canzone *Madonna, dir vi voglio*, lines 27-30 ("La salamandra audivi / che 'nfra lo foco vivi – stando sana; / eo sí fo per long' uso: / vivo 'n foc' amoroso"); by Inghilfredi, *Audite forte cosa*, line 8 ("E vivo in foco come salamandra"); by Carnino Ghiberti, the canzonetta *Disioso cantare* (which speaks "d'uno foco d'amore"), lines 37-38 ("La salamandra in foco, / secondo è [*che* in the sole V] detto, vive"). Then we have the cases in Guinizzelli and pseudo-Guinizzelli, here below. Cf. also Vuolo, in *Cultura Neolatina*, XVII (1957), 97 f. (= *Il Mare Amoroso*, Rome 1962, pp. 129 f.) (GC)

[15] See, by Bondíe, the canzone *Amor, quando mi membra* (in the only V), lines 49-60: "La salamandra ho 'nteso, / agendo vita in fuoco, / che fôra viva poco / se si partisse, tal è sua natura; / del pesce sono apreso / che 'n agua ha vita e gioco, / e, se parte di loco, / aggio visto c'ha vita picciol' ora. / Ed ogne altro alimento / notrica un animale, / ciò ho 'nteso, lo quale, / se se 'n parte, che viene a finimento." By Chiaro, the canzone (also in the only V) *Assai m'era posato*, lines 43-50: "Quatro son l'alimenta / c'ogni animal mantene / ed in vita li tene, / onde ciascun per sé vi s'acontenta; / la talpa in terra ha bene, / aleche in agua abenta, / calameon di venta, / la salamandra in foco si mantene." The subject can also be found, for example, in the *Tuscan Bestiary* of Garver and McKenzie, c. 18 (*Studj romanzi*, VIII [1912], 38-40): "Four are the creatures which God created in this world, which take no nourishment other than from the four elements of which the world is made... One of these creatures is called the mole... The other creature that lives only on water is a fish that is called a frog. And the other that lives only on air is a bird that man calls a chameleon. And the other that lives only on fire is a bird by the name of salamander, and it is white..."; or, in the *Acerba*, 1. III, c. VII. Other similar passages have been indicated by Milton Stahl Garver, in *Romanische Forschungen*, XXI, I (1907), 301-310; of singular importance is the *Bestiaire d'Amours* of Richart de Fornival, to be enjoyed in the masterly edition of Cesare Segre, Milan-Naples, 1957, pp. 36-37. The fact that Dante does not

not enough. Among the list of applicants for the salamander we also find Guinizzelli, at least with the canzone *Lo fin pregi' avanzato* (which is presumably not just Guittonian in style, but also the very poem the author sent to Guittone)[16]—since while we may or may not acccept that the canzone *Madonna, dimostrare* is Guinizzelli's, it is not to be believed that Dante, as some moderns have done, himself attributed it to the Bolognese master.[17] Thus it is from several points that the fire here burns Guido *ad hominem*.

And therefore if the reasons for poetry can be invoked to explain the invention itself, they should, *a fortiori*, be adopted in the area of investigation that appears to be their own. In this regard a question arises at once: Just as the structure displays novelties which, in linking back up with the more general story being told, introduce occurrences of a prophetic and sacred nature, so should they also prove to be novelties when subjected to linguistic analysis. And they are eminently lexical in character. In a typical line such as "E già per li splendori antelucani" (line 109), the arcane, solemn charm, foreshadowing the most stately utterances of the *Paradiso* (along the lines of "Esso litare stato accetto e fausto"), is realized in the final word, which, unless I am mistaken, here makes its first appearance in the Italian language, and no less in the line's stately Latin ascendancy than in its protracted extension, so evocative in phonetico-symbolic meaning. (Note that *splendore*, in its variants of *spre-*, *spie-*—from which derives *spe-* as well—and *spiandore* by way of Gallicism, attests instead to a passage through "popular" tastes.) These values, in this context, serve to highlight the theme of the opposition of light and darkness, not in any impressionistic or phenomenal sense, but without chiaroscuro—in short, a "trascendent light." The theme unfolds more explicitly in the tercets of the sunset (70-72) and the double comparison over the coming night (76-78).

---

mention the salamander can also be explained by the fact that Albertus Magnus calls the belief in the creature false (as well as that concerning the *allech*, the herring) in his *De animalibus* (cf. the Stadler edition, vol, II [Münster i. W. 1921, XVI, of the *Beiträge zur Geschichte der Philosophie des Mittelalters*"], pages 1571 and 1518, respectively. (GC)

[16] Cf. "Dante as Character/Poet," in this volume. The passage, lines 35-39, goes as follows: "lo meo core / altisce in tal lucore / che si ralluma come / salamandra 'n foco vive, / ché 'n ogne parte vive – lo meo core" (*foco* as a monosyllable is probably a Provençalism). (GC)

[17] The passage, lines 17-20, says: "Ca eo non o sentero / si salamandra nente, / che ne lo foco ardente / vive…" Concerning the error of attribution, cf. Contini, in *Atti del Convegno Internazionale di Studi Federiciani*, Palermo 1952, p. 368, note 2. It provides the bibliography for the undue Casini ascription, *Le rime dei poeti bolognesi del secolo XIII*, Bologna 1881, p. 327. (GC)

Let us look now at the first of these tercets: The adjective *immenso*, however odd it may seem, had not yet appeared in Dante, and will appear again in a highly Latinizing context in the *Paradiso* (XXIV 7); *orizzonte*, here deprived of an article and therefore treated preciously as a proper noun, is elsewhere used in normal, up-to-date fashion; *dispensa*, which should likewise be considered a Latinism (clearly a medieval one), appears for the first time and will be re-used metaphorically in the *Paradiso* (V, 39). Or let us examine the second example: *manse* and *pranse* (whatever the precise etymon of *manso*) are unique in Dante, and the same is said of *rapide* (though I can't convince myself that it means "rapacious"); *protervo* here appears for the first of two times (the second is in *Purg.* XXX, 70), and the only time bearing its literal, exquisite meaning ("haughty, arrogant"); *pecuglio* (which will reappear in a metaphorical function in *Par.* XI, 124) finds itself in the same situation (here highlighted perhaps by the preposition *lungo*, which in such a context smacks of a Gallicism, as an analogue of *selon(c)*, "near to"); and while the outward appearance of the modern tongue may allow us to spot it at once, it risks averting our attention from the fact that *pernotta*, in the same line, is no less "precious" a word to Dante and one never used elsewhere in the vernacular (the "*diu pernoctaviums* [or, better yet, *pernoctitavimus*] of Epistle V helps us to relocate its Biblical connotation). Naturally the connection to Latin is only one of the ingredients (compare it to *allotta*, to *grotta* and *roccia*, still now in the spoken tongue, and to the powerful image of *fasciati*) that go to make up this bright, emphatic, real passage: "io come capra..." (line 86). Anyone wishing to talk about a "bucolic" passage (let alone the fact that, technically speaking, the eclogue mustn't be assigned the highest style, being in fact the genre to which Theodulus,[18] among the *Auctores octo*, belonged) would simply be displaying a rather commodities-oriented notion of literary genres. And if that presumed tonal definition was supposed to refer to I know not what idyllic quality in the text, it would quickly butt up against the widespread opinion that the end of the *Purgatorio*, at least up until Beatrice appears, draws its inspiration from the representations of the Dolce Stil Novo.

---

[18] The letter to Cangrande, listing (32) poetic genres different from tragedy and comedy, names, in orderly fashion, "carmen bucolicum, elegia, satira, et sententia votiva"; and this approach to the elegy, which in the *De vulgari*'s hierarchy ranks below comedy, may be significant. On the medieval eclogue before Dante, see, most recently, the observations of Carlo Battisti, in *Studi Danteschi*, XXXIII, 2 (1955-1956), 71 ff. (GC)

But what, in the end, what do we mean when we speak of the stilnovismo of the Earthly Paradise episode? Perhaps that there are "arbuscelli" (134, "shrubs") as in Cavalcanti's canzonetta, *Fresca rosa novella* (which found itself attributed to Dante because it was dedicated to him)? Or that there are little flowers of vermilion and gold (*vermigli, gialli*, XXVIII, 55-56) more or less as in Guinizzelli's sonnet *Io vogli' del ver* (where, moreover, I would also note a distant echo of Arnaut Daniel's opening line, *Ar vei vermeills, vertz, blaus, blancs, grocs*?) Or do we mean instead that Leah as well as Matelda are stylized not only in the Cavalcantian manner, as comparisons clearly show,[19] but also indeed in the stilnovistic manner that came to be called "Dantean?" In this case the "ghirlanda" (102) would seem to be reviving the "ghirlandetta" of a famous little ballata, or the garland of the sestina; and the "giovane e bella" woman in the dream (line 97) would be a cousin of the *pargoletta* of the opening lines of *I' mi son pargoletta bella e nova* and *Perché ti vedi giovinetta e bella*.

Now look at this latter comparison through the lens of a superficial but well-fitting consideration: the radical difference lies in the fact that the paragogical binomial in the *Purgatorio* is included in a rhetorical hyperbaton with inversion and enjambment ("Giovane e bella in sogno mi parea / donna veder andar per una landa / cogliendo fiori"; lines 97-99). We are not dealing with some facile melodifying, but a strongly-felt recourse to a word order that seems inevitably and directly derived from Latin syntax, even though the use of hyperbaton, in the more recent culture of the time, proves more connected with the Guittonian *tendance*—more precisely, and quite copiously, with the poet Panuccio dal Bagno ("Magna medela a grave e perigliosa / del tutto infermità so che convene, / ché parva parvo, so, dà curamento"), whose name we should not forget among the forerunners of Dante's great moral *canzoni*.

Another scarcely stilnovistic detail, in terms of vocabulary, is the presence of a Gallicism such as *miraglio* (105), whose most immediate antecedents are to be found in Lotto di ser Dato (in the canzone, *Fior di beltà*, line 32), and in Bondíe Dietaiuti (in the canzone *Madonna, m'è avvenuto*, line 37, used metaphorically); and even, I daresay, in Guittone's own letters (XIII 102 Meriano, also used metaphorically).

---

[19] Comparisons made most recently by Natali, *art. cit.*, p. 201; by Gmelin, in a note to XXVII, 98; and by Sapegno, in the comment to XXVIII, 40, and XXIX, I. Comparisons to the Pargoletta, so illusory as to be based on the apocryphal *Era tutta soletta*, are made by Antonio Santi, in *Giornale Dantesco*, XXI (1913), 176-179. (GC)

The closer one gets to the strictly formal elements of the rhetoric, the more the same conclusions become clear. Typical in the canto is the alliteration, not only in a place that might be seen as a fitting topography for oratory, such as the penultimate line of Virgil's leave-taking and of the canto itself ("E *f*allo *f*ora non *f*are a *s*uo *s*enno"),[20] but also outside of this circumstance (line 88, "*P*oco *p*arer *p*otea lí *d*el *d*i fori"),[21] even with lesser accentuation (l. 19, "Vol*s*ersi *v*erso me"; 27, "*d*'un *c*apel *c*alvo"; 106, "*v*eder *v*aga"; 128, "*v*eduto" / "*v*enuto";[22] 130, "*T*ratto *t*'ho"). One cannot deny that such a design leads straight into the lap of Sicilian-Guittonian technique, however regenerated through direct recourse to the patron of the *trobar clus*, Arnaut Daniel (suffice it to recall, together with the opening cited above, the other pieces—*En breu brizara'l temps braus* and *Sols sui qui sai lo sobrafan que'm sorts*—compared to which the line put in Cacciaguida's mouth, *Par.* XV, 63, is a miracle of sobriety: "In che, prima che pensi,

---

[20] Erich Frhr. Von Richtofen cites only this line of our canto, giving examples from other passages (in *Zeitschrift für romanische Philologie*, LXVI [195], 288), in a careful examination of the phonetic values in Dante that should only be consulted with the greatest caution (it is the last section, pp. 279-302, of the essay *Zu den poetischen Ausdrucksformen in altromanischer Epik (Heldendichtung – Dante)*, the first part of which can be found, translated into Spanish, in the volume *Estudios épicos medievales*, Madrid [1954], pp. 231-294). On the one hand, Richthofen is in fact generous (though his procedure should be left for impressionistic amateurs) in considering phonetic aspects as intentional or in any case meaningful, whereas with those that are truly meaningul he neglects to study their topographical distribution or even their structural function; on the other hand he tends to attribute this technical approach to Dante alone, to the point that it could be used to argue in favor of the authenticity of the *Salmi penitenziali*, precisely where the only precedents (which should neither be ignored) would be Classical and specifically Virgilian. Concerning alliteration in Guittone, indeed in Guittone's prose, it would have been enough to cite an obligatory passage such as that on pp. 60-63 of Alfredo Schiaffini's *Tradizione e poesia* etc., 2nd ed. Rome, 1943. The same arguments as in that essay can be found in partly abbreviated, partly explanded and updated form (but without any competence in the vernacular literature that precedes Dante), in the second half of another volume by Richthofen (which we'll euphemistically describe as "adventurous"), *Veltro und Diana. Dantes mittelalterliche und antike Gleichnisse, nebst einer Darstellung ihrer Ausdrucksformen*, Tübingen 1956. In it he particularly asserts (with documentation, moreover, on p. 106, using *Purg.* XXVII, 22, as example) a greater concentration of the verse line in the transition from the *Inferno* to the *Purgatorio*, and even more so to the *Paradiso*. (GC)

[21] The widespread variant of this line, "Poco pareva lí del dí di fori" (from the critical apparatus of the Petrocchi edition) doesn't change the situation much. (GC)

[22] This example, like that of the quarrel evoked below, figures among the cases of *annominatio* listed by Curtius in *Romanische Forschungen*, LX, 2 (1947), 278. Curtius points out that the density of cases increases in the transition from one *cantica* to another, with Dante's discretion with respect to medieval Latin and French practice remaining always outstanding. (GC)

il pensier pandi"). Indeed it is so possessed of this technique that it is framed in a play of replication (of which an extreme example would be Lentini's legendary *Eo viso e son diviso da lo viso*) of varying type: "Ricorditi, ricorditi" (22); "Fatti ver'lei, e fatti far credenza" (20); "Pon giú omai, pon giú" (31); "pur fermo... pur fermo" (33-34); "poggiato... poggiato" (81);[23] "il sonno; il sonno che..." (92); "voler sopra voler" (121);[24] "Vedi... Vedi" (133-134); "puoi e puoi" (138).

[23] We would have a simple alliteration in the case of the variant "di posa" in the place of the second "poggiato"; this variant was notoriously favored by Barbi (in *Studi Danteschi*, XVIII [1934], 34-35), without, however, any examples given for the rhetorical argument. (And it is now also favored by Petrocchi.) (GC)

[24] It is clear that "voler" here is the "buon voler" of XII 124 (just as the "diletto" of line 75 pointedly replicates that of XII 126); but in the expression what predominates, even if not conceptually, is the echo between "Tanto voler sopra voler mi venne" and "Contra miglior voler voler mal pugna" in XXI, although the web of more internal interrelationships should also go so far as to include *Inf.* XXIII 10 ("E come l'un pensier de l'altro scoppia"). In the same way, in line 42 ("Che ne la mente sempre mi rampolla," rhyming with *solla*) one can draw a comparison with line 16 (for its equally metaphorical *rampolla*, rhymed with *insolla*) and with *Par*. IV 130 (for *rampollo*); yet belonging to the same internal pattern is, for example, *Inf.* VIII 111 ("Che no e sí nel capo mi tenciona"). However restricted or expanded the field of affinity, these connections bring out symmetries of some structural interest. The "pellegrin" [plural] of line 110 do not by accident echo the "novo pelegrin" [singular] of VIII 4: they were already beginning their ascent, whereas here (and the increased proximity to God is emphasized by Virgil in line 24) we are closer to the goal (thus making the variant of *piú* for *men* in line 111 [cf. Petrocchi's critical apparatus] rather inconvenient, even contextually). In this way line 123 ("Al volo mi sentia crescer le penne") stands in opposition, whether consciously intended to or not, with *Inf.* XXVI 125 ("Dei remi facemmo ali al folle volo"): "penne" as a synonym for "ali" (would the same hold as well for the highly similar "penne" of Bonagiunta, XXVI, 58?), and the constant "volo," underscore the just man's felicitously reversed "Ulyssesism," with equal voluntary phenomenology; Ulysses's flight is "folle" just like, in the passage studied above (the position inside the line is identical), the love radiating from Ciprigna (the "fole Amor" that Raison, in Jean de Meung, distinguishes from "fin Amor" and "bone Amor," the "loco Amor" opposed to the "buen Amor" in the Archpriest of Hita), love remaining the motor of the universe and specifiable as such. Sometimes, as I was insinuating concerning Bonagiunta's "penne," verbal coincidence, especially when in proximity, can perhaps orient our choice of interpretation. Centripitally with respect to our canto, the *fossa* in line 15 will seem the same as that in the nearby XVIII 121, thus alluding to corpselike pallor, not to the terror of being 'buried alive.' In one case (line 116) an admirable syncretism on Dante's part flashes before us. The commentators teach us that the "cura de' mortali" echoes Boethius's "mortalium cura"; except that the mirroring of this clause with "l'appetito de' mortali" (XXII 41), derived from Virgil's "*mortalia pectora*", puts us on the path of a contamination, since it is from the "sacra fame" that the other hungers ("fami") here descend, and likewise, at one remove, the image of the "dolce pome." (Though in *Inf.* V 121-123, the grafting of Boethius and Virgil is, to the say the least, a little shaky; cf. "Dante as Character/Poet," in this volume.) (GC)

And it goes well with the word-play, particularly in the sense intended by Antonio da Tempo (p. 162 Grion, "*bisteç*us est quando, una dictione semel nominata, postmodum in ipsa mutatur una vocalis vel plures in prolatione, firmis semper, remanentibus literis consonantibus, et semper cum eodem accentu"[25])—and no less than in the solemn and also repetitive line (133), "Fuor se' dell'*erte* vie, fuor se' dell'*arte*" (which proceeds etymologically backwards, issuing from the Vulgate Matthew's "*arcta via*").

This deference to archaic precedents is also visible, with some insight, in the area of thematics. And it is enough to indicate two *topoi* in this regard, that of Pyramus and Thisbe, and that of the boy (*fanciullo*). Concerning the former, which occurs in a famous tercet (lines 36-38)—"Come al nome di Tisbe aperse il ciglio / Piramo in su la morte, e riguardòlla, / allor che 'l gelso diventò vermiglio"; ["As at the name of Thisbe, Pyramus / on the verge of death, opened his eyelids and, looking at her / turned from chalky to vermilion"]—and is then resumed at the end of the Purgatorio (XXX, 69), Fergusson recently voiced the opinion[26] that it is significant in terms of content . Since he sees the theme of the canto as being the sacrifice for love, he surely finds the blood "shed in despair and by mistake"—blood which, moreover, alludes, "however weakly," to the mystical blood of Christ, cited, almost as a *Leitmotiv*, at the start of the chapter (line 2: "Là dove il suo Fattor lo sangue sparse"; "In the place where his Maker shed [his] blood"); and whose redness may actually, in turn, reflect the earlier flames. These, I fear, are fantasies, all the more extra-textual as they are pseudo-textual; whereas we are standing on firm ground when we note that, before it was ever Dantean, the preference for Pyramus (also Prïämo) and Thisbe (also Tísbia or Tisbía) is Sicilian and, as one says, Sicilian-Tuscan (having come down from the Troubadour[27] branch, into which it was probably introduced by

---

[25] "[W]ord-play [bisteçus] occurs when, in a single word once mentioned, one or more vowels are subsequently changed in the pronunciation, always with due regard to the remaining consonant letters, and always with the same accent..."

[26] *Op. cit.*, p. 167. (GC)

[27] Thisbe ("*Tibes*"), along with other illustrious lovers (Semiramis, Helen, Isolde, et al., as well as Dido and Tristan in one manuscript), appears in Arnaut de Maroill [Mareuil] (*Domna genser*, l. 159); and (alongside Pyramus) in a similar list in Matfre Ermengaut (*Breviari d'Amor*, l. 27839). Among the subjects that Cabra the jongleur doesn't know well, according to the famous *ensenhamen* of Giraut de Cabreira, lines 166-168, there is also "De Piramus / qui for los murs / sofri per Tibes passion" (cf. the edition of Martín de Riquer, *Los cantares de gesta franceses*, Madrid [1952], p. 400. For Rambaut de Vaqueiras (*Era·m requier*, line 12) as well, Pyramus's devotion to Thisbe is

the delightful French poem of *Piramus et Tisbé*). Look at Pier della Vigna, in his "canzonetta" *Amore in cui disio* (line 15). Or, among the Tuscans (aside from the anonymous *L'amoroso conforto*, lines 17-18), look at Schiatta Pallavillani, in the sonnet *Poi che vi piace* (in a *tenzone* exchange with Monte Andrea), lines 3-14; Rustico di Filippo, in the sonnet *Oi amoroso*, line 11; and most importantly, Chiaro Davanzati, indeed five times (in the canzoni *Madonna, lungiamente*, line 8, and *Di lontana riserva*, line 20; and in the sonnets *Ringrazo amore*, line 4, *Lo disioso core*, line 7, and *Desidero lo pome*, line 14). In Chiaro, on the other hand, one usually finds only Thisbe, who is used (like Morgana, Helen, and Isolde) as a paradigm of feminine attraction.

Such is the pattern inherent in the Dantean reference; even though Dante was concerned prinicipally with collating, almost ostentatiously, his usual source, Ovid's *Metamorphoses* (IV, 145-146, "*Ad nomen Thisbes oculos a morte gravatos Pyramos erexit*"[28]). The detail of the mulberry, added in the last line completing the tercet, must have seemed to readers like something extraneous to the text, if Fergusson felt the need to justify it as a representation of spilt blood. And Parodi before him, with impressionistic but also perhaps anachronistic finesse, wrote: "the last line—*allor che 'l gelso diventò vermiglio*—almost confers on the tragic moment the mysterious consecration of an awareness and participation on the part of nature." Granting for the sake of argument that it should be interpreted in strictly economic terms, we might just as well take it as a redirection, away from a much-abused commonplace in certainly less than admired lyric poetry (in the *Commedia*, Helen is alone, though Paris and Tristan rub elbows in *Inf.*, line 67), and back to a narrative already competently fulfilled in Ovid's original.

---

exemplary. In Italy after Dante, a quote probably from Petrarch (leaving aside the routinely cited *Tr. Cup.* III 20), that from the sonnet to Sennuccio del Bene, *Sí come il padre del folle Fetonte*, ll. 7-8 (Solerti ed., *Rime disperse*, Florence 1909, p. 110) appears to be more ancient; text also in Marino De Szombathely, *Le rime di Sennuccio del Bene*, Bologna-Trieste [1925], p. 29; *Rime antiche...*, published by Piero Ginori Conti, Florence 1940, p. 69; and cf. p. 10). A veritable Humanistic "revival" of the theme can be found in the *Innamoramento di Melone e Berta* (in Barini, *Cantàri cavallereschi dei secoli XV e XVI*, Bologna 1905, p. 208). Broader indications are given by Ramiro Ortiz in *Giornale storico della Letteratura italiana*, LXXXV (1925), 5-25 (cf. also *Varia Romanica*, Florence [1932], p. 77), and Francesco A. Ugolini, *I cantari d'argomento classico*, Geneva-Florence 1933, pp. 99-134. (GC)

[28] "At Thisbe's name [Pyramus] raised his dying eyes..." (Melville trans.)

We find a similar promotion of a cliché in the image of the boy (the *fanciul*, line 45, who is "vinto al pome," won over with an apple). The application of of child psychology to the naïve lover (and sometimes to his unconscious beloved) is clearly of troubadouric inspiration and common coin in the contemporary poetry. Even leaving aside Percivalle Doria and Pietro Morovelli, who liken the beloved (*madonna*) to a small child (the former in the last line of canzone *Come lo giorno*: "Tu doni e tolli come fa lo fante"; the latter in *Donna amorosa*, ll. 43-50: "come'l zitello / che de l'ausello va dilettando / finché l'auzide, tanto lo tira, / e poi lo mira, / forte s'adira; / ma tosta gira, / c'aisí delira[29] / e va giocando"); we have Mazzeo di Ricco (from Messina, but a correspondent of Guittone's): "Ben mi menò follia / di fantin veramente, / che crede fermamente / pigliar lo sol ne l'agua splendïente / e stringere si crede lo splendore / de la candela ardente" (from the canzone *Sei anni ho travagliato*, lines, 11-16).

And here is Bonagiunta, opening a sonnet:

> A me adovene com'a lo zitello
> quando lo foco davanti li pare,
> che tanto li risembla chiaro e bello,
> che stendive la mano per pigliare;
>
> e lo foco lo 'ncende, e fallo fello,
> ché no[n] è gioco lo foco toccare:
> poi ch'è passata l'ira, alora e quello
> disïa inver' lo foco ritornare [...];

But he also holds up the young boy as an example: "Saver che sente un picciolo fantino, / esser devria in signor' che son seguiti; schifa lo loco ov'ello sta al dicino / e teme i colpi i quagli ha già sentiti." And then, even closer to home, there's Chiaro Davanzati, in a tenzone con Monte Andrea:

> Come'l fantin ca ne lo speglio mira
> e vede a proprietà süa figura,
> sí gli abelisce, di presente gira,
> parte per quel veder da sé rancura,
> vole pigliare per traresi d'ira,
> non val neiente a contastar paura,

---

[29] Better Panvini's "traisi dell'ira" (in canzoniere *P* instead of *V*), confirmed by the words "per trarersi d'ira" in the parallel passage, just below, by Chiaro (where *ira* and *mira, gira*, come after Monte's presentation, though the contexts are closer to Morovelli). (GC)

> prende lo speglio e frangelo per ira,
> alora adoppia piú ed ànne arsura [...]

And there is Paolo Zoppo: "Ma faccio come fantino [variant: 'fa 'l fantin'], che crede, / quando sogna, essere gran veritate" (canzone *La gran nobilitate*, lines 38-39).[30]

As in the prior case, the convention stiffens by the time it reaches Dante (and it was certainly not among his preferred). And so he picks it up and, almost polemically, expands it, placing it in an interpretative framework of general signification. The situation of the child in Dante, highlighted by that ever so subtle linguistic sign that is the first person plural pronoun (44), "Volénci star di qua?" (don't we normally say to small children things like "How pretty we are today!"), is indicative of the prevalence of instinct in him, "contra coscienza" (33). To this instinctivity, Virgil is the "dolcissimo patre" (*Purg.* XXX, 50), indeed "mamma" (ibid, 44), just as the *Aeneid* was "mamma" to Statius (XXI, 97). And yet he is not enough; or, let us say that the fallen man in fact cannot attain "buona felicitade," not to mention the highest happiness, with the use of reason alone. He needs as well an irrational, or more violent, supra-rational impulse: Beatrice, with her efficacious name,[31] of which the name of Thisbe, love or Grace, is also a figure, so that the two topoi become entwined.

But where Dante's archaic culture can claim a resounding victory is in the canto's last line—and thus with a connotation of exception: "per ch'io te sovra te corono e mitrio" ("whereby I crown and mitre you myself").[32] Dante is his

---

[30] Gaspary (op. cit. p. 99) cites only the opening of the mentioned *Donna amorosa* by Pietro Morovelli ("Di me giucate / com'omo face / d'uno fantino, / che gio' li mosa / e gioca e ride; / da poi che vede / sua volontate, / lo 'nganna e tace," etc.); which he links, however cautiously, to a passage in the famous chanson of Aimeric de Peguilhan, *Si com l'arbres* (ll. 34-40), which I take here from the text of Shepard and Chambers, pp. 233-234: "o faitz de mi tot enaissi / cum de l'enfant qu'ab un maraboti / fai hom del plor laissar e departir, / e pueys quant es tornatz en alegrier / et hom l'estrai so que l donet e'l tol, / et adoncs plora e fai maior dol / dos aitans plus que non fetz de premier"). (GC)

[31] The efficacy of the invocation, the name's magical meaning (particularly in the Beatrice of the *Vita Nuova*), and the narrative delay in citing it (as happens for Matelda's as well) are all typical conventions in a medieval tale and quite plain to see, for example, in Chrétien de Troyes. Reto R. Bezzola wrote a brilliant exposition of this in *Le sens de l'aventure e de l'amour (Chrétien de Troyes)*, Paris (1947), pp. 33-61. (On the subject of the "späte Namensnennung," however, the Bernese thesis of Werner Ziltener is essential reading, in *Chrétien und die Aeneis. Eine Untersuchung des Einflusses von Vergil auf Chrétien de Troyes*, Graz-Köln, pp. 51-57). (GC)

[32] Singleton translation.

own overlord, king, and sovereign. Should we perhaps take this—along with "some interpreters, including l'Ottimo, Buti, Landino among the ancients, Venturi, Lombardi, Tommaseo, Bianchi among the moderns," with whom Casini, like Sapegno today, felicitously disagreed—to mean emperor and pope? (And do note that in the meantime, a highly authoritative exegete, Parodi himself, has joined their number: "...as though dressed doubly in purple, imperial and pontifical.") Casini and Sapegno base their arguments on internal data (even though the latter concludes: "The expression *corono e mitrio*... should be taken rather as a fixed formula, generic in meaning.")

And the rhetoricians are not lacking, even if we ignore the original one dug up by Scartazzini from a 13th-century text from Latium on Otto IV, "*mitratus et coronatus ivit cum domino Papa*." Synonymic dittologies at the end of a verse line, also from the Occitan tradition, were still the norm, even in Dante, even in this very canto: "fermo e duro" (34), "rapide e proterve" (77); and we should add, no matter what sophisticated distinctions are drawn by the glossers,[33] "con ingegno e con arte" (130, in an equivocal rhyme with another "*arte*," this one meaning "straits"), to be read as meaning "with full awareness," as is the case in the other example of the same binomial in *Par.* XIV, 11, and not too differently with the trinomial in *Par.* X 43 ("lo'ngegno e l'arte e l'uso").

(There is supposedly an additional case, according to Boccaccian tradition, appearing for example in the codex Casanatensis before the first *envoi*—which is missing, however from the Barbarerinian codex as well as from Ginori Conti, along with the second as well—of the canzone *Io sento sí,* line 95: "né cerchio né ad arte"; unless, of course, we are dealing with an editorial variant, meaning, that is, that the corrupter had his ears full of the *Commedia* and its synonymic values.)

Thus far we have proceeded by way of analogy. But if the binomial, or something very similar, proves well documented already in the surrounding vernacular culture, my suspicion will become a certainty. For this is exactly what we find in a sonnet by Guittone, the "*petroso*" composition we know as *De coralmente amar*. In it we read "ch'Amor di gioia mi corona e sagra," with the mitre popping up in the line that follows ("und'ho di ben piú ch'altr'om, piú che

---

[33] A serious argument could be inferred from the sole Dante text where the opposition is clearly manifest, the *De Vulgari*: "*arte scientiaque immunes, de solo ingenio confidentes*" (II iv 11). Leaving aside the difference of epoch, one will gather specifically that the distinction exists only in opposition, and not in juxtaposition. (GC)

metra") and even further on ("poi son d'Amore a maggior don ch'a metra.") As if this were not enough, that same sonnet is mirrored in another (which, moreover, was part of a correspondence) by Chiaro Davanzati, *Ki 'ntende intenda*, featuring, no less, the exact same binomial ("Ma pur d'atender mi corono e sagro"). It is quite instructive to note that Virgil takes his leave using the same formula as that of the very Guittone who has been so often defamed here, and as recently as in the prior canto. No longer isolated and merely virtuosic, but now included in the great dialectical game of the *Commedia*, which goes beyond it and gives it a functional meaning, even archaism becomes legitimate again, both as a direct recourse to the great Occitan sources and even in the mediation of the old school.[34]

[From *Studi in onore di Angelo Monteverdi*, Modena, Società Tipografica Editrice Modenese, 1959.]

---

[34] Here I relegate to a footnote remnants of a few linguistic interpretations. At the start of Canto XXVII, "Sí come quando i primi raggi vibra…, sí stava il sole" (where the second *sí*, according to Vandelli, Caselli and now Petrocchi, based on the paradigm of *Par*. XXX 88-89 and similar instances, is replacing an unaccented *si* perhaps not permissible in the vernacular at the time), we have an apparently tautological procedure that we might call definition through comparison (the most famous example of which is certainly *Inf*. V 126, "dirò come colui che piange e dice"): it offers a reduction of the contingency to a permanent type, the measure of eternity, and removes it from the accident of experience. In 124-125, "Come la scala tutta sotto noi / fu corsa," the passive voice, here not even accompanied by the agent as in the nearby XXV, 109-110 ("E già venuto a l'ultima tortura / s'era per noi") and in many other cases (*Inf*. XXVI 84, *Purg*. XII 45, XXII 85, XXXIII 121-122), represents the perfect action in its result; that is, it serves the purpose of waiting; and the logical subject appears not in the shadow of the usual *per*, but in a prepositional relationship that is local in nature and therefore objectivized ("sotto"). I will add a mention of a grammatical imperfection. In line 6 ("ci apparse"), one usually reads the *ci* (explicitly, in Casini) as a personal pronoun, in keeping with a great many examples of this verb with the dative pronoun expressed (*Inf*. I 45, *Par*. XV 74, XXVIII 75, etc.), including—though in the (archaic) form *n(e)*—that, precisely, of the first person plural (*Inf*. XIV 128); it nevertheless seems plausible that we are dealing here with the topicalizing form of the adverb, as is probably the case in the ballata, *I' mi son pargoletta*, line 19 ("un'angioletta che ci è apparita"). (GC)

An Example of Dante's Poetry
(Canto XXVIII of the Paradiso*)*

Once again, as every time I allow myself to be induced into a *lectura Dantis*, I feel compelled to justify my choice and excuse the label. It is almost as though the flowery, indeed Art-Nouveau style of the Institute, patently manifest even in its name, mirrored a lapsed *belle époque* of the historical method, while certain aspects in the canto selected would prove so distinctive as to legitimize its isolation as a paradigm and *pièce d'anthologie*. But what if the old positivists among our predecessors had some inkling that in the greatness of the *Commedia*, what dominates the construction and narrative development is the verbal execution, which one can verify with wonder and awe with each new turning of the page? In such a case this canto would represent a conventional extension of a verbal fabric suited to reconciling the immobility of contemplation with a minimum of motion.

Having rendered this generic homage to our forebears, one all the more thankful as it was unexpected, and having begun the research in keeping with the present concern whence this homage springs—a concern for an attention on the signified not curtailed by an attention on the signifier—we find, however, that the present canto is one of those proverbially theological ones more tolerated than admired by specialists, who cut up the poetry with not terribly complimentary scissors and are quite inclined to cast aspersions on its ideological uselessness (as though far more recent centuries hadn't continued to make brilliant contributions to the doctrine of the angels, for example in Rosmini's *Teosofia*). It is precisely a canto of this sort that proves to be, in compensation, an appropriate, indeed obvious subject for stylistic study, or more precisely, the very sort of criticism that coincides with one part of Leo Spitzer's activities and finds definition in the search for a fundamental, revelatory word. I do not thereby mean to imply that I adhere in any general way to the validity of this method, which essentially seems to track down the signs of a concern buried in the unconscious but difficult to contain and prone to eruptions. Quite to the contrary, the word that Dante most cherishes and repeats, *vero*, is so apparent as to lie directly under the brightest illumination of the conscious mind, indeed of conscious intention. The structures that modern explorations recognize in literary works are objective data that don't necessarily concern the reflected consciousness of the authors; in this case the attribute of intentionality is equivalent to a very special kind of visibility, which is differential and downright ostentatious.

For the sake of convenience, let us subdivide the canto into four periods or movements:

> 1) Dante's vision of the Primum Mobile, first through the eyes of Beatrice, then with his own;
> 2) the contents of this vision, a very bright point around which nine circles turn, enflamed, with decreasing speed away from the center, and with Beatrice providing the definition of this point;
> 3) the doubt, dispelled by Beatrice, concerning the contradiction between these mechanics and laws of the physical universe;
> 4) the list, also made by Beatrice, of the angelic hierarchies, according to (Pseudo) Dionysus the Areopagite, in opposition to Pope Gregory.

In each of these four parts, we find the key word.

In the first movement, Beatrice (in recapitulation of the end of the prior canto), "aperse 'L VERO" (my emphasis); and Dante compares himself to one who, standing in front of a mirror, turns "per veder se 'l vetro / li dice IL VERO." [1]

In the next movement, the radical of the term is technically missing, but a derived form is present when Dante uses his powers to predict[2] the brightest light of the circle as that closest to the "favilla pura," "però che piú di lei s'INVERA" (my emphasis, ll. 37-38).[3]

In the third, Beatrice's explanation like a wind the clears the sky of all mist, "e come stella in cielo IL VER si vide" (my emphasis, l. 87).[4]

---

[1] First quote: "...unlocked THE TRUTH"; line 2; second quote: "...to see whether the glass ; tells him THE TRUTH"; lines 7-8.

[2] For an entirely parenthetical reading of the initial "credo," it is useful to compare it (as shown by Mattalia) to the line "al modo, credo di lor viste interne" (*Par*. VIII, 21). (GC)

[3] First quote: "...pure spark"; second quote: "...for it entruths itself most with it [the spark]."

[4] "...and like a star in the sky, the truth was seen."

In the final movement, the angels, says Beatrice, experience delight in proportion to the depth of their intuitive immersion "NEL VERO in che si queta ogni intelletto" (my emphasis, l. 108).[5] And to conclude: if a simple man such as Dionysus could reveal "tanto SECRETO VER" (l. 136), it is because, she states, he received the news of it from the one (Paul) who, having beheld it in a vision, communicated it to him "con altro assai DEL VER di questi giri" (l. 139).[6]

Truth thus pursues and confirms itself. But, before the start of the *Paradiso*,[7] we'd only had a tenuous, antiphrastic, and derogatory foretaste of it in Maestro Adamo's quip to Sinon (*Inf.* XXX, ll. 112-114):

> [...] "Tu di' VER di questo;
> ma tu non fosti sí VER testimonio
> là 've del VER fosti a Troia richiesto."

The true, in the circle of the counterfeiters, is, by way of rapid hammering, obedient to a less-than-arduous rhetoric: mere antithesis to the false (to the point that Sinon replies: "S'io dissi FALSO, e tu FALSASTI il conio"). In the highest sky of Paradise this insistent echo across space represents, through phonetic physicality, the limit of approaching truth—in rapport or *aedequatio*—to reality. And in fact, we find that the true, *il vero*, is here exclusively a substantive (regularly articulated), except for the one case in which it actually passes into action and verb. The passage from *vero* the adjective to *vero* the substantive—which here is a passage from the moral *vero* to the theoretical *vero*, in a gradual process reflecting Dante's intellectual ethics, which are affirmed more explicitly further on in the canto when beatitude is ranked by intellectual criteria (being based "in the act of seeing, / not that of loving, which follows after"; "ne l'atto che vede, / non in quel ch'ama, che poscia seconda"; ll. 110-111)—gains prominence in the

---

[5] "...in the truth in which every spirit finds peace."

[6] "...with much more of the truth from these circles."

[7] Indeed Canto IV is characterized by a double replication with two definitions, "VER diciamo insieme" and "fonte ond' ogni VER deriva,"and "se 'l VER non lo illustra / di fuor dal dual nessun VERO si spazia," prepared by isolated mentions ("alcun VERO," "primo VERO"), followed and as it were continued by other mentions ("a piè del VERO," "un'altra VERITÀ"); but only in the diptych do formal *verità* and real *Verità* alternate. As for the opposition of *vero* and *falso*, the *Purgatorio* seems to be the seat of its realization in the form of litotes: "le cose che son fuori di lei [the soul] VERE"; and "i miei NON FALSI errori"; "per via non VERA, / imagini di ben seguendo FALSE." The collision of opposites is frontal in the PARADISO, in passages such as "tu vedi / ogni contradizione e FALSA e VERA"; "la vista pare e NON par VERA" (cf. also "credendo e NON credendo dicer VERO"). (GC)

relationship between this canto and the prior one, which closed with Beatrice's prophecy that "VERO frutto verrà dopo 'l fiore" ("true fruit will come after the flower"); whereas in fact, according to the Tuscan saying, "la pioggia continüa converte / in bozzacchioni le susine VERE" ("the endless rain turns true plums / into misshapen fruit"; *Par.* XXVII, 126-127). Through the echoing of *vero* (adjective) in the final line of the previous canto in the (substantive) *vero* at the start of the present canto (more precisely, in the second line), the two cantos are linked almost like the *coblas capfinidas* of the finest Occitan, Sicilian, and Tuscan canzoni. And the greater subdivisions of the poem, called *cantiche* in accordance with the line in the *Purgatorio* ("le carte / ordite a questa cantica seconda"; XXXIII, 140) and with the letter to Cangrande, are indeed canzoni, according to the *Inferno* ("de la prima canzon, ch'è de' sommersi"; XX, 3).

Let it be clear that such a link is exceptional and not systematic. But even in Dante's canzone, *Li occhi dolenti*, it is equally loose ("che si *n'è gita in ciel* subitamente, / e ha lasciato amore meco dolente. // *Ita n'è* Beatrice *in* l'alto *cielo*"; "non era degna di sí *gentil* cosa. // Partissi de la sua bella persona / piena di grazia l'anima *gentile*"; "Poscia *piangendo* [...] // *Pianger* di doglia [...]") and not general. In *La dispietata mente* it is barely hinted between the first and second stanzas ("*piacciavi* di mandar vostra salute, / che sia conforto de la sua virtute. // *Piacciavi*, donna mia, non venir meno"). In *E' m'incresce* it's stricter but limited to the first half of the composition ("dicendo 'Nostro lume porta *pace*!' // 'Noi darem *pace* al core, a voi diletto'"; "e partir la convene *innamorata*. // *Innamorata* se ne va piangendo"). Also in *Lo doloroso amor*, the device never goes beyond the first connection ("'Per quella moro c'ha *nome* Beatrice." // Quel dolce *nome*, che mi fa il cor agro"). In our current instance the object is to allude to the unity of the construction at the very point in which it is about to be crowned and concluded.

The first *vero* is therefore a revealed future—the imminent unfolding of the moral life on earth, from an indirectly implied Saint Peter to a new "Scipio" and reconfirmed by Beatrice at his side. But what follows is not a foretaste of the future, time flattened in eternity, but rather an object of vision outside of time: the divine vision. It is the end-point, first mediated (in the Beatrice-mirror) then unmediated, directly experienced, perceived, seen, to be precise: the *vero* that recalls *vedere*, as in "Non VIDE mei di me chi VIDE IL VERO."[8] And indeed: "come

---

[8] "e VEDERmi dir VERO" (*Par.* XIV, 137) is less close. (GC)

in lo specchio fiamma [...] / VEDE colui [...] / prima che l'abbia in VISTA [...] / e sé rivolge per VEDER se 'l vetro / li dice il VERO, e VEDE ch'el s'accorda [...]." Beatrice's mirroring function refers back to the first movement described in the passage in Paul: "*Videmus nunc per speculum in aenigmate, tunc autem facie ad faciem.*"[9] And it is Paul, at the end of the canto, who reveals to Dionysus what Dante now contemplates directly: Dante, bearer ("Io non Enëa, io non Paulo sono") of the new *Visio Pauli*; while its beginning actually allows us to witness the passage from "*nunc*" to "*tunc*," from "*per speculum*" to "*facie ad faciem*," and thus literally functions as a fulcrum. It is fitting, therefore, that it should be verbally represented in so particular a fashion. And perhaps we should push ourselves just one step further, since in the last passage quoted—"per VEder se 'l VEtro / li dice il VEro"—the alliteration is not accidental, but rather helps to focus and involve the mirror in the mediation between the subjectivity of vision and the objectivity of truth.

Leaving the second movement aside for a moment, we find that likewise in the third movement (which, in a highly curious circumstance, presents a variation on the verse line that had closed Dante's "credo," "e come stella in cielo in me scintilla"), *vero* links up with *vedere* ("il ver si vide"). If the sky is the place where truth is revealed like a star in the sky ("come stella in cielo"), this confirms that the allusion is to a central motif. Here the *vero* is the rationality immanent in a specific cosmogonic situation (however invented by Dante himself): that sort of Keplerian theorem (if I may call it such) whereby, as distance increases, the speed of the rotating entity does not equally increase, and indeed diminishes in Dante.[10] This presents itself in a visualization that is paradoxical

---

[9] "We see now through a glass darkly, but then face to face."

[10] This in keeping with a major premise in *De Monarchia* I, xi 15: "*omne diligibile tanto magis diligitur quanto propinquius est diligenti.*" The root—though not put forward but rather carefully implied—of the visual inversion is naturally the contraction of infinity into a single point, and thus the veering of the (spontaneous) geo- and anthropocentric representation into theocentrism, whereby Dante, in moving away from the earth, proceeds (tacitly) from great to greater: in this one, God was the greater entity in every volume; in the other one, He is the minor. In terms of the *Vita Nuova*, it is the contrast between "Oltre la spera che piú larga gira" (where, with verb and noun equally heavenly, a "new intelligence" ... "pulls") and "*Ego tanquam centrum circuli.*" Dante resolves the antithesis by interpreting the circularity retrospectively as purely symbolic and didactic: "*parvenza / de le sustanze che t'appaion* tonde"; further ahead he says: "*parendo* [il punto] inchiuso da quel ch'elli 'nchiude." The metaphors are geometrical; but geometry, as he'd explained in the *Convivio*, "si muove intra due repugnanti a essa, sí come tra 'l punto e lo cerchio [...]; e questi due a la sua

compared to the simplistic situation of the constant angular speed and the growing tangent line—a visualization consistent with that of the tree that "thins out" towards the bottom, or the tricolor trio of women.

In the final movement, the *vero* is infinite truth itself made visible, God indeed repeatedly connected with the act of vision: "e posson quanto a VEDER son sublimi. // [...] // [...] la sua VEDUTA si profonda / nel vero [...]. // Quinci si può VEDER come si fonda / l'esser beato ne l'atto che VEDE / [...] // e del VEDERE è misura mercede."[11] And in the end the *vero* is a matter of fact, the order of the angels according to Dionysus[12] instead of the *Moralia*, now an object of observation, experimental in its way: both for Dante as for, previously, Gregory, who laughs at himself ("di se medesimo rise")—just as Beatrice, in a place just as doctrinally renunciatory, had once smiled at a question concerning the moon's spots; or at the nearby "pueril coto" ("childish thought") regarding the "specchiati sembianti" ("mirrored likenesses"; *Par.* III, 26, 20, respectively). We know that this is in fact a genuine recantation, given that the second book of the *Convivio*, in illustrating the concept of "Voi che 'ntendete il terzo ciel movete"[13] *(Par.* VII, 37), had adopted none other than Gregorian theory. But even when contradicting and belying himself, Dante is peremptory as usual, and it is not clear whether his forcefulness is attenuated or instead reinforced by his invention of the vision, in which the intuition of theological theorems, now become testable, unites, through an appropriation of divine privilege, with the knowledge of human destinies.

---

certezza repugnano; ché lo punto per la sua indivisibilitade è immensurabile, e lo cerchio per so suo arco è impossibile a misurare a punto." Hardly by accident, of course, the last simile in the *Commedia* revolves around squaring the circle: the fantasy of the *Paradiso* itself moves between the two "immeasurable" extremes, and the paradox stems from this situation. (GC)

[11] "...and they can see how sublime they are. // [...] // [...] its sight so deep / in the truth [...]. // Whence one can see how the blessed being / arises in the act of seeing / [...] / and of sight is the merciful measure."

[12] Not for nothing is it thus evoked in the Sun's sky: "Appresso VEDI il LUME di quel cero / che giú, in carne, piú a dentro VIDE / l'angelica natura e 'l ministero" (note the verbal echo of the clausulae "VEDI LUME" and "VEDER l'alto LUME"). The details concerning the dispute over the order of angels are in Helen Wieruszowski, *Archivio italiano per la Storia della Pietà II* (1959), 182-183: Dante supposedly took Gregorian doctrine from the *Tresor* of Brunetto, who in turn supposedly came to know of it through Isidore; Dionysus's teaching is embraced and justified by Aquinas. The "*poi*" ("Ma Gregorio da lui poi si divise") seems to allude to the fact that Gregory, in a homily, had actually abided, at least in essence, by the other specification. (GC)

[13] "You who understand move the third heaven..."

Vero thus covers several different meanings: historical truth in prescience; conforming of the *intellectus* to the *res*; theorem in fact; theorem in its rationality; and finally, and most supremely, God himself, as an object of contemplation ("alta luce che da sé è vera";[14] *Par.* XXXIII, 54). All these significations become equalized in the experience of the direct vision. And if God is "Colui che mai non vide cosa nova" (*Purg.* X, 94),[15] Dante's somewhat paradoxical assumption is to represent eternity as a "cosa nova"—i.e., to temporalize it. For such an operation he again needs the mediation of Beatrice, whether because she resorts to a certain durable rationality and mathematical congruity concerning the relationship between the angels and God, or because she sets forth in the sole manner possible—that is, apodictically (though the *Convivio* had earlier made the effort to deduce at the very least their number from a trinitarian speculation)—the sequence of the hierarchies or terns and the angelic orders within them. The vision, clearly, can only be an object of memory—whence the fundamental mention of memory: "cosí la mia memoria si ricorda"[16] (line 10)—one which recurs at decisive points in the fabric of the poem: the invocation at the start of the journey, when indeed Dante readies himself to become the new Paul ("o mente che scrivesti ciò ch'io vidi";[17] *Inf.* II, 8); the repetition of the notion at the start of the *Paradiso* ("[…] dietro la memoria non può ire. // Veramente quant'io del regno santo / ne la mia mente potei far tesoro";[18] I, 10-11); the final vision ("e cede la memoria a tanto oltraggio"; "e l'altro a la mente non riede"; "a la mia mente / ripresta un poco"; "Un punto solo m'è maggior letargo"; "pur a quel ch'io ricordo").[19]

This raises the question of what truth really is for Dante. In Dante the character, in as much as he assumes the part, the "genre" of visionary, it is only that of an imagined experiment, which will in no way exempt him from the mediation of reasoned discourse, and in the dispute between intuition and rationality, he does, overall, favor rationality. But Dante the historical individual—with

---

[14] "lofty light that is true in itself…"

[15] "He that never saw anything new…"

[16] "so recalls my memory…"

[17] "o mind that wrote what I saw…"

[18] "the memory cannot go back. // Truly so much of the holy realm / I could make into a treasure in my mind."

[19] "the memory fails at such excess"; "what remains does not come back to mind"; "lend a little back / to my mind"; "but one moment is my greater forgetting"; "even concerning what I remember".

his frequent (and mostly hidden) recantations and contradictions, those we've mentioned concerning the angelic orders and lunar spots (where the *Paradiso* contradicts the *Convivio*), or the oft-cited conflicts between the relative nobility of Latin and that of the vernacular (*De vulgari* vs *Convivio*), or on the mutability of Hebrew (*Paradiso* vs *De vulgari*), or, why not? on the known land mass—seems more a man of themes than of theses, one concerned even conceptually with the formality of intellectual research, in the great wake of the Sophist tradition so clearly carried on by the practice of Scholastic disputation, just as in the speaker and poet pure formality becomes equivalent, when it doesn't prevail over it, to narrative invention.

The kind of truth here described balances intuition and discourse in a manner where the Neoplatonic presence of the *De coelesti Hierarchia* (so broadly commented upon by Hugh of Saint Victor) within the overall neo-Aristotelian framework—a presence moreover well in keeping with Aquinas—is a glaring symptom. But the treatment of the angelic question such as it unfolds in the *Paradiso* is, with respect to Dante's whole career, a final resolution and retrospective justification—already begun in the *Convivio* in a merely doctrinaire form—of the mediating, animating function of angels such as it is found in the stilnovista Dante. A similar recuperation occurs when, in the reconciliation of theoretics and will through an intellectual, non-mystical solution found in the act of seeing that precedes love, Dante seems to lean strongly back to his first conclusion.

But what is Dante's essential cognitive tool? In the stilnovistic mode, "belli occhi / onde a piglar*lo* fece Amor la corda."[20] *Corda*: rope, or, if you will, fishing line, noose, net, or, even better, a prisoner's shackles. It is as if we are in the presence of the customary troubadorian or Petrarchian *agudeza* of the ensnared lover, with the related derivation of *Amore* from *amo* ("hook"), clearly embraced by Dante in his usual spiralling mode of procedure which here is no longer exhaustive. At this height, in fact, Love is no longer limited to the banal courtly hypostasis; rather, it is infinite love of which Dante is the object, God-as-Love aimed at his salvation, perhaps by means of theological stratagems. Love, in other words, has a heuristic value with respect to knowledge.

---

[20] Altered by the author for illustrative purposes from *Par.* XXVIII, 11-12, "...belli occhi / onde a pigliar*mi* fece Amor la coda": "Beautiful eyes / which which Love fashioned the rope to catch me" (Contini changes "me" to "him" in the above phrase.)

In the canto that follows the angels will become "amori," as emanations of the "l'etterno Amore"; and here too, already, the Primum Mobile is the "miro e angelico templo / che solo amore e luce ha per confine"—a chiastic variation on what was said in the prior canto on the Empyrean in relation to the Primum Mobile: "Luce ed amor d'un cerchio lui comprende."[21] But what is stressed is the paradoxical aspect, the verbal contradiction inherent in the utterance—even if for Dante *templum*, independent of the etymon (he may have Isidore's suggestion in mind, "*templa dicta quasi tecta ampla*,"[22] which in the original, however, is followed by the insinuation "*a contemplatione*"),[23] could only have been a sacred enclosure, a privileged, limited space where light and Love, whether separate or fused in the equalizing binomial, are by definition entities of limitless extension, such that the utterance holds up a limit that is a non-limit.

The analysis of the signifier, involving correlations and linguistic-conceptual memories, has immediately transformed itself into an analysis of the signified. If we may resort to a subjective analysis, the relationship of Dante's word *vero* with the contexts in which it is placed came to him, finding shape and expression in much the same way, in another epoch, the word *forma* came to DeSanctis: the clue lies in a predominant conceptual intention. In this light, Dante's constant proposition of novelty and linguistic renovation must find precise form in the most visible, illuminated sphere, the vocabulary. Whence the utterly unusual, repeated prodding of the word *vero*; not to mention the abundance of lexical outcroppings—that is, neologisms. It is not only a question of quantity (the neologistic pressure is everywhere in the *Commedia*), but of the systematic, somehow categorical nature of the neologisms. We are at the end of the *Paradiso*: independently of the unprecedented experience to be communicated, captured in the summary of transmutation and transhumanation, there is not a lot of space in which Dante can strike, and thus the concentration—one might say the ostentation—of his instruments must needs increase.

Let us begin with what can be broken down into series, into grammar—where, however, the facility (that is, the massive, infallible efficacy) of the second phenomenon (neologism) finds itself joined by the first (repetition). If the

---

[21] Respectively: "...wondrous angelical temple / whose only limits are love and light" (ll. 53-54); "Love and light enclose it in a circle" (*Par.* XXVII, 112).

[22] "they are called temples because of their ample roofs"

[23] While Dionysus "a CONTEMPLAR questi ordini si mise" (line 31)["set to contemplating these orders"]. (GC)

repetition involved the word *vero*, then in the embedded example, *s'invera* ("in the vicinity of the real Truth we proceed ontologically"), it is prolonged within the chapter of neologisms thanks to the insertion into the series of parasynthetic verbs with the prefix *in-*: all reflexive verbs, as we can see, or, more precisely, middle verbs—that is referring to the subject, ontologically described and animated, but never actually proceeding into action. In truth, there is one exception in the very first tercet, in the verb that sets the tone to this aspect of the canto, the transitive *(i)mparadisa* (similar to the already used *inciela*); it differs from the remaining series, and differently from *inciela*, because, among other things, it's not rhymed (the rhyming position, a marked point of the rhythm, even when not actually the final rhyme of the tercet, highlights the import of the neologism). But then the tercet comes to a close with *s'immilla* and *s'interna* (if this goes, as it certainly does, with TERNI), which belong to the same derivative family as *s'imploa*, *s'inzaffira*, *t'insusi*, *s'indova*, *s'insempra* (the sole neologism at the very end of a canto), *s'inluia*, *t'inmii* (with *m'intuassi* trailing behind it), *t'inlei*, and especially the numerical branch of *s'incinqua*, *s'intrea* (and also *s'addua*). This, clearly, is the grammar of metamorphosis.

We are still close to the realm of grammar when we look at the accents (*collòca*) and the word endings (*vonno, terminonno*). The commentators have not failed to point out the respectively Umbrian and West-Tuscan character of the *–onno* ending[24] and to cite the Pisan example of *andonno* in the *De vulgari*. The colorful rustic tinge—which is, moreover, regional, not local—would be all the more violent if the verb *terminare* (which in the context is also violently alliterative) happened, as some suspect, to be used not according to its everyday meaning but to the technical meaning of "to define." The much-lamented obscurity of the *per che* connection preceding it in the same line (105) leads one to wonder whether by any chance Dante hadn't intended to mean that, just as the lower order, "angels," being the least extensive, serves as the name for all the separate intelligences,[25] so the lower order of the first hierarchy gives its name to the hierarchy itself. Naturally, however, the uniqueness of the lexical lemmata

---

[24] *Vonno* is a permutation of *vanno* even strictly within the language of Dante, and indeed the poem, and the *cantica*, given that the line phonically varies the preceding one, "in queste stelle che 'ntorno a lor vanno" (*ponno*, moreover, in a rhyme, is quickly replaced by *posson* inside a verse line). (GC)

[25] Pseudo-Dionysus (in John Scotus Eriugena's translation, *Patrologia Latina* CXXII1048): "*theologi omnes quidem simul caelestes essentias angelos vocant*." (GC)

was even more obviously explored—not to mention the odd *roffia* and *paroffia*; such Latinisms as *alo, circumcinto, rape*; *osannar*; the first appearance in Dante of *ubi* as a substantive (earlier it was just *dove*) and *vimi* (both repeated in the canto that follows, but in the singular); the previously used but nevertheless rare words *igne, arto*, and *arti* (the latter an element clearly considered well-suited to phonetic games—*ampi e arti* [line 64], an assonanced binomial belonging to the same family as the play on words in *Purg.* XXVII, 132: "fuor se' de l'erte vie, four se' de l'arte"). As for *vimi* (line 100), starting with the plural is quite understandable: it is an homage to Guinizzelli, whose highly sophisticated sonnet to Guittone, *O caro padre meo* (Dante should have addressed the same words to Guido himself), features "debel' vimi" in rhyme, among other things.

The culmination of this ever so composite expressiveness is easily recognizable in *roffia* and *paroffia*, regarded with severity from one scholar to whom readers of the *Commedia* are more indebted than most others, namely Giuseppe Vandelli. The worthy Vandelli does not refrain from pointing out that, if you eliminate "the slightly vulgar words *bazzoffia* and *battisoffia*" the only two remaining were these two words, to which the poet adapted the context. You couldn't really say he was terribly convinced by the famous testimonial of l'Ottimo (that is, Andrea Lancia, as is now generally believed): "and he said *tempio*, not *chiesa* [in the Farinata episode], to speak more precisely, not because he was constrained by the rhyme. I heard a writer say to Dante that he never used a rhyme to say anything other than what he intended; but that oftentimes he had words in his poems [*rime*] say other than what they were used to express by other speakers."

Without too demurely insisting on the need for these two very hard stones in Dante's workshop, we must nevertheless try to interpret them from a more proper angle. How can you assert that *paroffia*—that is, the Greek rival of *parrocchia* ("parish, group"), as magisterially discovered by Schiaffini—"is probably used here, in a facile metaphor, to mean 'part'"? The suitability of the metaphor, if we may say so, lies in the fact of applying to the heavens a subdivision that is, admittedly, earthly, but also ecclesiastical. The pertinent examples are administrative in character. The meaning of "team, assembly, crowd" that we find documented in Boccaccio, in Sacchetti, in *Il Pataffio*, comes to us from contexts too much under Dante's influence to attribute to the term, as Parodi does, an independent, plebeian origin instead of such an affiliation, however equivocal (especially in Boccacccio's *Teseida*, where it's used to rhyme with *soffia*); and if it were in fact a genuine jargonization, it would postdate Dante and not concern him at all. More or less the opposite is true for *roffia*—which (I quote Parodi from Vandelli) "formerly meant 'cleaning and trimming of tanned hides'; and it was a small step to transition from this meaning, which is certain, to that of 'rubbish, refuse, gargage, filth' in general." Here too this position, however simplified, comes from Parodi, who is too concerned with documenting the Tuscan dialect: "it should be connected," as he well knows, with the Old-French *roife* and the Northern Italian *rofia* and nouns of similar meaning "*forfora, crosta, desquamazione delle labbra*" ("dandruff, crust, labial desquamation"). But this, and not the technical meaning of skinners, which is a specialized one, is indeed the present definition, as others have not failed to point out; it is the leprosy of the heavens, which the mistral blows away, the *roife* already in literary use, between Gautier de Coincy and the chanson of *Ami et Amile* (the latter being a text in which we find a foreshadowing, on a child's lips, of the argument of Ugolino's sons: "tu ne vestisti / queste misere carni, e tu le spoglia").

The canto's language is therefore marked by an intentional effort of differentiation. But now we must examine it beneath the threshold of consciousness—that is, within the sphere of those internal echoes that should be considered entirely spontaneous and preceding all planning.

Rather than a typological order, we should follow the flow of the discourse itself topographically. And the beginning of the canto already offers us something decisive: that which, in the system of metaphors related to the vision, ammasses around the mirror. The more general theme is the coincidence between the thing and the reflected image, which we are anxious to verify here. We had one antithetical, bi-polar realization of the theme (which is indeed defined through antithesis: "per ch'io dentro a l'error contrario corsi / a quel ch'accese amor tra l'omo e l'fonte" ["for I rushed into the opposite error / to what kindled the love between the man and the font'"; *Par*. III, 17-18], calling to mind the "*specchio* di Narcisso" in Maestro Adamo's canto) in the moonlit sky, where the faces of the blessed, comparable to those reflected "per *vetri* trasparenti e tersi" ("through clean transparent sheets of glass"; Par. III, 10), were interpreted as "*specchiati* sembianti" ("mirrored likenesses," line 20), so that, "to see whose they were, I twisted my eyes" ("per veder di cui fosser, *li occhi torsi*": a syntagmatic cluster that recalls Ugolino's "li occhi torti"). If the mirrored image demands comparison with the real image, this latter, if attenuated, is then presumed to be mirrored. But since the comparison brings a torch (*doppiero*) before the mirror (*specchio*, which equals *vetro*), there is one "che se n'alluma retro" ("that lights up behind"); and this can be related to real mirrors as well, those of the optical experiment suggested by the moon's spots: "*Rivolto* ad essi, fa che *dopo il dosso* / ti stea un lume"[26] (the mirror here is defined as "vetro / lo qual di retro a sé piombo nasconda" ("glass / behind which hides lead")—but Virgil, reflecting on the same concern as Dante in this continuous bouncing back and forth between reality and image, had already spoken "di piombato vetro"[27]). And there was also mention of a light behind one's back in Statius's comparison—"Facesti come quei che va di notte, / che porta *il lume dietro* e sé non giova, / ma dopo sé fa le persone dotte" ("You did as one who goes at night, / carrying the light behind him, not for his own good, / but makes the people after him wiser")—where we actually witness the birth of the semantic-phonetic nexus of "*il lume dietro*" (from which the author's impressed memory derives "alluma retro"), since the passage is notoriously a variation of the opening of a sonnet by Paolo Zoppo, quite lax in its stretching of the alternating-rhyme quatrain ("Sí come quel che porta la lumera / la notte quando passa per la via / aluma asai piú gente de la spera / che sé medesmo che l'a in balía [...]"; "Just as he who carries the lamp / at night when going down the street / brightens far more people with the glow / than himself who has it in his hand"). The Primum Mobile chapter, with its three elements of the light behind, the (real) mirror, and the act of turning round, incorporates and summarizes, through recapitulation, the combination (in *Paradiso* II) of "light behind" (in its pure state in *Purgatorio* XXII) and mirrors (real ones), which includes the phrase "rivolto ad essi", and the combination (in *Paradiso* III) of a (believed) mirror and the act of turning round.

The first-degree comparison, however, is not enough for Dante, and, as always in moments of great illumination, he introduces another analogy, in a perspectival suite of concentric circles—a procedure typical of this poet, who straddles the line betweeen idealism and realism and who never reproduces pure, raw reality, but always brightens it with analogues that are all intensely real and contained within one another like Chinese boxes. The second degree analogy, with respect to the sameness of direct light and reflected light, is the sameness of the *note* and "suo metro" ("its measure", line 9) of musical realization and the schema proposed. Observe, in fact, the synonymy between "questo

---

[26] "Turned towards them, make it so that behind your back / there is a light..."

[27] "Vetro terminato con piombo" and "vetro piombato," are the exact definitions of the mirror given in book III of the *Convivio* (the commentary of Busnelli and Vandelli, vol. I, pp. 369 ff., transcribes or otherwise indicates the Scholastic sources). (GC)

metro" (*Inf.* XIX, 89) and "cotai note" (*Inf.* XIX, 118), in the bitter rebuke addressed to Nicolò III, and also essentially between the "dolenti note" (*Inf.* V, 25) and the "ontoso metro" (*Inf.* VII, 33), as far as concerns the substantive. If *nota* fundamentally implies musical execution, we understand that *notare* can stand for "to sing in unison" (which we hear particularly in the angels who "notan / sempre / dietro a le note de li etterni giri"), and more generally for "to conform, to comply," which seems to be the meaning most fitting for "quando / Amor mi spira, noto" (*Purg.* XXIV, 53; and therefore more or less equivalent to "vo significando," line 64) and also in "Bene ascolta chi la nota" (*Inf.* XV, 99; a proverb alluding to the usefulness of learning that can only be verified in the conformity of action). Petrarch, in writing of Laura (in the sonnet *Ripensando a quel ch'oggi*), "e come intentamente ascolta e nota / la lunga istoria de le pene mie," shows that he derives the usage from the passage in question and at the same time echoes it to the ear, however valid the point being made here for dissociating the meaning of "make a note in my mind" from this archaic use of *notare*.

Moving forward, however little, we encounter the "belli occhi / onde a *pigliarmi* fece Amor la corda" as instruments of knowledge. The attested memory is recent, from the prior canto, where Dante wants to return to Beatrice's eyes, which contain more beauties in them than any other spectacle in nature: "e se nature o arte fe' pasture / da *pigliare* occhi"... These eyes being talked about are those of the one contemplating, captive, not captivating eyes: the verbal connection, indeed the contiguousness between eyes and the verb *pigliare* (*fé* and *fece* are also common) thus indicates, in this case as well, a more primary notion, to be realized in contradictory, polarizing fashion. But the connection can also be merely phonetic; that is, it might conform to a rhythmic-tonal abstraction. This is what immediately happens next, with "quandunque nel suo giro ben s'adocchi," where the placement of *ben* before the verb forcefully takes us back into a contextually rather misshapen clause appearing in the bolgia of the falsifiers (*Inf.* XXIX, 138), namely: "e te dee ricordar, *se ben t'adocchio*."

We are by now in the sphere of the *punto*—an image rather dear to Dante, if he is able to use it, in the (clearly Latinized) *auctoritas* of the *Metaphysics*, to replace the "*principio*" of the original ("*Ex tali igitur principio dependet caelum et natura*"[28]). An excellent geometric representation of extreme reduction, the image of the "point" can be applied, as here, to space; and also in the same

---

[28] "On such a principle depend heaven and nature."

general part of the poem (canto XXX): "il triunfo che lude / sempre dintorno al *punto* che mi *vinse*." But immediately afterwards, it is interpreted thematically: "Da questo passo [that is, the beauty of Beatrice in the Primum Mobile] vi concedo / piú che già mai da punto di suo tema / *soprato* fosse comico [thus like him, the author] o tragedo"; then temporally, in the final canto: "Un *punto* solo m'è maggior letargo [...]" (which is not far indeed from "perché foco d'amor compia in un punto / ciò che de' sodisfar chi qui si stalla" (*Purg.* VI, 38-39); where, we may add, *punto* as "*punctum temporis*" is an identical rhyme with *punto* as "thematic point."

Let it be said incidentally that the final passage, that of the *punto* that is *letargo*, seems to prove right the much-debated line (not too far away in the text, since it is on Saint Bernard's lips), "Ma perché 'l tempo fugge che t'assona" ("It's time that flies that makes you sleepy"; *Par.* XXXII, 139). Time, in being crushed down, reduced to a point towards eternity, brings sleep and oblivion. One important fact links the last few passages cited, though they are applied to different aspects of the *punto*: whether it is spatial or temporal or thematic, whether it triumphs or overcomes, the "point" corresponds to a risk or supreme test for the subject, a watershed that confirms the word's true identity. The "punto che mi vinse" (spatial) and the "punto solo" (temporal) branch out—in contrast to the convergence and imbrication we saw above (which are two possible ways of effecting the same kind of internal echo)—from Francesca's famous statement (where the *punto* is thematic): "ma *solo un punto* fu quel *che ci vinse*." (This line was surely in Petrarch's mind when, in the canzone *Quel antiquo mio dolce empio signore*, he wrote "Né costui né quell'altra mia nemica / ch' i' fuggia, mi lasciavan *sol un punto*.") From such a sinful occasion to a vision of the divine, what an abyss! What an unintentional lineage! The bond between *punto* and *vinse*, however, lies in the virtual definition whereby the *punto* is what is able to overcome a force: it is a sort of semantic abstraction underlying the rhythmic-phonetic abstraction. Meanings of this kind seem undoubtedly primordial, more profound than the mantle of culture upon which centuries of interpreters have focused their attention.

A few other minute formal abstractions follow.[29]

---

[29] We can confine to a note, as being purely verbal, the cross-referencing of "chiuder conviensi" (said of the "viso") to the prior "conviene insieme chiudere e levare" (said of the eyes), as advanced by one of the commentators most sensivite to internal echoes, Daniele Mattalia. Additionally, in the same critic, the echo of "parrebbe luna" (said of "quale stella") with the also prior verse opening

The circle of fire (of the Seraphim) "si *girava sí ratto, ch(e)* [...]": here there is a clear echo, and no less antithetical in context, of the banner of slothful, "che girando correva tanto ratta, / che…" (*Inf.* III, 53-54).

"Con l'ordine ch'io veggio *in quelle rote*": a glance at the rhyming dictionaries shows how easily *rote*, "enheavened" in rhyme in the *Paradiso*, will attract the demonstrative adjective to precede it, appearing only once as "quelle rote" (in Forese we read "Non hanno molto a volger *quelle rote*"); but there are many other cases, such as, in the *Paradiso*, the indivisible "queste rote", particularly (for the *in*) Cacciaguida's "Però ti son mostrate *in queste rote*" (*Par.* XVII, 136).

Divino as "sublime," as in "veder le volte tanto *piú divine*" (that is, "faster"), attracts the comparative. While, for *divino*, one can only properly invoke the eyes of Beatrice, "pieni / di faville d'amor *cosí divini*," the likening becomes more forceful, and still in the rhyming position, with the synonym (*dia*, for "divine"), as in "nella luce *piú dia* / del minor cerchio" (said of Solomon), and "e farai *dia / piú* la spera suprema (Gabriel's words). To this we may add by way of solid confirmation, "De' Serafin colui che piú s'in*dia*" (*Par.* IV, 28); the prominence here confirms the pertinence of an analogous similarity involving another exquisite adjective, *poco*, when intended to mean "small": "e quale stella par

"parrebbe nube" (said of "Qualunque melodia") cuts deeper into the phonetic substance; here, however, we continue till the end of the tercet in a binary rhythm ("che squarciata tona"). In our location the progress of subtlety produces, in a rather different melodic context, the transition to a ternary rhythm ("locata con esso"), which is perfectly concomitant with the culmination of alliterative play and etymological repetition ("luna locata,"; "con… come … con… colloca"; "stella… stella"; but also, further up, "acuto… acume"). Also important, in Mattalia's study, is the breaking up of "lume acuto," an image so central two stanzas earlier, in an enjambment; whereas "la virtú / che si distende" is enjambed just as "si distende / la virtú" is in the *Purgatorio*. The same goes for "quanto ponno," in a clausula like "quanto puote" in the *Inferno*, which is just the Scholastic "in quantum potest" that we also find in the *De vulgari*. (Since "quanto puote" refers to "segue," it would seem we should infer that likewise "quanto ponno" refers to "seguono" and not to "somigliarsi," so that "per somigliarsi al punto," with its nevertheless finalizing value, should be put in quotation marks. Further confirmation would appear to be given by the context in the *Purgatorio* where we find, internally, the formula "che quanto posson dietro al calor vanno." Except that what decisively settles the question of the reference to *somigliarsi* is the parallelism with a point in De Monarchia, I viii: "*humanum genus bene se habet, et optime quando, secundum quod potest, Deo assimilatur. Sed genus humanum maxime Deo assimilatur quando* etc.…."). Finally, highly useful comparisons can be made between "l'ultimo è tutto d'Angelici ludi" and "Di [and not *De'*, as Petrocchi rightly informs] violenti il primo cerchio è tutto," and between "di su (s'ammirano)" / "e di giú (vincon)" and the prior "di su prendono e di sotto fanno." (GC)

quinci *piú poca*," just above (line 19); "Quell'altro [i.e., Michele Scotto] che ne' fianchi è *cosí poco*" (*Inf*. XX, 115)—and we are omitting "sí poco" or "sí poco" in rhymes and using the normal meaning.

Once past the critical boundary marked by Beatrice's revelation, we are offered another little system, one that makes the present canto again seem recapitulative: "non altrimenti *ferro disfavilla* / che *bolle*" echoes the passage from the beginning of the *Paradiso* in which the sun is seen to "*sfavillar* dintorno, / com *ferro* che *bogliente* esce dal foco" (I, 60); but the series in which this slice in integrated—"[…] sfavillaro"; "[…] ogni scintilla"; "[…] (i)l numero loro"; "[…] s'immilla"[30]—itself imbricates in turn the memory of Jupiter's M in the sky, "innumerabili faville" (XVIII, 101); "piú di mille / luci" (103), which follows "lo sfavillar de l'amor che lí era" (71). Interpolated between these self-memories is "piú che 'l doppiar de li scacchi s'immilla" (XXVIII, 93)—naturally with, in addition, an awareness of what was said in the *Convivio*: "E però lo mille significa lo movimento del crescere; ché in nome, cioè di questo 'mille,' è lo maggiore numero, e piú crescere non si può se non questo multiplicando" ("And yet the thousand signifies the motion of growth; for in name, this 'thousand,' that is, is the greatest number, beyond which we cannot go except by multiplying it")—an allusion to a very well-known Provençal (and not necessarily troubadour-related) and French topos. The closest seems to be a passage of Peire Vidal ("Mil tans es doblatz sos bes / Que'l comptes de l'escaquier"), which one can now read with proper commentary in the fine edition of D'Arco Silvio Avalle.

What does it mean that Dante defers to this (perhaps overly intellectualized and too unnatural) commonplace and others? Usually inspired by a genuine observation of nature, his lists of comparisons contain a sincere homage to reality, however cut up into series and catalogues and abecedarian syllabifications of the Great Book. With his prodigious inventiveness, Dante expands the lists at every step (but they're all lists from the very beginning: think of the bestiaries), showing *in vivo* what this rhetorical convention attests in the state of the "source," and which for us is only an object of erudite curiosity: the concomitance of an inspiration by reality (a rustic, non-urban inspiration, ancient, not modern, later lost to the average mind) and a culture that denies realism any autonomy. In the same way, by composing in a quotable way, in a proverbial,

---

[30] Compare the places inferred by Busnelli and Vandelli (vol. I, p. 135) in their comment on the phrase "quasi innumerabili" in the *Convivio*. (GC)

peremptory style, Dante broadens and even ruptures the Classical custom of the *auctoritates*, while the framework remains perfectly perceptible.

I shall now separate, from the echoes that remain more or less verbal and conceptual, those that are purely rhythmical. For our example, let us take the line (which, in reference to the cosmogonic knot, refers to the difference between heavenly "essemplo" and earthly "essemplare"): "tanto, *per non tentare*, è fatto sodo." It is quite unusual how the causal infinitive here, with its passive meaning following *per non*,[31] forces a break in the rhythm, such as we had elsewhere identified, though with a slight syntactical variation, in the canzone *Tre donne*: "*per non usar*, vedete, son turbate—at least if we take *vedete* as parenthetical and not governing. Or consider the "cerchio *che piú* ama *e* che *piú* sape": we have here the same distribution (of the emphasized words) as in "nome *che piú* dura *e piú* onora." Or take the parenthetical phrase dropped in the middle of the two lines: "al punto fisso che li tiene a li *ubi*, / *e terrà sempre*, ne' quai sempre fuoro"; it retraces, at the summit of Paradise, a rhythm born at the bottom of Hell: "[...] onde mi vien riprezzo, / e verrà sempre, de' gelati guazzi." And together they go to make up the figure so instructively imitated by Petrarch, as much in the sestina *Giovene donna* ("[...] i' l'ò dinanzi agli occhi, / *ed avrò sempre*, ov'io sia, in poggio o 'n riva") as in the canzone *Una donna piú bella* ("[...] et èvvi ancora, / *e sarà sempre*, fin ch'i' le sia in braccio.") Dante's figure is indeed imitated, but also gothically altered, slackening the parentheticality into fragmentation and replacing the earlier poet's potent hypotaxis with the addition of new segments.

Finally, there is a noteworthy phonetic closeness (*sí che* in the same position after the verb)[32] between the line "e di giú vincon sí, che verso Dio" (compare this, for example to "che pria turbava, sí che 'l ciel ne ride") and an-

---

[31] It should be pointed out that the meaning of *per* in this context is that of "because," such as is carried sometimes by the word *for* in English as well, and that the passive voice Contini evokes here means that the phrase *per non tentare* should be read as "for not having been tried" or "because it was never tried."

[32] We find a slightly different distribution of the words in the lines, which are nevetheless central, "non trasmutò, sí ch'amendue le forme" and "s'appiccar sí, che 'npoco la giuntura" (a bit before, but not after the verb, "ad alber sí, come l'orribil fiera") along with "m'impigliar sí, ch'i' caddi; e lí vid'io." The quotations are from the predominant version of the time; but comparisons show that the punctuation needs revision. (And indeed Petrocchi would be the first to do this, suppressing the comma in the first and the last of these examples; whereas in the last of the text he puts a semicolon between piangëa and sí che.) (GC)

other middle tercet line, though near canto's end, and at any rate in a quasi polar location (though it's again in Francesca's chapter) and "l'altro piangëa sí, che di pietade." The main difference is that the rhyme here shares with its rhyming mate in the tercet (*-irano*) both the tonic vowel (itself not an infrequent occurrence) and the final vowel, while the tonic persists in the next stanza's rhymes (*-ise*) and in the final stanza's (*-iri*).

Becoming accustomed to the formal values employed by Dante allows one to work out and insinuate hypotheses that could not otherwise be put forward, but are made plausible, indeed quite fitting, thanks to the great mass of similarities in the different cases. At the opening of the canto in question, the "vita presente / de' *miseri mortali*" renews, as the commentators have not failed to point out, a typically Virgilian syntagma, found in Book XI of the *Aeneid* ("*Aurora interea* MISERIS MORTALIBUS *almam Extulerat lucem*") as well as in Book III of the *Georgics* ("*Optima quaeque dies* MISERIS MORTALIBUS *aevi Prima fugit*"), thus displaying, within Virgil, given the sameness of morphology and position, an internal self-imitation of the sort we are examining in Dante, by the author's own hand. But this is not the only instance where *mortali* as a noun has a scent of Virgil about it. In Statius's rendering, *mortalia pectora* (which occupies a similar position in his hexameter—"*Vi potitur, quid non* MORTALIA PECTORA *cogis*"—as the prior syntagma), becomes, in *Purg.* XXII, 41, "l'appetito de' mortali."

Piecing together further data well established by exegesis, we find that in addition to Virgil there is another more or less classic paradigm at work here: Boethieus, whose "*mortalium cura*" (in one of his prose works) is reflected in the first "cura de' mortali" (in *Purgatorio*, XXVII), which Dante typically revives, and this time in rhyme, in a famous opening in *Paradiso* XI, "O insensata cura de' mortali," even though the line, as a whole, is closer to an opening by Persius's "*O curas hominum.*" A similar borrowing was effected from a Biblical sourse, the "*Quis [...] hominum*," of the Latin version of the Book of Wisdom, rendered in *Paradiso* XIX with "a voi mortali." For our concerns, the enjambment of the present canto is ordered in a manner quite akin to what we find in another opening tercet line, however distant and heterogeneous its location (*Inferno* XIV): "la tresca / de le *misere m*ani"—a syntagma likewise held together by alliteration. Is this simply a coincidence? The fact remains, however, that one can provide yet another example of the same phenomenon (from *Inferno* III): "Questo *misero m*odo"—which leads one to suspect that crouching all the while behind this alliterative figure, before being retraced in plain language, is still

Virgil's "MISERIS Mortalibus." This opens new avenues of research, in addition to those already being explored concerning Dante's memories of himself and of his readings—which were first and foremost in Latin, and only sparingly in the vernacular. Beyond what has been suggested above, the intelligence of the angels in the rhyming position ("in ciascun *cielo*, a sua *intelligenza*") seems, through the attraction of *cielo*, to pay homage yet again to Guinizzellli, and this time to the great canzone *Al cor gentil*, one of whose most solemn stanza openings is "Splende 'n la 'ntelligenzïa del *cielo*."

With the fibres thus detached on our dissecting table and left to dry in the anatomical archives, we remain curious to glimpse the physiology itself in operation, the better to discern, without metaphor, and by slowing things down, the movement imposed on the most celebrated loci in the canto, which are pleasant even to those who find the ensemble to be vexatious. But first a preliminary statement is in order, concerning a nexus we've already analyzed:

> in questo miro e angelico templo
> che solo amore e luce ha per confine.

We are in the custom of extracting these lines and reading them thus, "on the downbeat," so to speak. But in the context the nexus is eminently "on the upbeat." Indeed it is the conclusive element of a protasis stripped of independence: "Onde, se 'l mio disio dee aver fine / in questo [etc.], / udir convienmi ancor [etc.]". Freed from the suspensive intonation of its heteronomy and functionality, the distich is made an anthology piece by means of philological abuse and poetic legitimacy: and in such a paradox lies the life of all of Dante's poetry and the guarantee of its surviving the culture that shapes it.

The most rigorous list concerns, clearly, the purity of the now cloudless sky and the second angelic tern. The first passage,

> Come rimane splendido e sereno
> l'emisperio de l'aere, quando soffia
> Borea da quella guancia ond'è piú leno,
>   per che si purga e risolve la roffia
> che pria turbava, sí che 'l ciel ne ride
> con le bellezze d'ogni sua paroffia;
>   cosí fec'ïo [...]

features an expressive intentionality that we examined above (as concerned the unusual words of the rhyme). It is, moreover, intensely historical, in that the gentle, cathartic value of the Mistral (which is not compromised by the *bonhomie* contained in the folksy metaplasm *leno*) can be understood only if one has experienced it blowing in the Romagna province in which Dante probably composed this conclusion to the *Paradiso*, where, existing as the perfect opposite of the scirocco that blows "per la pineta in su 'l lito di Chiassi," it becomes "*serenaro*"[33]—from *sarnêr* (its lovely Romagnolo name, which also graces a fine modern collection of dialect poetry). Formally, we can add that we view the spectacle in all its dynamism, thanks to the progress of the subordinations (*quando, per che, sí che*, and including intermediary and perspectival conjuctions *ond(e)* and *che*) and the preparation of its glorious arrival in the double hendiadys: the adjectival one moving through the slow dactyl or *sdrucciolo* (*tardus* is the double-dactyl *cursus*, "*non sine quodam tempore profertur*": a line of the Heavens ending with two dactyls in the *De vulgari*), "splendido e sereno" (not unlike, with the same adjective, "lucido sereno," "plenilunïi sereni"); and the verbal one of increasing mass, "purga e risolve," all effected through Latin (and therefore luminous) means.

Nevertheless, we must not forget that the scene, aside from having a culturally concentric development (due to the learned insertion of *Borea*—of which it is not clear Dante recognized its successor in the *bora* [north wind]—and its iconography), also serves as a metaphor: an allegory of truth unveiled in all its purity. And if it culminates phonetically in the shrill "*ride*" ("laughs"), the image, intensely in the thrall of the light, recalls (aside from the line for Paolo Orosio, "Ne l'altra piccioletta luce ride"; X, 118) the celebrated lines at XXIII, 26-27, "Trivïa ride tra le ninfe etterne / che dipingon lo ciel per tutti i seni."[34] Undoubtedly an expressive high point, these lines must likewise be read contextually "on the upbeat," as they are included in a comparison and cloaked in mythological equivalents. The enchantment is thus, dare I say indirect? but certainly mediated and anything but impressionistic.

As for the second sample of sublimity:

> L'altro ternaro, che cosí germoglia
> in questa primavera sempiterna
> che notturno Arïete non dispoglia,

---

[33] That is, "rende sereno": it "clears the sky," as the Mistral indeed does (*cielo sereno*, in Italian, meaning "clear sky.")

[34] "Tutti i seni," still referring to the sky, is the equivalent of "ogni sua paroffia." The same tonality, associated with the same verb, as in "faceva tutto rider l'orïente" (said of Venus). (GC)

> perpetüalmente 'Osanna' sberna
> con tre melode, che suonano in tree
> ordini di letizia onde s'interna;

The first question that arises is: Why is the summit of poetic intelligence not admitted to the summit of the hierarchy? At this point a noteworthy imbalance appears between the material and the verbal register. The springtime unfolding of the theme entails something truly central: Aries is the sign of creation, the sign under which Dante moves, as evoked in careful periphrasis at the start of the poem, at the end of the *Purgatorio*, and at the start of the *Paradiso*. It is the troubadour topos of rebirth, now corresponding to the passage from time to eternity. But the realization of the theme (a new reason for pause for anyone drawn to manipulating the plumb-line of rationality) is not representative, but indeed suggestive. "Notturno Arïete non dispoglia": this nexus, whose fascination has been universally sung, and is indeed incontrovertible, is not a visualization, but rather a conceit ("it is not subject to changing with the season, when Aries is nocturnal and no longer diurnal"). And it is curious to note the privative nature of *Ariete* (in keeping with the precious precedent we find in the *petrosa* lyric, *Io son venuto*: "Passato hanno lor termine le fronde / che trasse fuor la vertù d'Arïete"), whereas the present efficacy of the sign is entrusted to the mentioned instances of periphrasis—"quelle stelle / ch'eran con lui" and similar cases. The suggestion of season, assigned to such words as *germoglia*, *primavera*, and to a technical verb such as *sberna* (compare to the lines of the Anonymous Sicilian of the Vatican *canzoniere* close to Dante's: "Quando fiore e foglia la rama / e la primavera s'adorna [...] / e gli auscelletti per amore / isbèrnano sí dolzemente [...]), joins with that of eternity, active in the terms *sempiterna* and *perpetüalmente*, thanks to a physical extension of the syllabic mass predominating over the simple rendering of the notion. Here the poetry of Dante breaks through the confines of the "plan" and finds a measure of the irrational. Thus does a canto appearing so "planned" lead us to the ineffable, bursting forth, we must admit, with violence.

[From the *Lectura Dantis Scaligera, Paradiso*, Florence, Le Monnier, 1969; in which it is dated "March 1965," the year when it was first published in issue 32 of *Approdo letterario*.]

Appendix

An American Book on Dante

It is not an exaggeration to state that from this small work, so brief and spirited, so elegantly produced and written, so intelligent (yet not without some ostentation of intelligence), and in which the element of surprise plays a large role—surprise concerning as much what is new and legitimate as what might perchance prove irritating—comes a wind of respirable air over what is for the most part a barren, limitless, desert land, that is, the continent of Dantean bibliography. The scholarly apparatus, reduced to a minimum, retreats almost entirely into the notes; and what emerges is the great care taken, as is only fitting for a brilliant essayist, that the text be readable even to those who know neither Italian nor Latin (the quotations, not always in the original, are in any case always translated). These are all outward aspects, of course, but from the very opening they underscore the distinguished Harvard alumnus's intention not to appear any less modern and pragmatic than humanistic. The merits and even the less positive qualities that characterize this fascinating text are equally linked to such a position.

Singleton's basic goal is to describe the poetic authenticity of the *Commedia* and to reform the trivial allegorical interpretation that negates the work's literal meaning by taking it as exclusively a function of something else. I'm not sure how much it helps his thesis to oppose Croce's judgment and more generally the presumed imperialism of his aesthetics. "[O]ne sees a hill that is not a hill, one gazes at a sun that is not the sun, and one encounters three wild beasts that are and are not wild beasts..." At least formally speaking, such a proposition is unexceptionable (but we are in fact in the zone that Singleton himself grants to Dante-as-"us" more than to Dante-as-"I", and so he cannot avoid understanding things according to what, with the *Convivio*, he defines as "the allegory of the poets"); and it is obviously the right of the critic to judge in accordance with his own aesthetics, considering the poetics preceding the text as irrelevant or even immanent within it. Rediscovering this poetics is certainly an important philological task, and like all such operations, in as much as it serves to verify the facts, it is useful to the prehistory of the aesthetic judgment to be made (especially *ad hominem*, according to Croce's logic, which equates existential judgment and value judgment); but this does not imply in the least that the critic should infer his categorical tables from the poetics. Indeed the opposite is true: the philologist does not dismiss perspective or, so to say, historical stereoscopy, whereas the critic, as such, attracts by his modernity, through persistent, constitutional anachronism. Given this contemporaneity, we can instead speculate as to what help the modern successors to Symbolism—let's say, just to remain on the East Coast of the U.S., Pound and Eliot (though we might be on more solid ground citing the great figures of post-Romantic fiction, Melville and Kafka)—may provide to an understanding the analogical poetics of the Middle Ages. But what gain accrues, with the new procedure, to the "poetry" of Dante? Will it add something to Beatrice's arrival or Lucifer's *patibulum*, no matter how many times their dynamic unfolding has been presented and re-presented to the unprejudiced eyes of pilgrims and contemplators alike?

In reality, since the literal meaning of the text does not stand for its hidden meaning but stands in force beside it, the re-evaluation so usefully performed by Singleton of the letter of Dante's journey, the journey of an "I" determined in an actual bodily space and a genuine historic time, would indeed be quite appropriate for reconfirming a faith in the three-dimensional Dante of tradition, a tradition from which neither De Sanctis nor Croce departs. If poetic novelties are to be expected, we might be better off looking for them in an analysis of the style and not of the "writing," at least not in the sense employed by Singleton. But why dwell on a superfluous polemic? It is quite enough that the new interpreter has made an irrefutable contribution to the definition of Dante's poetics.

As with anything essential, this contribution is quite easily defined. From the *Convivio* the writer takes the distinction made there between the "allegory of the poets," which reduces the letter to a mere cipher, and the "allegory of the theologians," which juxtaposes the literal, historical meaning with an allegorical or moral or anagogical, or in any case mystical or spiritual meaning. The *Convivio*, Singleton persuasively argues, is an attempt to divert the first kind of allegory and apply it to the *Vita Nuova*, which is clearly dripping with symbolic and analogical elements, but is not, however, allegorical. Indeed the fact that the story breaks off suddenly can be ascribed (and this sort of hypothesis has all our sympathy) to the dissatisfaction the author felt at the outcome of his attempt. But the *Commedia*, which is popularly interpreted according to the allegory of the poets, is inspired by the allegory of the theologians: this was still understood by ancient hermeneuts such as Benvenuto, and is declared openly in Dante's letter to Cangrande—a document that Singleton, with instictive sagacity, treats as authentic mere months before Francesco Mazzoni showed this to be true through a flawless technical demonstration. The book that the *Commedia* is imitating structurally is the book of God, the Bible, which is full of mystical meanings, but whose letter carries events that actually occurred in time. With the difference that God speaks not only in the Bible, but in nature as well, which, for a true Christian such as Augustine, Hugh of Saint Victor, or Bonaventure, is entirely open to symbolic interpretation. One must not stop at the thing itself, says Augustine, and one must not stop at the work of art as such, as Cato seems to admonish when reproaching the unmoving souls around Casella (*Purg.* II), who have forgotten their status as pilgrims ("pilgrims" in the sense of Hebr. XI, 13). From this comes the distinction, perhaps the sharpest of Singleton's perceptions, between Dante's allegorism and his symbolism: the former being inherent in the book, in that it imitates the Bible, the latter in that it imitates nature, whose objects are at once thing and sign. As concerns allegory, the junction between alluded meaning and literal meaning is established through poetic, or, let us say, linguistic ambiguity: the "I" that in the prologue of the *Inferno* stands primarily for "we," Everyone, the human race, and enacts itself outside any bodily space and historical time, becomes, in the actual journey, a genuine "I," as individuated as Aeneas or Saint Paul (the letter to Cangrande is concerned with supporting the possibility of vision). Consonant with the individuation of the subject is the plausibility of the space and the time: physical space and unrepeatable time. At intervals—that is, at salient points in the construction—the abstract dimension of the "we" reappears within the confines of the historical, irreversible plain, as can be said about the leopard (*lonza*) re-evoked at the entrance to Malebolge and the cord for catching it (*Inf.* XVI, 108 ff.)

(And here we might do well to point out, as I mentioned above, that the merely allegorical sections should be treated with the yardstick of the allegory of the poets. Virgil and Beatrice are labels—but Dante, of course, is a realist, as Singleton rightly points out, "realist" as opposed to "nominalist," that is—labels that designate, turn by turn, historical or symbolic characters; two functions that complement each other and are not identical, but recurrent and spatially separate. And from this fact stems the important divergence between the Biblical exegete and the demiurge imitating the holy book. But let's leave aside, or within these parentheses, the manner in which this elementary consideration can be developed.)

Singleton elaborates these truths in his first two chapters, called, respectively, "Allegory" and "Symbolism"—the second of which, aside from being an excellent essay, is the only previously unpublished part of the book—and in the appendix, called "Two Kinds of Allegory." The third chapter, "The Pattern at the Center," perceptively points out how, in the Christian masterpiece that is the *Commedia*, which is a human poem participating in the divine poem through analogy, the appearance of Beatrice should be interpreted as an apparition of Christ, and how this episode constitutes an organic continuation of the death of Beatrice in the *Vita Nuova*, which for its part is clearly inspired by the death and Ascension of the Redeemer. Such a Beatrice-Christ analogy, already explored by the author in a previous "Essay on the *Vita Nuova*," posits for him a "third dimension"—that is, it allegedly makes the *Commedia* also an imitation of history, of events as they happen, and not just an imitation of nature and of events being fashioned (the Bible). The literal meaning—the journey into the afterlife—may allude to ways of life in the here and now, and this alone would be allegory in the strict sense; it may allude to universal history (in time), and this would be analogy. I don't know how many readers will feel certain that the passage of Bonaventure's *Breviloquium* (p. 49) on the length of Scripture need be quoted; an any rate, here, where we have had to double the Biblical dimension, we are at the limit of this Biblical imitation, between formal structure and (Christian) substance.

A similar hint of reserve, accompanied in equal measure by praise, is spurred by the final chapter, "The Substance of Things Seen," which is said to describe, the preface assures us, a fourth dimension, perhaps the supreme dimension. In it Singleton asks himself what the truth of the *Commedia* might be, this framing of the investigation being prompted by the Aristotelian pronouncement the poet makes in his letter to Cangrande: "*Sicut res se habet ad esse, si se habet ad veritatem*" ("As each thing is in respect of being, so it is with respect to truth"). I fear, however, that the instrument adopted for this approximation—i.e., a comparison with Platonic myth—may not prove to be the most economical tool for dealing with, historically, the material in question; and it is quite possible that at the end of the laborious operation the conclusion might actually fall short for being too simplistic. Singleton's final formula, wittily parodying Scholastic modules ("*fides quaerens visionem*," "*praecedit fides, sequitur visio*")[1], spar-

---

[1] "Faith seeking vision"; "faith precedes, and vision follows" (ironic reformulations of Augustine's *fides quaerens intellectum* and *praecedit visio et sequitur effectio*).

kles more than it constitutes anything original. That Brunetto Latini is damned, despite the poet's private predilection, for things Dante can do nothing about because the *Commedia* is a genuine vision, is a circumstance that has nothing specific about it. It is well known that Flaubert and Tolstoy both felt determined to choose the destinies of their characters: the objective necessity of imagined events—let us call it their providentiality—is identical to both transcendental and immanentistic premisses, both theological and secular. Faith and the (ironic) ontological crisis of the creators—say, Dante and Ariosto (even provisionally accepting Singleton's objections)—are universal polarities with which poetry criticism, which I will call religious, operates. In Dante, if anything, the distribution of justice and mercy, so liberally dispensed in the literal meaning of the afterlife, signifies and represents, according to the allegorical sense discussed in the letter to Cangrande, the selflessness of divine decision: Grace.

Other of Singleton's observations carry far more weight. First of all, that if the truth of an artistic representation lies, in keeping with Augustine's *Soliloquies*, in its fiction and falsity, the formal certainty of the *Commedia* lies in the "I" revealing the vision (Singleton wisely avoids typologizing this phenomenon, which would yield I know not what results if applied, for example, to first-person novels of late Antiquity); and this explains the cultural precedent set by the *Commedia* in the lyric genre. There is, however, one essential element of this tradition that Dante goes so far as to reject: the hypostasis of Love. After the famous Chapter XXV of the *Vita Nuova*, which justifies its purely metaphorical import retrospectively, there would be no more talk of Love unless in keeping with philosophical truth (or at least as concerned participating in true Love): as an accident in substance, not a substance in itself. Substantial Love, in keeping with all of Christian mysticism, can only be God Himself: *"Deus caritas est"* (see the final line of the *Commedia*). But this point, too, was covered in the "Essay." If the establishment of a link between substance and formal structure is needed, I would say that it should be found in a progressive renunciation of poetic licence—a renunciation at first purely rational (at the moment of the *Convivio*) and crowned by the realization, even theoretically superior, of the allegory of the theologians and the imitation of the Bible.

What we can probably already glimpse from these surveys is a slight imbalance between general exegesis and specific exegesis. In the final chapters, it did not seem to me inevitable that the exegesis of specific points in the texts, however exhaustive (and already put forward in the Essay) or wanting (Brunetto), should give rise to any structural inferences. But also, on the other hand, contestable examples are cited in connection with generalizing arguments—clever propositions and speculations so subtle as to border on cavils, but which do not, all the same, undermine any of the solidity and groundedness of those arguments. And it is not clear to me whether the same Cato episode, in which the worldly distractions condemned do not spare even the noblest such activity, actually implies an intention to affirm the semantic heteronomy of art (whereas a bit more could perhaps be advanced on the subject of that same canzone, on that same Amore that reasons in the mind, in connection with the problematics of the hypostasis of Love and the dual nature of allegory). In the non-literal *fiumana* in *Inf.* II, 108, which for Singleton either represents or alludes to the sea surrounding the mountain of Purgatory, one may or may not recognize, according to his suggestive comparison, the waters of concupiscence discussed by Augustine and Hugh. In either case, Singleton's general thesis remains neither confirmed nor belied. And the same holds all the more true for the more resolutely unacceptable positions: within a comparison, the *perduta strada* of *Purg.* I, 119, is considered by Singleton an allusion to the lost straight-and-narrow (p. 6, where topographical constants are persuasively cited); also in a comparison, the *pelago* of *Inf.* I, 23, is taken as a reprise of the *lago del cor* of three lines earlier, *piaggia* as ambiguous between "shore" and "bank," and *corpo lasso* as due to the effort of exiting the *pelago* (pp. 11-12).

Or take his analysis of Lucifer's punishment: on the basis of Dante's quotation of the *Vexilla regis*, Singleton excogitates that the hymn, which is processional, induces the reader to await the arrival of the banner, an expectation disappointed by the immobility of that anti-Cross that lies at the center of the Earth; and this irony would in fact supposedly be another aspect of justice. Worse yet, the procession (and the verb *proceder*, in *Inf.* XXXIV 37), on the one hand, and the verb *spirare*, on the other, are alleged to allude to the technical terms *processio* and *spiratio* that teleologically designate the relationships between the persons of the Trinity. But these are accidental, verbal coincidences, and for the critic who probes them, apparent refinements; but one cannot infer the principle from the suspect nature of the corollary. It is likely that Singleton's intention was to pull together into a conceptual unity general ideas and discoveries made over the course of his readings and re-readings of Dante and Patristics. But it doesn't matter. What matters is that in so confined a space he was able to bring together so many general truths and so many novelties and hypotheses of a specialized nature. And it is of interest to us that he should prepare to resume the discussion soon. Coming from him, it will presumably be yet another discussion that will change the status of the question—one which, even in the most modest of outcomes, will remain open to debate, meaning that it is worthy of discussion, which one cannot say for too many such works.

[First published as a review in *Romance Philology* in 1956. Note that the second volume of the second volume of the series, titled *Journey to Beatrice*, came out in 1958.]

Dantean Postscript

These notes belong ideally to what would be an addendum for a possible, and certainly desirable, third edition to my commentary on Dante's *Rime*; and since the book won the generous approval of Ernst Robert Curtius,[1] they will not demure from the present occasion for textual analysis and exegesis, however modest their scope. Whatever syllable they serve to restore will be a syllable of Dante's, just as any improved comprehension of the compositions will be his gain.

The version adopted for that volume was clearly the one established, though not generally demonstrated, by Michele Barbi. Recent probings allow me to say that, leaving aside the need for explication of evidence, it is not hard to find documentary material to be added presumably to that already known by the finest Dantean scholar. One such songbook would be the Magliabechiano *canzoniere*, number VIII.25, of the Nazionale di Firenze,[2] a fifteenth-century collection which contains, among the more modern poems with their labeled attributions, anonymous fourteenth- and even thirteenth-century texts that have escaped the attentions of specialists (even though the codex was already well known in particular to Casini, for his edition of Bolognese poets). Among these we find the Dantean sonnet, *Un dí si vene* (no. LXII in Barbi), until now known only from the Vaticano Barberiniano 3953,[3] which was transcribed in 1330 for

---

[1] In *Romanische Forschungen*, LX (1947-48), 245-250 and 289. (The present essay was first published in a collection in honor of Curtius.) (GC)

[2] The codex, originally from Marmi, is described by Mazzatinti in *Inventari dei manoscritti delle biblioteche d'Italia*: Biblioteca Nazionale di Firenze, III, 176-179. Some publishing suggestions: S. Morpurgo, *Supplemento* to the *Opere volgari a stampa dei secoli XIII e XIV*, by F. Zambrini, Bologna 1929, p. 263; add to this the Corsi edition of *Dittamondo e le Rime* of Fazio degli Uberti, Bari 1952, II 355, no. 31. (Now see also D. De Robertis, in *Studi danteschi*, XXXVII (1960), 201, ff.). (GC)

[3] There it is attributed to "Danti Aligieri da Florenza," (p. 150 of the Lega ed., Bologna 1905). (GC)

the Trevisan Nicolò de' Rossi[4] in a form redolent of the Veneto dialect. Even if only for the advantage—with respect to the Barberiniano (B)—of having it in Florentine form with no need for translation, however mildly inflected towards vernacular usage, it is worthwhile to present it here in accordance with the Magliabechiano (*M*), cc. 115*v*-116*r*, with the usual arrangements:[5]

> Un dí si viene a me Malinchonia,
> e disse: "Io voglio un poco star con teco";
> e parve a me che la menasse seco
> Dolore e Ira per sua compagnia.
>   Et io le dissi: "Partiti, va' via";
> et ella mi rispuose come un greco;
> e ragionando a grande agio con meco
> guardai e viddi Amor, che venia
>   vestito di nuovo d'un drappo nero
> e sopr'al capo portava un cappello
> e certo lacrimava pur di vero.
>   Et io li dissi: "Che hai tu, captivello?"
> E lui rispuose: "Io ho grave pensiero,
> ché nostra donna muor, dolce fratello."

With respect to our version, *M* has a clear error (*viene* as opposed to the perfect *vene*, line 1) and a banalization (*grave* instead of *guai e*, line 13), and appears to have modernized the text at two different points (*tu*, line 12; and *lui* instead of *el* in line 13). It is at least indifferent in one instance (*e sopr'al* instead of *e nel so'*,[6] line 10), and in another it allows the poem to gain a syllable by abandoning a suspect diaeresis (*con*, line 7; cf. also *star con teco*, line 2, against the nevertheless acceptable *stare tego*). *M*, however, is hypometric like *B* in line 8 (with *amor*; Barbi: *Amore*), so that the confirmation of the accentual pattern in

---

[4] The other canzoniere of Nicolò's, the Sevillian one discovered and illustrated by Signora Scudieri Ruggieri, features a sonnet imitating ours in the opening, *Un die se vene a mi la Sagura* (cf. *Cultura Neolatina*, XV 1955, 102). Now published in the M.S. Elsheikh edition, Milan-Naples, 1973, p. 97, now in the F. Brugnolo ed., Padua 1974, p. 70. It also has an echo of the first quatrain in line 3 ("e menò sego en sua compagnia"). (GC)

[5] The abbreviation & is rendered with *et* before a vowel (4), and *e* before a consonant (2, 7, 8, 10, 11). (GC)

[6] On the subject of this line, it was Barbi himself who proved that wearing a hat ("portava il cappello") was a sign of mourning, in *Rassegna bibliografica della letteratura italiana*, xxiii (1915), 241. Now cf. the Barbi-Maggini commentary to the *Rime della "Vita Nuova" e della giovinezza*, Florence 1956, pp. 273-274. (GC)

line 9 appears undecided. And the fact that *B* and *M* drew in part from common sources becomes clear from the presence of several of the same sonnets: *Voi che portate la sembianza humile* (*M*, c. 115v, just before *Un dí*, whose Dantean authorship is thus outwardly confirmed); *Senno non vale a chi fortuna è contra* (*M*, c. 117r); *Fior di virtú si è gentil coraggio* (*M*, c. 117v). Among these I do not include *L'uomo ch'è saggio non corre legiero* (*M*, c. 115r), which later proved to be merely a remake of the famous Guinizzelli sonnet (in *B*, in fact, and given to Guittone). At the current state of studies, a serious comparison can be established only for *Senno non vale*, of which one critical edition, however unsatisfying, exists, by merit of Aldo Francesco Massèra,[7] based on Riccardiano 2908, in addition to *B*: and its contents reveal, among other things, the erroneous agreement between *B* and *M* as to *senno* (as opposed to *forza*) in line 2, and *né* (as opposed to *non*) in line 13. It is, in conclusion, a second useful testimonial, but of a usefulness limited by its lineage.

Aside from the sonnet studied, and the poem *Voi che portate* from the *Vita Nuova* (I am not counting *Fior di virtú*, which has nevertheless been attributed not only to Folgore and Cino, but also to Dante), *M* contains a third sonnet that happens to be sometimes attributed to Dante[8] and which not even Barbi excluded *a priori* from his edition (it is number XXIX of the "Rime dubbie"). I trascribe it here from *M*, cc. 116v-117r, again with the usual arrangements,[9] so that it may serve as a point of reference:

---

[7] *I sonetti di Cecco Angiolieri*, Bologna 1906, pp. 70 and 192-193. The version appears slightly retouched in the *Sonetti burleschi e realistici dei primi due secoli* (reprinted by Russo, Bari 1940, pp. 136 and 340). To this should be added the partial Sicilian re-edition, published most recently by G. Cusimano, *Poesie siciliane dei secoli XIV-XV*, I (Palermo 1951), p. 95 (and cf. p. 19). See also E. Vuolo, in *Cultura Neolatina*, XI (1951), 255-272. (The text in *M* was later reprinted and commented on pp. 383-385 and 396 of my "Paralipomeni angiolsiereschi," in *Saggi e ricerche in memoria di Ettore Li Gotti*, I, Palermo 1962 [=*Centro di Studi filologici e linguistici siciliani, Bollettino*, 6.]) (GC)

[8] For more information on this sonnet, see *Indice delle carte di Pietro Bilancioni*, Bologna 1893 (excerpted from *Propugnatore*), p. 36; G. Gnaccarini, *Indice delle antiche rime volgari a stampa che fanno parte della biblioteca Carducci*, Bologna 1909, I, 348 (M 214); Morpurgo, *op. cit.*, p. 215. Also: M. Pelaez, *Di un codice Barberino di rime antiche* (XLIV.129), Lucca 1902 (excerpted from vol. XXXI of the *Atti della R. Accademia lucchese di Scienze, Lettere ed Arti*), pp. 9 and 29 (no. 95); where it is wisely said, against Zingarelli's doubts: "I do not see the problem in attributing it to the young Dante." (GC)

[9] The abbreviation & is rendered with *et* before a vowel (7), and *e* before a consonant (11, 12). (GC)

> Molti, volendo dir che fusse amore,
> dissen parole assai; ma non potero
> di lui dir cosa che assembrasse vero,
> né diffinir qual fusse il suo valore.
>   Ben fu alcun che disse ch'era ardore
> di mente ymaginando per pensiero;
> et alcun disse che era disidero
> di voler dentro per piacer di fuore.
>   Ma io dico che amor non ha substanza
> né cosa corporal ch'abbi figura:
> dico ch'è passïone e disïanza,
>   piacer di fuore e dentro per natura,
> sí che 'l voler di quore ogn'altro avanza;
> e questo basti infin che l'amor dura.

Given our reasons for quoting the texts, there's no need to insist on the mistakes (line 9 has *ha* in the place of *è*) and other variants (lines 3, 6, 11, 12, 14) that distinguish *M*'s version from the one Barbi established—though we cannot but point out in any case that *M* is missing the "two strong but suspicious diereses" (my own prior comment) of line 9 (the commonly accepted version has no *Ma*) and line 11 (the standard version has *anzi è* [for *dico ch'è*]). For what I say below, it will be enough simply to restore line 8, with Barbi, to *nato per piacer del core*.

The thesis of the non-substantiality of Love—not a "cosa per sé," nor a "sustanzia corporale," but rather an "accidente in sustanzia"—takes up the decisive chapter XXV of the *Vita Nuova*, which describes what can be called the metaphorical moment of stilnovistic poetics—a moment that Dante will soon leave behind (but not Cavalcanti, and this will be the source of Guido's "disdain" for Beatrice), but which in the meantime unites Dante and Cavalcanti (the probable allusion, moreover, of the definition of Amore as an "accident" in the latter's canzone, *Donna me prega*). Such a coincidence is food for thought, without, however, constituting decisive proof of attribution. The thesis of the *Vita Nuova* is, with more or less philosophical ostentation, the same as that of Notaio Lentini and Jacopo Mostacci in the polemic with the Abate of Tivoli and Pier della Vigna (a polemic more literary than speculative, of course). The most authoritative precedents are thus from *tenzoni*. And this constitutes a rather solid basis, rendering superfluous the dubious support offered by Santangelo's suggestive but unilateral hypothesis (in *Le tenzoni poetiche nella letteratura italiana delle origini*, Geneva 1928), according to which sonnets figuring among those closest to the both the first and second definitions cited in *Molti volendo* were supposedly originally parts of *tenzoni* (nor does the third such definition differ perceptibly much from the second, except for the addition of "passion," which, however, is no less present in Andreas Cappellanus than in, say, Aquinas).

As for the first definition, that of ardor, we have: the "ardore" and the "figura [...] imaginata" of ser Pace[10] (*imaginare* is a technical term for Lentini, corresponding to Cappellanus's *cogitatio*), not to mention the "continovo pensiero" of mastro Francesco;[11] for the second definition, that of desire, we have: "il disio de l'arma" of maestro Torrigiano,[12] the "benivolo volere" or "disianza" that resides in the heart.[13] Here, naturally, what matters most is Lentini's definition ("Amor è un desio..."), precisely in the second of the *tenzoni* mentioned, with Mostacci and Piero. And another *tenzone* comes to mind: that of Vaticano 3793 between two anonymous poets (in whom Santangelo, however, believed he recognized the Abate and Lentini), with *Non truovo chi mi dica* as the *proposta* (in which Love is "volere" consequent to the convergence of "piacere e pensare e disianza"), and *Io no lo dico* as the *risposta* (where "Amor non è [...] cosa c'om possa veder né toccare").[14] The latter *tenzone* explicitly cites the general problematics of love and refutes widespread preconceptions; another fact no less important concerning what will be said later, is that the first sonnet will reappear, removed from the *tenzone*, attributed to a certain Pietro da Siena (is this Dietisalvi? Canterino?), and even metrically refashioned (with the quatrains featuring an ABBA rhyme scheme instead of ABAB), in a fifteenth-century manuscript of the Estense, which also features *Molti volendo* under Dante's name.[15] That this poem might have been part of a *tenzone* is therefore by now a rather plausible working hypothesis.

At first glance, upon studying the *M* codex itself, and an isolated sonnet of correspondence (c. 117r), one might think it possible to find a text with the

---

[10] The sonnet is called *Novella gioia* (Santangelo, *op.cit.*, p. 199). (GC)

[11] The sonnet is called *Molti l'amore* (*op. cit.*, p. 98). (GC)

[12] The sonnet is called *Né volontier* (*op. cit.*, p. 97). (GC)

[13] Anonymous sonnet (which Santangelo attributed to Lentini), *Dal cor si move* (*op. cit.*, p. 125). (GC)

[14] *Op. cit.*, pp. 121-123. (Republished by B. Panvini, *Le rime della Scuola Siciliana*, I, Florence 1962, pp. 645 ff. Also republished here are the three prior sonnets [on pp. 307, 316, 582, respectively]). (GC)

[15] A. Cappelli, *Che cosa è amore? Sonetti tratti da un codice Estense del secolo XV*, Modena 1873 (for the Sighinolfi-Zoccoli Gambigiani wedding). (GC)

requisites for qualifying as the *proposta* for which the *risposta* is *Molti volendo*. The metrical scheme is the same (2 ABBA, 3 CD), sharing the A rhymes in the first part (*-ore*), with, as the rhyming words, *amore* (1) and *valore* (5/4); and, after the abovementioned restoration, *piacer del core* (4/8); while in the sirima we find a correspondence of the C rhyme of the one with the D rhyme of the other (*-ura*), with the rhymed words being *figura* (9/10), *natura* (13/12), as well as *dura* (adjective 11/ verb 14). These are the very canons of the most ancient form of correspondence in verse, such as they were elucidated by Santangelo, and they illustrate in this case the so-called Sicilian-Tuscan phase of lyric poetry, since this was when the cross-rhymed quatrain was first introduced, possibly by Guittone.[16] It is perhaps to this phase, which notably includes the activity of the young Dante, that the peculiar meaning of *fonte* in the opening line—which recalls the "fonte del gentil parlare" (line 12) of Dante's sonnet *Due donne*, and the "fonte / Che spandi di parlar sí largo fiume" of *Inf.* I, 79)—would appear to allude, if we could verify the vocative. Here too, to facilitate comparison, we present the version in *M*:[17]

> Dimmi, o fonte, donde nasce Amore;
> e qual cagion lo fa esser sí degno
> che pigli nelli human' corpi ritegno;
> se vien dalli occhi o dal piacer del core;
>   o qual virtú gli dá tanto valore;
> o il qual parte sta il suo contegno,
> non sapendo veder per quale ingegno
> né per che modo si facci signore.
>   Ancor vorrei saper s'egli ha figura
> o per sé forma a·ssimiglanza altrui,
> o se suo passïon è dolce o dura.
>   Chi l'à servito e fidasi di lui,
> doverebbe saper la suo natura:
> et io dimando a voi come de' sui.

The connection of the new text with the Sicilian, or Sicilianizing literature, adduced for *Molti volendo* is no less evident in this case. See, in particular, the paired poems, *Non truovo – Io no lo dico* (in the first: "Non truovo chi mi dica

---

[16] Cf. L. Biadene, *Morfologia del Sonetto nei secoli XIII e XIV*, Roma 1888 (=*Studi di filologia romana*, fasc. 10), pp. 27-30. (GC)

[17] The abbreviation & is rendered with *e* before a consonant (line 12), despite the *et* in line 2. (GC)

chi sia Amore, / Ove dimori o di che cosa è nato, / Perché la gente il chiama per segnore"; and in the second: "Che este amore e di che nasce e quando / E qual parte de l'om ponsi a sedere"). There are many obvious comparisons to be made on the respective roles of the eyes and the heart: one need only recall, among the sonnets cited above, *Amor è un desio* by Lentini, or *Dal cor si move*; or *Como lo sol*, which finds itself attributed to Cino, or *D'Amor volendo*.[18] As for line 10 (where one should, naturally, read *o simiglianza*), the echo of the line "Amore a nulla cosa à simiglianza," from the sonnet *Amor discende*,[19] is rather clear; in the same poem one also reads "Assai che aman non san che sia Amore."

But the supposed rediscovery mentioned is, moreover, well known. With a non-hypometric opening, *Deh, dite o* [but also *(i)l*] *fonte donde* [or *dove*] *nasce Amore*, it appears in many manuscripts as well as a few recent editions,[20] indeed as a suggestion, but one to which the other sonnet, *Per util, per diletto, o per onore*, in fact responds. And according to the attributions, the exchange seems to have occurred between Fra Antonio da Ferrara (or Cino da Pistoia) and Petrarch, or, inversely, between Petrarch (or Lancillotto da Piacenza, or an anonymous author) and Antonio. Or between others. Must we therefore conclude that the established connection was illusory? No, quite the contrary: that connection helps us to recognize the clear stylistic divergence between the archaic, pseudo-theoretical, in short, "Sicilian-Tuscan" design of the *proposta,* and the moralizing, indeed *trecento* nature of the *risposta* and the condemnation of "carnale amor," or indeed "carnal furor" (where, moreover, the "piacer di forma," line 10, derives, according to Barbi's solid version, from line 12 of *Molti volendo*, from which perhaps descends as well the phrase *per natura*, in the rhymed position in line 13 in his version).

To adjust it to the new use—that is, to a correspondence entirely, and no longer only partially, in rhymed poetry—the sonnet was provided with a line

---

[18] Santangelo, *op. cit.*, pp. 173-174 respectively (with a doubtful attribution to Maestro Francesco), and 183. (GC)

[19] *Op. cit.*, p. 201. (Now also in Panvini, *op. cit.*, pp. 619-620. (also pp. 628-629.), for the two preceding.) (GC)

[20] The *proposta* and *risposta*, with plentiful bibliographical information, are published in A. Solerti, *Rime disperse di Francesco Petrarca o a lui attribuite*, Florence 1909, pp. 90-91; to be read in conjunction with E. Levi, "Antonio e e Nicolò da Ferrara" (in *Atti e Memorie della Deputazione Ferrarese di Storia Patria*, XIX, fasc. II [1909]), pp. 327 (no. 31) and 342-343 (no. 110); idem., "Maestro Antonio da Ferrara rimatore del secolo XIV," Rome 1920 (from *Rassegna Nazionale*), pp. 127-128; D. Bianchi, in *Studi Petrarcheschi*, II (1949), especially pp. 113-118. (GC)

of refrain, or coda, a true sign of the times:[21] "ch'io non ne son, né posso, né già fui." On the other hand the sonnet, as Francesco Zambrini[22] pointed out, is closely related to Guido Orlandi's sonnet to Cavalcanti, *Onde si muove e* [var. *o*] *donde nasce Amore?*—which sixteenth-century philologists already spotted as a *proposta* to *Donna me prega*, and which in this respect links back up ("è sustanza o accidente?") with the problematics of chapter XXV of the *Vita Nuova*. First of all, a quick comparison shows that the connections between this other sonnet—or let's call it the *proposta* of a *tenzone*—and our *tenzoni* are rather rich. The sonnet *Per util*, which we saw through one detail draw inspiration from *Molti volendo*, seems to take its rhymed use of *furore* from Orlandi; and in the sonnet from the source, the "piacer del core" (line 4), which we nevertheless found confirmed by Barbi's version of *Molti volendo*, has a competitor in the *valor* [that should be corrected to *voler*] *di core* in Solerti's version, which turns out to be identical in the corresponding line of Orlandi's and reappears in the penultimate line of *Molti volendo*.[23] In the memoirs, as in the tradition (the pseudo-Petrarchian *tenzone* is, for example, in the same Estense codex as *Molti volendo*), the group was supposed to be close-knit. *Molti volendo*, however, cannot have Orlandi's sonnet as its target, instead of the sonnet of the source, because Orlandi's text, among other things, is missing *valore* and *dura* in rhyming positions; and it is not easy to determine whether the former is a variation of the latter, as people were apparently inclined to presume when thinking, generally and specifically, of Orlandi's personality; or whether it may not be instead the second, witty variation of the first, and aimed at the greater Guido. The atmosphere in the poem is, in any case, either that of early stilnovismo or that of the prior generation on its way out. An attribution to Dante da Maiano would be too confining; an attribution to Dante Alighieri, or in any case to those close to Dante, falls more prudently into a framework of verisimilitude.

[From the collective Freundesgabe für Ernst Robert Curtius zum 14. April 1956 (edited by Max Rychner and Walter Boehlich), Bern 1956, pp. 95-102. The toast of the homage barely managed to see the proofs of the Festschrift, which came out after his death.]

---

[21] Cf. Biadene, *op. cit.*, pp. 66-67. (GC)

[22] *Opere volgari*, cit., 4th ed. (Bologna 1878), coll. 943-944. (GC)

[23] Here one might add that the "passione" of *Molti volendo* moves from the sonnet of the source, *M* codex version (the Solerti version has "*potestade*") and reappears in *Per util*. (GC)

Postscript on Celestine

To the documents on the ill fame of Pope Celestine V (born Pietro Angelerio, 1215-1296) collected by Giorgio Padoan, I am in a position to add a new testimonial that the legendary context would seem to indicate dates from not long after the events, perhaps still during the papacy of Boniface VIII. In a long series of mostly "comic" sonnets that take up the most ancient segment of the codex Magliabechiano VII.1034, probably from no later than the fourteenth century, alongside uncredited compositions by Guittone, Chiaro, Guinizzelli, Cavalcanti, Angiolieri and all the way down to Faitinelli, Bonichi, Pucci and others,[1] we find (c. 53v) the eulogy of wine that I transcribe below without alteration (though the version is not entirely satisfying), except for a few small supplements and deletions, which I've marked with brackets and parentheses respectively.[2]

      Io ò per peggio chi·mmi ghastigassi
de ber del vin(o), s'io non sia [di]sperato,
che·ss'e' mi fosse dato nel chostato
da una persona ch(ed) io mai no·mmi atassi.
      Or non è me(lglo) ch'io el bea che s'i' verssassi
A gittare el vin(o), ch'è sí gran peccato?
Alchun me n'à piú volte ghastigato,
ch'e' basterebbe s'elgli el mi rachassi.
      Quand ò bene armata la gha[l]ea,
parmi esser(e) papa, ma non Celestino;
allor no·mmi suggiuoga la giudea.

---

[1] Some information on the codex can be found in my *Paralipomeni angioliereschi* (p. 393, note). (GC)

[2] Note that the first letter in *bene* (line 9) is from correction (over a *v*?), and the first *e* in Celestino (line 10) looks rather like an *o*. (GC)

> Per lui non sia né chiesa né molino,
> a que' che·mmi riprende ch'io non bea
> chosí sancta chosa chom'è el buon vino.

The *galea* is probably a play on words with the wine recipient named—just to limit ourselves to this genre of poetry—by Cecco Angiolieri (in the sonnet *A questo mondo*): "Ma chi lo staio ha pieno o la galleta." *La giudea*, "quella strega" ("that witch"), is surely the feminine of Angiolieri's *can giudeo* (compare also to Cino's *O voi che siete ver' me sí giudei*).

[From volume XXXVIII (1961) of *Studi danteschi*, following upon Padoan's text, "*Colui che fece per viltà il gran rifiuto*."]

Sicilian Stylemes in the Detto d'Amore

Introducing, into a Dantean context such as the present conference,[1] what is conventionally known, in the manner of its discoverer Salomone Morpurgo, as the *Detto d'Amore*, is equivalent to assuming Dante as its author. It is perhaps a good idea to preface matters by stating that this thesis is not demonstrable through direct but indirect evidence. The stylistic arguments set forward by Morpurgo and Parodi have proved with the most desirable sorts of evidence that the *Detto*, and the so-called *Fiore*, issue from the same hand. But since the *Fiore*, for well-known external reasons and for stylistic considerations developed on other occasions, must be assigned to Dante, then likewise the *Detto*—a composition so remote from the Alighieri we know for certain that it was believed that its final premise might be a *reductio ad absurdum*—is Dante's.

We cannot escape the vicelike grip of the syllogism. Even with the wisdom of hindsight, it is hard to find anything but the most tenuous clues that would link the *Detto* inconstestably to Dante. I will list them in topographical order, leaving out any measurement of their provability.

DDA line 40: we find the verb *s'adona* in the reflexive form and the rhyming position, which is more comparable to *Purg*. XI 19 than to *Inf*. VI 34. (In the present case the surest echo is back to the source, which, with the verb *s'adona* rhyming with *dona* immediately above in a context of exclusively *settenari a rima equivoca*, that is, seven-syllable lines of homonymous rhymes, can only be lines 62 ff. of canzone V CCXLIII of Chiaro Davanzati [p. 154 in the Menichetti ed.]; using *s'adona* to close a *settenario*—though the sirima is different and missing the *aequivocatio*—is also authorized by line 5 of an anonymous canzone, in *V* LXVI (p. 74 in *Rime*, Panvini ed.) whose Pisan or Lucchese origin is proved, as Casini already pointed out, by the rhyme of *fermesse* with *volesse*.)

---

[1] Which was on "Dante e la Magna Curia," held in Sicily in November 1965. This lecture was presented in Catania. (GC)

DDA line 106: *or te ne getta* (cf. also the *Fiore*, XL 13, *non me ne getti*), possibly comparable to the important variant *se ne gitta* (or *getta*) in *Inf.* XVI 69 (in the standard version "o se del tutto se n'è gita fore").

DDA line 178: [*s*]*ciglia*, with Parodi's supplement perfectly in keeping with Barbi's, *dis*[*c*]*igli*, in line 44 of Dante's canzone (*Rime*, LXVIII) *Lo doloroso amor*. (Another Tuscan example, *mi sciglia* or *m'isciglia*, should of course be acknowledged in line 24 of the abovecited V LXVI, instead of the inadmissible *stillia* ['to make drip,' 'express tears'] in the Filologica Romana version, unfortunately still followed by Panvini.)

DDA line 233: *quando va per via*, identical to the clausula of a famous line (32) in the canzone *Donne ch'avete*.

DDA line 288: *Per neente*, a Provençalism or Gallicism for "in vain," associated with a verb in the second person singular ("Per neente t'aggire"), as in the *Fiore*, CCV, 14 ("Per niente bele"), but also as at the end of another youthful sonnet of Dante's (*Rime*, LIX), *Volgete gli occhi* ("…Dunque vuo' tu per neente / a li occhi tuoi sí bella donna tòrre?").

DDA, line 343: *salmo* in the rhyming position with a metaphorical meaning ("Or sí t'ho letto il salmo") as in the *Fiore*, though in the plural, at XLV, 4 ("ché non potresti apprender miglior salmi"), but also—and this an irrefutable link between *Fiore* and *Commedia*—in *Inf.* XXXI, 69 ("cui non si convenian piú dolci salmi").

DDA, line 378: *cò* in the verb formation of *far cò* (to "make capital," "draw advantage"), which we find in great variety of Dantean syntagmas (*Purg.* III, 128: "in cò del ponte," and in rhyme as in the *Detto*, in *Inf.* XX 76: "mette cò."

DDA, line 435: *devisar li 'ntagli*, with the meaning of "to design, to plan embroideries or decorations," a usage one certainly does not find in Dante, but which nevertheless recalls *Purg.* X, with its *intagli* ("bas reliefs")—and *intagliato*—as the object of *avvisar* (in the sense of "contemplate"), following a purely phonetic relationship that has been heavily documented in the *Commedia*.

Missing from my list is only the comparison of *DDA* 256 ff. with Dante's canzone (*Rime*, L), *La dispietata mente*, line 22 ("per man d'Amor là entro [in the heart, that is] pinta sete") and with his sonnet (*Rime*, LIX), *Volgete li occhi*, lines 9 ff. (where love "pinge" a woman "ne la mente"), because what matters more than a repetition of a commonplace is the *Detto*'s faithfulness in quoting. More of this below.

Now that we've confirmed, by far more solid indirect evidence, that the *Detto* is indeed by Dante, rather than feel scandalized by its disparity with respect to the canonical oeuvre—a disparity that is actually quite consistent with the richness and contradictory nature of Dante's formal culture—we might benefit from using it as an indicator as to the author's earliest literary frequentations. Indeed we might need to define such readings as "Sicilian," on the condition of not separating too cleanly the real Sicilians, who remain quite present, from the so called Sicilian-Tuscans. The two groups go together, as in the legendary verse that unites Lentini, Guittone, and Bonagiunta in the *canzoniere* Vaticano 3793 (*V*), which is so similar to the collection used by Dante and from which a pair of hardly negligible Tuscan texts have come down. And this is the context that the metrical trappings of the *Detto* call first to mind: the distich of *settenari*, as in Brunetto Latini's *Tesoretto* and *Favolello*, but implacably using rich rhymes and even homonymous rhymes; the compendium of facts and exaggeration that so wondrously suit Dante. Rich rhymes, for the author of the *Fiore*, clearly evoke the second part of the *Roman de la Rose*, considering that Jean de Meung makes rich rhymes obligatory for masculine endings (as is not the case with unfixed feminine endings), whereas in Guillaume de Lorris they were simply optional. Jean's artifice restored, or established, a subtle balance: given that a feminine rhyme formally provides a bisyllabic sameness, the point was to extend this feature to the masculine. And this clear example was enough to mark as distinct the strategy of the *Detto*, in which the oxytonic rhymes are, in Italian fashion, in a very small minority (even if we wanted to include such broken rhymes as *assempr'è* with *ma' sempre*, which sound flat to the ear, in accordance with the practice in the *Commedia*, with such examples as *non ci ha* and *Dí dí*).

We must therefore look elsewhere: among canzoni intewoven with *settenari* with homonymous rhymes, the archetype of which, at least for Dante, would have to be Guittone's canzone (XI), *Tuttor, s'eo veglio o dormo* (found in several manuscripts, particularly *V* CXLI), whose strophe ends with three distichs and is connected to the *Detto* by other rhetorical details as well (possible broken rhymes of the sort described above; the inclusion in homonymous rhymes of place names belonging to the usual comparative hyperbole, such as "como / eo n'acquistasse Como"; while in *Detto*, line 270, we find "[piú] che s'io avesse Valenza"). That this canzone of Guittone's might have been composed in response to another by Chiaro Davanzati (V CCXXIII) with the same meter—*Sovente il mio cor pingo*—as Casini believed (cf. Menichetti ed., p. 90) is not at all borne out by a careful reading of the text, even leaving aside the *envoi* to the poet's beloved in Arezzo: the lines "ché lo 'gengo mio dàme / ch'i' me pur provi d'onne / mainera, e talento ònne," clearly state that Guittone is trying his hand at something never before attempted; while Chiaro, who is surely addressing him, concentrates on the task at hand. What's more, Guittone's canzone is at the center of a broad game of imitation in which also take part, as Casini and Menichetti observe, two canzoni (V CXCII ss.) by the Florentine Finfo del Buono, *Se long'uso mi mena* and *Vostro amoroso dire*, sent respectively to Monte and and of course to Guittone; but also two canzoni by Panuccio del Bagno (missing from *V*, having been handed down only by the Rediano canzoniere), *Di dir già piú non celo* and *Poi che mia voglia varca*; not to mention, also from Pisa, the canzone by Galletto, *Credeam' essere, lasso*, with its rhymed response from Lunardo del Guallacca, *Sí come 'l pescio al lasso* (both in *V* CXII ff.), in which, moreover, the form of the sirima is retouched (one rhymed couplet is dropped) and the homonymy, at least in Lunardo, is altered and diminished.

The author of the *Detto* may well have had some of these sources in mind, and here above seems to have sampled another questionable text by Chiaro, V CCXLIII, (and his play on *membra*, *DDA* 165, probably comes from this, since both Panuccio and Gallo also have it, similarly sharing with him the plays on *cera*, *DDA* 171, and *matto*, *DDA* 361, though we don't know whether these are meaningful or coincidental). All the same, Guittone's precise fingerprint is evident in the *Detto*'s echo (line 259) of the former's *incipit*—"s'i' dormo o veglio"—all the more so as the styleme takes a somewhat different shape in the real Sicilians. For example, in Lentini's descort (also in *V*, v), line 72, we find "ca·ss'io veglio – o sonno piglio"; and in Tomaso di Sasso's canzone, *D'amoroso paese* (also V, XXI), line 12, we find "s'io veglio o dormento." Other possible or even probable clues, such as the plays on *gioia* (*DDA* 181-182), on *somma* (*DDA* 331-332.), and *agio* (*DDA* 345 ff.), fade in importance in comparison to the quotation (with variation) on Guittone's opening, which defined his lyric.

A more detailed examination of the *Detto* reveals the presence of Sicilian stylemes, some of them generic but others extremely precise and bearing the signatures of the classic authors of the school. Without listing them in any hierarchy—a proposition that might lead to pointless hairsplitting—here they are in topographical order.

DDA 142: *Amor amar è*. A famous play on words (cf. Menichetti, p. 74).

DDA 147: *Or come vivere' 'o?* The writing here may seem extravagant and incorrect, but one can easily challenge anyone to find a better way to represent the meeting and crasis of the final *e* of *vivere'* and the first *e* of *eo* (the manuscript, which shows *uiue reo* as identical to what in the next line is represented as *vive reo*, pointedly indicates, with these two graphic words, the need for analysis). The graphic inconsistency betrays a phono-syntactical anomaly, one which can be traced back to a famous Sicilian verse line, also a *settenario*, also interrogative and, in the verb, antiphrastic, and which the author may well have read in a *canzoniere* very close to the Vatican one: "Adunque morire' eo?", line 9 of the canzone, *Madonna, dir vo voglio*, the first composition in the *V* codex. This version, also present (but it's not the only common mistake) in the 1288 Bolognese memorial (which moreover features, at least, the word *Donqua*), and tolerated only by para-Bédier publishers such as Langley and Vitale, is, aside from the form, contextually incongruous, and publishers of Lachmannian persuasion all agree in rejecting it, publishers, that is, such as the author of the present text (who accepts, as an instance of *lectio difficilior*, "mor' u viv'eo") and Panvini himself (who, perhaps spurred also by the "moro" or "morò" of the Palatino codex, nevertheless returns to the correction "moriraio eo" of the Valeriani). The heavy-handed Tuscanization provides in any case a strong indicator as to the ascendancy of the *Detto*.

DDA 171: *la sua piacente cera*. This is a variation in word order, of the sort we saw with the quotes of "dormo o veglio," with respect to the Sicilians' "Vostra cera plagente," line 33 of Lentini's canzone, *Madonna mia, a voi mando* (which was also in *V* XIII, though it has now fallen out), and *La dolce cera piagente*, the opening of a canzonetta which (according to *V* LX) appears to belong to Giacomino Pugliese (though according to the less reliable Palatino and Chigiano codices was written by Pier della Vigna). But we cannot help but compare it as well to "la piagente sua cera vermiglia" in Rustico Filippo's sonnet (*V* 856) for Messerino.

DDA 179: *ben voltati*. Referring to eyebrows, a requisite in the *Roman de la Rose* (as is often the case for poets of *langue d'oïl*), in the *Mare amoroso*, and, in the context of *V*, of Chiaro Davanzati (cf. the Menichetti ed., p. 140). In *Mare*, we find *avolti*, in Chiaro, *vólti*.

DDA 197 ff.: *Alèna* keeps to the widespread Gallicizing form (in *V* alone, we find it in Lunardo, Chiaro, Guittone, and Guido Orlandi), and is featured in rhyming position in such canzoni as *In gioi mi tegno*, by Rinaldo d'Aquino (V XXXIII), line 3; and the anonymous descort *De la primavera* (V LIII), toward the end (Panvini, p. 470). In the *Detto* itself, it is the homonymy with *alena* that snags the much-sought panther[2] (most recently by Menichetti, p. LVI): in Ing-

---

[2] A reference (with thanks to L. Ballerini) to a metaphor in the *De vulgari* concerning the pursuit of the perfect language for poetry (*ubique redolentem et necubi apparentem*...).

hilfredi, at least, we have *lena*, in the canzone *Dogliosamente* (anonymous in V XCVIII), line 32. But the phrase *dolce alena* in rhyme echoes line 4 of the anonymous canzone (V CCLXIII), *Cotanta dura pena*, where, however, unless the line is incomplete, "dolze alena" presents an unusual dieresis (the "douce aleine" of Guillaume de Lorris, *Rose* 535, is too generic).

DDA 209: *la dia*. A banal Sicilianism (also limited to forms with the article), from Re Giovanni, Rinaldo d'Aquino, and Cielo.

DDA 241: *serena*. Another wide-ranging topos (examples in the Vuolo edition, 1962, of the *Mare amoroso*, pp. 143-144).

DDA 245: *l'aria* [...] *chiara*. Echo of the famous opening of a sonnet (by Lentini, but listed as anonymous in V 389) which in the V codex appears as *All'aira chiara ò vista plogia dare* (whereas the rest of the tradition has *a(i)re* in the masculine).

DDA 256 ff.: *Ma Amor l'ha sí a punto / Nella mia mente pinta, / Ch'i' la mi veggio pinta / Nel cor*. Notoriously inspired by Lentini's canzone *Meravigliosamente* (which is also in V, appearing second in the series), particularly (and here the "painter" is the lover himself) in the lines "In cor par ch'eo vi porti, / pinta come parete" (in the *Detto*, the play on sounds, instead of revolving around *portare* and *parere*, as here, is based on *punto/pinto*, and thus tighter). Clearly the first *pinta*, as Parodi correctly interprets, is intended to mean *spinta* ("pushed," "made to enter"), thus distancing itself somewhat from the *pinger (di) f(u)or(e)* common to both the *Fiore* (IV 4) and *Commedia* (*Inf.* IX 1 and *Purg.* XXXI 14).

DDA 260 *Assessino al Veglio* (which is followed, with absolute fidelity, by *Presto a Dio*, with the former rhymed with *presto*, exactly as in the *Fiore* II 11). It is another commonplace (cf. Vuolo, pp. 110 ff.), here particularly close to the manner of the *Mare* and of Neri Poponi, who appears in V. Still we must for other reasons cite the famous passage of Guido delle Colonne from his canzone *Gioiosamente canto* (also in V XXIII, part of the transmission to Mazzeo di Ricco), lines 23-24, "per ch'eo son vostro piú leale e fino / che non è al suo signore l'assessino," as the one that can best account for the subsequent passage in the *Detto* (455-456), "ché non tien lean fino / chi va come l'alfino." Parodi's glossary understands *fino* as "*fine, scopo*"—i.e., as "end, objective"—and we have, moreover, only one distich later, in a more flaunted show of skill, a "perfect" *fino* rhyming with *fino* as a form of *finare* (another Sicilianism, in Re Enzo et al.). Strictly speaking, however, the similarity to Guido delle Colonne, though undeniable, may simply be acoustic. Nevertheless, the overwhelming likelihood is that *tien leal-fino* (line 455), which should be printed in this fashion to emphasize graphically the fusion of the neutral binomial, is intended to mean "si attiene a integra lealtà" ("abides by absolute loyalty").

That the memory of a presumably very young Dante was crammed with memories of Sicilian precedents is thus more broadly documented in the *Detto d'Amore* than in the lyrical compositions left out of the *Vita Nuova*.

[From the *Minutes* of the Conference, edited by the Centro di Studi filologici e linguistici siciliani, Palermo 1966.]

A Crux of Medieval Culture:
Roman de la Rose – Fiore – Divine Comedy

1.

Allow me to begin with an experience from a few months ago. By force of circumstance, I happened to consult a text by Joseph Bédier and another by Francesco Novati just a few minutes apart. Quite curiously, I found the same hostility, the same impatience towards the *Roman de la Rose*—the *Roman de la Rose* of Jean de Meung, that is—at an interval of mere moments. We'll get back to the details shortly, but for now, suffice it to say that Bédier called the romance *sic et simpliciter "monstre"*; and, as for Novato, he says, yes, the romance became a model, but there is nothing to celebrate in this. What this brings to our attention, and into focus, I think, is a rather unusual paradox. In order to read the *Roman de la Rose*, one must be a Romanist; Romance philology is the tool that allows us to attack the book, since it is the most illustrious late-medieval work of vernacular writing by far, if we exclude, that is, the *Divina Commedia*, which now enters the discussion for the first time. And it is precisely Romance philology, through the mouths of its most eminent representatives, which now slings mud at the text. The considerations that follow involve Romanists exclusively, since, thanks to Chaucer and the Anglo-Saxon Symbolists, the *Rose* enjoys favor among the Anglicists, all the way down to the scholarly and penetrating, even when exegetically irksome, volume of John V. Fleming, *The Roman de la Rose. A Study in Allegory and Iconography*, an important work particularly for the attention paid to the illuminations richly adorning the book.

And so we ask ourselves what is the value, what is the stock-market price of this fundamental study? It must be admitted that the value is low, even non-existent, and one would be hard pressed to cite an authoritative reference to it. Of course, there had already been one life spent on the *Roman de la Rose* in putting together a monumental critical edition that still today appears to be of the highest quality: that published by Langlois in the nineteenth century. (Who was naturally the least famous, the least commonly accepted of the philologists named Langlois. One can scarcely forget the little book by Péguy entitled *Langlois tel qu'on le parle*. But the individual thus pilloried was a different Langlois, a director-general of the national archives who'd managed to step on Péguy's toes. He was Charles-Victor. Ours is Ernest Langlois.)

Well, this Ernest Langlois was, I would say, an aesthetically neutral character. Such was the condition necessary for him to devote his entire life first to the sources, then to the majority of the manuscripts, and finally to the elaboration of the critical text. It is the only fully scholarly edition of the *Roman*, and it is extremely exhaustive. And I believe that even the anastatic reprinting, currently in bookshops, has sold like hotcakes. Some may object that there's also the edition of Félix Lecoy available. But Lecoy's in an ostentatiously Bédierian edition, therefore a book based on *one* testimony, even if his Bédierism is tempered by the sensibility of Mario Roques; the edition is thus organized on the basis of a comparative codex with three others in the context of a tradition that counts somewhat more than 250 manuscripts. And to this is added the discredit hurled upon what we shall call Lachmannian ideology. Nor do I know whether my colleague Lecoy can nevertheless consider himself, like his predecessor, aesthetically neutral.[1]

But an entirely different spectacle presents itself when we try to determine the highest level of the *Rose*'s admirers. Leaving Dante aside, it seems to me that the most notable would be Chaucer (a character who, incidentally, would come to enjoy a certain Italian notoriety by the same means by which Luchino Visconti vaulted Mahler into the popular imagination[2]). It is well known that Chaucer once wrote in a preface that he had translated the *Roman de la Rose*, and so people set about looking for this translation. They looked for it and sometimes found it, managing to identify it through certain fragments. Chaucer, however—as much in the *Canterbury Tales* as in other works, particularly *The Book of the Duchess*—literally translates, albeit in extremely brilliant fashion, broad passages of the *Roman de la Rose*.

---

[1] Later another edition based on a single manuscript (but including unavoidable interventions) was provided by Daniel Poirion (Paris 1974), though the codex is the same as that followed by the old Méon and one of Lecoy's three assistants. (GC)

[2] An apparent allusion to Pier Paolo Pasolini's cinematic interpretation of a selection of *The Canterbury Tales*.

The period of the *Rose*'s flowering (if you'll excuse me the *calembour*) can, however, be seen to be longer. Langlois's preface gives us some precious indications in this regard. For example, Etienne Pasquier places Guillaume and Jean before Dante and all the Italians. We find more of this sort of thing in Sibilet, and we could add reference upon reference, jumping from luminary to luminary, including the testimonies of Baïf[3] and even Ronsard. But around the end of the fifteenth century and the start of the sixteenth, there were quite a few printings of the *Roman* in circulation, and we shall have occasion to point out a few details connecting these editions to the prior manuscript tradition. You all know that we owe one such text, modernized, to none other than Clément Marot—a modernization of which one reproduction was recently curated by an Italian scholar. In short, if we ask ourselves what is the "topical hour" of the *Roman de la Rose*—and by this I mean above all the *Roman de la Rose* of Jean de Meung—well, we can say that it is the autumn of the Middle Ages down to and including the Pléiade. A point, therefore, far more removed from our sensibilities as Romantics or post-Romantics, and in effect a point that is almost erased by the efforts of the Romantic *poussée*. You will cite Sainte-Beuve in objection: there's the *Tableau de la poésie française au XVIe siècle*, after all. But Sainte-Beuve is a tepid admirer of medieval literature in general and the *Rose* in particular.[4] The phrase, the "autumn of the Middle Ages," moreover, is a category invented not by a lover of poetry, not by a literary critic, but by a great cultural historian. And it's quite unusual: one Burgundian-Flemish myth of Johan Huizinga is, one could say, a local myth for this Dutchman, but also consistent with this geographical circumstance is the fact that the two ancient translations of the *Roman de la Rose* are in Middle-Netherlandish. And if we try to imagine the readers of the *Rose*, we will picture them with the coiffures and even the profiles—just to see them through the eyes of geniuses—of the subjects of Van Eyck and Petrus Christus.[5] If we try to visualize the figures from the *Ro-*

---

[3] The codex belonging to Lazare and most likely inherited by his son Jean-Antoine is still exant (Arsenal 2988). (GC)

[4] I mean Jean de Meung, of course, which he too held up against Guillaume. But now that survey course held in *Liège on L'Ancienne littérature (Partie Médiévale)* (1848-49) has been published (Dehousse 1971), one notes that the lectures he devoted to them are offhanded and evasive. (GC)

[5] On the subject of the *Annunciation* in the Louvre, Roberto Longhi (in *Carlo Braccesco*) writes: "on the small shelf on which sparkle some finely bound editions, there may also figure the *Roman de la Rose*." (GC)

man de la Rose, we find that, while there naturally is also—as we shall see—a legitimately philological visualization available, our thoughts race at once to the *Très riches Heures* of the Duc de Berry or other pages of the same sort. And when we we wish to see these allegorical entities plastically, figuratively embodied, we think not so much of the Maestro delle Vele di Assisi—the artist whose identity and relationship to Giotto is so hotly debated, and to whom a few strokes in Dante may refer—no, we think rather, for example, of the Church or the tottering Synagogue of Konrad Witz. Huizinga, now that I've mentioned him, has no difficulty establishing a connection, an actual cultural continuity between the *Roman de la Rose* and the high Renaissance, which leads him even to mention the name of Sandro Botticelli—and we have to say it is rather the trembling Botticelli he evokes, the weepy, Savonarolan Botticelli.

All of this explains why Romance philology, that typical product of Romanticism, could never accept or embrace the *Roman de la Rose*. Its qualification was the "popular" explosion of poetry that one could discover in the Romanesque sense of the *chansons de geste*, or perhaps in the troubadour lyrical tradition, despite its extreme erudition. One need only know that the first grammarian of Romance linguistics, Friedrich Diez, worked to an equal extent on Provençal poetry. And if Romance philology, as a product of Romanticism, embraced the Gothic, I am reminded, as concerns the *Commedia*, of the confessions of a German Dante scholar, now deceased, by the name of Schneider, who said: For us Germanic folks the *Commedia* is much more current, much more alive than for you, even in its structure, even in its unusual verticalities, even in its stylistic flourishes. It is the verticality of a construction built around a violent eruption of poetry, whereas the *Roman de la Rose* is literary and continuous; there are no ruptures in its levels.

But let's go back to Bédier and Novati. What was this about? I shall begin with some information on Novati. I was looking for his work one of the last fabliaux authors, one of the late bourgeois poets of northern France—actually from a region that is now Belgium—Jean de Condé, son of Baudoin de Condé, searching for the edition of the *Dit du Coc* contained in the Casanatense manuscript (which also features, among other things, the *Roman de la Rose*), published by Novati in the founding volume of his *Studi medievali* in 1905. Novati observes that Jean de Condé, like his father, proceeds by way of repetition and amplification ad infinitum. "Nor can this be said to be peculiar to him: more or less all the trouvères writing allegorical and moral compositions at the end of the thirteenth and start of the fourteenth centuries had the same custom.

In this respect, too—and there's no reason to congratulate him for it—Jean de Meung established a model."[6] From the very start, Novati seems a pure scholar, and thus neutral in the sense used above. It is true that he published passages from Sire Thomas, but he similarly published not quite the Venetian *Brandano*, but an alphabetized series of proverbs. Novati is nevertheless the precursor of some outstanding trends, and at least in part that represented by Curtius. In other words, Novati is concerned, and perhaps the first to be so, with establishing the continuity, in both directions, of Romance culture with Latin culture, as amply demonstrated on the one hand by his volume on the *Origini*, which unfortunately remained unfinished though later completed by Monteverdi, and on the other by his edition of the correspondence with Coluccio Salutati. Being, in essence, a historian of medieval Latin culture, he is the historian of a possibility, a continuously renewed temptation towards "renaissances." His position speaks for a substantial formalism, and it is this formalism that leads him to abhor such infinite dilation as we saw above. It is hardly an accident that the author who prevails in his critical production is Dante, whereas for his own part he considers him a decadent and accuses his fierce positivism of mannerism. Not for nothing was he an art collector—in the area of decadent Lombard art, the painting of the *scapigliati*.[7] It is curious to note that in the preamble to his rejection of the *Rose* he finds himself coinciding precisely with Sainte-Beuve (cited above).

And now let's look at Bédier. In his youthful book, his thesis on the *Fabliaux*, written in 1893 and published in 1894, Bédier compares the realistic world of the fabliaux with the idealistic world of the Round Table, with the former aimed at a bourgeois readership, the latter at an aristocratic audience, and he concludes: "these two worlds co-exist. More than that, they interpenetrate. –Is not the symbol of this coexistence and this interpenetration the monster that is the *Roman de la Rose*, where Jean de Meung naïvely believes he is carrying on the work of Guillaume de Lorris, whereas in fact he contradicts it and juxtaposes both ideals?" (Giovanni Macchia, too, moreover, though he'd analyzed the *Romance* with sympathy and intelligence, speaks of an "almost monstrous... book" and of a "monstrous ensemble.") Anyone who knew Bédier—and here I appeal

---

[6] In his proper panning of Jean (as opposed to Guillaume), "Il codice dell'amor profano," (in *Freschi e minii del Dugento*), Novati, noting the severity of "modern criticism" in his regard, does not fail to find him already a "monster," starting with Gaston Paris and to conduct, to Jean's detriment, a parallel with Dante, citing Jean Lemaire de Belges. (GC)

[7] See note 1 to page 79.

to the good Italo Siciliano, since our friendship was born at a seminar on Bédier—can easily picture the exquisite, impeccable gentleman at his ease with the great sentimental authors, with Thomas of Britain and the various Tristans, with *Roland* and the various *chansons*, as with Chénier as well; and when he deals with somewhat humbler authors, say, Jean Renart or Colin Muset, especially in the studies of his youth, they are not, however, specifically realistic authors. It is actually quite curious that he attacks the fabliaux; I am not sure whether the subject was entirely of his own choosing, but the problem is that *Les Fabliaux* become a question of origins—that is, the very content of those tales turns evanescent and disappears, because *Les Fabliaux* are the first structural text not so much of French culture but of ecumenical culture in general. Even Propp deigns to cite them at some point, though I think that Levi-Strauss at first didn't even know the book. That late nineteenth-century dissertation, *Les Fabliaux*, actually founded critical structuralism. The book therefore serves as a pretext for an eminently intellectual question. What is of interest to us here, however, is that Bédier is anxious to capture realism in its pure state, leaving behind idealism in its pure state—and therefore to separate clearly the aristocratic river bed from the bourgeois river bed. He abhors the blending effected in Jean de Meung, and I would add that this position, which gives rise to a penetrating though clearly violent simplification, is a reflection of the literary events of Bédier's time—a reflection, that is, of the post-Romantic split between naturalism/*verismo* on the one hand, between the heritage of Flaubert and Zola, just to put it in rather broad terms, and the Symbolist current, from Baudelaire to Mallarmé, on the other. This, therefore, is why this response, this rebellion on Bédier's part, seems just as significant to literature as Novati's.

One might, perhaps, object that I am engaging more the criticism of the *Rose* than actually examining the *Rose* itself; but the fact is that we must not fall prey to the naturalist deception and must realize that a work of literature lives through its interpreters, that the *Commedia,* for example, lives through its readers, and that the temptation to touch the object of one's research directly, without any screens—the screen here being the history of criticism—is in fact an illusion. Epistemologically it is, I think, entirely correct to attempt to reach subjects through their objectification in the history of criticism. I shall therefore try to conceive of the *Roman de la Rose*, or Dante, on the basis of the judgment provided me by the critics. This creates pressure to introduce an argument based on the affinity such judgement appears to have caught by surprise between the evanescent criticism of the *Roman de la Rose* (there actually isn't much interest in the romance itself, and therefore the judgments are summary) and the nevertheless macroscopic body of criticism of the *Commedia*. And what name clearly comes to mind? I am thinking not of the endless names in cultural history that one could cite, but of the only two that can be invoked if one believes in poetry as a value and at the same time senses a certain reluctance to proclaim the literary values of the late Middle Ages: De Sanctis and Croce. They constitute two absolutely obligatory roads one must travel.

For De Sanctis, then, I think naturally of the opposition between "poetry" and "poetics," between "real world" and "intentional world"; I think of the notion that Dante is a poet in as much as he acts in a manner contrary to his premises, in that the vitality contradicts his initial propulsion, and that his poetry is not only different from his culture, but irreconcilable with it. And as far as Croce's theorems are concerned, I think of the fragmentation of Dante's poetry, of the rupture not of the inner unity, but of the intentional, external unity of the *Commedia*; that unity which is a simple support—a structure, in the Crocian sense of course, not in the sense in fashion today—for the birth of poetry. I think that one may conclude, as of this moment, that the considerations on which Novati's and Bédier's condemnation of Jean de Meung is based correspond to the coincidence of his poetry—or non-poetry, if you prefer—with his poetics, his structure.

So let us now ask ourselves whether Novati and Bédier are interchangeable with De Sanctis and Croce. That is, let us try to imagine the latter two as critics of the *Rose*—a perhaps laughable hypothesis as far as De Sanctis is concerned, as his culture is extremely limited outside the literature he learned in his youth. Given, on the other hand, the infinite reading knowledge of Croce (even if not in this special domain), it is clear that the absence of any mention is a sign of scant attention paid to the subject. It would appear that the answer is to be found directly in the famous words De Sanctis used in his argument for Dante's poetics, when he writes that "the allegory of science" and "the exposition of science in direct form" are both prejudicial to art, and that "the thought does not fit into the image, the figuration does not fit into the figure"; whereas in reality, as far as Dante's vitality is concerned—note too that Bédier's own terms jump out here—"the pure real and the pure ideal are two abstractions; every reality carries with it its own ideal." And therefore De Sanctis's imaginary *Rose* could only be the object of a bad review, and yet this imaginary Rose seems to me a legitimate entity if we sincerely reassert our sense of difficulty in the face of the comprehensiveness of a great thirteenth/fourteenth-century work, were it even the *Commedia*. At this point one might even think that Croce's imaginary *Rose* is equally negative; but I'm not quite as certain as to this conclusion. The point is that if we recall those famous pages in *La Poesia di Dante* on the "forest that is not a forest," the "wild beasts that are not wild beasts," then this can only be a panning of the *Rose* in its most central aspect; but a similar judgment on the structure could, it seems to me, have led Croce to work out the concept of a cycle (*collana*)—not, of course, a cycle of lyric poems, but a cycle of passages in the "low," ironic tone, in a prosaic tone, a cycle of, in short, literary literature, or entertainment literature. In this case I think a rescue using Crocian tools can work, and quite well.

These imaginary hypotheses are not gratuitous amusements; they are sequential approximations similar to those used by mathematicians to define and solve problems. Here the problem, or the question, is: How does Dante deal with the *Rose*? Up until this point, we have argued as if the *Rose* and the *Divine Comedy* were analogues of each other; now, however, the goal is to try and determine a genetic relationship between the two, a cultural continuity. There is only a general sway exercised by the *Rose* over the *Commedia* as the founding work of its genre, a genre that we may define as the "allegorical epic," in a line that runs, let's say, from Prudentius to Alain de Lille by way of the *prosimetra* of Martianus Capella and Boethius. Provided, however, that this allegorical epic be rendered first and foremost encyclopedic; and when I use this word, I am using it in the medieval sense, not in the modern sense of a rationalized planning, but in accordance with a connection both rhetorical and dialectical such as we find in medieval *summae*. Secondly, and more importantly, provided that the work be in the vernacular ; that is, outside the clerical monopoly on expression. Jean de Meung, for one, was a professional translator. In a letter-preface to Philippe le Bel he lists his translations, probably, according to Langlois, in chronological order, in the same way that Chrétien de Troyes, at the start of his *Cligés*, lists his own romances. We need only cite his adaptations of Vegetius and Boethius, and to note that Chaucer used the latter by combining the direct translation of the Latin and the indirect translation through French. Jean de Meung, therefore, is a popularizer and translator in the fullest sense of the term. He is, moreover, linked to a political power, and this is essential, even if it is by chance not only *not* the same power as that idealized by Dante, but actually opposed to it, considering the relations Jean had (or hoped to have) with the Capet dynasty (remember the letter to Philippe le Bel) and actually with the Angevin branch, to the point that one of his idols, in the second *Rose*, is indeed Charles d'Anjou.

Naturally, on this occasion it is perfectly normal to set aside the ingenious "artistic discovery" whereby Dantean symbolism, realized through "representative characters," goes well beyond, as Gilson magisterially demonstrated, the symbolism of the *Rose*, which proceeds by "personified abstractions." Aside from the inevitable but generalized sway, there are also individual and absolutely undeniable dependencies of the *Commedia* on the *Rose*. For the moment I will leave out of consideration the presence of the *Fiore*, and briefly recall some rather famous arguments, such as that made by D'Ovidio, who claimed to recognize, in the white rose (*candida rosa*) at the end of the *Paradiso*, a sublimated allusion to the *rose* of the romance, in its most profane, secular sense. And there would be reason to cite the relationship between the landscape of the earthly paradise in which Matelda dwells and Guillaume de Lorris's[8] initial description, and so on in this fashion. But what speaks most for a direct derivation is the presence of a signature identified as author-character in both texts. Naturally, the situation of the *Rose* is quite peculiar to itself, since the romance has two authors, and the second author identifies Guillaume, the first author, with the first-person character-narrator and then introduces the prophecy of the advent of Jean de Meung, after Guillaume dies.

At any rate, the evidence of a direct relationship is decisive. And so one becomes curious to know where and how Dante came to know the *Roman de la Rose*. One answer has been ventured by my friend Francesco Mazzoni, the best informed of present-day Dante scholars. He thinks there was a mediation by Brunetto Latini. Brunetto was supposedly a kind of exchange official for all French culture among his compatriots, a kind of press agent even after repatriating to Italy after Benevento (or at any rate in 1266). For all that, there has been no ineluctable adherence to the theses of, for example, L.F. Benedetto, who sees Latini's *Tesoretto* as being under the influence of both *Roses*. Note that it is generally accepted that the *Roman de la Rose* was completed around 1280, or in any case before 1282, whereas the *Tesoretto* was composed during Brunetto's exile in France, therefore between 1260 and 1266. But there is indeed a continuity of cultural relations and interactions with France in all of Brunetto's work. For example, if the *Rose* was completed, as I said, in 1280, there are, in the *Tresor*, which nevertheless belongs to Brunetto's French period, historical chapters of

---

[8] Connections between Matelda (and Leah) and Guillaume's Oiseuse have been brought to light by Köhler (in *Zeitschrift für romanische Philologie*, 1962). (GC)

later events, such as the death of Manfred and the triumph of Charles d'Anjou—the same two characters in whom Jean de Meung embodies ill luck and good luck. And here I am leaving aside the affinities of taste that manifest themselves for example in the *Tesoretto*, whose structure presents no curvature or circularity, but is, if I may use a biological term, strictly metameric. And yet I must confess that I doubt that there was any knowledge of the French poem on Dante's part in Italy. My reluctance, you see, is based essentially on the absences, and *ex silentio* arguments are somewhat limited in value. I must recognize that of course a great deal, in the interim, has been lost; it's enough to realize that we do not possess a single line handwritten by Dante, and the lacunae concerning the *Rose* are considerable. What are the dates of the most ancient manuscripts of the *Rose*? It is well known that some, but not very many, have been ascribed perhaps to the end of the last decade of the thirteenth century, if not to the early fourteenth. I call to our attention that the most ancient dated manuscript is, if I am not mistaken, a codex not studied by Langlois because it only recently became known to the public, ever since it has become accessible in what I will call the Fondazione Cini of Switzerland, and that is the Bodmer Library of Cologny. The codex of the Fondation Martin Bodmer, having passed through the hands of a great many owners from a variety of countries, including, apparently, Francis I of France,[9] bears in fact the date of 1308, which takes us rather further down the line. What's more, there's but one manuscript containing only the part by Guillaume de Lorris (among other texts) with a very brief continuation also archived elsewhere (Fr. 12786 of the Bibliothèque Nationale in Paris). To this we must add the manuscript preferred by far by Langlois and followed in systematically Béderian fashion by Lecoy, the Fr. 1573, in which the hands are similar but distinct, with one transcribing Guillaume de Lorris, the other transcribing Jean de Meung. If, therefore, nearly all trace of Guillaume by himself has been lost, and even the earliest tradition of Jean is likewise missing, then it would, I think, be difficult even to argue *ex silentio*.

I would, however, like to add a geographical argument, which is that there are very few manuscripts of the *Roman de la Rose* in Italy, with the understandable exception that must be made for Turin, since, in the disaster that struck

---

[9] I cannot let this name be invoked without recalling that it was for this same sovereign that the most royally illustrated copy of the *Rose* was executed, a text that has been recently added to the treasures of the Pierpont Morgan Library of New York (M. 948), notably to the ten other manuscripts of the *Roman*. (GC)

that city with the fire at the Biblioteca Nazionale, which followed shortly after the collapse of its bell-tower, all the manuscripts of the *Roman de la Rose* went up, alas, in flames, with their charred remains now resting in a sort of libarary cemetery. And so, with this Piedmontese exception,[10] there are not many manuscripts of the *Rose* in Italy; and they are all originally from France. I don't know whether the one cited in the Estense library or the one, probably abridged, which Petrarch gave to a Gonzaga, were also French. At any rate, I can tell you that the Marciano codex was also drafted in France, in fifteenth-century *bâtarde* script, which I point out not out of any noble sense of civic duty, but simply because in some collections one can find misleading clues, and specifically because, enclosed in the late binding of this ample manuscript, in folio in appeareance—that is, of a post-fourteenth-century typology—was a small slip of paper featuring a Provençal text written in Northern Italy, probably in the Veneto. Manuals that cite this codex for its Provençal-Italian text—such as that published by my late lamented teacher Brunel—speak of an "Italian" manuscript, but in reality the principal manuscript was without a doubt composed in France, or by the hand of a French scribe. (On this matter I would, as an aside, appeal to the Veneto school of philology that has studied that Provençal-Italian text not only to situate our knowledge of it in the context of a whole tradition, but above all to gather further information on that little letter on the back of which it was written, which has remained somewhat in the shadows.) And so, if these arguments *ex silentio* yield any clues, without going so far as to say they have any evidentiary value, one may legitimately suspect that Dante could have come to know the poem in France.

A further consideration serves to buttress this suspicion, and this is the moment to bring the so-called *Fiore* into the discussion. It turns out that the only extant codex of the *Fiore* has all the appearance of having always been in France. We are only able to trace its history starting from a relatively recent epoch, and it informs us that the codex was present in the famous Dijon library of the Bouhier family: that is, at least since the seventeenth-century, the time of Jean III Bouhier.[11] But the manuscript now at Montpellier, though drafted by a

---

[10] Also from the Piedmont is the fragment (studied by Ruggieri in *Archivium Romanicum* in 1930), donated by Bertoni to the Estense of Modena. (GC)

[11] He lived from 1607 to 1671. The codex now in Montpellier is registered all the way back to Bouhier's catalogue (cf. A. Vernet and R. Etaix, in A. Ronsin, "La Bibliothèque Bouhier etc." = *Mémoires de l'Académie des Sciences, Arts et Belles-Letters de Dijon*," t. CXVIII [1971], p. 227).

Florentine hand, has what one can call a typographical structure and pagination that are decidedly French in appearance. In addition, the folios containing an incomplete version of a text very close to the *Fiore*, which its discoverer, Salomone Morpurgo, called the *Detto d'Amore*, turn out to have come from the same ancient manuscript. These were found in the Ashburnham fund of the Laurentian Library, which indicates that they were dredged up by the famous Guglielmo Libri in some provincial French library.[12] Therefore the two elements making up the ancient manuscript both point to France. It thus seems to me highly likely that the Dante's acquaintance with the *Romance of the Rose* occurred in France.

But let us ask ourselves a somewhat less imaginary question, in case our fantasy might seem too overweening or far-fetched in the preceding considerations. Let us ask, I say, how Dante may have viewed the *Rose*, how he may have interpreted it. I would say that he saw it as possessing an incessantly progressing linearity, to which the curvature of the *Commedia*, with its ascending spiral, its submission to the numbers imposed by the rules of art, stands in stark contrast. The plot of the *Rose* is so elementary as to be almost nil; it is the quest for the heroic deed from the start to its physiological conclusion, and it matters little whether this end shines with Guillaume de Lorris's courtly candidature or with the insolent phanerogamia of Jean de Meung. With both ends well established, the whole thing becomes a sort of vast *entre-deux*—and I will be forgiven, I trust, for advancing a concept in reference to a surely great French writer and an indisputable masterpiece of that country's literature, no less a work than *A la recherche du temps perdu*. Proust stated that he wrote the last page immediately after the first, and that everything in between is an immense *entre-deux*. Well, one can, with due irony, say something similar about the *Roman de la Rose*. Naturally it is easy to understand the sense of freedom, indeed license, with which a continuator might work on a plot so wanting—such as, for example, Ariosto car-

---

The year 1721, inscribed in the codex, as both Mazzatini and Parodi have reported, is the date of the cataloguing done by Jean IV, grandson of Jean III (*op. cit.*, p. 219). The library was, moreover, founded by Jean I, great-great-grandfather of Jean III, in the early 1500s. (GC)

[12] In all likelihood at Troyes, where Libri had been working as a kleptomaniac from 1840 (*op. cit*, pp. 151-152). The Bouhier library, confiscated by Revolutionary authorities from the Cistercians of Clairvaux (who had bought it in 1782), had been transferred in 1795; but in 1804 some parts of it were assigned to a variety of libraries, with an important bundle going to Montpellier (*op. cit.*, p. 150). The manuscript of the *Fiore*, notoriously bound together with one of the *Rose* (at the time of Jean III Bouhier?), had thus left Burgundy quite some time before, and the pages with the *Detto* were probably scattered at the time of the binding. (GC)

rying on Boiardo, and of course Jean with respect to Guillaume. The *Commedia* is clearly something else entirely. The *Commedia* is the metamorphosis of the lost man into the saved man. And if the *Rose* had followed Dante's great work, we would say that the *Rose* is a parody of the *Commedia*; but since the *Rose* comes before it, we will say that there is, in the *Commedia*, a sort of anti-parody of the *Rose*—in the same way as one speaks of anti-matter, or of pre-image (*antimmagine* in Italian) in mathematics. The non-durability, the instantaneousness of the *Rose*'s physiological conclusion should, I think, be compared to the instantaneousness of the beatific vision in so far as this appears to a living man and is immediately nullified. All this occurs within the common framework of a "comic" work. "Comic" in quotation marks, of course, meaning "comedic," with a happy ending following prior troubles, even though Dante's opening is truly grim, while Guillaume's is so sedate that Dante, as we've seen, was able to draw inspiration from it for his earthly paradise. Indeed, the landscape through which Guillaume de Lorris's first-person narrator/character moves is once called "*parevis terrestre*" in the text. A clear representation of Dante's curvature, as opposed to the progressive, metameric linearity of the *Rose*, lies in his adoption of the *terzina* as opposed to the octosyllabic distichs of the French text. The tercet, with its terza rima, contains a movement of continuous, partial return, while Guillaume's and Jean's schema presents a total openness. Thus, on the one hand, the pattern is ABA, BCB, and so on, on the other, it's simply AA, BB, and so on, up to ZZ.

This problem—upon which I must insist, for it is a major point that was luminously covered by Pio Rajna, and with a perspicacity surprising to us moderns who think ourselves so discerning—this problem, I say, opens the way to a rather delicate question, which is that of interpolations. One might object that it is impossible to interpolate anything into the *Commedia*. The fact is, however, that it is not, strictly speaking, impossible, since there is some interpolation in the work: a few tercets, or even two whole cantos, brought to our attention by Ignazio Giorgi. But it is a teratological phenomenon, a minor occurrence in the overall arc of the tradition. Whereas the tradition of the *Rose*, on the contrary, offers a whole panorama of continuous interpolations. These interpolations are thus as facilitated and fomented by the structure as they are discouraged in Dante's schema. But how do we evaluate them? Are they falsifications? The known existence of many dozens of manuscripts of the *Rose* stirs some doubt in my mind, since in a number of cases the interventions are fragments, obviously distichs, marked in the margin or at the bottom of the page, and thus must come from a collation. The most important thing, however, is the fact that a notable quantity of these so-called interpolations, when collated with the basic text of the *Fiore*, appear very much to have already been present—which leads me to strongly suspect that the insertions made into Guillaume de Lorris's text may possibly come, at least in part, from Jean de Meung, and those in Jean's text from later editions of his contribution. The question seems to me to be still open, even though I do not think it has yet been raised in clear enough terms. It is true that Langlois—and let this be said to his credit—noticed with typical accuracy which of these passages are documented in the *Fiore*, but of course at the time nobody realized that the *Fiore* was by Dante, to the point that even just a few years ago the work's sonnets were anthologized in a selection of minor Trecento poets.

And I would add that one can conjecture as to another reservation that Dante may have had towards the Rose, aside from those reservations of an ideological and poetic nature that we have already mentioned, an equally tacit reservation. "Dante, you know," Curtius once said to me, "was a great mystifier." Indeed, sometimes a rejection serves to camouflage a debt owed, to cloak it with a disparaging association, when it is a debt that troubles the author. Let us not forget the quotation or quotations of Guittone and Brunetto himself. If we base our position on the ideal envisioned in the *De vulgari*, we can put forward the proposition that the *Commedia* is a synthesis of required comic and tragic elements, and that essential to its constitution is the assumption of a subject corresponding at once to the three *magnalia* of the *De vulgari*: *Salus*, *Amor*, and *Virtus*.[13] And so we ask ourselves what the *Rose* must have seemed like to Dante from this perspective. It must have seemed a "comedy" of the lowest style, one not figuring in what has been called the "encyclopedia" of styles. And it is legitimate to doubt that its content, even the purely pretextual content of its external structure, is "Amor." Worst of all, however—worst, that is, not for Leopardi or for Freud, but for a courtly poet of the Middle Ages—is that this "love" is not only abstract, but entirely separate from death. For a courtly poet, says Guittone: "AMORE quanto A MORTE vale a dire" (my emphasis); "Amor dogliosa morte si pò dire, / Quasi en nomo logica sposizione, / Ch'egli è nome lo qual si pò partire / En A e MOR, che son due divisione, / E MOR si pone MORTE a difinire"; or Federigo dall'Ambra: "AMOR dai savi quasi A-MOR s'espone; / Guarda s'amore a morte s'apareggia." In the face of all this, I believe that the

---

[13] Salvation, Love, and Virtue.

Roman de la Rose enjoys the singular distinction of being the only *large* work of world literature (I'm not sure we can call it "great") in which death is absent. There are, of course, characters who die. For example, Malebouche is strangled to death and has his tongue cut out, but he's a fictional abstraction, down to his very name; historical figures such as Manfred and Conrad die, but only to justify the fortunes of Charles d'Anjou; mythological characters such as Narcissus and ancient and paradigmatic figures such as Nero and Virginia also die, but the list ends there. When, instead, we think of the *Commedia*, the whole thing is an extraordinary Nékyia; there is only one character who is not dead, not *yet* dead, that is, and that's the one who says "I." And contemporaries were actually so struck by this fact that the illustrators, the illuminators of the *Rose* (of whom we'll speak more later), were sought as sources of inspiration for the illuminators of the *Commedia*. A few of the manuscripts have an enormous abundance of illustrations which I would call miniated in a general sense. (The precision is necessary because the manuscript I am about to mention features watercolor illustrations rather than illuminations in the strict sense.) I believe the *Rose* codex containing the greatest number of miniatures is one of the two Laurentian ones (no. 153 of the Acquisti e Doni group). Well, in these watercolors, the painter depicts with great fervor the massacre of these mythical characters—all remote historical figures, or simply allegorical—clearly to get a bit of blood throbbing in the veins of the cerebral text.

So far, we have no mediation between the *Roman de la Rose* and the *Divina Commedia*. We have even taken care to set the *Fiore* aside. But now the moment has come to introduce the so-called question of the *Fiore*—that is, the question concerning the attribution of the *Fiore* to Dante. I'll not go into all the details, because I don't wish to repeat tediously what has already been published, even by the present author (particularly in the chapter on the *Fiore* in the volume devoted to Dante by the review *Cultura e Scuola*, and later in entry on the *Fiore* in the *Enciclopedia Dantesca*). But I would like to underscore that a curious illusion has emerged: namely, that, with all this effort, the question of the *Fiore* had reached a certain maturity. If there is indeed something that bears repeating, it is that the *Fiore*'s first publisher (that is, Ferdinand Castets in 1881) had already presented essentially all the arguments—all the external ones, that is—favoring the identification of Dante Alighieri as its author.

Let me recapitulate these arguments at supersonic speed. First, the presence of a signature. The signature of *Durante* or *ser Durante* appears twice, in sonnets LXXXII and CCII: thus the signature, or identity, of a character saying

"I"; and the first passage is the one in which Guillaume de Lorris is named. A second argument concerns something that does not appear in the *Rose*; namely, a character of common interest to both the author of the *Fiore* and to Dante: the philosopher Siger of Brabant. Yes, there is a Siger in the *Rose* (*frere Seier* or *Sohier*), but apparently, if it is not a fictitious name (and I don't think that Langlois's opinion on the matter is plausible), it probably alludes to an illustrious personage par excellence, such as he was, from the time of Louis VI or Louis VII: the reformer of the abbey of Saint-Denis. And so, what, in the place of *frere Seier*, do we have in the *Fiore*? There is Frate Alberto, who we immediately realize is Alberto della Magna.

A third argument can be gleaned from sonnet XCVII, in the story of the wolf that becomes a lamb, of which we have only one erratic version—more precisely, the first quatrain, with slight modification, which turns out to be vague and attributed (specifically by an ancient commentator, the one called pseudo-Boccaccio) to the legend of Dante. What's more, there is a sonnet by Dante to Brunetto—but we should read this (with the captions of the codices) as a Brunelleschi—which speaks of a maiden (*pulzelletta*) who comes with him "to celebrate Easter" ("la pasqua a fare"); some have interpreted this maiden to be the *Fiore* itself. At any rate, the writing does not seem easily understood, but at the home of the addressees there are "molti frati Alberti"—here's one element common to both the *Fiore* and the *Commedia*—"many Brother Albertis" who are able to understand "what is put into their hands" ("ciò ch'è posto loro in mano"); and if they perchance are not able to respond, one must turn to messer Giano, who may very well be Jean, that is, the *ipsissimus* author of the second part of the *Rose*.

All of these arguments were put forward particularly by Guido Mazzoni and Francesco D'Ovidio, but it is the latter who adds, as already mentioned, the hypothesis of the *Rose*: in other words, that the *Commedia*, as an anti-parody of not only the *Rose* but also the *Fiore*, departs from that insolent phanerogamia and sublimates the *candida rosa*. Pio Rajna, for his part, stressed the metrical aspect, since, with its section in tercets, the *Fiore*'s corona—that is, the cycle of sonnets (the *Fiore* being the most extended corona, more than Guittone's, and more than anything by the pseudo-Cavalcanti)—seems to foreshadow the invention of *terza rima*.

These arguments are all of the external variety—very solid, in truth, but what we need are internal arguments, involving stylistic questions, and much livelier. Among such we even find correspondences brought forward by critics opposing the identification of Dante as the author of the *Fiore*. One is advanced by D'Ancona himself, another by a less prominent opponent, the Italian-American nun Mary Dominic Ramacciotti, who composed a diligent and moreover perfectly inconclusive dissertation on the *Fiore*. Advocates of a Dantean identification such as Basserman, mocked by those (especially Vossler) who thought they knew better, do their part to contribute. As do illustrious specialists, who nevertheless play it safe as to the core principle. For example, Vanelli has given us an important examination of the question; yet he remains neutral, psychologically intimidated by the fact that Barbi leaned towards rejecting the attribution. And while he does refrain from taking a position as to the beginning, we have a major contribution from Domenico De Robertis in his *Libro della 'Vita Nuova'*; I'm not sure whether it is correct to speak of neutrality on his part, however, since De Robertis emphasizes that the problem needs to be re-examined *da capo*. And if it turns out that that my own research on the question has any merit, the inescapable precedent to such research lies in that book by De Robertis.

Still, there are other internal arguments, which for the sake of brevity I will break down into four categories. Lexical arguments above all—that is, the presence of syntagmae typical on the one hand of the *Fiore*, and on other of the *Commedia*: such as, for example the "buona speranza" that nourishes the author, and which we also find in sonnet III, line 13, of the *Fiore* (and to this one should add the "bona spera" of XXXV, 4) and is comparable to the "speranza buona" feeding him in *Inferno* VIII, 107. Naturally, this example—and I will give one for each category—represents only the top of a list that is often very long. Then there are the lexical correspondences in rhyme, where the semantic and phonetic aspects coincide: the "miglior' salmi," for example, a burlesque metaphor from *Fiore* XLV 4 in the rhyming position, comparable to the "piú dolci salmi" of *Inferno* XXXI 69. The third category consists of what I would call associative lexical correspondences. For example, in *Fiore* VII 4, the text says "Se Pietate e Franchezza no·ll'acora," where *acora* carries a literal meaning (*accorare* signifying "to kill by running the heart through"; it's a word that Tuscan peasants still use when they slaughter a pig). Here, however, *acora* is a verb referring to the subject, *Pietà*, which calls to mind *Inferno* XIII 84: "Ch'i' non potrei, tanta pietà m'accora." Finally, for the fourth category, a series of purely phonic correspondences, as in sonnet XIV, which contains, among many other coincidences, the line "Di non far grazia al meo domandamento"; in *Inferno* II 79 we have a line with the same pattern, with a considerable number of syllables in the same positions: "Tanto m'aggrada il tuo comandamento," where *tuo*, naturally, is a permutation of the original *meo*.

After reaching this point, I believed that the field of external arguments was far outstripped by that of the internal arguments, and this convergence of semantic and phonetic elements seemed to me incontestably obvious. But what is incontestability? And what is obviousness? Because the fact is that there are, bibliographically speaking, some protests to be counted against this supposed obviousness. More specifically, there are two small books by a Swiss colleague of mine, a man of signal civility in this polemic, Remo Fasani, and in these two opuscules he maintains: first, that the *Fiore* is not by Dante; and second, that it is the work of ... But that's just it. This is where the problem starts, because his first booklet claims that it is by a certain author, whose name is Folgóre da San Gemignano, and the second booklet claims instead that it is by a certain other author, whose name is Antonio Pucci. This variability, of course, renders the thesis rather difficult to defend, at first glance; but there is only one thing here that worries me, which is that what I thought was obvious is not obvious at all, since what I also thought to be incontestable has been indeed contested. And so I cannot avoid the need to take the measure of my position, and this counteroffensive will consist of endeavoring to demonstrate that the chronological sequence is *Rose-Fiore-Commedia*, because if this is the case, then we can no longer take into consideration a so-to-speak burlesque-realistic *rimatore* of the ilk of either Folgóre or that of Antonio Pucci, and the likelihood of bringing the question back into the Dantean fold becomes so great as to be considered decisive. And so I shall leave you, for now, in suspense. Tomorrow I shall present the arguments proving the sequence of *Roman de la Rose – Fiore – Divina Commedia*. The evening lecture will be preceded by a seminar on the cases in which the text handed down to us by the sole manuscript of the *Fiore* deserves, for internal reasons or for reasons of comparison with the *Roman de la Rose*, to be corrected.

II.

As we seek a more decisive resolution, one essential element of our demonstration will be to establish the sequence of *Roman de la Rose – Fiore – Divina Commedia*, and from this the proof of Dante's authorship of the *Fiore* will emerge reinforced. A friend of mine, one of the most illustrious of the so-called "hermetic" critics, insists that one can engage in decent philology only if one bears in mind the second law of thermodynamics at all times. And in this sense, what I am about to give is a demonstration of entropy. In the writings I cited yesterday, I was able to establish some relationships that had seemed to me causal and some that seemed non-causal, between passages in the *Fiore* and passages in the *Commedia*. For example, in the same sonnet (XIV) from which we took the line "Di non far grazia al meo domandamento" we find the line (10), "Molt'è crudel chi per noi non vuol fare." This line to me seemed clearly and immediately to recall Ugolino's tragic line: "Ben se' crudel, se tu già non ti duoli." The rhythm is identical, more anapestic than dactylic, if interpreted as ascendent; *crudel* is in the exact same position; as is the negation. Let us admit that there is nothing, in and of itself, to be surmised from this, although to me it seems we may infer that the *Fiore* was written by the same hand as the *Inferno*. But it is essential to establish the sequence, and here only one point of external reference will prove decisive. Which is to say that, if the text of the *Rose* is closer to one of these places than the other, it will be clear that the order is *Rose* – the closer text – the less close text, as in *Rose-Fiore-Commedia*; otherwise it will be necessary to work out an impossibly uneconomical solution, which would be that an imitator of the *Commedia* brought the letter of his text, by dint of hammerings, close to the letter of the *Rose*. Now the abovecited line of the *Fiore* surely refers back to the lines of Guillaume 3315-3316 (I still use Langlois's numbering, not Lecoy's, which is slightly different): *"Mout par est fel e deputaire / Qui por nos deus ne viaut rien faire."*

This figure crops up several other times, and you will have, I trust, the indulgence to hear a few demonstrations of this. In the *Fiore* LXXVI 13, we read a verse that begins: "Per altra via andrai." Who doesn't hear in these words lines 91 and 92 of *Inferno* III: "Per altra via, per altri porti / Verrai a piaggia"? And yet this passage too appears in the *Rose* (line 10,232 of Jean): *"Ailleurs vostre chemin querreiz."* On top of this—and here things become a little more complicated—consider the line (*Inf.* XV, 9): "Anzi che Chiarentana il caldo senta." Armed with this information, we find in the *Fiore* (XVII 9-10): "Quando Bellacoglienza sentí 'l caldo / Di quel brandon." *Sentire* linked with *caldo* creates one of those connections whose probative import I pointed out yesterday, as also in (CXLV 7-8), "te, che dê' sentire / Il caldo del brandon." Well, these passages have meaning only if referred back to the *Rose*, but there's no longer any relationship between the *Rose* and the *Commedia*; the relationship we could fictitiously establish in the previous cases here can no longer be proposed in any way. And indeed we see, in Guillaume 3473-3474: *"Bel Acueil, qui senti l'aier Dou brandon…"* And here I must add a gloss even for those with expertise in Old French. *Aier* is almost an *unicum*; you'll find it all alone in the great Tobler and Lommatzsch dictionary, and it is rendered imperfectly, in my opinion, by the philologists. Langlois, to whom I have otherwise paid homage as a valuable scholar and will continue to do so, claims that we are dealing here with a version of *aïr* with a meaning of "help", and so he derives it from the (archaic) verb *aidier*. Apparently Lecoy found himself in the same aporia, but his solution is no more felicitous, since he looks back to AER—apparently, that is, to the accusative AEREM. But in fact, here *aier* is the same as *desierre* and *ocierre* for *desire* and *ocire*, in other words, *aïr*: that same word that gave the Italian language the word *aíre* ("impetus"), and is therefore, in this case, the force coming from that torch. Also worth noting in the *Rose* is line 12753, "*Bien sai le brandon sentireiz.*" Here the passage is truly gradual, inching forward in fits and starts.

The same circumstance seems similarly demonstrative in the following case. Let us begin with the *Commedia*, *Inferno* XXXII 12, "Sí che dal fatto il dir non sia diverso," rhymed with *verso* as a noun. The combinations of *fatto* and *dir* are frequent in the *Commedia*; take *Inferno* IV 147, "Che molte volte al fatto il dir vien meno"; or *Paradiso* XVIII 39, "Né mi fu noto il dir prima che il fatto." But it's the former passage that comes to mind when we see *Fiore* CIII 11, "Ma molt'è il fatto mio a·dir diverso," it, too, rhyming with *verso* as a noun. Here it is crucial to establish whether this passage of the *Fiore* corresponds to any context in the *Rose*, and indeed it does, with Jean 11222, "*Mout sont li fait aus diz* [variant: est li faiz au dit] *divers*," with *divers* rhymed with *vers* as a noun.

And there's more. In a passage of the *Inferno*, a very famous one, which speaks of a Friar Gomita as a "sovereign swindler," the line (XXII, 87) "Barattier fu non picciol, ma sovrano" may well be an invention of Dante's, but we start to smell a rat when we read *Fiore* LXXXVIII 66, "Che re de' barattier' tu sí sarai" ("that thus king of swindlers shall you be"), which corresponds literally to a line of the *Rose*, where the expression, moreover, carries a technical meaning. It is line 10938 of Jean, "*Tu me seras reis des ribauz*," and here *ribauz* is an administrative term designating a police superintendent or prefect. Clearly the author of the *Fiore* interpreted "king of the ribalds" in a general, not technical manner, and the author of the *Commedia* then borrowed this incorrect transposition as if it were essentially a straightforward image.[14]

---

[14] In realtity the synonymy of "rex ribaldorum" and "baracteriorum rex," even in 14h-century Tuscany, was well demonstrated by Luciano Rossi in "Notula sul Re dei Ribaldi,"in *Cultura Neolatina*, XXXIII (1973), 217-221. I will add that the Occitan term is "rei dels arlotz" (Guilhèm de Tudela, str. 19, v. 1, *La Chanson de la Croisade alibigeoise*, Martin-Chabot ed., I, Paris 1931, p. 55. N. 2)]. (GC)

A further observation: *Fiore*, CXII 4, "se·llo scritto non erra" (referring to the Bible) is a passage mirroring *Rose* 2269, "*se la lettre ne ment*" (also referring to the Bible), though in a different context. Now look at how the *Inferno* combines the text of the *Fiore* with the memory of Guillaume: "Di parecchi anni mi mentí lo scritto" (XIX, 54).[15]

I will give one last example, to avoid taking advantage of your indulgence, adding only that there are many more in the dossier: "E 'nganno ingannatori e ingannati" (*Fiore* CXVIII 14). There are also parallel passages in which the Italian uses the same term, *ingannare*, and one finds the same play on words, except the term used in the *Fiore* context is different, and we are thus looking at a process of condensation typical of the paraphrastic reworking of the *Fiore*. *Rose* 11531 (I'm sorry to keep citing these reference numbers like a Quaker preacher, but I suppose someone in the audience may be interested in immediately checking the source): "*Lobant lobez e lobeeurs*" stands for the first *Fiore* passage above, but 12237 and the lines that follow, "*Maint vaillant ome ai deceü... Mais ainz fui par mainz deceüe*," find their counterpart in (*Fiore* CXLIX 1 ff.) "Molti buon'uomini i'ò già ingannati... Ma prima fui 'ngannata tanti mesi." We thus have a condensation process from which the next locus (*Fiore* CLXXIX 8-9) descends, "mi credette ingannare: / Ingannar mi credette, i' l'ò 'ngannata"; followed by *Inferno* XVIII 2-3, "Isifile ingannò, la giovinetta / Che prima avea tutte l'altre ingannate." And thus the working hypothesis, however expertly and copiously confirmed—namely, that a certain element of derivation proceeds directly from the *Rose* to the *Commedia*, and that this is indirectly further reflected in the *Fiore*, by another hand from the early, or even possibly the late, fourteenth century—proves to be utterly absurd and counterproductive. We can call the process not entropic (as in the second law of thermodynamics), but what mathematician-physicist Luigi Fantappiè would have called syntropic. It calls to mind what his former pupil Leonardo Sinisgalli said about his Roman lectures: he would project a film backwards and have the class witness the return of the chick to the egg. It is an eminently unnatural process.

Thus, although I had succeeded in transferring the so-called question of the *Fiore* from an external argument to an internal one, and although the corroboration of phonetic and semantic data seemed decisive to me, I was contradicted in the matter by scholars who had presented contrary hypotheses. Now, it

---

[15] "The book has lied to me by many years." (Mandelbaum)

would seem to me that the sequence of *Rose-Fiore-Commedia* has been proven incontrovertibly. In this case the *Fiore* can only have been composed by a master active between the year 1280 (the end of the *Rose*) and the start of the composition of the *Commedia*. I do not rule out that one could proceed further along this gradation. This evening, however, I would like you to turn your benevolent attention to the limit I have at the moment reached, which is the following: Echoes of the *Rose* can be found, as we have seen, in great quantity, by *force majeure*, in the *Fiore*, but also in the *Commedia*; and yet they can be found, to a lesser degree, in other works of Dante, either certifiably by Dante or probably by Dante or in any case by the same hand that gave us the *Fiore* and Morpurgo's *Detto d'Amore*. What is important to bear in mind is that these steps do not coincide—that is, the derivations of the *Fiore*, the derivations of the *Detto*, the derivations of the *Commedia*, the derivations of possible other minor works of Dante from the *Roman de la Rose*, do not repeat themselves (except in the graduated instances we examined); rather, they integrate themselves with one another. And this argument, to me, seems decisive.

I will give two bits of information in this connection. The first sonnet of the *Fiore*, the opening sonnet, mirrors the passage that begins at line 1681 of the *Rose*—of the first part, to be exact, the part by Guillaume de Lorris. And never mind that the poem is also a summary and a string of allusions to prior loci. Still, the suspicion might arise, since the very first part of the *Rose* has no counterpart in the *Fiore*, that the latter text is acephalous. Indeed this very suspicion was promoted at least to the status of working hypothesis and then correctly refuted by Egidio Gorra. And in fact, if one studies the morphology of this sonnet in the manuscript, even only in its physical aspects, one sees that it comes with no captions nor with the usual adornments: which means that it was a sonnet with a function—a function of demarcation, as the structuralists would say. In other words, it was supposed to be the very first sonnet, for which the final special ornamentation was never obtained, and meanwhile the regular decorations for the other sonnets in the middle of the text are missing here. Now, the fact is that the opening of the *Rose* is reflected in other works of the Dantean oeuvre, especially in the *Commedia*. As I have had occasion to point out elsewhere, some of the recurrent themes from the beginning of the *Roman de la Rose* (themes which, by way of fourteenth-century French poetry, manage to reach Chaucer, for example) are: vision; deep sleep; the age of the sleeper, who is twenty years old in Guillaume ("*Ou vintieme an de mon aage*"), and midway through life for Dante; the season—which, in accordance with a topos that we find already in the ancient troubadours, is presented antithetically at the start of sonnet III in the *Fiore*, where the poem says that the event takes place "Del mese di gennaio, e non di maggio" ("In the month of January, not May"), and thus in opposition to a text in which it occurs in May, which is, of course, the start of the *Rose*, which corresponds more or less with the *Commedia*. And then there is the landscape of delight I mentioned yesterday, called "*parevis terrestre*" in the *Roman de la Rose*, which perfectly matches Dante's earthly paradise, where Matelda dwells. One could even cite the precise passage in the *Rose,* and the corresponding passage in the *Purgatorio*, proceeding, if one so desired, from the later text to the earlier one—from "Allor si mosse contra il fiume, andando / Su per la riva" to the movement towards the mountain in the *Rose*, thus making the derivation absolutely clear: "*Lors m'en alai par mi la pree, / Contreval l'eve esbaneiant, / Tot le rivage costeiant*." Note that this all refers back not to Jean de Meung's part of the text, not to the skillfully realistic part, but to the "idealistic" part—to use what we might call Bédier's terminology. Other features could likewise be cited, such as the theme of true-to-life dreams—"se presso al mattin del ver si sogna"—which also figures in the *Rose*, where *auctoritas* plays an important role in the person of Macrobius. And the same goes, generally speaking, for the presentation of the allegorical figures.

A second example, and the proof of integration will be sufficient, I think. In the *Rose* we find the "Commandments of Love"; clearly it's a tablet—not that there are only ten, but they are, in short, the "tablets of the law." These commandments do not reappear in the *Fiore*, where they are in fact replaced by a similarly sacred image, the list of the four Evangelists. In compensation, however, the "commandments" appear in the *Detto d'Amore*. Thus the *Detto* does not coincide with the *Fiore*, it completes it; its material derived from the *Roman* integrates that found in the *Fiore*.

And here we would do well to remember some other motifs related to Dante's oeuvre. I will cite two that seem to me particularly significant. One is the theme of the retention of memory; and it involves lines 2053 ff. of Guillaume (of which I understand there exists a famous source, famous because it is the proem of the *Dicta* or *Distichia Catonis*, a Scholastic text believed to be by Cato the elder but which in reality is by a certain Dionisio Catone of the fourth century AD):

> Li maistres pert sa poine toute
> Quant li deciples qui escoute
> Ne met son cuer au retenir
> Si qu'il l'en puisse sovenir.

Another theme—though this one is actually in the *Vita Nuova*—is that of the "screen," which one also finds in lines 2687 ff. of Guillaume:

> Mais vers la gent tres bien te cele
> E quier autre achoison que cele
> Qui cele part te fait aler,
> Qu'il est granz sens de soi celer.

If this mosaic means anything at all, it seems to me that the only possible solution is that the *Fiore* comes from Dante's hand; but also, in addition, that it represents something organic in his career—that it constitutes, in short, a first attempt at adapting the *Rose*, a first effort, though in fact a maximalist effort, in as much as it is a reduction to an exclusive realism, the *Roman de la Rose* boiled down to pure storytelling. If you can indeed recall the compositional formula of which Bédier spoke, you find in the *Fiore* a *Rose* that no longer blends idealism and realism (imagining both concepts of course in quotation marks), but is reduced to pure realism. It is the introduction to a "bourgeois" ideal that makes all the idealistic and chivalric stuff disappear. It is a first rehearsal of the "comedic" vein, the completely comedic: not, of course, the comedic that will eventually lead to the *Commedia*'s encyclopedia of styles; but the comedic in its pure state. It linguistic caricature is hyperbolic. However vast, however shocking the abundance of Gallicisms in the text may seem, there even are certain instances we might call hypergallicisms. I won't attempt to give a complete catalogue thereof, especially as one need only pick up Parodi's glossary and look for the French forms in it.

Not all these examples can be attested to in the *Rose*, however. For instance, the first that comes to hand in alphabetical order is *adreza*—from *adrece*—which finds itself in the rhyming position at CLXXXIII 7 and CCXIV 3, but it is nowhere to be found in the corresponding passages of the French original. It is therefore a supplemental Gallicism that was inserted into the text. And there are other examples that can attest to this reading of the *Fiore* as a first experiment at equalling the *Rose*—metrical instances we've already seen in connection with the development of the *terzina*, which is one of Ser Durante's great discoveries. One particular novelty that came out in this morning's seminar is that there is, in the text, a mobile dialectical relationship, not very apparently univocal, between the *endecasillabo* and the *octosyllabe*: sometimes it involves expanding the content of the verse line, while at other times it's to shorten it brusquely.

What I've laid out here is probably the essential part, the nucleus of the demonstration, but I would like to call to our attention many other details as well, first of all the physical appearance of the manuscript of the *Fiore*. I've already alluded to this physical aspect, but meanwhile a familiar expression of Bédier's comes to mind: "*Ces manuscrits* (and he would mime the gesture of caressing the codices) *sont notre seul bien.*" In other words, the only certain, palpable reality in philology are the manuscripts. Since we have in this case something indeed tangible, we may ask: What does it look like from the outside? It is in fact a highly unusual object, or at least I know of no other to which it could be closely related. It is a collection with two columns on each page: in the left-hand column are two sonnets, and in the right-hand column two more sonnets, as in, to my knowledge, no other collections of the same period. This kind of pagination seems to me—if you'll allow me the term—Franco-Italian: the verse beginnings alternate in color between blue and red, a very obvious detail,[16] and this is a near constant—that is, constant with the exception of the first sonnet, which I've already mentioned, and the last sonnets, where it is clear that work ordered by the patron was never completed. And there are captions, but they do not correspond to any system: they merely explain which character is speaking, or who he/she is speaking about.

It is clear that whoever drafted the manuscript of the *Fiore* was imitating the manuscript of the *Rose*. Almost all of the *Rose* manuscripts have each page divided into two columns. There are some exceptions, of course, though I haven't seen all the codices. One has three columns (the Parisian Fr. 378), and it is one of the oldest and contains other texts as well; and there are other with only one column per page, such as the Madrileño 10319 and the abovecited Laurentian one, but this latter is an oddity that also caught the attention of Langlois, because the manuscript is very narrow, tall and cramped as if it were a normal two-column manuscript cut lengthwise. It is an ingenious, exquisitely manneristic curio (if one may speak of mannerism in connection with the production of a codex).

And what about the captions? The captions either accompany the illuminations (which I will discuss presently) or they indicate that a specific character is speaking. These captions are only slightly less constant in the tradition of the *Rose*. But I also know of manuscripts where the captions appear in the same way as the title headings in our present-day volumes. Such as the Parisian Fr. 1574; or number 364 of the Bibliotheca Bongarsiana of Bern, which owns two,

---

[16] Less obvious, however, is the fact that the alternation of blue (with little red threadings) and red (with little blue threadings) is irregular, in the sense that each side contains two blue initials and two red. (GC)

one that looks normal, and another which was given its barbarously pathological appearance by I know not what reader or user, who cut it up as if with a razor blade, not in order to insert any illuminations (and indeed those that do figure in the manuscript are unusually crude), but for the pure thrill of destruction. Well, this same vandalized document is nevertheless essential to our purpose, because in this case the captions represent a running title, therefore something very close to their use in the *Fiore*.

A more clearly pleasant, and less brutally archivistic feature is that the great majority of manuscripts of the *Rose* are adorned with illuminations (almost all of the *Rose* manuscripts, but not the *Fiore*), with an almost limitless possiblity of expansion, to the point of the extraordinary richness found, for example, in the Laurenziano Acquisti e Doni. Despite this dynamism, I think it is impossible not to recognize the existence of an early nucleus, or at least a common group linked to Guillaume de Lorris. There are certain manuscripts that feature illuminations only for the first part of the romance, that by Guillaume (such as the abovecited Fr. 378), with sometimes one or very few additions for Jean de Meung's text (as in Fr. 1569). From this fact we can gather that, in all probability, Jean inherited a text by Guillaume that already featured illustrations, and that others were later added within Jean's text by means of a gradual extension. These variations are of great import from the perspective of textual criticism: if until now the genealogy of texts has been based on reasons of content, on the basis of the version—an entirely unambiguous matter—in terms of mistakes and innovations one also encountered another physical fact, that is, the presence of one or another type of illumination. We are thus taken far back in time. I can cite, for example, the fact that when the first illumination of the poem (which I will talk about in a moment) is quadrilobate, it bears the symbol of a specific family, which helps to identify it, in the same way as the presence of a given interpolation or a certain variant in the printing. The models are invariable, even if the style may change, and thus this search for variation in the updating of a text, starting from a common thematic foundation, is an extraordinary test. I will cite two examples that are among the most outstanding testimonials I've ever laid my hands on: the manuscript of Sainte-Geneviève (that is, no. 1126, the illuminated one), and one from the Vaticani Reginensi (no. 1492). The Sainte-Geneviève manuscript is inspired by an extremely archaic Gothic taste; the illuminations are sumptuous and gilded, and in a kind of delayed Romanesque style. The Reginense, on the other hand, features a flowery, cosmopolitan, International Gothic style, on a level with the material represented.

This leads us to a question, if not yet to a solution. What is the significance of such visualization? On the subject of the absence of death in the *Rose*, we spoke of certain historical or legendary or ancient personages whose situations are recounted, especially the tragic ones. There is (for example Fr. 1565, and in the Geneva codex) an illumination depicting Charles d'Anjou killing Manfred with his own hands; in the Sainte-Geneviève it's Conrad who's killed, and Virginia beheaded like a martyr. These illuminations of historical-mythological subjects belong to the added portion; that is, they are not part of the central nucleus, the archetypal part.

Let us examine the minimum with which a considerable number of manuscripts of the *Rose* content themselves (these include the French 797, 800, 804, 812, 1572, and our own Riccardiano). What is the significance of the opening illumination, which depicts a sleeping man? Clearly it is a sign directed at the reader to alert him to the fact that what is discussed in those pages is a "*songe*," or an "*avision*."[17] Then there is a curious modification, also of great interest from a hermeneutical perspective: the figure portrayed is doubled; that is, accompanying the horizontal character is a vertical one, who is the same character, but his "double." One is the sleeper, the other is the sleeper in the dream, the character who says "I." The split between the author and the character who says "I" is marked by the passage from the horizontal state to the vertical state. This, too, is an initial declaration of a twofold register of great exegetical importance; it is not made in words, however, but presented directly in an image. Further on, there is sometimes a variation that clearly corresponds to an alteration in the original situation: that is, the vertical character is equipped with a club or leafy stick; the same object upon which he rests his head or dozes off, as the text of the *Fiore* splendidly tells us. This character's name is Dangier (in the *Fiore*, he is Schifo). Curiously, this figure armed with this sort of flowery or leafy club is actually found again in an illustration that reaches well beyond the time of the codexes—that is, the beginnings. If you take in hand an extremely accessible manual such as the *Dizionario delle Opere*, published by Bompiani, you will find reprinted therein the opening woodcut of a Quattrocento edition, showing precisely a figure holding a sort of club. This is the evolution of the initial il-

---

[17] This is the fitting solution offered by Breiger, co-author (with Meiss and Singleton) of the *summa* of Dantean illustrations, to the sole instance (Egerton codex) where Dante is initially represented as asleep in bed and simultaneously beside himself, walking. Might the same figuration in the *Rose* not be the source for this? (GC)

lumination, and a minimization of the figurative representation. To a later time belongs the presentation of allegorical characters such as the Vices, or the god of Love replete with crown, wings, bow and arrows. And the most commonly illuminated part in Jean de Meung is of the very same nature; particularly notable in this is the representation (more or less constant) of Faux Semblant. This character obviously belongs to the ecclesiastical realm, and given the polemic against the medicant orders (Franciscan and Dominican) at the University of Paris, one recognizes, in his white garment under a black cloak, the typical garb of the Dominicans. That this representation is found in a good number of manuscripts (Sainte-Geneviève or Fr. 380 or Mazarine 3874)[18] is hardly an accident, but it indicates the presence of an archetypal situation. At any rate, with these manuscripts, it becomes clear that, the older they are, and the more repeated, and probably archetypal, the more exegetical they are, and the less ornamental. In short, the *Roman de la Rose* appears to have been, at its origin, an illustrated book. At times words like "*point*" or "*portrait*" appear (as in "*Aprés fu pointe Convoitise*"; or "*Aprés refu portraite Envie*," etc.). Well these are indications to be taken even literally, as in: *I will describe for you in words the images you see here opposite*.

I do not remember how the observation that the *Roman de la Rose* was born as an illustrated book was made in earlier cases. It is Columbus's egg in miniature, but this egg perhaps deserves to be tasted at other tables, since the notion raises a great many questions concerning medieval books in general (beyond, of course, those like the *Danses macabres*, the various *Trois morts et trois vivants*, the *Mors de la Pomme*, and similar works, which are intentionally based on a symbiosis of word and vignette). I confess that the observation makes me anxious to go digging through almost every medieval text to see if they could have initially been illustrated volumes, and clearly for certain texts the answer is obvious, whereas for others it's only probable or possible. It certainly is clear for Francesco da Barberino, who also executed the illustrations for the the only partially autograph copy of the *Documenti d'Amore*,[19] whereas for the entirely autograph specimen he had a good illuminator at hand. As for *Intelligenza*, an anonymous narrative poem in *nona rima* on "intelligence," might it too have been born as an illustrated book, since, like the first *Rose*, it features descriptions

---

[18] A few other indications include Fr. 1567; Arsenal 2988; Morgan 324 and 503, etc. (GC)

[19] An early 14th-century book of illuminations and verse by Barberino that features references to the first two *cantiche* of the *Divina Commedia*.

of the figurative representations? Unfortunately, the tradition of *Intelligenza* is very spare (two codices), and the illumination is reduced to a minimum (and here too the opening illustration is in the only non-acephalous specimen), but the suspicion is legitimate (Gervais's *Fauvel* presents a similar but less insubstantial situation). An unusual case, though belonging to the domain of a genre still waiting to be studied (I'm thinking above all of Giacomino da Verona), is that of an extremely modest writer, Pietro da Bersegapè, whose only codex was illustrated by a distinguished illuminator whom Roberto Longhi has recently discovered also painted wood panels. And what about the *L'Acerba*?[20] *L'Acerba* is, to all appearances, a treatise deserving to be accompanied by visual plates, and indeed one part of its tradition is a figurative translation of extreme importance due to its presence in the great Laurentian manuscript. Some have described *L'Acerba* as an anti-comedy. But of course the question first arises in connection with the *Divina Commedia*.

Was the *Commedia* originally an illustrated book? I am not in a position to provide a definitive answer to this question, and I must also admit that it seems to me likely, at a glance, that the *Commedia* did not come into the world as an illuminated book. Some will say that the question is anything but innocent, since two solemn volumes were recently devoted to the illustrations of the *Commedia* by a group of three American scholars, at least two of whom are assiduous Italophiles. It does not, however, seem to me that these eminent scholars have asked themselves this specific question—whether or not the *Commedia* was originally an illustrated book—since the American book's splendid apparatus of illustrative plates features more images of standout scenes than canonical scenes, the very kinds of scenes whose convergence would seem to be the only argument in favor of such a hypothesis. And while I do not think that the *Commedia* was born as an illustrated book, we all know how the author, in a page of the *Vita Nuova*, claims he is able to "draw figures of angels" (*disegnare figure d'angeli*) "on certain small panels" (*sopra certe tavolette*). All the same, I would say that the *Commedia* is a book that could be illustrated—that is, a book authorized by the author for illustration, since it contains important passages that invite visual representation: just think of the topography of the *Purgatorio*. What I mean is that, just as the *Commedia* becomes a text that can be sung, it similarly becomes popular poetry for Sacchetti's blacksmith and donkey driver—something

---

[20] A long verse composition from 1327 by Cecco d'Ascoli.

the importance of which Sacchetti, a middle-class mediocrity, doesn't remotely realize, just as his popularizing adaptation would itself stand to demonstrate how the work could be illustrated in the manner of a *Biblia pauperum*: call it a *Comœdia pauperum*.

It is legitimate to ask, concerning this point, what is the fundamental difference—and I would like to end my presentation with this consideration—what is the fundamental difference between the *Roman de la Rose* and the *Commedia*? When we speak of Dante's ability to be illustrated, and his authorization of such, we are thinking of the question in opposition to authors who were against any representation of their fantasies. The most authoritative example of this would be Flaubert, who was terrified at the thought that *Madame Bovary* might fall into the hands of an illustrator. Well, things went quite differently in the Middle Ages, and not only then (Manzoni himself instigated the undertaking with Gonin[21]). In my opinion, the *Roman de la Rose* calls out mostly for an exegetical sort of visualization. Indeed at first such illustration refers back to the allegorical information; the non-allegorical information will be added later. The *Commedia*, on the contrary, aims at the memory; that is, it wants to shake up and tear apart the reader's memory. Here, then, moreover, is a distinction that one should not be too inflexible about, among other reasons because the *Commedia* grants licence to the illustrator, one that will give us objects of such lofty aesthetic dignity as to call to mind the problematics of Oderisi and Franco Bolognese. And allow me to cite only the case of the great illuminator, also from Bologna, Maestro Falvano, who illumnated the *Commedia* codex today divided between the Ricciardiana and the Braidense.

But there's another reason why the distinction must not be too inflexible: because the *Rose* itself works on our memory, just as the *Commedia* will do afterwards. But I will go out on a limb and say that the *Rose* worked on specialized memories, the memories of particularly equipped individuals, one of whom might be named Chaucer and the other Dante. I would like here to present the proof regarding Dante, which will be the last example I submit for your consideration. What is this proof that the *Rose* worked on Dante's memory? Well, first of all, there is the fact that the master of the *Fiore* jumps from one place to another in his paraphrasing or remembrance of the *Rose*. I shall give a few samples among the countless possible ones, because almost every sonnet could

---

[21] I.e., to have *I promessi sposi* (The Betrothed) illustrated by Francesco Gonin.

serve for considerations of that nature; but these few should suffice, and then I will cite a borderline case, from which a few meager numbers can be inferred to make the point.

Sonnet II of the *Fiore* mirrors the passage of the *Rose*, lines 1181 ff. (clearly Guillaume de Lorris). But line 13 of the sonnet, whose subject is the kiss, the kiss of investiture whereby the lover becomes a *fedele d'Amore*, harks back to passage much farther forward in the *Rose*, lines 1935 ff., while another similar passage crops up at line 1957 ("sa bouche baisa la moie"), in such a way as to call to mind Ginevra's or Francesca's kiss. But there's more. The formulation appears in rhyme, sort of as filler, but it has a kind of ritual significance: "sanz'altro aresto," which is a refection of "senz'arest," found at various and mutually distant points in the *Rose*, one at line 788, another at line 2798, naturally always in an important and demarcating spot such as the rhyming position. Dante's mind thus attests to a wonderful cybernetics, which enabled him to hop blithely from one passage to another in such an extended poem. Let us also take sonnet IV, which mirrors the passage in lines 1999 ff. in the *Rose*, but then the penultimte line reproduces two lines much further on in the *Rose*, 2183 and 2184:

> Amant sentent le mal d'amer
> Une eure douz e autre amer;

But, as Parodi remarked in the margins of the copy of the Mazzatinti-Gorra edition belonging to the Facoltà di Lettere di Firenze, lines 5 and six reproduce, for their part, the *Rose*'s lines 4272 and 4273:

> il est mes sires,
> E je ses on ligies entires.

Please note that the sonnet in question here is doubled. In the transition from the *Rose* to the *Fiore*, there is sometimes a process of condensation, other times one of gemmation. Sonnet V is a doubling of the previous one, in which the Gospels replace the commandments, as we pointed out before. We are thus at the start of Guillaume's text; and yet there's a passage in the *Fiore* poem—line 12, and again it was Parodi who discovered it—which mirrors a line deep into Jean de Meung's text, line 10368: "*En vostre lei mourir e vivre*." And so on and so forth, since one can say that hardly any sonnet in the *Fiore* is immune to this game, this extraordinary exercise.

And now let me cite the borderline case, represented by sonnet VIII, which speaks of "mastro Argus[so] che fece la nave." Melded together in this Argus[so] are al-Khuwarizmi—that is, the Arab algebrist who invented the algorithm, which is named after him—and the *Argo*, the ship named after its builder, Argus; and he is mentioned in reference to a list that can only be numerated by a specially equipped mathematical mind. The sonnet stands between sonnet VII (equivalent to lines 2765 ff. in Guillaume) and sonnet IX (equivalent to lines 2971 ff.). As Castets observed, sonnet VIII reproduces nothing less than lines 12790 ff. (which are Jean de Meung's). But why such a great leap? Why such an anomaly? I myself have wondered whether this sonnet, which does not in any way fit the order in which it appears, was not perhaps a "stray" sonnet, drafted independently, and then dropped completely from circulation.

Looking at things more closely, I think that one can in fact answer the question in sufficiently satisfying fashion. One thing to note is that the passage on Maestro Argusso is an odd sort of excerpt that must have made strong a impression on readers. The two greatest readers of the *Rose*, Dante and Chaucer, both agree on the need to reproduce this passage. One part in Chaucer's *Book of the Duchess* reproduces and translates it with the same faithful wit as Dante, and it is not reasonable to assume that Chaucer had the *Fiore* in his hands. As for the *Fiore*, let us have a quick look at the surrounding sonnets to see if we can determine whether this presumed sonnet VIII was really supposed to fall of necessity between numbers VII and IX, even though it represented the equivalent of a passage occurring much later in the original source text. Its position in the *Fiore* does not seem very convincing. Why not? We know that in the prosody of the *Fiore*, the sonnet tends to become a strophic entity, and the corona of sonnets tends to become a continuous text. One detail of this continuity is found in the repetition of words from the prior sonnet in the one that follows; in a way the two sonnets are related to each other in a manner similar to the *coblas capfinidas* in troubadour poetry, and the repetition thus involved should of course be included in the general historical context of the canonical *interpretatio*.

Well, sonnet VII and sonnet IX are linked by the presence of the word *vilmente*, in the first and second lines, respectively, of the two poems, and by the presence of the word *villano* in the respective seventh and first lines. Let us try moving number VIII a little backwards: can this sonnet directly follow sonnet VI? It seems unlikely, because *villano* links line 11 of sonnet VI and line 7 of sonnet VII, while the expression *lo Schifo* (with a capital S, of course, corresponding with *Dangier* in the original) reproduces the word from line 13 of the prior sonnet in line 2 of the sonnet that follows. Nor does number VIII seem to fit well after sonnet V, because in this case we really are looking at strict *capfinidas* strophes, as in certain famous canzoni of Guinizzelli or even Dante himself, in as much as number V ends with *si parte* and number VI begins with *Partes*[*i*]. (This is the exact same formula—noting of course that *si parte* cannot appear in an opening because of the Tobler-Mussafia law—but reproduced in the only syntactically possible way.) But there is, perhaps, a chance to fit the sonnet in question in after number IV, by resorting to the same argument—that is, the repetition of words, because the sonnet in question, the sonnet of Maestro Argusso, contains the little golden key with which Amore locked the lover's heart; it is mentioned in line 10, but it reproduces the key discussed at the start of sonnet IV, which makes it seem that we may have found the best placement for this stray sonnet. You can see what kind of elasticity this involves, where not only can neighboring tesserae of a complex mosaic evoke very remote passages, but a sonnet may somehow be dislodged from its original spot. That this placement is particularly interesting stems from the fact that the sonnet comes to settle in after number four. But what does this mean? Sonnet IV: I II III IV. The sonnet in question ends up, after all that—but it's only after the first sheet, which as we said, contains four sonnets—as the first sonnet, not the last, on the second sheet.

Of course the memory here denoted is not so much the memory we invoke by preference when discussing Dante—that is, an explosive action exerted on the reader or listener—as it is the poet's extremely, almost monstrously receptive memory; which is, however, the precondition for the former. And therefore, if we must not rigidify the distinction between the *Rose* as a visualized poem and the *Commedia* as an eminently vocal poem, a poem whose realization is acoustic, then I would say that, on the whole, the principle holds true. And the conclusion we may draw from this is actually itself a truism: namely, that great literature, for which the *Rose* can be taken as a symbol, has, as one of its specific contents, an intellectual mediation, whereas great poetry, such as the *Commedia*, demands execution. The difference and opposition between the two narrative poems is the difference and opposition between literature and poetry.

[An ever so lightly revised transcription of two lectures held at the Fondazione Cini in Venice, published in the anthological volume, *Concetto, storia, miti e immagini del medio evo*, edited by Vittore Branca (Sansoni, Florence 1973), after having appeared in *Lettere italiane*.]

Postscript (1984)

This essay, like the preceding one, is part of the preparation for a critical edition of the two poems proceeding from the *Roman de la Rose*: *Il Fiore* and the *Detto d'Amore*, both attributable to Dante Alighieri, Gianfranco Contini, ed., Mondadori, Milan 1984; and can be read together with the commentary included immediately afterwards in the *Opere minori* of Dante Alighieri, tome I, Part I, Ricciardi, Milan-Naples 1984. It was perfectly irrelevant to incorporate into the preparatory text the few adjustments of aim that would have made it exactly like the supposedly definitive volume.

Specifically, Guglielmo Libri's appropriation of the object called the *Detto d'Amore* should have occurred not in Troyes (see page 270, note 12), but rather at Montpellier, and by resection, as the edition relates on p. LII and as Chabaneau had written as early as 1891without (and this should be amended) any scholars even noticing. I recounted that philological "mystery" to the best of my ability.

A French-speaking colleague reproaches me for my proposed etymology for *aier* (see p. 278). He sticks with Lecoy as his source, a source kept hidden because he admired the work being negatively judged, according to the little note signed *Réd.*, the mark of Roques. This is the noteworthy article by Jenkins (Romania, LII 349 ff.); which may induce one to take up the question again, but for the moment it does not seem to resolve the matter of our *aier*, which it is not easy to admit reflects an AEREM with the accented Greek ἀέρα. The Greek accusative is usually continued with AĔRA, whence the Italian *aria*, but also the numerous French examples of *aire* (Tobler-Lommatzsch, I 250 at the end).

Lastly, a sleeping Dante in a continuous narrative between the opening illustrations of the *Commedia* can also be found in other codexes: such was the case at the Mostra del Gotico at Siena in 1982, with codex Perugino L 70 (whose illuminations were considered autograph works by no less a master than Pietro Lorenzetti) and Laurenziano 40.3 (both reproduced in the catalogue).

G.C.

www.ingramcontent.com/pod-product-compliance
Lightning Source LLC
Chambersburg PA
CBHW030147100526
44592CB00009B/153